W0081647

PRACTICAL DMX QUERIES for

Microsoft® SQL Server® Analysis Services 2008

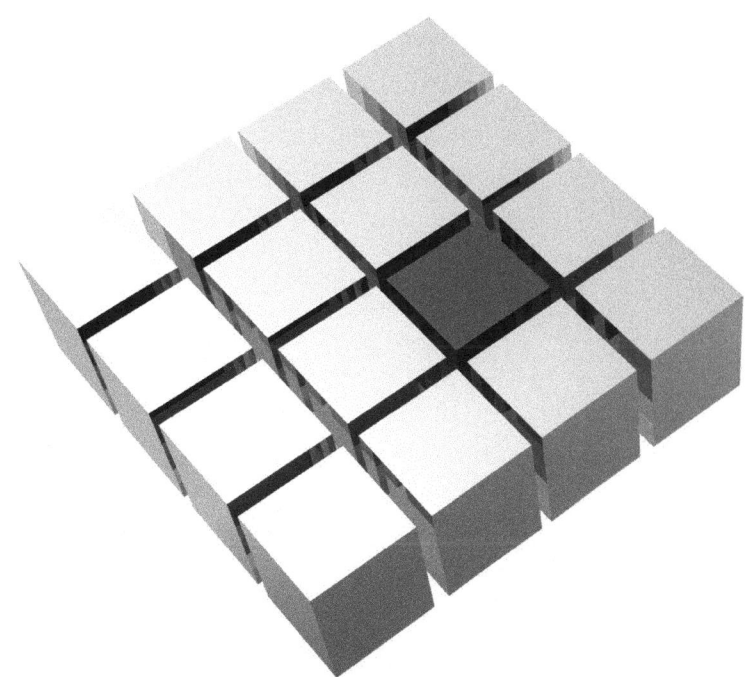

About the Author

Art Tennick (Brighton, U.K.) has worked in relational database design and SQL queries for over 20 years. He has been involved in multidimensional database design, cubes, data mining, DMX, and MDX queries for 10 years. Based in the United Kingdom, he has been a software consultant, trainer, and writer for some 25 years. Recently, he has worked with several major retail and banking corporations to implement BI solutions using Microsoft SQL Server, SSAS, SSIS, SSRS, and Excel 2007/2010. This is his eighteenth book and he has also written over 300 articles for computer magazines in the U.S., the U.K., and Ireland. His web site is www.MrCube.net.

About the Technical Editor

Dejan Sarka focuses on development of database and Business Intelligence applications. Besides projects, he spends about half of the time on training and mentoring. He is the founder of the Slovenian SQL Server and .NET Users Group. Dejan Sarka is the main author or coauthor of eight books about databases and SQL Server. Dejan Sarka also developed two courses for Solid Quality Mentors: Data Modeling Essentials and Data Mining with SQL Server 2008.

PRACTICAL DMX QUERIES for

Microsoft® SQL Server® Analysis Services 2008

Art Tennick

Mc
Graw
Hill

New York Chicago San Francisco Lisbon
London Madrid Mexico City Milan
New Delhi San Juan Seoul Singapore
Sydney Toronto

The McGraw·Hill Companies

Cataloging-in-Publication Data is on file with the Library of Congress

McGraw-Hill books are available at special quantity discounts to use as premiums and sales promotions, or for use in corporate training programs. To contact a representative, please e-mail us at bulksales@mcgraw-hill.com.

Practical DMX Queries for Microsoft® SQL Server® Analysis Services 2008

1234567890   DOC DOC   109876543210

ISBN   978-0-07-174866-7
MHID   0-07-174866-0

Sponsoring Editor Wendy Rinaldi	**Indexer** Ted Laux
Editorial Supervisor Patty Mon	**Production Supervisor** George Anderson
Project Manager Deepti Narwat Agarwal, Glyph International	**Composition** Glyph International
Acquisitions Coordinator Joya Anthony	**Illustration** Glyph International
Technical Editor Dejan Sarka	**Art Director, Cover** Jeff Weeks
Copy Editor Margaret Berson	**Cover Designer** Jeff Weeks
Proofreader Laura Bowman	

For Lorna and Emma

Contents at a Glance

Contents

Acknowledgments

A s always, thank you to my editor, Wendy Rinaldi. She encouraged me every step of the way. Joya Anthony helped to bring the book to production, and Melinda Lytle helped with the graphics—thank you. Dejan Sarka was a remarkable technical reviewer—he helped me, in a big way, to complete the book with his incredible knowledge of DMX.

Introduction

DMX

Business Intelligence (BI) is a very rapidly growing area of the software market. Microsoft's core product in this field is SQL Server Analysis Services (SSAS). It is revolutionizing the way companies view and work with data. Its purpose is to turn data into information, giving meaning to the data. There are two main objects in SSAS that support this goal—cubes and data mining models. If these can be visualized easily, then the information they contain is transformed into intelligence—leading to timely and effective decision making. Cube information can be extracted and visualized with Multidimensional Expressions (MDX) queries. Data mining model information can be extracted and visualized with Data Mining Extensions (DMX) queries. This book is devoted to data mining and the DMX language. It takes you from first principles in DMX query writing and builds into more and more sophisticated queries. The book is a practical one—with lots of syntax to try on nearly every page (and you can copy and paste from the download files for this book, if you prefer not to type).

Prerequisites

You will need two databases. First, the SSAS Adventure Works DW 2008 database (called Adventure Works DW in SSAS 2005), which contains the Adventure Works mining models—the DMX queries are written against those models. Second, the SQL Server AdventureWorksDW2008 database (called AdventureWorksDW in SQL Server 2005), which provides the source data required by the SSAS Adventure Works DW 2008 database. If you already have the SSAS database, you don't need the SQL Server source. However, if you have not yet processed the SSAS database, the SQL Server source database is necessary.

Installing Adventure Works

You can download the required SSAS database (with the Adventure Works mining models) and the SQL Server database from www.codeplex.com (both 2008 and 2005 versions). As of this writing, the URL was http://www.codeplex.com/MSFTDBProdSamples/Release/ProjectReleases.aspx?ReleaseID=16040. Choose SQL Server 2008 or SQL

Server 2005 from the Releases box. URLs can change—if you have difficulty, search for Adventure Works Samples on www.codeplex.com.

SSAS 2008

Before you begin the download, you might want to check the two hyperlinks for Database Prerequisites and Installing Databases. Download and run SQL2008. AdventureWorks All Databases.x86.msi (there are also 64-bit versions, x64 and ia64). As the installation proceeds, you will have to choose an instance name for your SQL Server. When the installation finishes, you will have some new SQL Server databases including AdventureWorksDW2008 (used to build the SSAS Adventure Works mining models). You will not have the mining models just yet.

SSAS 2005

The download file is called AdventureWorksBICI.msi (there are also 64-bit versions, x64 and IA64). With 2005 you can also go through Setup or Control Panel to add the samples—this is not possible in 2008. Unlike 2008, the download and subsequent installation do not result in the new SQL Server source database appearing under SQL Server in SSMS. You have to manually attach the database. You can do this from SSMS (right-click the Databases folder and choose Attach) if you have some DBA knowledge. Or you might ask your SQL Server DBA to do this for you. If you click the Release Notes hyperlink on the download page, you will find out how to do this from SQL—but this is a DMX book! You will not have the mining models just yet.

Creating the Adventure Works Mining Models

These are the mining models used by all the DMX queries in this book:

1. Navigate to C:\Program Files\Microsoft SQL Server\100\Tools\Samples\ AdventureWorks 2008 Analysis Services Project (C:\Program Files\Microsoft SQL Server\90\Tools\Samples\AdventureWorks Analysis Services Project for 2005).

2. Depending on your edition of SSAS, open the Enterprise or Standard folder.

3. Double-click the Adventure Works.sln file. This will open BIDS.

4. In Solution Explorer, right-click on the Adventure Works project, which is probably in bold. If you can't see Solution Explorer, click View, Solution Explorer. The project will be called Adventure Works DW 2008 (for SSAS 2008 Enterprise Edition), Adventure Works DW 2008 SE (for SSAS 2008 Standard Edition), Adventure Works DW (for SSAS 2005 Enterprise Edition), or Adventure Works DW Standard Edition (for SSAS 2005 Standard Edition).

5. Click Deploy (then click Yes if prompted). After a few minutes, you should see a Deploy Succeeded message on the status bar and Deployment Completed Successfully in the Deployment Progress window.

If the deployment fails, try these steps:

1. Right-click on the project and choose Properties. Go to the Deployment page and check that the Server entry points to your SSAS (*not* SQL Server) instance—you might have a named SSAS instance rather than a default instance, or your SSAS may be on a remote server.
2. Right-click on Adventure Works.ds (under the Data Sources folder in Solution Explorer) and choose Open. Click Edit and check that the Server name entry points to your SQL Server (*not* SSAS) instance—you might have a named SQL Server instance rather than a default instance, or your SQL Server may be on a remote server.
3. Try to deploy again.

Source Code

All of the source code for the queries in this book is available for download. You can simply copy and paste into the query editor to save you typing. You can copy and paste individual queries or copy and paste blocks of code. If you do the latter, make sure that you highlight only the relevant code before you run the query.

You can download the source code from www.mhprofessional.com/computingdownload.

Acronyms

The following acronyms are used in this book:

- ► **ASSL**   Analysis Services Scripting Language
- ► **BI**   Business Intelligence
- ► **BIDS**   SQL Server Business Intelligence Development Studio
- ► **DMX**   Data Mining Extensions
- ► **KPI**   Key Performance Indicator
- ► **MDX**   Multidimensional Expressions
- ► **SQL**   Structured Query Language
- ► **SSAS**   SQL Server Analysis Services
- ► **SSIS**   SQL Server Integration Services

> ▶ **SSMS**   SQL Server Management Studio
> ▶ **SSRS**   SQL Server Reporting Services
> ▶ **XMLA**   XML for Analysis

SSAS 2008 or SSAS 2005?

The DMX queries in this book are primarily for SSAS 2008. Fortunately, over 99 percent also work with SSAS 2005. One minor exception is the ability to hold out and filter mining structure cases introduced in SSAS 2008—this will affect only two or three queries in this book.

Enterprise/Developer Edition or Standard Edition?

It makes little difference which edition you use. All of the queries work with the Enterprise/Developer Edition and the Standard Edition of SSAS.

Writing Queries

1. Open SSMS.
2. If prompted to connect, click Cancel.
3. Click File | New | Analysis Services DMX Query.
4. Click Connect in the dialog box.
5. From the drop-down on the toolbar, choose the Adventure Works DW 2008 database.
6. Make sure the relevant mining model is selected in the Mining model drop-down just to the left of the query editor window. The model metadata should be visible in the Metadata pane.
7. Type, or type and drag, or copy and paste to create the query.
8. Click the Execute button on the toolbar.

There are many other ways of opening the query editor. Here's a popular alternative:

1. In Object Explorer, right-click on the SSAS database Adventure Works DW 2008 (Adventure Works DW in SSAS 2005).
2. Click New Query | DMX.
3. Make sure the relevant mining model is selected in the Mining model drop-down just to the left of the query editor window. The model metadata should be visible in the Metadata pane.

Chapter Content

The DMX you learn can be used in many places. These include SQL Server Reporting Services (SSRS), SQL Server Integration Services (SSIS), and your own .NET Windows forms and web pages. In addition, you can extend your SQL queries by embedding DMX code. By and large, all of the DMX in the book is divided into chapters based on functionality. The chapters are as follows:

Chapter 1, "Cases Queries"

Cases are the relational database records (or cube attributes and measures) used to initially populate a data mining structure. These cases are then available to train (and, optionally, later test) the data mining models within the mining structure. This is your source data. This chapter explores ways of viewing the cases within structures and models. A good knowledge and understanding of the cases will help you achieve more accurate and meaningful data mining results. We use DMX Cases queries to look at the cases.

Chapter 2, "Content Queries"

Data mining models are trained using the cases (source data) that populate the data mining structure to which the model belongs. The results of the model training are referred to as the *model content*. When you browse a model graphically, you are looking at the content. You can also examine the content of a model from a DMX query—DMX Content queries are the subject of this chapter. The nature of the content depends upon the algorithm on which the model is based. For example, you can view cluster profiles or you can examine probabilities and support of predictable columns. The content of a model is based on existing data. New data is analyzed with a DMX Prediction query.

Chapter 3, "Prediction Queries with Decision Trees"

This chapter demonstrates how to perform DMX Prediction queries with mining models based on the Decision Trees algorithm. Cases queries reveal the original source data for the model. Content queries show the result of training the model and the patterns, clusters, and correlations discovered. Both Cases and Content queries are based on existing data. Prediction queries, on the other hand, work on new data (one exception to this rule is the Time Series algorithm, which usually makes predictions based on existing data—this feature is not available in the Standard Edition). They do so by comparing the new data with the results discovered during model training. For example, a Prediction query might show the possibility and probability of a new customer being a bike buyer. Although this chapter focuses on the Decision Trees algorithm, the techniques learned are generally applicable to all the data mining algorithms.

Chapter 4, "Prediction Queries with Time Series"

Data mining models based on the Time Series algorithm also support Prediction queries. Most mining algorithms use new data (through a prediction join) to make predictions. The Time Series algorithm is an exception—its predictions (that is, forecasting future trends) are based on existing data and not on new data. Therefore, a prediction join is not required to analyze new data against existing content data. The predictions are generally extrapolations of existing figures and trends. There are two minor exceptions to this rule—EXTEND_MODEL_CASES and REPLACE_MODEL_CASES, which can be used to simulate new data. This chapter concentrates on DMX Prediction queries with models based on the Time Series algorithm.

Chapter 5, "Prediction and Cluster Queries with Clustering"

Mining models based on the Clustering algorithm may or may not have a predictable column—both varieties of models are explored in this chapter. A cluster model with a predictable column (for example, Bike Buyer) supports Prediction queries (for example using the Predict() function). All cluster models support a range of functions that are specific to clusters (for example, the Cluster() function)—I have called these Cluster queries to distinguish them from Prediction queries. This chapter shows you how to perform Prediction and Cluster queries against models based on the Clustering algorithm. Cluster queries are useful for profiling and anomaly detection. Prediction queries are useful for indicating potential future behavior.

Chapter 6, "Prediction Queries with Association and Sequence Clustering"

This chapter contains yet more Prediction queries. The DMX queries this time are written against mining models based on two algorithms, Association and Sequence Clustering. Both algorithms appear in the same chapter as they share a lot of common characteristics. Although every mining algorithm has lots of uses, these two algorithms are typically used in market basket analysis. Market basket analysis is the focus of this chapter, and there are quite a few Prediction queries devoted to identifying cross-selling opportunities. However, it's important to realize they can be used in other applications— for example, Sequence Clustering can be used to analyze click-stream data on web sites. The main difference between the two algorithms is quite subtle. Association, for example, can show purchasing combinations for all customers—it's generic. Sequence Clustering, by contrast, can show purchasing combinations for individual groups (clusters) of customers—it's specific.

Chapter 7, "Data Definition Language (DDL) Queries"

DMX DDL queries are used to create, alter, drop, back up, and restore data mining objects. In addition, they are used to train the mining models. The source data used for cases and model training in this chapter is both relational (using embedded SQL) and multidimensional (using embedded MDX). You will learn how to specify the usage and content of structure and model columns as well as build all the mining objects you will ever need.

Chapter 8, "Schema and Column Queries"

This chapter focuses on two main areas, Schema queries and Column queries. Schema queries are all about metadata (data about data). For example, you can list all of the algorithms available, all of your mining structures, all of your mining models, all of your structure or model columns, and more. DMSCHEMA_MINING_SERVICE_ PARAMETERS is very useful for showing the various parameters for each algorithm and what they mean. Column queries are used to examine the values (or states) of all your discrete, discretized, and continuous structure columns.

Chapter 9, "After You Finish"

Throughout this book, you'll be using SSMS to write your DMX queries and display the results. It's unlikely that your users will have SSMS—indeed, it's not recommended for end users as it's simply too powerful and potentially dangerous. This chapter presents some alternative software and methods for getting DMX query results to the end user.

Appendix A, "Graphical Content Queries"

The previous chapters showed the syntax for DMX queries and involved entering the syntax manually in SSMS. However, it is possible to generate the DMX syntax behind the scenes using the graphical user interface. This and the following two appendixes show various ways of running DMX queries graphically, without the need to enter any syntax. This first appendix demonstrates how to return data mining model content using graphical tools. In particular, it uses both SSMS and Excel 2007/2010 to generate queries graphically and to display the results graphically too.

Appendix B, "Graphical Prediction Queries"

You can also generate Prediction queries graphically. This appendix shows how to do so in SSMS, SSAS, SSRS, SSIS, and Excel 2007/2010.

Appendix C, "Graphical DDL Queries"

This third appendix demonstrates how to generate DDL queries graphically. Such queries are for creating and training data mining models. You can do this from Excel 2007/2010 or from BIDS. There are also a number of features in SSIS that help you create and train data mining models with little or no syntax involved. Here you get to see how it can be done in Excel 2007/2010, SSAS, and SSIS.

Chapter 1

Cases Queries

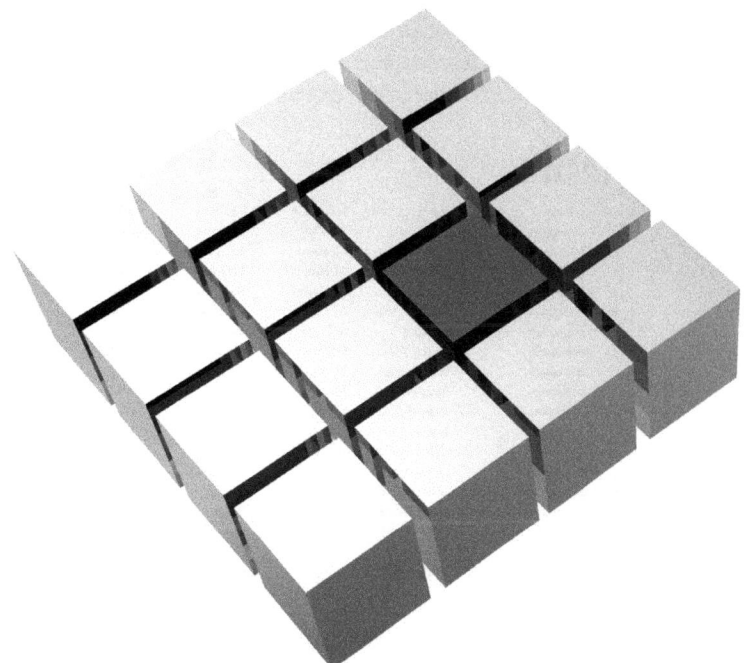

Cases are the relational database records (or cube attributes and measures) used to initially populate a data mining structure. These cases are then available to train (and, optionally, later test) the data mining models within the mining structure. This is your source data. This chapter explores ways of viewing the cases within structures and models. A good knowledge and understanding of the cases will help you achieve more accurate and meaningful data mining results. We use DMX Cases queries to look at the cases.

▶ **Key concepts**   Mining structure cases, mining model cases, nested case tables, training and testing (hold out) cases, drill-through, subqueries

▶ **Keywords**   Select, Distinct, Top, Flattened, From, Where, Order By, .cases, .sample_cases, IsInNode(), IsTrainingCase(), IsTestCase(), StructureColumn()

Examining Source Data

The source data is the data originally used to populate a mining structure. This data (or a subset) is then used to train the mining models within the structure. You can optionally store a copy of the source data permanently inside the mining structure—this is now independent of the initial relational or multidimensional source. To examine this stored copy of the original source, you will need a DMX Cases query on the mining structure.

Syntax

```
-- select all cases from structure
-- this is a comment as is the line above
select * from mining structure [customer mining].cases;
```

Result

Subcategories		Customer Counts	Commute Distance	Education	Gender	Home Owner	Marital Status	Number of Cars ...	Number of Childr...
⊞	Subcategories	Jon V. Yang	1-2 Miles	Bachelors	Male	Yes	Married	0	0
⊞	Subcategories	Eugene L. Huang	0-1 Miles	Bachelors	Male	No	Single	1	3
⊞	Subcategories	Ruben Torres	2-5 Miles	Bachelors	Male	Yes	Married	1	3
⊞	Subcategories	Christy Zhu	5-10 Miles	Bachelors	Female	No	Single	1	0
⊞	Subcategories	Elizabeth Johnson	1-2 Miles	Bachelors	Female	Yes	Single	4	5
⊞	Subcategories	Julio Ruiz	5-10 Miles	Bachelors	Male	Yes	Single	1	0
⊞	Subcategories	Janet G. Alvarez	5-10 Miles	Bachelors	Female	Yes	Single	1	0
⊞	Subcategories	Marco Mehta	0-1 Miles	Bachelors	Male	Yes	Married	2	3
⊞	Subcategories	Rob Verhoff	10+ Miles	Bachelors	Female	Yes	Single	3	4
⊞	Subcategories	Shannon C. Carl...	5-10 Miles	Bachelors	Male	No	Single	1	0
⊞	Subcategories	Jacquelyn C. Su...	5-10 Miles	Bachelors	Female	No	Single	1	0
⊞	Subcategories	Curtis Lu	10+ Miles	Bachelors	Male	Yes	Married	4	4
⊞	Subcategories	Lauren M. Walker	1-2 Miles	Bachelors	Female	Yes	Married	2	0
⊞	Subcategories	Ian M. Jenkins	0-1 Miles	Bachelors	Male	Yes	Married	3	0
⊞	Subcategories	Sydney Bennett	1-2 Miles	Bachelors	Female	No	Single	3	0
⊞	Subcategories	Chloe Young	5-10 Miles	Partial College	Female	No	Single	1	0
⊞	Subcategories	Wyatt L. Hill	5-10 Miles	Partial College	Male	Yes	Married	1	0
⊞	Subcategories	Shannon Wang	5-10 Miles	High School	Female	Yes	Single	2	0

Analysis

The name of the mining structure is followed by .cases. The data from the cases is displayed. The results will vary from structure to structure. In this example, the Customer Mining structure contains a nested case table called Subcategories. You can view the contents of this nested table by expanding it. When you design the structure in SQL Server Business Intelligence Development Studio (BIDS), there is a CacheMode property. In order to see the cases, this property has to be set to KeepTrainingCases. The other setting for this property is ClearAfterProcessing—this means that a copy of the source data is not stored in the structure after the models in the structure are trained, and a Cases query will not return any data. The semicolon at the end of the query is optional, but is considered good practice as it explicitly delineates the query if you have more than one query.

Flattened Nested Case Table

The key word Flattened is useful in many areas of DMX—it's used many times in this book whenever there is a nested table in the query results. Here, we are flattening or expanding the Subcategories nested table seen in the previous query.

Syntax

```
-- select flattened all cases from structure
select flattened * from mining structure [customer mining].cases
```

Result

Subcategories.Internet Sales Amount	Subcategories.Subcategory	Customer Counts	Commute Distance	Education	Gender	Home Owner	Marital Status
5719.98	Mountain Bikes	Jon V. Yang	1-2 Miles	Bachelors	Male	Yes	Married
21.98	Fenders	Jon V. Yang	1-2 Miles	Bachelors	Male	Yes	Married
2384.07	Touring Bikes	Jon V. Yang	1-2 Miles	Bachelors	Male	Yes	Married
33.98	Tires and Tubes	Jon V. Yang	1-2 Miles	Bachelors	Male	Yes	Married
34.99	Helmets	Jon V. Yang	1-2 Miles	Bachelors	Male	Yes	Married
53.99	Jerseys	Jon V. Yang	1-2 Miles	Bachelors	Male	Yes	Married
5694.98	Mountain Bikes	Eugene L. Huang	0-1 Miles	Bachelors	Male	No	Single
21.98	Fenders	Eugene L. Huang	0-1 Miles	Bachelors	Male	No	Single
28.96	Bottles and Cages	Eugene L. Huang	0-1 Miles	Bachelors	Male	No	Single
53.99	Jerseys	Eugene L. Huang	0-1 Miles	Bachelors	Male	No	Single
8.99	Caps	Eugene L. Huang	0-1 Miles	Bachelors	Male	No	Single
539.99	Road Bikes	Eugene L. Huang	0-1 Miles	Bachelors	Male	No	Single
34.99	Helmets	Eugene L. Huang	0-1 Miles	Bachelors	Male	No	Single
5694.98	Mountain Bikes	Ruben Torres	2-5 Miles	Bachelors	Male	Yes	Married
2384.07	Touring Bikes	Ruben Torres	2-5 Miles	Bachelors	Male	Yes	Married
34.99	Helmets	Ruben Torres	2-5 Miles	Bachelors	Male	Yes	Married
5694.98	Mountain Bikes	Christy Zhu	5-10 Miles	Bachelors	Female	No	Single
14.98	Bottles and Cages	Christy Zhu	5-10 Miles	Bachelors	Female	No	Single

Analysis

There are now six records for Jon V. Yang instead of the single record as in the last query. Jon V. Yang is an individual customer, and his data (for example, his education) is used for the Customer Clusters (clustering or profiling) data mining model that is part of the Customer Mining data mining structure. The six records in the expanded nested table show which subcategories he bought. The subcategory purchase information from all customers is used by the Subcategory Association (association or market basket analysis) mining model in the same structure. The same source data in a single structure can be used for different purposes by different mining algorithms. You can view each structure and the model(s) it contains in BIDS or in Object Explorer in SQL Server Management Studio (SSMS).

Specific Source Columns

Instead of displaying all the columns from the source data, you might find it helpful to concentrate on a few columns at a time. Understanding the source data helps to analyze why your structure/models are producing accurate results (or not). Mining is iterative— it's good practice to experiment with differing combinations of source columns as you refine your mining models.

Syntax

```
-- select flattened all cases from structure, specific columns only
select flattened [customer counts] as Customer,
(select [Subcategory], [internet sales amount] as Sales
from [subcategories]) from mining structure [customer mining].cases
```

Result

Customer	Expression.Subcategory	Expression.Sales
Jon V. Yang	Mountain Bikes	5719.98
Jon V. Yang	Fenders	21.98
Jon V. Yang	Touring Bikes	2384.07
Jon V. Yang	Tires and Tubes	33.98
Jon V. Yang	Helmets	34.99
Jon V. Yang	Jerseys	53.99
Eugene L. Huang	Mountain Bikes	5694.98
Eugene L. Huang	Fenders	21.98
Eugene L. Huang	Bottles and Cages	28.96
Eugene L. Huang	Jerseys	53.99
Eugene L. Huang	Caps	8.99
Eugene L. Huang	Road Bikes	539.99
Eugene L. Huang	Helmets	34.99
Ruben Torres	Mountain Bikes	5694.98
Ruben Torres	Touring Bikes	2384.07
Ruben Torres	Helmets	34.99
Christy Zhu	Mountain Bikes	5694.98
Christy Zhu	Bottles and Cages	14.98
Christy Zhu	Caps	8.99

Analysis

There are a few important points to note in this query. One, the key word Flattened is again used to expand the nested table. Two, the columns are aliased. Three, individual columns within a nested table are manipulated within a subquery. The subquery is the inner Select and is enclosed within parentheses—note that it uses the name of the nested table in its From clause. This DMX subquery is very similar to an SQL subquery. The acronym DMX stands for Data Mining eXtensions—this means that DMX is an extension to SQL. The MDX language (for querying SSAS cubes) is a completely separate language and is not an extension to SQL—MDX stands for MultiDimensional Expressions (not eXtensions).

Examining Training Data

Here we have a subtle variation on the last few queries. Please note the addition of a Where clause. Beginning with SQL Server Analysis Services 2008 (SSAS), it's possible to stipulate that not all of the source data copied into the mining structure is used for training. You may wish to keep some of the data for post-training testing of your mining models in the structure.

Syntax

```
-- training cases only - 2008 only
select flattened [customer counts] as Customer,
(select [Subcategory], [internet sales amount] as Sales
from [subcategories]) from mining structure [customer mining].cases
where IsTrainingCase()
```

Result

Customer	Expression.Subcategory	Expression.Sales
Rob Verhoff	Tires and Tubes	2.29
Rob Verhoff	Touring Bikes	2384.07
Rob Verhoff	Helmets	34.99
Shannon C. Carlson	Mountain Bikes	5669.98
Shannon C. Carlson	Tires and Tubes	2.29
Shannon C. Carlson	Touring Bikes	2384.07
Shannon C. Carlson	Helmets	34.99
Jacquelyn C. Suarez	Mountain Bikes	5694.98
Jacquelyn C. Suarez	Touring Bikes	2384.07
Jacquelyn C. Suarez	Caps	8.99
Curtis Lu	Mountain Bikes	5694.98
Curtis Lu	Touring Bikes	2384.07
Curtis Lu	Jerseys	53.99
Lauren M. Walker	Tires and Tubes	46.27
Lauren M. Walker	Helmets	34.99
Ian M. Jenkins	Tires and Tubes	43.98
Ian M. Jenkins	Helmets	69.98
Sydney Bennett	Tires and Tubes	43.98
Sydney Bennett	Helmets	69.98

Analysis

The query returns only those cases or records actually involved in training the models in the structure. The Where clause has the IsTrainingCase() function. The training cases may be all of the cases from the source data or a subset. This is determined by the HoldoutMaxCases and/or the HoldoutMaxPercent properties on the structure in BIDS. In the Customer Mining structure, neither of those properties is set—no data is held back for retrospective testing. Therefore, all of the source cases are training cases. If you were to stipulate a non-zero value for HoldoutMaxCases, then our query would return a subset of the original data. DMX queries do not show the number of records returned, so it can be difficult to ascertain whether functions like IsTrainingCase() are successful.

Examining Specific Cases

Maybe a particular case is of interest. For example, you might have some customer clusters and drill through to see the customers in a particular cluster (drill-through is covered later in the book). You can extend the Where clause to return specific cases.

Syntax

```
-- subset of training cases - 2008 only
select flattened [customer counts] as Customer,
(select [Subcategory], [internet sales amount] as Sales
from [subcategories]) from mining structure [customer mining].cases
where IsTrainingCase() and [customer counts] = 'Eugene L. Huang'
```

Result

Customer	Expression.Subcategory	Expression.Sales
Eugene L. Huang	Mountain Bikes	5694.98
Eugene L. Huang	Fenders	21.98
Eugene L. Huang	Bottles and Cages	28.96
Eugene L. Huang	Jerseys	53.99
Eugene L. Huang	Caps	8.99
Eugene L. Huang	Road Bikes	539.99
Eugene L. Huang	Helmets	34.99

Analysis

Eugene L. Huang is the customer of interest. The flattened nested table shows the subcategories he purchased. You can establish that he is a valid customer by, for example, drilling through a cluster. If you had set HoldoutMaxCases or HoldoutMaxPercent in BIDS, then it's possible that Eugene L. Huang may be in your test cases and not in your training cases. If that were so, he would not have appeared during drill-through on the cluster and this query would not have shown him. In that situation, you can omit the IsTrainingCase() function (that's how you would have to do it in SSAS 2005). There is also an IsTestCase() function in SSAS 2008 that would have returned his data, even if it had been held out for testing.

Examining Test Cases

In SSAS 2005, you can examine all the cases (records) that populate a mining structure and are available to mining models within the structure. You can do the same in SSAS 2008. However, in SSAS 2008, you have the option of seeing only the training cases or only the test cases. This query shows you how to look at the test cases only—these are used for post-training validation of your models, maybe in a Mining Accuracy Chart lift chart in BIDS or SSMS.

Syntax

```
-- test cases only - 2008 only
-- HoldoutMaxCases
-- With Holdout
select flattened [customer counts] as Customer,
(select [Subcategory], [internet sales amount] as Sales
from [subcategories]) from mining structure [customer mining].cases
where IsTestCase()
```

Result

Analysis

There is no result! The Customer Mining structure does not have any holdout or test cases (HoldoutMaxCases and/or HoldoutMaxPercent properties in BIDS). If you were to create structures programmatically from DMX rather than graphically in BIDS, you could use the With Holdout statement, which will keep back some data for testing. With Holdout is covered later in the book.

Examining Model Cases Only

All of our queries so far have returned cases from a mining structure. The cases used to train the individual mining models within a structure may or may not be the same as those in the structure. Viewing model cases, as opposed to structure cases, is called *drill-through*. Model cases can differ from structure cases in two respects. Firstly, the model might use only some of the available columns from the structure (these are called the *structure columns*). Secondly, the model might use only a subset of the available cases in the structure training cases. This is called *filtering* (Filter property in BIDS or With Filter from DMX) and became available in SSAS 2008.

Syntax

```
-- select all cases from model (cluster)
select * from [Customer Clusters].cases
order by [customer counts 1]
```

Result

Customer Counts 1	Commute Distance	Education	Gender	Home Owner	Marital Status	Number of Cars ...	Number of Childr...	Occupation
Aaron A. Allen	1-2 Miles	High School	Male	Yes	Single	2	1	Manual
Aaron A. Hayes	2-5 Miles	Partial College	Male	Yes	Married	1	0	Skilled Manual
Aaron A. Zhang	2-5 Miles	Bachelors	Male	Yes	Married	0	1	Management
Aaron Alexander	5-10 Miles	High School	Male	Yes	Married	2	0	Skilled Manual
Aaron B. Adams	5-10 Miles	Partial College	Male	Yes	Single	1	0	Skilled Manual
Aaron Bryant	10+ Miles	Bachelors	Male	Yes	Single	2	0	Management
Aaron Butler	5-10 Miles	Partial College	Male	Yes	Married	2	0	Professional
Aaron C. Campbell	2-5 Miles	Graduate Degree	Male	Yes	Single	1	0	Professional
Aaron C. Diaz	1-2 Miles	Bachelors	Male	Yes	Married	0	0	Professional
Aaron C. Scott	5-10 Miles	Partial College	Male	Yes	Married	1	0	Skilled Manual
Aaron C. Yang	5-10 Miles	High School	Male	Yes	Married	2	0	Professional
Aaron Chen	2-5 Miles	Bachelors	Male	Yes	Married	0	3	Professional
Aaron Coleman	5-10 Miles	Partial College	Male	Yes	Single	1	0	Skilled Manual
Aaron E. Baker	2-5 Miles	High School	Male	Yes	Married	2	2	Skilled Manual
Aaron E. Evans	0-1 Miles	Graduate Degree	Male	No	Single	0	0	Professional
Aaron Edwards	1-2 Miles	Bachelors	Male	Yes	Married	4	2	Management
Aaron Flores	0-1 Miles	Bachelors	Male	No	Single	1	0	Professional
Aaron Foster	0-1 Miles	Graduate Degree	Male	Yes	Married	1	0	Professional

Analysis

Here we are drilling through to the cases used to train the Customer Clusters model. It's a deceptively simple query—there's a lot to it! The key phrase, Mining Structure (in all of the previous queries), has been removed from the From clause. There is an optional Order By clause. The result does not return the Subcategories nested case table column—this structure column is not part of the model columns. The algorithm for the model (Clustering) supports drill-through; not all algorithms do so. Finally, the ability to return model cases is determined by the AllowDrillThrough property on the model in BIDS. You can also control this programmatically if you create the model in DMX (With Drillthrough) rather than graphically in BIDS.

If you scroll down far enough, you will see both Jon V. Yang and Eugene L. Huang, whom we met earlier.

Examining Another Model

Not all of the models in the same structure have to use the available containing structure in the same way. Here we are drilling through another model in the same structure.

Syntax

```
-- select all cases from model (association)
select * from [Subcategory Associations].cases
```

Result

Customer Counts 1	Subcategories
Jon V. Yang	⊞ Subcategories
Eugene L. Huang	⊞ Subcategories
Ruben Torres	⊞ Subcategories
Christy Zhu	⊞ Subcategories
Elizabeth Johnson	⊞ Subcategories
Julio Ruiz	⊞ Subcategories
Janet G. Alvarez	⊞ Subcategories
Marco Mehta	⊞ Subcategories
Rob Verhoff	⊞ Subcategories
Shannon C. Carlson	⊞ Subcategories
Jacquelyn C. Suarez	⊞ Subcategories
Curtis Lu	⊞ Subcategories
Lauren M. Walker	⊞ Subcategories
Ian M. Jenkins	⊞ Subcategories
Sydney Bennett	⊞ Subcategories
Chloe Young	⊞ Subcategories
Wyatt L. Hill	⊞ Subcategories
Shannon Wang	⊞ Subcategories
Clarence D. Rai	⊞ Subcategories

Analysis

All of the customer demographics (used by the clustering) have disappeared. The customer name column is only used to link subcategory purchases (in the nested table) together so we can perform market basket analysis—we need to establish who bought what to search for cross-selling opportunities. Again, the algorithm (here it's Association) must support drill-through and it must be enabled (AllowDrillThrough property in BIDS).

Expanding the Nested Table

The last query contained a nested table. Here it's expanded to easily reveal further information.

Syntax

```
-- select flattened all cases from model (association)
select flattened * from [Subcategory Associations].cases
```

Result

Customer Counts 1	Subcategories.Subcategory
Jon V. Yang	Mountain Bikes
Jon V. Yang	Fenders
Jon V. Yang	Touring Bikes
Jon V. Yang	Tires and Tubes
Jon V. Yang	Helmets
Jon V. Yang	Jerseys
Eugene L. Huang	Mountain Bikes
Eugene L. Huang	Fenders
Eugene L. Huang	Bottles and Cages
Eugene L. Huang	Jerseys
Eugene L. Huang	Caps
Eugene L. Huang	Road Bikes
Eugene L. Huang	Helmets
Ruben Torres	Mountain Bikes
Ruben Torres	Touring Bikes
Ruben Torres	Helmets
Christy Zhu	Mountain Bikes
Christy Zhu	Bottles and Cages
Christy Zhu	Caps

Analysis

Once more, the key word Flattened expands the nested table. Now, it's easier to see the subcategory purchases of each customer. For example, Jon V. Yang bought mountain bikes and touring bikes while Eugene L. Huang bought mountain bikes and road bikes.

All of this information is used to show which product subcategories were bought together by all customers when you browse the model. You can browse models in SSMS or BIDS. These are not end-user tools—your end users can browse models graphically in Excel or as facts and figures in an SQL Server Reporting Services (SSRS) report based on a DMX query.

Sorting Cases

Just like SQL, DMX has Order By and Where clauses. They function in exactly the same way. This query is simply a sort of the cases from the mining model.

Syntax

```
-- select flattened all cases from model (association), sorted
select flattened * from [Subcategory Associations].cases
order by [customer counts 1]
```

Result

Customer Counts 1	Subcategories.Subcategory
Aaron A. Allen	Mountain Bikes
Aaron A. Hayes	Road Bikes
Aaron A. Hayes	Mountain Bikes
Aaron A. Hayes	Bottles and Cages
Aaron A. Zhang	Road Bikes
Aaron A. Zhang	Tires and Tubes
Aaron A. Zhang	Helmets
Aaron Alexander	Shorts
Aaron B. Adams	Tires and Tubes
Aaron B. Adams	Helmets
Aaron B. Adams	Jerseys
Aaron Bryant	Jerseys
Aaron Bryant	Caps
Aaron Bryant	Tires and Tubes
Aaron Bryant	Helmets
Aaron Butler	Bottles and Cages
Aaron C. Campb...	Road Bikes
Aaron C. Campb...	Helmets
Aaron C. Diaz	Road Bikes

Analysis

Your DMX queries can employ Where and Order By clauses much as they can in SQL. Their syntax and functionality in DMX and SQL are similar. However, you will find that not *all* of the SQL functionality is available to you—there are certain limitations. Our query here is sorting the customers alphabetically (as in SQL, by default it's an ascending sort). In the result you will see that Aaron A. Allen has a narrow range of interests, while that of Aaron A. Zhang is rather wide.

Model and Structure Columns

To reiterate, data mining structures define the cases and the columns in those cases that are available for your mining. The structure can contain zero, one, or more than one model—although a structure with no models is not very helpful. The data mining model(s) within a structure may only be trained with a subset of all of the available cases by filtering the model. In addition, the data mining model(s) within a structure may only be defined and trained with a subset of the columns available from the structure. Here the query not only shows the mining columns but also references an unused column from the structure.

Syntax

```
-- StructureColumn
select flattened *, StructureColumn('Education') as Education
from [Subcategory Associations].cases
order by [customer counts 1]
```

Result

Customer Counts 1	Subcategories.Subcategory	Education
Aaron A. Allen	Mountain Bikes	High School
Aaron A. Hayes	Road Bikes	Partial College
Aaron A. Hayes	Mountain Bikes	Partial College
Aaron A. Hayes	Bottles and Cages	Partial College
Aaron A. Zhang	Road Bikes	Bachelors
Aaron A. Zhang	Tires and Tubes	Bachelors
Aaron A. Zhang	Helmets	Bachelors
Aaron Alexander	Shorts	High School
Aaron B. Adams	Tires and Tubes	Partial College
Aaron B. Adams	Helmets	Partial College
Aaron B. Adams	Jerseys	Partial College
Aaron Bryant	Jerseys	Bachelors
Aaron Bryant	Caps	Bachelors
Aaron Bryant	Tires and Tubes	Bachelors
Aaron Bryant	Helmets	Bachelors
Aaron Butler	Bottles and Cages	Partial College
Aaron C. Campb...	Road Bikes	Graduate Degree
Aaron C. Campb...	Helmets	Graduate Degree
Aaron C. Diaz	Road Bikes	Bachelors

Analysis

The Subcategory Associations model does not include the Education column from the structure. To reference an unused structure column while querying model cases, you use the StructureColumn() syntax. Here we are looking at the Education column. Of course, you could also simply write a mining structure cases query as we did at the start of this chapter.

Specific Model Columns

Let's go back to the Customer Clusters mining model. This contains a large number of columns for the demographics of each customer. Suppose you wish to concentrate on a particular demographic. You do so by explicitly requesting the column in your query.

Syntax

```
-- specific column
select Education from [Customer Clusters].cases
```

Result

Education
Bachelors
Bachelors
Bachelors
Bachelors
Bachelors
Bachelors
Bachelors
Bachelors
Bachelors
Bachelors
Bachelors
Bachelors
Bachelors
Bachelors
Bachelors
Bachelors
Partial College
Partial College
High School
Partial College

Analysis

The result shows the Education column for each customer case. To return all columns, specify an asterisk (*). To return a few columns, specify a comma-separated list of column names. As it stands, this is not a very informative query. More useful would be an enumeration of the possible values of Education—this is covered in the next couple of queries.

Distinct Column Values 1/2

Rather than show the Education of every individual customer, you might want to see the possible values. Maybe a Distinct might help?

Syntax

```
-- distinct specific column 1/2
select distinct Education from [Customer Clusters].cases
```

Result

```
Executing the query ...
Error (Data mining): DISTINCT is not allowed in the type of SELECT statement found at line 2, column 1.

Execution complete
```

Analysis

Unfortunately, adding a Distinct generates an error. You can't have a Distinct with a Cases query. But don't worry! The next query shows you how to do it.

Distinct Column Values 2/2

There is a very small change this time. We've dropped .cases after the name of the model.

Syntax

```
-- distinct specific column 2/2
select distinct Education from [Customer Clusters]
```

Result

```
Education

Partial High School
High School
Bachelors
Graduate Degree
Partial College
```

Analysis

This is not a Cases (there is no .cases after the model name) query as such. Here you are querying the model itself directly. This time, Distinct is fine. You should see a list of all the possible values for the Education column (including the missing value). This is a handy technique when you want to look at the possible values for a discrete column in your models. It's not so useful for continuous values where there are many, many possible values—in fact, you'll only get one value in the result (the average). We'll return to the continuous value problem in a later chapter. Please note the empty row at the top of the result.

Cases by Cluster 1/4

If your cases belong to a clustering model, it's possible to further analyze the cases by cluster. The next few queries investigate this further. Here we have a base query to get us started—it's a repeat of an earlier query. We are also going to do some more sorting of data.

Syntax

```
-- IsInNode (cluster) with Order 1/4
select * from [Customer Clusters].cases
order by [customer counts 1]
```

Result

Customer Counts 1	Commute Distance	Education	Gender	Home Owner	Marital Status	Number of Cars ...	Number of Childr...	Occupation
Aaron A. Allen	1-2 Miles	High School	Male	Yes	Single	2	1	Manual
Aaron A. Hayes	2-5 Miles	Partial College	Male	Yes	Married	1	0	Skilled Manual
Aaron A. Zhang	2-5 Miles	Bachelors	Male	Yes	Married	0	1	Management
Aaron Alexander	5-10 Miles	High School	Male	Yes	Married	2	0	Skilled Manual
Aaron B. Adams	5-10 Miles	Partial College	Male	Yes	Single	1	0	Skilled Manual
Aaron Bryant	10+ Miles	Bachelors	Male	Yes	Single	2	0	Management
Aaron Butler	5-10 Miles	Partial College	Male	Yes	Married	2	0	Professional
Aaron C. Campbell	2-5 Miles	Graduate Degree	Male	Yes	Single	1	0	Professional
Aaron C. Diaz	1-2 Miles	Bachelors	Male	Yes	Married	0	0	Professional
Aaron C. Scott	5-10 Miles	Partial College	Male	Yes	Married	1	0	Skilled Manual
Aaron C. Yang	5-10 Miles	High School	Male	Yes	Married	2	0	Professional
Aaron Chen	2-5 Miles	Bachelors	Male	Yes	Married	0	3	Professional
Aaron Coleman	5-10 Miles	Partial College	Male	Yes	Single	1	0	Skilled Manual
Aaron E. Baker	2-5 Miles	High School	Male	Yes	Married	2	2	Skilled Manual
Aaron E. Evans	0-1 Miles	Graduate Degree	Male	No	Single	0	0	Professional
Aaron Edwards	1-2 Miles	Bachelors	Male	Yes	Married	4	2	Management
Aaron Flores	0-1 Miles	Bachelors	Male	No	Single	1	0	Professional
Aaron Foster	0-1 Miles	Graduate Degree	Male	Yes	Married	1	0	Professional

Analysis

As a reminder, this query will fail in the "real world" if AllowDrillThrough is not enabled for the model design in BIDS. This is a book about DMX queries—graphical structure and model design including Properties windows in BIDS are outside our scope. When we design structures and models in a later chapter, we will do so from code—from DMX itself! Thus, you will learn how to create and design a model programmatically. For example, to enable drill-through so that Cases queries work, we'll use With Drillthrough in a DMX script rather than discuss how to set the AllowDrillThrough property in BIDS. The DMX With Drillthrough syntax will automatically set the AllowDrillThrough property for you. This leads to an important point. When you create SSAS mining (or cube) objects graphically, they can be referenced from DMX (or MDX) code. Conversely, when you create mining objects from DMX queries, they can be opened and viewed graphically in BIDS (as well as in SSMS).

I was tempted to write the same about MDX. Many people start in SQL, move on to MDX (and unlearn SQL!), and only then try DMX (and learn SQL again). There are fundamental differences in the three languages. SQL is a data manipulation language (DML), a data definition language (DDL), and a data control language (DCL). DMX is a DML and DDL language; you can't use it to set security. MDX is a DML language (with just a few DDL capabilities). MDX is not used to create cubes—its purpose is to query cubes. The DDL/DCL language for cubes is XML for Analysis/Analysis Services Scripting Language (XMLA/ASSL). That's why SSAS queries in SSMS give you the choice of DMX or MDX or XMLA queries. Confusingly for newcomers, you can also use XMLA as a DDL language for data mining, as well as DMX. Even more confusingly, XMLA can also function as a DML language for mining (or cubes) if you embed your DMX (or MDX) inside the XMLA.

Cases by Cluster 2/4

The Customer Clusters model is based on the Clustering algorithm. All of the input cases are assigned to a particular cluster (there are usually ten clusters by default). The clusters are part of the model content rather than a property or column of the cases themselves. This query returns the cases that have been assigned to a particular cluster.

Syntax

```
-- IsInNode (cluster) with Order 2/4
select * from [Customer Clusters].cases
where IsInNode('005')
order by [customer counts 1]
```

Result

Customer Counts 1	Commute Distance	Education	Gender	Home Owner	Marital Status	Number of Cars ...	Number of Childr...	Occupation
Aaron Bryant	10+ Miles	Bachelors	Male	Yes	Single	2	0	Management
Aaron Hill	10+ Miles	Bachelors	Male	Yes	Single	3	0	Professional
Aaron Powell	5-10 Miles	Bachelors	Male	Yes	Married	1	0	Professional
Abby J. Sanchez	10+ Miles	Bachelors	Female	Yes	Married	3	0	Professional
Abby Martinez	0-1 Miles	Bachelors	Female	No	Single	2	0	Management
Abby T. Raman	10+ Miles	Bachelors	Female	Yes	Single	3	0	Professional
Abigail I. Ross	1-2 Miles	Bachelors	Female	Yes	Married	2	0	Management
Abigail Johnson	5-10 Miles	Bachelors	Female	Yes	Married	1	0	Management
Abigail L. Flores	1-2 Miles	Graduate Degree	Female	Yes	Married	2	0	Management
Abigail Patterson	10+ Miles	Bachelors	Female	Yes	Married	1	0	Management
Abigail Rogers	10+ Miles	Partial College	Female	No	Married	1	0	Professional
Abigail Walker	5-10 Miles	Graduate Degree	Female	Yes	Single	2	0	Management
Abigail Washington	10+ Miles	Bachelors	Female	No	Single	3	0	Professional
Adam Adams	1-2 Miles	Graduate Degree	Male	No	Married	2	0	Management
Adam H. Evans	10+ Miles	Bachelors	Male	Yes	Married	3	0	Professional
Adam L. Wang	10+ Miles	Graduate Degree	Male	Yes	Married	2	0	Management
Adam R. Phillips	10+ Miles	Bachelors	Male	Yes	Single	3	0	Management
Adam W. Hernandez	1-2 Miles	Graduate Degree	Male	No	Married	2	0	Management

Analysis

The Where clause includes the IsInNode() function. You can think of a node as a cluster in this example. The parameter for the IsInNode() function is the node ID of the cluster. By default, the node IDs are 001 through 010. Later in this chapter we'll see how to check the node IDs of the clusters. Here, you should be looking at the subset of cases that have been assigned to the fifth cluster. There is an important point to make here—data mining algorithms do not always return the same results (they can be non-deterministic), and your result may be different if you rebuild the model.

Cases by Cluster 3/4

Our query here is the same as the last query but with an explicit (rather than implicit) ascending sort by customer name.

Syntax

```
-- IsInNode (cluster) with Order 3/4
select * from [Customer Clusters].cases
where IsInNode('005')
order by [customer counts 1] asc
```

Result

Customer Counts 1	Commute Distance	Education	Gender	Home Owner	Marital Status	Number of Cars ...	Number of Childr...	Occupation
Aaron Bryant	10+ Miles	Bachelors	Male	Yes	Single	2	0	Management
Aaron Hill	10+ Miles	Bachelors	Male	Yes	Single	3	0	Professional
Aaron Powell	5-10 Miles	Bachelors	Male	Yes	Married	1	0	Professional
Abby J. Sanchez	10+ Miles	Bachelors	Female	Yes	Married	3	0	Professional
Abby Martinez	0-1 Miles	Bachelors	Female	No	Single	2	0	Management
Abby T. Raman	10+ Miles	Bachelors	Female	Yes	Single	3	0	Professional
Abigail I. Ross	1-2 Miles	Bachelors	Female	Yes	Married	2	0	Management
Abigail Johnson	5-10 Miles	Bachelors	Female	Yes	Married	1	0	Management
Abigail L. Flores	1-2 Miles	Graduate Degree	Female	Yes	Married	2	0	Management
Abigail Patterson	10+ Miles	Bachelors	Female	Yes	Married	1	0	Management
Abigail Rogers	10+ Miles	Partial College	Female	No	Married	1	0	Professional
Abigail Walker	5-10 Miles	Graduate Degree	Female	Yes	Single	2	0	Management
Abigail Washington	10+ Miles	Bachelors	Female	No	Single	3	0	Professional
Adam Adams	1-2 Miles	Graduate Degree	Male	No	Married	2	0	Management
Adam H. Evans	10+ Miles	Bachelors	Male	Yes	Married	3	0	Professional
Adam L. Wang	10+ Miles	Graduate Degree	Male	Yes	Married	2	0	Management
Adam R. Phillips	10+ Miles	Bachelors	Male	Yes	Single	3	0	Management
Adam W. Hernan...	1-2 Miles	Graduate Degree	Male	No	Married	2	0	Management

Analysis

This is an explicit ascending sort. As in SQL, an ascending sort is the default, so adding Asc to the Order By clause is optional but recommended. In SQL you can sort on multiple columns by having a comma-separated list of column names. In DMX, you are limited to sorting on only one column at a time—or on more than one column, but only if you concatenate the column names with a plus sign (+).

Cases by Cluster 4/4

Sorting in descending order is the same as in SQL.

Syntax

```
-- IsInNode (cluster) with Order 4/4
select * from [Customer Clusters].cases
where IsInNode('005')
order by [customer counts 1] desc
```

Result

Customer Counts 1	Commute Distance	Education	Gender	Home Owner	Marital Status	Number of Cars ...	Number of Childr...	Occupation
Zoe Peterson	0-1 Miles	Bachelors	Female	Yes	Married	3	0	Management
Zoe D. Morgan	10+ Miles	Bachelors	Female	Yes	Married	2	0	Management
Zachary Wang	1-2 Miles	Graduate Degree	Male	Yes	Married	2	0	Management
Zachary Russell	2-5 Miles	Bachelors	Male	Yes	Single	1	0	Management
Zachary Powell	0-1 Miles	Bachelors	Male	No	Single	1	0	Management
Zachary K. Garcia	10+ Miles	Graduate Degree	Male	Yes	Married	2	0	Management
Zachary Anderson	1-2 Miles	Bachelors	Male	Yes	Married	2	0	Management
Yolanda M. Goel	10+ Miles	Bachelors	Female	No	Married	3	0	Professional
Yolanda J. Kumar	10+ Miles	Bachelors	Female	Yes	Married	4	0	Professional
Yolanda Bhat	2-5 Miles	Bachelors	Female	Yes	Married	1	0	Professional
Yolanda A. Nath	1-2 Miles	Graduate Degree	Female	No	Married	2	0	Management
Xavier R. Peterson	10+ Miles	Graduate Degree	Male	Yes	Single	2	0	Management
Xavier R. Cox	1-2 Miles	Bachelors	Male	No	Married	2	0	Management
Xavier R. Bryant	1-2 Miles	Graduate Degree	Male	Yes	Married	2	0	Management
Xavier R. Bell	10+ Miles	Bachelors	Male	Yes	Married	2	0	Management
Xavier Martinez	10+ Miles	Bachelors	Male	Yes	Married	2	0	Management
Xavier L. Mitchell	0-1 Miles	Bachelors	Male	No	Married	1	0	Management
Xavier L. Clark	1-2 Miles	Graduate Degree	Male	Yes	Married	2	0	Management

Analysis

Your result should now be in the reverse order. Note the addition of Desc to the Order By clause.

Content Query

All of the queries so far have been Cases queries. Cases queries return a copy of the source data that gets stored in the mining structure (or possibly a subset that is used to train each individual mining model within the structure). This, by contrast, is a Content query. Content queries operate on individual models, not on the structure itself. The results are the patterns or trends or clusters or associations or probabilities discovered after a model is trained.

Syntax

```
-- getting node name (cluster)
select * from [Customer Clusters].content
```

Result

MODEL_CATALOG	MODEL_SCHEMA	MODEL_NAME	ATTRIBUTE_N...	NODE_NAME	NODE_UNIQUE...	NODE_TYPE	NODE_GUID	NODE_CAPTION	CHILDREN_
Adventure Works ...		Customer Clusters		000	000	1		Cluster Model	10
Adventure Works ...		Customer Clusters		001	001	5		Cluster 1	0
Adventure Works ...		Customer Clusters		002	002	5		Cluster 2	0
Adventure Works ...		Customer Clusters		003	003	5		Cluster 3	0
Adventure Works ...		Customer Clusters		004	004	5		Cluster 4	0
Adventure Works ...		Customer Clusters		005	005	5		Cluster 5	0
Adventure Works ...		Customer Clusters		006	006	5		Cluster 6	0
Adventure Works ...		Customer Clusters		007	007	5		Cluster 7	0
Adventure Works ...		Customer Clusters		008	008	5		Cluster 8	0
Adventure Works ...		Customer Clusters		009	009	5		Cluster 9	0
Adventure Works ...		Customer Clusters		010	010	5		Cluster 10	0

Analysis

The query operates against the model, not the containing structure. There is one fundamental change from earlier queries—.cases has been replaced by .content. Content queries return data that is specific to a particular algorithm. This is a Content query against a Clustering model. You may have to scroll horizontally to see all of the columns; there are quite a few.

Important columns in this example include NODE_UNIQUE_NAME, NODE_CAPTION, NODE_DESCRIPTION, and NODE_SUPPORT. The Node ID is NODE_UNIQUE_NAME; it is the parameter you need in an IsInNode() function.

Decision Tree Cases

Let's query a Decision Tree model for a change. This is a Cases query.

Syntax

```
-- IsInNode (decision tree)
select * from [TM Decision Tree].cases
where IsInNode('0000000010403')
order by age
```

Result

Age	Bike Buyer	Commute Distance	Customer Key	Education	Occupation	Gender	House Owner Flag	Marital Status
38	1	0-1 Miles	24368	Graduate Degree	Management	F	0	S
38	1	0-1 Miles	17288	Graduate Degree	Management	M	0	S
38	1	0-1 Miles	29190	Graduate Degree	Management	F	0	S
38	1	0-1 Miles	24367	Graduate Degree	Management	M	0	S
38	1	0-1 Miles	22913	Graduate Degree	Management	F	1	S
38	1	0-1 Miles	15591	Graduate Degree	Management	M	1	S
38	1	0-1 Miles	27459	Graduate Degree	Management	M	1	M
44	0	1-2 Miles	17395	Graduate Degree	Management	F	0	S
44	1	0-1 Miles	15770	Bachelors	Management	M	0	S
44	0	1-2 Miles	23469	Graduate Degree	Management	F	0	S
44	1	0-1 Miles	21271	Bachelors	Management	M	1	M
44	0	0-1 Miles	19686	Graduate Degree	Management	M	1	M
44	1	1-2 Miles	28076	Graduate Degree	Management	M	0	S
44	1	0-1 Miles	15964	Bachelors	Management	M	0	S
44	1	1-2 Miles	21205	Graduate Degree	Management	F	0	S
44	1	0-1 Miles	29222	Bachelors	Management	M	1	M
44	1	1-2 Miles	16691	Graduate Degree	Management	F	0	S
44	0	0-1 Miles	11269	Graduate Degree	Management	M	1	M

Analysis

The Where clause means we only see a subset of the cases used to train the model. Just like Clustering models, Decision Tree models have nodes—nodes or splits in the tree. But this time, the Node ID used as a parameter in the IsInNode() function is not so obvious. You'll require a Content query (coming next) in order to establish the parameter you want. If you retrain this model, you may see a different result—the mining algorithms are often non-deterministic.

Decision Tree Content

Here we have a Content query against a Decision Tree model.

Syntax

```
-- getting node name (decision tree)
select * from [TM Decision Tree].content
```

Result

MODEL_CATAL...	MODEL_SCHEMA	MODEL_NAME	ATTRIBUTE_N...	NODE_NAME	NODE_UNIQUE...	NODE_TYPE	NODE_GUID	NODE_CAPTION
Adventure Wor...		TM Decision Tree		0	0	1		
Adventure Wor...		TM Decision Tree	Bike Buyer	000000001	000000001	2		All
Adventure Wor...		TM Decision Tree	Bike Buyer	00000000100	00000000100	3		Number Cars Owned = 0
Adventure Wor...		TM Decision Tree	Bike Buyer	00000000101	00000000101	3		Number Cars Owned = 3
Adventure Wor...		TM Decision Tree	Bike Buyer	00000000102	00000000102	3		Number Cars Owned = 1
Adventure Wor...		TM Decision Tree	Bike Buyer	00000000103	00000000103	3		Number Cars Owned = 4
Adventure Wor...		TM Decision Tree	Bike Buyer	00000000104	00000000104	3		Number Cars Owned = 2
Adventure Wor...		TM Decision Tree	Bike Buyer	0000000010400	0000000010400	3		Yearly Income < 26000
Adventure Wor...		TM Decision Tree	Bike Buyer	0000000010401	0000000010401	3		Yearly Income >= 26000 an...
Adventure Wor...		TM Decision Tree	Bike Buyer	0000000010402	0000000010402	3		Yearly Income >= 58000 an...
Adventure Wor...		TM Decision Tree	Bike Buyer	0000000010403	0000000010403	3		Yearly Income >= 106000
Adventure Wor...		TM Decision Tree	Bike Buyer	000000001040300	000000001040...	4		Region = 'Europe'
Adventure Wor...		TM Decision Tree	Bike Buyer	000000001040301	000000001040...	3		Region not = 'Europe'
Adventure Wor...		TM Decision Tree	Bike Buyer	00000000104030100	000000001040...	4		Total Children = 2
Adventure Wor...		TM Decision Tree	Bike Buyer	00000000104030101	000000001040...	4		Total Children not = 2
Adventure Wor...		TM Decision Tree	Bike Buyer	000000001040200	000000001040...	3		Number Children At Home = 0
Adventure Wor...		TM Decision Tree	Bike Buyer	000000001040201	000000001040...	3		Number Children At Home = 3
Adventure Wor...		TM Decision Tree	Bike Buyer	000000001040202	000000001040...	3		Number Children At Home = 1

Analysis

Again as in a Clustering model, important columns in this example include NODE_ UNIQUE_NAME, NODE_CAPTION, NODE_DESCRIPTION, and NODE_ SUPPORT. The Node ID is NODE_UNIQUE_NAME; it is the parameter you need in an IsInNode() function.

Now you could go back and amend the previous Cases query—this is a useful technique you can employ with your own decision tree.

Time Series Cases

Differing data mining algorithms require that you organize the source data in different ways. Here you'll see the typical cases used by a Time Series model.

Syntax

```
-- select all cases from model (time series)
select [Model Region], [time index] as [Date], Quantity, Amount
from [Forecasting].cases
```

Result

Model Region	Date	Quantity	Amount
M200 Europe	200107	6	20324.94
M200 North America	200107	6	20324.94
M200 Pacific	200107	19	64424.81
R250 Europe	200107	25	89456.75
R250 North America	200107	35	125239.45
R250 Pacific	200107	40	143130.8
R750 Europe	200107	5	3495.491
R750 North America	200107	7	4893.6874
R750 Pacific	200107	3	2097.2946
R750 Pacific	200108	6	4194.5892
R750 North America	200108	5	3495.491
R750 Europe	200108	5	3495.491
R250 Pacific	200108	44	157443.88
R250 North America	200108	40	143130.8
R250 Europe	200108	25	89456.75
M200 Pacific	200108	18	60899.82
M200 North America	200108	7	23724.93
M200 Europe	200108	6	20349.94
M200 Europe	200109	5	16949.95

Analysis

There are four columns in the result. Model Region is the case key (a case key is similar to a primary key)—if you look at the Content property of the structure in BIDS, you'll notice it's set to Key. Incidentally, the structure and the model share the same name, Forecasting. The Time Index column, aliased as Date, is the case time key (Content property is Key Time). Quantity and Amount are continuous value input columns. They are both predictable columns as well.

The cases are organized in such a way to enable forecasting quantity and amount sold by model region by time.

Sequence Clustering Cases 1/2

Sequence Clustering models are often used to analyze and to predict the sequence in which events (for example, purchases or web page visits) have occurred or are likely to occur—and the likelihood of that happening. Here we have a Cases query on a Sequence Clustering model.

Syntax

```
-- select all cases from model (sequence)
select * from [Sequence Clustering].cases
```

Result

Order Number	v Assoc Seq Line Items
S051176	⊞ v Assoc Seq Line Items
S051177	⊞ v Assoc Seq Line Items
S051178	⊞ v Assoc Seq Line Items
S051179	⊞ v Assoc Seq Line Items
S051180	⊞ v Assoc Seq Line Items
S051181	⊞ v Assoc Seq Line Items
S051182	⊞ v Assoc Seq Line Items
S051183	⊞ v Assoc Seq Line Items
S051184	⊞ v Assoc Seq Line Items
S051185	⊞ v Assoc Seq Line Items
S051186	⊞ v Assoc Seq Line Items
S051187	⊞ v Assoc Seq Line Items
S051188	⊞ v Assoc Seq Line Items
S051189	⊞ v Assoc Seq Line Items
S051190	⊞ v Assoc Seq Line Items
S051191	⊞ v Assoc Seq Line Items
S051192	⊞ v Assoc Seq Line Items
S051193	⊞ v Assoc Seq Line Items
S051194	⊞ v Assoc Seq Line Items

Analysis

The cases are based on individual orders and the line items of those orders showing the sequence of the line items and the product model purchased. In the source data, there is a one-to-many relationship between the order and the order line items. Thus, the line items are represented by a nested table within each order. You can expand the nested table to see the line items.

Sequence Clustering Cases 2/2

As usual, it's helpful to show a nested table directly by flattening it.

Syntax

```
-- select flattened all cases from model (sequence)
select flattened * from [Sequence Clustering].cases
```

Result

Order Number	v Assoc Seq Line Items.Line Number	v Assoc Seq Line Items.Model
SO51176	1	Road-250
SO51176	2	Road Bottle Cage
SO51177	1	Touring-2000
SO51177	2	Sport-100
SO51178	1	Mountain-200
SO51178	2	Mountain Bottle Cage
SO51178	3	Water Bottle
SO51179	1	Road-250
SO51179	2	HL Road Tire
SO51179	3	Road Tire Tube
SO51179	4	All-Purpose Bike Stand
SO51180	1	Road-250
SO51180	2	Road Bottle Cage
SO51180	3	Water Bottle
SO51180	4	Sport-100
SO51180	5	Long-Sleeve Logo Jersey
SO51181	1	Road-250
SO51181	2	Road Tire Tube
SO51181	3	HL Road Tire

Analysis

Superficially, this looks like classic market basket analysis—what was bought with what. That's often done in an Association model. A Sequence Clustering model is subtly different. Firstly, it takes note of the sequence in which products were purchased. Secondly, it performs this sequence analysis by dividing the orders into clusters based on purchase sequence similarity.

You might like to compare these results with the cases for the Association model. However, in Adventure Works, drill-through for the Association model is disabled. You'd have to change the AllowDrillThrough property in BIDS.

Neural Network and Naïve Bayes Cases

There are two more algorithms or models for you to try—the first is a Neural Network model, the second a Naïve Bayes one.

Syntax

```
-- select all cases from model (neural)
select * from [TM Neural Net].cases

-- select all cases from model (naive bayes)
select * from [TM Naive Bayes].cases
```

Result

```
Executing the query ...
Error (Data mining): Drillthrough (SELECT ... FROM model.CASES) is not enabled for the 'TM Neural Net' model.

Execution complete
```

Analysis

Not much luck! If you are familiar with the BIDS environment, you might be tempted to set the AllowDrillThrough property for each model to True. Only you won't have much joy. Of the seven major algorithms or model types, Neural Network and Naïve Bayes do not support drill-through.

There are actually nine algorithms. Linear Regression is a variation of the Decision Tree algorithm. Logistic Regression is a variation of the Neural Network algorithm. Neither Linear Regression nor Logistic Regression are covered in this book. Instead, we are looking at the other seven base algorithms (Association, Naïve Bayes, Neural Network, Decision Trees, Clustering, Sequence Clustering, and Time Series). Most of our DMX will be written against five of those seven algorithms (Association, Decision Trees, Clustering, Sequence Clustering, and Time Series).

Order By with Top

Here's an interesting way to present a Cases query. In addition to Where and Order By, it also has Top.

Syntax

```
-- select top (time series)
select top 5 [Model Region], [time index] as [Date], Quantity, Amount
from [Forecasting].cases
where [model region] = 'R250 Pacific'
order by [time index]
```

Result

Model Region	Date	Quantity	Amount
R250 Pacific	200107	40	143130.8
R250 Pacific	200108	44	157443.88
R250 Pacific	200109	45	161022.15
R250 Pacific	200110	45	161022.15
R250 Pacific	200111	42	150287.34

Analysis

You can use such a query to perform ad-hoc historical sales analyses. It shows sales in the first five time periods recorded for the R250 Pacific model and region.

Apart from .cases, this looks pretty much like an SQL query. Unlike SQL, however, Top does not support Percent nor does it support With Ties.

Sequence Clustering Nodes 1/2

Sequence Clustering alone supports a variation on .cases, namely .sample_cases.

Syntax

```
-- sample cases (sequence)
select * from [Sequence Clustering].sample_cases
where IsInNode('7')
order by [order number]
```

Result

Order Number	v Assoc Seq Line Items
S051176	⊞ v Assoc Seq Line Items
S051177	⊞ v Assoc Seq Line Items
S051178	⊞ v Assoc Seq Line Items
S051179	⊞ v Assoc Seq Line Items
S051180	⊞ v Assoc Seq Line Items
S051181	⊞ v Assoc Seq Line Items
S051182	⊞ v Assoc Seq Line Items
S051183	⊞ v Assoc Seq Line Items
S051184	⊞ v Assoc Seq Line Items
S051185	⊞ v Assoc Seq Line Items
S051186	⊞ v Assoc Seq Line Items
S051187	⊞ v Assoc Seq Line Items
S051188	⊞ v Assoc Seq Line Items
S051189	⊞ v Assoc Seq Line Items
S051190	⊞ v Assoc Seq Line Items
S051191	⊞ v Assoc Seq Line Items
S051192	⊞ v Assoc Seq Line Items
S051193	⊞ v Assoc Seq Line Items
S051194	⊞ v Assoc Seq Line Items

Analysis

Sample cases are not the same as cases. Only Sequence Clustering models support sample cases. Cases represent actual source data used to train a model. Sample cases represent fictitious cases generated during training to assist the algorithm in reaching its conclusions. You can't use sample cases to view a copy of the source data stored in the mining structure that contains a Sequence Clustering model.

Just like Decision Tree and Clustering models, a Sequence Clustering model has nodes, so you can use the IsInNode() function.

Sequence Clustering Nodes 2/2

This is a Content query, not a Cases query. It's a Content query against a Sequence Clustering model.

Syntax

```
-- getting node name (sequence)
select * from [Sequence Clustering].content
```

Result

MODEL_CATAL...	MODEL_SCHEMA	MODEL_NAME	ATTRIBUTE_N...	NODE_NAME	NODE_UNIQUE...	NODE_TYPE	NODE_GUID	NODE_CAPTION	CHILDREN,
Adventure Wor...		Sequence Clust...		0	0	1		All	16
Adventure Wor...		Sequence Clust...		1	1	5		Cluster 1	1
Adventure Wor...		Sequence Clust...		2	2	5		Cluster 2	1
Adventure Wor...		Sequence Clust...		3	3	5		Cluster 3	1
Adventure Wor...		Sequence Clust...		4	4	5		Cluster 4	1
Adventure Wor...		Sequence Clust...		5	5	5		Cluster 5	1
Adventure Wor...		Sequence Clust...		6	6	5		Cluster 6	1
Adventure Wor...		Sequence Clust...		7	7	5		Cluster 7	1
Adventure Wor...		Sequence Clust...		8	8	5		Cluster 8	1
Adventure Wor...		Sequence Clust...		9	9	5		Cluster 9	1
Adventure Wor...		Sequence Clust...		10	10	5		Cluster 10	1
Adventure Wor...		Sequence Clust...		11	11	5		Cluster 11	1
Adventure Wor...		Sequence Clust...		12	12	5		Cluster 12	1
Adventure Wor...		Sequence Clust...		13	13	5		Cluster 13	1
Adventure Wor...		Sequence Clust...		14	14	5		Cluster 14	1
Adventure Wor...		Sequence Clust...		15	15	5		Cluster 15	1
Adventure Wor...		Sequence Clust...		1081327	1081327	13		Sequence level ...	38
Adventure Wor...		Sequence Clust...		1081328	1081328	14		Transition row f...	0

Analysis

You can use this type of query to determine the NODE_UNIQUE_NAME for a node. Then you can use that in an IsInNode() function.

Chapter 2

Content Queries

Data mining models are trained using the cases (source data) that populate the data mining structure to which the model belongs. The results of the model training are referred to as the *model content*. When you browse a model graphically, you are looking at the content. You can also examine the content of a model from a DMX query—DMX Content queries are the subject of this chapter. The nature of the content depends upon the algorithm on which the model is based. For example, you can view cluster profiles, or you can examine probabilities and support of predictable columns. The content of a model is based on existing data. New data is analyzed with a DMX Prediction query.

▶   **Key concepts**   Mining model content, predictable columns, names and values of predictable columns, probability and support of predictable columns, cluster membership, updating cluster captions

▶   **Keywords**   .content, Update, attribute_name, attribute_value, [Support], [Probability], NODE_CAPTION, NODE_DESCRIPTION, NODE_DISTRIBUTION, NODE_SUPPORT, NODE_TYPE, NODE_UNIQUE_NAME, VBA!Format

Content Query

While a Cases query shows the data used to train a model, a Content query shows the results produced by the model after training is finished. The results returned will vary from algorithm to algorithm. For example, a Content query on a Clustering model will show the properties of the clusters detected by the Clustering algorithm. Cases queries can be written against mining models or mining structures. Content queries can only work against models.

Syntax

```
-- content (cluster - no predict column)
select * from [Customer Clusters].content
```

Result

MODEL_CATAL...	MODEL_SCHEMA	MODEL_NAME	ATTRIBUTE_N...	NODE_NAME	NODE_UNIQUE...	NODE_TYPE	NODE_GUID	NODE_CAPTION	CHILDREN_CA
Adventure Wor...		Customer Clusters		000	000	1		Cluster Model	10
Adventure Wor...		Customer Clusters		001	001	5		Cluster 1	0
Adventure Wor...		Customer Clusters		002	002	5		Cluster 2	0
Adventure Wor...		Customer Clusters		003	003	5		Cluster 3	0
Adventure Wor...		Customer Clusters		004	004	5		Cluster 4	0
Adventure Wor...		Customer Clusters		005	005	5		Cluster 5	0
Adventure Wor...		Customer Clusters		006	006	5		Cluster 6	0
Adventure Wor...		Customer Clusters		007	007	5		Cluster 7	0
Adventure Wor...		Customer Clusters		008	008	5		Cluster 8	0
Adventure Wor...		Customer Clusters		009	009	5		Cluster 9	0
Adventure Wor...		Customer Clusters		010	010	5		Cluster 10	0

Analysis

This is a Content query on a Clustering model. Consequently, many of the columns returned are the properties of clusters. In the next few queries, we'll look at some of these content columns in more detail. The Customer Clusters model is pure clustering only—there is no predictable column.

Updating Cluster Captions

By default, clusters have generic names (to be precise, we should call them captions)—for example, Cluster 2. When users browse the model (say, in Excel), these are the names they see. Or maybe you write a Content query in DMX and show the results in an SSRS report. Once again, users will see the default names or captions. The following query demonstrates a simple technique for providing more meaningful results for the end user. Please note, in order to browse models in Excel 2007 or Excel 2010, you need to download the Excel data mining add-in. It's currently available from www.sqlserverdatamining.com and is also part of the SQL Server Feature Pack.

Syntax

```
-- changing cluster names
update [Customer Clusters].content
set node_caption = 'Interesting!'
where node_unique_name = '002'
```

Result

```
Executing the query ...
Execution complete
```

Analysis

NODE_CAPTION is the column that contains the name or caption the user sees when browsing the model. Our example will change the caption from 'Cluster 2' to 'Interesting!'. Yes, you're right—our new name is not that much more meaningful than the original. In reality, you need to browse the clusters graphically or run a few more Content queries to help you profile the clusters and come up with better names.

Content with New Caption

The purpose here is simply to validate that the previous query did function as intended.

Syntax

```
-- testing name change
select * from [Customer Clusters].content
```

Result

MODEL_CATAL...	MODEL_SCHEMA	MODEL_NAME	ATTRIBUTE_N...	NODE_NAME	NODE_UNIQUE...	NODE_TYPE	NODE_GUID	NODE_CAPTION	CHILDREN_CA
Adventure Wor...		Customer Clusters		000	000	1		Cluster Model	10
Adventure Wor...		Customer Clusters		001	001	5		Cluster 1	0
Adventure Wor...		Customer Clusters		002	002	5		Interesting!	0
Adventure Wor...		Customer Clusters		003	003	5		Cluster 3	0
Adventure Wor...		Customer Clusters		004	004	5		Cluster 4	0
Adventure Wor...		Customer Clusters		005	005	5		Cluster 5	0
Adventure Wor...		Customer Clusters		006	006	5		Cluster 6	0
Adventure Wor...		Customer Clusters		007	007	5		Cluster 7	0
Adventure Wor...		Customer Clusters		008	008	5		Cluster 8	0
Adventure Wor...		Customer Clusters		009	009	5		Cluster 9	0
Adventure Wor...		Customer Clusters		010	010	5		Cluster 10	0

Analysis

To see the new caption in the NODE_CAPTION column, you might have to scroll across. Your new caption will now be visible in your Content queries and graphically when users browse the model. There is one other place where this caption can be helpful. When you create clusters graphically in BIDS, you have the option to save the clusters as a new SSAS cube dimension and to show the clusters in an existing or new cube. Users can browse the cube in a pivot table in Excel. They will be able to analyze, say sales, by cluster, or to filter on a cluster. Here meaningful names are very important—Cluster 2 is not going to convey much to users!

Changing Caption Back

It would be a shame to alter the original SSAS Adventure Works database and its data mining models permanently. This query simply resets the cluster caption back to its original state.

Syntax

```
-- changing back
update [Customer Clusters].content
set node_caption = 'Cluster 2'
where node_unique_name = '002'
```

Result

```
Executing the query ...
Execution complete
```

Analysis

In your own data mining, you probably want to rename all the clusters—by default, you will normally have ten clusters.

Content Columns

Here we dig a little deeper into the columns of a Content query. Some columns are more immediately useful than others. This query looks at some of the columns you'll often need.

Syntax

```
-- useful columns
select node_unique_name, node_type, node_caption,
node_description, node_distribution, node_support
from [Customer Clusters].content
```

Result

node_unique_name	node_type	node_caption	node_description	node_distribution	node_support
000	1	Cluster Model	All	⊞ node_distribution	18484
001	5	Cluster 1	Number of Cars Owned =0 , Education=Graduate Degree , Number of...	⊞ node_distribution	2901
002	5	Cluster 2	0 <=Number of Children At Home <=3 , Yearly Income=40000 - 70000...	⊞ node_distribution	2578
003	5	Cluster 3	Number of Cars Owned =2 , Commute Distance=5-10 Miles , Educatio...	⊞ node_distribution	2490
004	5	Cluster 4	0 <=Number of Children At Home <=1 , Occupation=Manual , Yearly I...	⊞ node_distribution	2154
005	5	Cluster 5	Occupation=Management , Number of Children At Home =0 , Yearly I...	⊞ node_distribution	1985
006	5	Cluster 6	Yearly Income=130000 - 170000 , Yearly Income=100000 - 120000 , ...	⊞ node_distribution	1916
007	5	Cluster 7	Number of Cars Owned =1 , Yearly Income=40000 - 70000 , Number ...	⊞ node_distribution	1810
008	5	Cluster 8	Yearly Income=10000 - 30000 , Occupation=Manual , Education=Part...	⊞ node_distribution	1168
009	5	Cluster 9	Yearly Income=80000 - 90000 , Total Children >5 , 0 <=Number of Chi...	⊞ node_distribution	911
010	5	Cluster 10	4 <=Total Children <=5 , 4 <=Number of Children At Home <=5 , Occu...	⊞ node_distribution	571

Analysis

There's quite a lot of interesting data in this result. NODE_UNIQUE_NAME is just what you need for an IsInNode() Cases query. It's also used in the Where clause when you update a cluster's caption. NODE_TYPE tells you whether it's a cluster or the model itself. NODE_CAPTION is used when displaying the clusters to end users. NODE_DESCRIPTION is a high-level, generalized profile of a cluster. NODE_DISTRIBUTION, which is nested, is a more detailed profile of the cluster. NODE_SUPPORT tells you how many in each cluster and in the model itself.

Node Type

Every row (or node) returned by a Content query on a Clustering model has a NODE_TYPE column. Here it's part of the Where clause.

Syntax

```
-- clusters only
select node_unique_name, node_type, node_caption,
node_description, node_distribution, node_support
from [Customer Clusters].content
where node_type = 5
```

Result

node_unique_na...	node_type	node_caption	node_description		node_distribution	node_support
001	5	Cluster 1	Number of Cars Owned =0 , Education=Graduate Degree , Number of C...	⊞	node_distribution	2901
002	5	Cluster 2	0 <=Number of Children At Home <=3 , Yearly Income=40000 - 70000 , ...	⊞	node_distribution	2578
003	5	Cluster 3	Number of Cars Owned =2 , Commute Distance=5-10 Miles , Education...	⊞	node_distribution	2490
004	5	Cluster 4	0 <=Number of Children At Home <=1 , Occupation=Manual , Yearly Inc...	⊞	node_distribution	2154
005	5	Cluster 5	Occupation=Management , Number of Children At Home =0 , Yearly Inc...	⊞	node_distribution	1985
006	5	Cluster 6	Yearly Income=130000 - 170000 , Yearly Income=100000 - 120000 , 0...	⊞	node_distribution	1916
007	5	Cluster 7	Number of Cars Owned =1 , Yearly Income=40000 - 70000 , Number of ...	⊞	node_distribution	1810
008	5	Cluster 8	Yearly Income=10000 - 30000 , Occupation=Manual , Education=Partia...	⊞	node_distribution	1168
009	5	Cluster 9	Yearly Income=80000 - 90000 , Total Children >5 , 0 <=Number of Child...	⊞	node_distribution	911
010	5	Cluster 10	4 <=Total Children <=5 , 4 <=Number of Children At Home <=5 , Occup...	⊞	node_distribution	571

Analysis

A NODE_TYPE of 5 indicates a cluster. The model itself has a NODE_TYPE of 1. The node types are documented in SQL Server Books Online (BOL).

Flattened Content

If you flatten the last query, you'll discover all kinds of interesting information.

Syntax

```
-- flattened result
select flattened node_caption, node_description, node_distribution,
node_support from [Customer Clusters].content
where node_type = 5
```

Result

node_caption	node_description	node_distribution.ATTRIBUTE...	node_distribution...	node_distribution...	node_distribution...	node_distribution...	node_distribution...
Cluster 1	Number of Cars Owned =0 , Educati...	Commute Distance	Missing	0	0	0	1
Cluster 1	Number of Cars Owned =0 , Educati...	Commute Distance	10+ Miles	0	0	0	4
Cluster 1	Number of Cars Owned =0 , Educati...	Commute Distance	0-1 Miles	1994.08351973...	0.72167246326...	0	4
Cluster 1	Number of Cars Owned =0 , Educati...	Commute Distance	2-5 Miles	365.950657078...	0.13244004552...	0	4
Cluster 1	Number of Cars Owned =0 , Educati...	Commute Distance	5-10 Miles	0	0	0	4
Cluster 1	Number of Cars Owned =0 , Educati...	Commute Distance	1-2 Miles	403.107859568...	0.14588749121...	0	4
Cluster 1	Number of Cars Owned =0 , Educati...	Education	Missing	0	0	0	1
Cluster 1	Number of Cars Owned =0 , Educati...	Education	Partial High Sch...	0	0	0	4
Cluster 1	Number of Cars Owned =0 , Educati...	Education	High School	0	0	0	4
Cluster 1	Number of Cars Owned =0 , Educati...	Education	Bachelors	754.485629282...	0.27305350913...	0	4
Cluster 1	Number of Cars Owned =0 , Educati...	Education	Graduate Degree	1870.16748643...	0.67682640335...	0	4
Cluster 1	Number of Cars Owned =0 , Educati...	Education	Partial College	138.488920662...	0.05012008750...	0	4
Cluster 1	Number of Cars Owned =0 , Educati...	Gender	Missing	0	0	0	1
Cluster 1	Number of Cars Owned =0 , Educati...	Gender	Female	1368.66304844...	0.49532851747...	0	4
Cluster 1	Number of Cars Owned =0 , Educati...	Gender	Male	1394.47898793...	0.50467148252...	0	4
Cluster 1	Number of Cars Owned =0 , Educati...	Home Owner	Missing	0	0	0	1
Cluster 1	Number of Cars Owned =0 , Educati...	Home Owner	No	544.034681059...	0.19688987171...	0	4
Cluster 1	Number of Cars Owned =0 , Educati...	Home Owner	Yes	2219.10735531...	0.80311012828...	0	4

Analysis

This is really going to help you profile each cluster and devise meaningful captions. There are now multiple rows for each cluster, instead of the single rows in the previous query. Let's take a quick look at the Education of customers who've been assigned to Cluster 1 during model training. NODE_DESCRIPTION indicates Graduate Degree (you might have to widen the column). But the NODE_DISTRIBUTION.ATTRIBUTE_NAME column has other values for Education. If you check the NODE_DISTRIBUTION .SUPPORT column, you'll see that Graduate Degree is simply the most likely. NODE_ SUPPORT (as opposed to NODE_DISTRIBUTION.SUPPORT) is the total number of customers in the cluster.

Flattened Content with Subquery

The NODE_DISTRIBUTION column has been replaced by a Select on the column itself. This is possible as the column is actually a table. This type of construct, with a Select within another Select, is called a *subquery*. As we'll see over the next few queries, this gives you total control over your Content queries.

Syntax

```
-- flattened with subquery
select flattened node_caption, (select * from node_distribution)
from [Customer Clusters].content
where node_type = 5
```

Result

node_caption	Expression.ATTRIBUTE_NAME	Expression.ATTRIBUTE_VALUE	Expression.SUPPORT	Expression.PROBABILI...	Expression.VARI...	Expression.VAL...
Cluster 1	Commute Distance	Missing	0	0	0	1
Cluster 1	Commute Distance	10+ Miles	0	0	0	4
Cluster 1	Commute Distance	0-1 Miles	1994.08351973265	0.721672463260562	0	4
Cluster 1	Commute Distance	2-5 Miles	365.95065707842	0.132440045520767	0	4
Cluster 1	Commute Distance	5-10 Miles	0	0	0	4
Cluster 1	Commute Distance	1-2 Miles	403.107859568223	0.14588749121867	0	4
Cluster 1	Education	Missing	0	0	0	1
Cluster 1	Education	Partial High School	0	0	0	4
Cluster 1	Education	High School	0	0	0	4
Cluster 1	Education	Bachelors	754.485629282322	0.273053509138809	0	4
Cluster 1	Education	Graduate Degree	1870.16748643477	0.676826403352526	0	4
Cluster 1	Education	Partial College	138.488920662201	0.0501200875086648	0	4
Cluster 1	Gender	Missing	0	0	0	1
Cluster 1	Gender	Female	1368.66304844654	0.495328517472804	0	4
Cluster 1	Gender	Male	1394.47898793276	0.504671482527196	0	4
Cluster 1	Home Owner	Missing	0	0	0	1
Cluster 1	Home Owner	No	544.03468105966	0.196889871710156	0	4
Cluster 1	Home Owner	Yes	2219.10735531964	0.803110128289844	0	4
Cluster 1	Marital Status	Missing	0	0	0	1

Analysis

Instead of two columns in a comma-separated column list, you have one column followed by a Select on the second column. Notice please that the inner Select has altered the column names from NODE_DISTRIBUTION.

Subquery Columns

Having a subquery gives you total control over the individual columns within a nested table column. Here the nested column names are specified individually in the subquery.

Syntax

```
-- selected columns in subquery
select flattened node_caption as [Cluster],
(select [attribute_name], attribute_value, [support], [probability]
from node_distribution) from [Customer Clusters].content
where node_type = 5
```

Result

Cluster	Expression.attribute_name	Expression.attribute_value	Expression.support	Expression.probability
Cluster 1	Commute Distance	Missing	0	0
Cluster 1	Commute Distance	10+ Miles	0	0
Cluster 1	Commute Distance	0-1 Miles	1994.08351973265	0.721672463260562
Cluster 1	Commute Distance	2-5 Miles	365.95065707842	0.132440045520767
Cluster 1	Commute Distance	5-10 Miles	0	0
Cluster 1	Commute Distance	1-2 Miles	403.107859568223	0.14588749121867
Cluster 1	Education	Missing	0	0
Cluster 1	Education	Partial High School	0	0
Cluster 1	Education	High School	0	0
Cluster 1	Education	Bachelors	754.485629282322	0.273053509138809
Cluster 1	Education	Graduate Degree	1870.16748643477	0.676826403352526
Cluster 1	Education	Partial College	138.488920662201	0.0501200875086648
Cluster 1	Gender	Missing	0	0
Cluster 1	Gender	Female	1368.66304844654	0.495328517472804
Cluster 1	Gender	Male	1394.47898793276	0.504671482527196
Cluster 1	Home Owner	Missing	0	0
Cluster 1	Home Owner	No	544.03468105966	0.196889871710156
Cluster 1	Home Owner	Yes	2219.10735531964	0.803110128289844
Cluster 1	Marital Status	Missing	0	0

Analysis

This is very similar to the last query. Here the column names are individually specified within the subquery. There are quite a few square brackets! The rules for using square brackets in DMX are the same as those in SQL (or in MDX, for that matter). Square brackets are obligatory if a name contains spaces, for example, [Customer Clusters]. Square brackets are also required if the name is a reserved word, for example, [Cluster] or [support] or [probability]. Otherwise, in general, square brackets are optional; for example, [attribute_name] does not need square brackets.

Subquery Column Aliases

It's easy to override built-in column names—you use aliases just as in SQL.

Syntax

```
-- aliases in subquery
select flattened node_caption as [Cluster],
(select [attribute_name] as Demographic, attribute_value as [Value],
[Support], [Probability] from node_distribution)
from [Customer Clusters].content
where node_type = 5
```

Result

Cluster	Expression.Demographic	Expression.Value	Expression.Support	Expression.Probability
Cluster 1	Commute Distance	Missing	0	0
Cluster 1	Commute Distance	10+ Miles	0	0
Cluster 1	Commute Distance	0-1 Miles	1994.08351973265	0.721672463260562
Cluster 1	Commute Distance	2-5 Miles	365.95065707842	0.132440045520767
Cluster 1	Commute Distance	5-10 Miles	0	0
Cluster 1	Commute Distance	1-2 Miles	403.107859568223	0.14588749121867
Cluster 1	Education	Missing	0	0
Cluster 1	Education	Partial High School	0	0
Cluster 1	Education	High School	0	0
Cluster 1	Education	Bachelors	754.485629282322	0.273053509138809
Cluster 1	Education	Graduate Degree	1870.16748643477	0.676826403352526
Cluster 1	Education	Partial College	138.488920662201	0.0501200875086648
Cluster 1	Gender	Missing	0	0
Cluster 1	Gender	Female	1368.66304844654	0.495328517472804
Cluster 1	Gender	Male	1394.47898793276	0.504671482527196
Cluster 1	Home Owner	Missing	0	0
Cluster 1	Home Owner	No	544.03468105966	0.196889871710156
Cluster 1	Home Owner	Yes	2219.10735531964	0.803110128289844
Cluster 1	Marital Status	Missing	0	0

Analysis

This is turning into quite a nice query. There are a couple of aliases. Demographic probably looks better than attribute_name. In addition, the non-aliased columns are capitalized correctly, like [Support]. All ten clusters are returned, but you'll have to scroll down to see all of them.

Subquery Where Clause

This time, there are two Where clauses. Our original Where clause is on the outer Content query. The new Where clause is on the inner subquery on the columns of the nested table.

Syntax

```
-- and only where there is support above 100
select flattened node_caption as [Cluster],
(select [attribute_name] as Demographic, attribute_value as [Value],
[Support], [Probability] from node_distribution where [Support] > 100)
from [Customer Clusters].content
where node_type = 5
```

Result

Cluster	Expression.Demographic	Expression.Value	Expression.Support	Expression.Probability
Cluster 1	Commute Distance	0-1 Miles	1994.08351973265	0.721672463260562
Cluster 1	Commute Distance	2-5 Miles	365.95065707842	0.132440045520767
Cluster 1	Commute Distance	1-2 Miles	403.107859568223	0.14588749121867
Cluster 1	Education	Bachelors	754.485629282322	0.273053509138809
Cluster 1	Education	Graduate Degree	1870.16748643477	0.676826403352526
Cluster 1	Education	Partial College	138.488920662201	0.0501200875086648
Cluster 1	Gender	Female	1368.66304844654	0.495328517472804
Cluster 1	Gender	Male	1394.47898793276	0.504671482527196
Cluster 1	Home Owner	No	544.03468105966	0.196889871710156
Cluster 1	Home Owner	Yes	2219.10735531964	0.803110128289844
Cluster 1	Marital Status	Married	1708.35680530535	0.618266011234048
Cluster 1	Marital Status	Single	1054.78523107394	0.381733988765952
Cluster 1	Number of Cars Owned	0	2763.1420363793	1
Cluster 1	Number of Children At Home	0	2763.1420363793	1
Cluster 1	Occupation	Skilled Manual	665.838341084459	0.240971449284216
Cluster 1	Occupation	Manual	282.488920662201	0.102234672319763
Cluster 1	Occupation	Clerical	996.992311645602	0.360818335981026
Cluster 1	Occupation	Professional	736.321512413045	0.266479791020041
Cluster 1	Total Children	1.30088696423142	2763.1420363793	1

Analysis

The new inner Where clause on the subquery results in fewer rows being returned. Unfortunately, DMX (unlike SQL and MDX) does not tell you the record count anywhere. This query has suppressed some of the least important demographic attribute values for each cluster. In particular, all of the Missing values have gone. We are looking only at those values where the number of customers is more than 100. Such a query allows you to concentrate on the most important characteristics of a cluster. This, in turn, helps you to profile and rename each cluster.

Individual Cluster Analysis

The outer Where clause has been extended. Syntactically, it's the same as SQL.

Syntax

```
-- narrowing down the clusters
select flattened node_caption as [Cluster],
(select [attribute_name] as Demographic, attribute_value as [Value],
[Support], [Probability] from node_distribution where [Support] > 100)
from [Customer Clusters].content
where node_type = 5 and (node_caption = 'Cluster 3'
or node_caption = 'Cluster 6')
```

Result

Cluster	Expression.Demographic	Expression.Value	Expression.Support	Expression.Probability
Cluster 3	Commute Distance	0-1 Miles	271.337582302108	0.112810226260638
Cluster 3	Commute Distance	5-10 Miles	1300.99449126103	0.54089625800377
Cluster 3	Commute Distance	1-2 Miles	774.37574494529	0.321951357629347
Cluster 3	Education	Partial High School	408.964231826572	0.170029330745258
Cluster 3	Education	High School	1261.37852036761	0.524425680643628
Cluster 3	Education	Partial College	730.816993618311	0.303841545670618
Cluster 3	Gender	Female	1199.58985696979	0.498736673469939
Cluster 3	Gender	Male	1205.66710683778	0.501263326530062
Cluster 3	Home Owner	No	1164.50108426658	0.484148305893751
Cluster 3	Home Owner	Yes	1240.75587954099	0.51585169410625
Cluster 3	Marital Status	Married	1226.51146879469	0.509929494956369
Cluster 3	Marital Status	Single	1178.74549501289	0.490070505043631
Cluster 3	Number of Cars Owned	1.99085336813029	2405.25696380757	1
Cluster 3	Number of Children At Home	0	2405.25696380757	1
Cluster 3	Occupation	Skilled Manual	1485.2292534923	0.61749296471889
Cluster 3	Occupation	Clerical	347.069608567952	0.144296270124309
Cluster 3	Occupation	Professional	531.27075395395	0.220879000434505
Cluster 3	Total Children	1.56682751081063	2405.25696380757	1
Cluster 3	Yearly Income	10000 - 30000	850.157381869241	0.353458027421496

Analysis

Maybe you don't want to analyze all of the clusters at once. This query focuses on just two clusters. Cluster 3 has three values for Education while Cluster 6 has five. Education has discrete values. It pays to look at the support for each value. Yearly Income also has multiple values. It looks as though these are discrete values, too. But if you check the properties of each column in the containing structure (Customer Mining) in BIDS, you'll notice that the Content property for the Yearly Income column is Discretized and not Discrete. Some attributes have only a single numeric value. Please have a look at Total Children. Here the Content property is Continuous. For continuous value attributes, the Content query displays the mean value for each cluster.

Demographic Analysis

Here the inner Where clause has been extended. This is an in-depth, detailed analysis.

Syntax

```
-- narrowing down the demographics
select flattened node_caption as [Cluster],
(select [attribute_name] as Demographic, attribute_value as [Value],
[Support], [Probability] * 100 from node_distribution
```

```
where [Support] > 100 and [attribute_name] = 'education')
from [Customer Clusters].content
where node_type = 5 and (node_caption = 'Cluster 3'
or node_caption = 'Cluster 6')
```

Result

Cluster	Expression.Demographic	Expression.Value	Expression.Support	Expression.Expression
Cluster 3	Education	Partial High School	408.964231826572	17.0029330745258
Cluster 3	Education	High School	1261.37852036761	52.4425680643628
Cluster 3	Education	Partial College	730.816993618311	30.3841545670618
Cluster 6	Education	Partial High School	152	7.90772987413508
Cluster 6	Education	High School	411.040408679571	21.3841876262641
Cluster 6	Education	Bachelors	557.653601816571	29.0116713585785
Cluster 6	Education	Graduate Degree	259.460223226821	13.4982984102664
Cluster 6	Education	Partial College	542.015623104946	28.1981127307561

Analysis

This query concentrates on the education of customers. Many customers in Cluster 6 have bachelor or post-graduate degrees. The customers in Cluster 3 seem to be less well-educated. Once again, you should be aware that when you process the model, it may return different results from those shown here.

Renaming Clusters

You are now in a position to give your clusters sensible and meaningful names. Please note, you should run the two Update queries separately; otherwise, you'll get an error.

Syntax

```
-- now rename
update [Customer Clusters].content
set node_caption = 'Non Graduates'
where node_unique_name = '003'
--
update [Customer Clusters].content
set node_caption = 'Graduates'
where node_unique_name = '006'
```

Result

```
Executing the query ...
Execution complete
```

Analysis

Our Content queries are beginning to do very useful things. If you recall, NODE_ CAPTION is what the end user sees when she browses the mining model graphically in Excel.

Querying Renamed Clusters

Renaming clusters is not only for end users. It also helps you write your DMX queries. Notice the change in the outer Where clause.

Syntax

```
-- and redo the select with new captions
select flattened node_caption as [Cluster],
(select attribute_value as [Education], [Support],
[Probability] * 100 as [Probability] from node_distribution
where [Support] > 100 and [attribute_name] = 'education')
from [Customer Clusters].content
where node_type = 5 and (node_caption = 'Non Graduates'
or node_caption = 'Graduates')
```

Result

Cluster	Expression.Education	Expression.Support	Expression.Probability
Non Graduates	Partial High School	408.964231826572	17.0029330745258
Non Graduates	High School	1261.37852036761	52.4425680643628
Non Graduates	Partial College	730.816993618311	30.3841545670618
Graduates	Partial High School	152	7.90772987413508
Graduates	High School	411.040408679571	21.3841876262641
Graduates	Bachelors	557.653601816571	29.0116713585785
Graduates	Graduate Degree	259.460223226821	13.4982984102664
Graduates	Partial College	542.015623104946	28.1981127307561

Analysis

Content queries done in this way are almost ready to be used in SSRS reports on your data mining models.

Clusters with Predictable Columns

The last few queries have been using the Customer Clusters model in the Customer Mining structure. Now we switch to the TM Clustering model in the Targeted Mailing structure. This new model also uses the Clustering algorithm. There is an important difference between the two models. Customer Clusters is pure clustering—it's concerned with demographics and profiles based on those demographics. TM Clustering is also clustering, but it now includes a predictable column. If we analyze this model correctly, we can profile customers (existing and new customers) just the same as we can with the previous model. However, we can also predict what they will buy!

Syntax

```
-- content (cluster - predict column)
select * from [TM Clustering].content
```

Result

NODE_CAPTION	CHILDREN_CA...	PARENT_UNIQ...	NODE_DESCRI...	NODE_RULE	MARGINAL_RU...	NODE_PROBA...	MARGINAL_PR...	NODE_DISTRIBUTION
Cluster Model	10		All			1	1	⊞ NODE_DISTRIBUTION
Cluster 1	0	000	Occupation=Ma...			0.12185628357...	0.12185628357...	⊞ NODE_DISTRIBUTION
Cluster 2	0	000	Yearly Income >...			0.11769625913...	0.11769625913...	⊞ NODE_DISTRIBUTION
Cluster 3	0	000	Age < 36 , Total...			0.11744861802...	0.11744861802...	⊞ NODE_DISTRIBUTION
Cluster 4	0	000	Number Cars O...			0.11245670464...	0.11245670464...	⊞ NODE_DISTRIBUTION
Cluster 5	0	000	Occupation=Cle...			0.10958583761...	0.10958583761...	⊞ NODE_DISTRIBUTION
Cluster 6	0	000	Total Children=2...			0.10871220262...	0.10871220262...	⊞ NODE_DISTRIBUTION
Cluster 7	0	000	Age >= 87 , Age...			0.10784666691...	0.10784666691...	⊞ NODE_DISTRIBUTION
Cluster 8	0	000	Education=Grad...			0.08429897652...	0.08429897652...	⊞ NODE_DISTRIBUTION
Cluster 9	0	000	Occupation=Ma...			0.06768702250...	0.06768702250...	⊞ NODE_DISTRIBUTION
Cluster 10	0	000	Number Childre...			0.05241142843...	0.05241142843...	⊞ NODE_DISTRIBUTION

Analysis

If you scroll across, you'll see the NODE_DISTRIBUTION nested table column just as before. But if you expand, in addition to the demographics, there are also three rows for Bike Buyer. This is a predictable column. If you select this column in the model in BIDS, you'll notice that its Usage property is Predict.

Narrowing Down Content

You would like to see the forest despite all the trees in the way? Once again, we are narrowing down our Content query to focus on what's most useful to us.

Syntax

```
-- just the clusters and three useful columns
select node_caption, node_description, node_distribution
from [TM Clustering].content
where node_type = 5
```

Result

node_caption	node_description	node_distribution
Cluster 1	Occupation=Manual , Region=Europe , 10000 <=Yearly Income <=38598.4744402891 , Number Children At Home=2 , Commute Distance=0-1 Miles ,...	⊞ node_distribution
Cluster 2	Yearly Income >160198.447718381 , Number Cars Owned=4 , Commute Distance=10+ Miles , Number Children At Home=1 , Number Children At Hom...	⊞ node_distribution
Cluster 3	Age < 36 , Total Children=0 , Number Children At Home=0 , 10000 <=Yearly Income <=65163.0844941386 , Commute Distance=5-10 Miles , Number ...	⊞ node_distribution
Cluster 4	Number Cars Owned=1 , Age=41 - 48 , 36225.7340386609 <=Yearly Income <=89522.3146656865 , Education=Bachelors , Age=48 - 53 , Region=P...	⊞ node_distribution
Cluster 5	Occupation=Clerical , Total Children=1 , Number Cars Owned=0 , Region=Europe , 14512.4596352767 <=Yearly Income <=53610.2209525522 , Com...	⊞ node_distribution
Cluster 6	Total Children=2 , Number Cars Owned=2 , Education=Partial High School , Education=High School , Age=59 - 64 , Age=53 - 59 , Commute Distance...	⊞ node_distribution
Cluster 7	Age >= 87 , Age=74 - 87 , Total Children=5 , Occupation=Management , Age=71 - 74 , Number Cars Owned=2 , Total Children=4 , 37094.886377814...	⊞ node_distribution
Cluster 8	Education=Graduate Degree , Number Cars Owned=0 , 40438.8305232694 <=Yearly Income <=82521.57773445 , Age=36 - 41 , Region=North Amer...	⊞ node_distribution
Cluster 9	Occupation=Management , 61964.7458395401 <=Yearly Income <=152313.701058421 , Age=41 - 48 , Education=Bachelors , Number Cars Owned=...	⊞ node_distribution
Cluster 10	Number Children At Home=5 , Commute Distance=10+ Miles , Region=Pacific , Number Cars Owned=4 , Number Cars Owned=3 , Age=36 - 41 , Total ...	⊞ node_distribution

Analysis

Here are three specific columns and a NODE_TYPE that shows the clusters and hides the model.

Flattening Content Again

There's nothing new syntactically here. However, the content returned now includes a predictable column.

Syntax

```
-- with flattening
select flattened node_caption, node_description, node_distribution
from [TM Clustering].content
where node_type = 5
```

Result

node_caption	node_description	node_distribution.ATTRIBUTE_NAME	node_distribution.ATTRIBUTE_VALUE	node_distribution.SUPPORT	node_distribution.PROBABILITY
Cluster 1	Occupation=Manual...	Age	Missing	0	0
Cluster 1	Occupation=Manual...	Age	< 36	409.50101948396	0.181807208556561
Cluster 1	Occupation=Manual...	Age	36 - 41	433.528386563174	0.192474699795387
Cluster 1	Occupation=Manual...	Age	41 - 48	520.639898524978	0.231149819195273
Cluster 1	Occupation=Manual...	Age	48 - 53	446.880785474777	0.198402798281147
Cluster 1	Occupation=Manual...	Age	53 - 59	274.13053935449	0.121706432386785
Cluster 1	Occupation=Manual...	Age	59 - 64	120.161134981053	0.0533482445426465
Cluster 1	Occupation=Manual...	Age	64 - 71	37.6266799168939	0.0167052127283157
Cluster 1	Occupation=Manual...	Age	71 - 74	8.41393767467333	0.00373555729733942
Cluster 1	Occupation=Manual...	Age	74 - 87	1.3430399744797	0.000596272871427108
Cluster 1	Occupation=Manual...	Age	>= 87	0.16612366266022	7.37543447939678E-05
Cluster 1	Occupation=Manual...	Bike Buyer	Missing	0	0
Cluster 1	Occupation=Manual...	Bike Buyer	0	1156.0163186756	0.51323950355263
Cluster 1	Occupation=Manual...	Bike Buyer	1	1096.37522693554	0.486760496447371
Cluster 1	Occupation=Manual...	Commute Distance	Missing	0	0
Cluster 1	Occupation=Manual...	Commute Distance	5-10 Miles	6.08161337121527	0.00270006934765205
Cluster 1	Occupation=Manual...	Commute Distance	2-5 Miles	436.00696490253	0.193575120521165
Cluster 1	Occupation=Manual...	Commute Distance	1-2 Miles	467.802348458606	0.207691397781231

Analysis

If you examine each of the ten clusters, there's a Bike Buyer attribute. This attribute
has three values—Missing, 0, and 1. Bike Buyer is a predictable column. A value of
1 means a bike was bought by the customers in a cluster. A value of 0 indicates no bike
was bought.

Some Tidying Up

This is the last query redone with a subquery and some simple aliasing.

Syntax

```
-- a few columns only from subquery and some outer query aliases
select flattened node_caption as [Cluster], node_description as
Demographics,(select [attribute_name], [attribute_value],
[Support], [Probability] * 100 from node_distribution)
from [TM Clustering].content
where node_type = 5
```

Result

Cluster	Demographics	Expression.attribute_name	Expression.attribute_value	Expression.Support	Expression.Expression
Cluster 1	Occupation=Manual , Region=Europe , 10000...	Age	Missing	0	0
Cluster 1	Occupation=Manual , Region=Europe , 10000...	Age	< 36	409.50101948396	18.1807208556561
Cluster 1	Occupation=Manual , Region=Europe , 10000...	Age	36 - 41	433.528386563174	19.2474699795387
Cluster 1	Occupation=Manual , Region=Europe , 10000...	Age	41 - 48	520.639898524978	23.1149819195273
Cluster 1	Occupation=Manual , Region=Europe , 10000...	Age	48 - 53	446.880785474777	19.840279828147
Cluster 1	Occupation=Manual , Region=Europe , 10000...	Age	53 - 59	274.13053935449	12.1706432386785
Cluster 1	Occupation=Manual , Region=Europe , 10000...	Age	59 - 64	120.161134981053	5.33482445426465
Cluster 1	Occupation=Manual , Region=Europe , 10000...	Age	64 - 71	37.6266799168939	1.67052127283157
Cluster 1	Occupation=Manual , Region=Europe , 10000...	Age	71 - 74	8.41393767467333	0.373555729733942
Cluster 1	Occupation=Manual , Region=Europe , 10000...	Age	74 - 87	1.3430399744797	0.0596272871427108
Cluster 1	Occupation=Manual , Region=Europe , 10000...	Age	>= 87	0.166123662666022	0.00737543447939678
Cluster 1	Occupation=Manual , Region=Europe , 10000...	Bike Buyer	Missing	0	0
Cluster 1	Occupation=Manual , Region=Europe , 10000...	Bike Buyer	0	1156.0163186756	51.323950355263
Cluster 1	Occupation=Manual , Region=Europe , 10000...	Bike Buyer	1	1096.37522693554	48.6760496447371
Cluster 1	Occupation=Manual , Region=Europe , 10000...	Commute Distance	Missing	0	0
Cluster 1	Occupation=Manual , Region=Europe , 10000...	Commute Distance	5-10 Miles	6.08161337121527	0.270006934765205
Cluster 1	Occupation=Manual , Region=Europe , 10000...	Commute Distance	2-5 Miles	436.00696490253	19.3575120521165
Cluster 1	Occupation=Manual , Region=Europe , 10000...	Commute Distance	1-2 Miles	467.802348458606	20.7691397781231

Analysis

The only new thing here is the calculation applied to the Probability column.

More Tidying Up

It may be a good idea to build your DMX queries gradually and incrementally as we're doing here. It can be quite tricky to write a sophisticated query without adopting this step-by-step approach.

Syntax

```
-- and a subquery alias
select flattened node_caption as [Cluster], node_description as
Demographics,(select [attribute_name], [attribute_value], [Support],
[Probability] * 100 as [Probability] from node_distribution)
from [TM Clustering].content
where node_type = 5
```

Result

Cluster	Demographics	Expression.attribute_name	Expression.attribute_value	Expression.Support	Expression.Probability
Cluster 1	Occupation=Manual , Region=Europe , 10000 <=Yearly In...	Age	Missing	0	0
Cluster 1	Occupation=Manual , Region=Europe , 10000 <=Yearly In...	Age	< 36	409.50101948396	18.1807208556561
Cluster 1	Occupation=Manual , Region=Europe , 10000 <=Yearly In...	Age	36 - 41	433.528386563174	19.2474699795387
Cluster 1	Occupation=Manual , Region=Europe , 10000 <=Yearly In...	Age	41 - 48	520.639898524978	23.1149819195273
Cluster 1	Occupation=Manual , Region=Europe , 10000 <=Yearly In...	Age	48 - 53	446.880785474777	19.840279828147
Cluster 1	Occupation=Manual , Region=Europe , 10000 <=Yearly In...	Age	53 - 59	274.13053935449	12.1706432386785
Cluster 1	Occupation=Manual , Region=Europe , 10000 <=Yearly In...	Age	59 - 64	120.161134981053	5.33482445426465
Cluster 1	Occupation=Manual , Region=Europe , 10000 <=Yearly In...	Age	64 - 71	37.6266799168939	1.67052127283157
Cluster 1	Occupation=Manual , Region=Europe , 10000 <=Yearly In...	Age	71 - 74	8.41393767467333	0.373555729733942
Cluster 1	Occupation=Manual , Region=Europe , 10000 <=Yearly In...	Age	74 - 87	1.3430399744797	0.0596272871427108
Cluster 1	Occupation=Manual , Region=Europe , 10000 <=Yearly In...	Age	>= 87	0.166123662666022	0.00737543447939678
Cluster 1	Occupation=Manual , Region=Europe , 10000 <=Yearly In...	Bike Buyer	Missing	0	0
Cluster 1	Occupation=Manual , Region=Europe , 10000 <=Yearly In...	Bike Buyer	0	1156.0163186756	51.323950355263
Cluster 1	Occupation=Manual , Region=Europe , 10000 <=Yearly In...	Bike Buyer	1	1096.37522693554	48.6760496447371
Cluster 1	Occupation=Manual , Region=Europe , 10000 <=Yearly In...	Commute Distance	Missing	0	0
Cluster 1	Occupation=Manual , Region=Europe , 10000 <=Yearly In...	Commute Distance	5-10 Miles	6.08161337121527	0.270006934765205
Cluster 1	Occupation=Manual , Region=Europe , 10000 <=Yearly In...	Commute Distance	2-5 Miles	436.00696490253	19.3575120521165
Cluster 1	Occupation=Manual , Region=Europe , 10000 <=Yearly In...	Commute Distance	1-2 Miles	467.802348458606	20.7691397781231

Analysis

Confusingly, I am aliasing Probability as Probability! This is necessary as the calculation returned a column name of Expression.Expression—not the friendliest of names.

Looking at Bike Buyers

You are digging deep in the mine again. This query is beginning to answer a fundamental mining question—what type of customer is likely to make purchases? There's now a Where clause in the subquery.

Syntax

```
-- where clause in subquery, bike buyer attribute only
select flattened node_caption as [Cluster], node_description as
Demographics,(select [attribute_name], [attribute_value], [Support],
[Probability] * 100 as [Probability] from node_distribution
where [attribute_name] = 'Bike Buyer') from [TM Clustering].content
where node_type = 5
```

Result

Cluster	Demographics	Expression.attribute_name	Expression.attribute_value	Expression.Support	Expression.Probability
Cluster 1	Occupation=Manual , Region=Europe , 10000 <=Yearly I...	Bike Buyer	Missing	0	0
Cluster 1	Occupation=Manual , Region=Europe , 10000 <=Yearly I...	Bike Buyer	0	1156.0163186756	51.323950355263
Cluster 1	Occupation=Manual , Region=Europe , 10000 <=Yearly I...	Bike Buyer	1	1096.37522693554	48.6760496447371
Cluster 2	Yearly Income >160198.447718381 , Number Cars Owne...	Bike Buyer	Missing	0	0
Cluster 2	Yearly Income >160198.447718381 , Number Cars Owne...	Bike Buyer	0	1297.26576960579	59.6316786335617
Cluster 2	Yearly Income >160198.447718381 , Number Cars Owne...	Bike Buyer	1	878.211884212823	40.3683213664382
Cluster 3	Age < 36 , Total Children=0 , Number Children At Home=...	Bike Buyer	Missing	0	0
Cluster 3	Age < 36 , Total Children=0 , Number Children At Home=...	Bike Buyer	0	1446.84018130394	66.6463992657408
Cluster 3	Age < 36 , Total Children=0 , Number Children At Home=...	Bike Buyer	1	724.08007431995	33.3536007342592
Cluster 4	Number Cars Owned=1 , Age=41 - 48 , 36225.73403866...	Bike Buyer	Missing	0	0
Cluster 4	Number Cars Owned=1 , Age=41 - 48 , 36225.73403866...	Bike Buyer	0	683.832237640226	32.8979061857917
Cluster 4	Number Cars Owned=1 , Age=41 - 48 , 36225.73403866...	Bike Buyer	1	1394.81749094209	67.1020938142082
Cluster 5	Occupation=Clerical , Total Children=1 , Number Cars Ow...	Bike Buyer	Missing	0	0
Cluster 5	Occupation=Clerical , Total Children=1 , Number Cars Ow...	Bike Buyer	0	579.80133005962	28.6239006575953
Cluster 5	Occupation=Clerical , Total Children=1 , Number Cars Ow...	Bike Buyer	1	1445.78329236944	71.3760993424046
Cluster 6	Total Children=2 , Number Cars Owned=2 , Education=P...	Bike Buyer	Missing	0	0
Cluster 6	Total Children=2 , Number Cars Owned=2 , Education=P...	Bike Buyer	0	1158.97147565363	57.6764461228922
Cluster 6	Total Children=2 , Number Cars Owned=2 , Education=P...	Bike Buyer	1	850.464877592181	42.3235538771078
Cluster 7	Age >= 87 , Age=74 - 87 , Total Children=5 , Occupation...	Bike Buyer	Missing	0	0

Analysis

You should be seeing the three values or states of Bike Buyer for each cluster. In addition, you can see the support (number of customers) for each state and the probability of the state being true.

Who Are the Best Customers?

The inner Where clause has been extended. Our query is going to show the figures for those customers who bought bikes—we are hiding figures for those who did not.

Syntax

```
-- where clause bike buyer attribute = 1
select flattened node_caption as [Cluster], node_description as
Demographics,(select [Support], [Probability] * 100 as [Probability]
from node_distribution where [attribute_name] = 'Bike Buyer'
and [attribute_value] = '1') from [TM Clustering].content
where node_type = 5
```

Result

Cluster	Demographics	Expression.Support	Expression.Probability
Cluster 1	Occupation=Manual , Region=Europe , 10000 <=Yearly Income <=38598.4744402891 , Number Children At Home=2 , Com...	1096.37522693554	48.6760496447371
Cluster 2	Yearly Income >160198.447718381 , Number Cars Owned=4 , Commute Distance=10+ Miles , Number Children At Home=1 ,...	878.211884212823	40.3683213664382
Cluster 3	Age < 36 , Total Children=0 , Number Children At Home=0 , 10000 <=Yearly Income <=65163.0844941386 , Commute Dista...	724.08007431995	33.3536007342592
Cluster 4	Number Cars Owned=1 , Age=41 - 48 , 36225.7340386609 <=Yearly Income <=89522.3146656865 , Education=Bachelors ,...	1394.81749094209	67.1020938142082
Cluster 5	Occupation=Clerical , Total Children=1 , Number Cars Owned=0 , Region=Europe , 14512.4596352767 <=Yearly Income <=...	1445.78329236944	71.3760993424046
Cluster 6	Total Children=2 , Number Cars Owned=2 , Education=Partial High School , Education=High School , Age=59 - 64 , Age=53 ...	850.464877592181	42.3235538771078
Cluster 7	Age >= 87 , Age=74 - 87 , Total Children=5 , Occupation=Management , Age=71 - 74 , Number Cars Owned=2 , Total Childr...	661.345710017975	33.1761398772574
Cluster 8	Education=Graduate Degree , Number Cars Owned=0 , 40438.8305232694 <=Yearly Income <=82521.57773445 , Age=36 ...	918.627454559559	58.955069960928
Cluster 9	Occupation=Management , 61964.7458395401 <=Yearly Income <=152313.701058421 , Age=41 - 48 , Education=Bachelo...	708.700886618012	56.6450032362232
Cluster 10	Number Children At Home=5 , Commute Distance=10+ Miles , Region=Pacific , Number Cars Owned=4 , Number Cars Owne...	453.593102432431	46.8214097490077

Analysis

Both the attribute_name and the attribute_value columns are being used to show statistics for only those customers who bought bikes. The state or value of Bike Buyer for those customers is 1. The customers in Cluster 5 are pretty good—please look at the Probability column.

How Did All Customers Do?

To examine all customers, we need to see the model itself and not just individual clusters. The outer query Where clause has gone.

Syntax

```
-- all customers as well as clusters, 9132 customers bought bikes
select flattened node_caption as [Cluster], node_description as
Demographics,(select [Support], [Probability] * 100 as [Probability]
from node_distribution where [attribute_name] = 'Bike Buyer'
and [attribute_value] = '1') from [TM Clustering].content
```

Result

Cluster	Demographics	Expression.Support	Expression.Probability
Cluster Model	All	9132	49.4048907162952
Cluster 1	Occupation=Manual , Region=Europe , 10000 <=Yearly Income <=38598.4744402891 , Number Children At Home=2 , Commut...	1096.37522693554	48.6760496447371
Cluster 2	Yearly Income >160198.447718381 , Number Cars Owned=4 , Commute Distance=10+ Miles , Number Children At Home=1 , N...	878.211884212823	40.3683213664382
Cluster 3	Age < 36 , Total Children=0 , Number Children At Home=0 , 10000 <=Yearly Income <=65163.0844941386 , Commute Distance...	724.08007431995	33.3536007342592
Cluster 4	Number Cars Owned=1 , Age=41 - 48 , 36225.7340386609 <=Yearly Income <=89522.3146656865 , Education=Bachelors , A...	1394.81749094209	67.1020938142082
Cluster 5	Occupation=Clerical , Total Children=1 , Number Cars Owned=0 , Region=Europe , 14512.4596352767 <=Yearly Income <=53...	1445.78329236944	71.3760993424046
Cluster 6	Total Children=2 , Number Cars Owned=2 , Education=Partial High School , Education=High School , Age=59 - 64 , Age=53 - 5...	850.464877592181	42.3235538771078
Cluster 7	Age >= 87 , Age=74 - 87 , Total Children=5 , Occupation=Management , Age=71 - 74 , Number Cars Owned=2 , Total Children...	661.345710017975	33.1761398772574
Cluster 8	Education=Graduate Degree , Number Cars Owned=0 , 40438.8305232694 <=Yearly Income <=82521.57773445 , Age=36 - 4...	918.627454559559	58.955069960928
Cluster 9	Occupation=Management , 61964.7458395401 <=Yearly Income <=152313.701058421 , Age=41 - 48 , Education=Bachelors ,...	708.700886618012	56.6450032362232
Cluster 10	Number Children At Home=5 , Commute Distance=10+ Miles , Region=Pacific , Number Cars Owned=4 , Number Cars Owned=...	453.593102432431	46.8214097490077

Analysis

When you want the total model as well as individual clusters, you have to remove the NODE_TYPE filter. Out of all our customers, 9132 bought bikes. This is approximately 49 percent of all customers.

Decision Tree Content

We've just been looking at the TM Clustering model that's part of the Targeted Mailing structure. That structure was designed to find out which potential customers are likely to buy bikes from Adventure Works. The structure contains other models including TM Decision Tree. This model also has content that relates customers to bike buying. This and the next few queries work with the content of the TM Decision Tree. As you might guess from its name, it's based on the Decision Trees mining algorithm.

Syntax

```
-- also for decision tree
select * from [TM Decision Tree].content
```

Result

NODE_DESCRIPTION	NODE_RULE	MARGINAL_RU...	NODE_PROBA...	MARGINAL_PR...	NODE_DISTRIBUTION	
					⊞	NODE_DISTRIBUTION
All	<compound-pre...		1	1	⊞	NODE_DISTRIBUTION
Number Cars Owned = 0	<compound-pre...	<predicate op="...	0.22927937675...	0.22927937675...	⊞	NODE_DISTRIBUTION
Number Cars Owned = 3	<compound-pre...	<predicate op="...	0.08899588833...	0.08899588833...	⊞	NODE_DISTRIBUTION
Number Cars Owned = 1	<compound-pre...	<predicate op="...	0.26417442112...	0.26417442112...	⊞	NODE_DISTRIBUTION
Number Cars Owned = 4	<compound-pre...	<predicate op="...	0.06822116425...	0.06822116425...	⊞	NODE_DISTRIBUTION
Number Cars Owned = 2	<compound-pre...	<predicate op="...	0.34932914953...	0.34932914953...	⊞	NODE_DISTRIBUTION
Number Cars Owned = 2 and Yearly Income < 26000	<compound-pre...	<predicate op="...	0.06151265959...	0.17608796654...	⊞	NODE_DISTRIBUTION
Number Cars Owned = 2 and Yearly Income >= 26000 and < 58000	<compound-pre...	<compound-pre...	0.11566760441...	0.33111352021...	⊞	NODE_DISTRIBUTION
Number Cars Owned = 2 and Yearly Income >= 58000 and < 106000	<compound-pre...	<compound-pre...	0.15921878381...	0.45578442000...	⊞	NODE_DISTRIBUTION
Number Cars Owned = 2 and Yearly Income >= 106000	<compound-pre...	<predicate op="...	0.01293010170...	0.03701409323...	⊞	NODE_DISTRIBUTION
Number Cars Owned = 2 and Yearly Income >= 106000 and Region ...	<compound-pre...	<predicate op="...	0.00568058861...	0.43933054393...	⊞	NODE_DISTRIBUTION
Number Cars Owned = 2 and Yearly Income >= 106000 and Region ...	<compound-pre...	<predicate op="...	0.00724951309...	0.56066945606...	⊞	NODE_DISTRIBUTION
Number Cars Owned = 2 and Yearly Income >= 106000 and Region ...	<compound-pre...	<predicate op="...	0.00216403375...	0.29850746268...	⊞	NODE_DISTRIBUTION
Number Cars Owned = 2 and Yearly Income >= 106000 and Region ...	<compound-pre...	<predicate op="...	0.00508547933...	0.70149253731...	⊞	NODE_DISTRIBUTION
Number Cars Owned = 2 and Yearly Income >= 58000 and < 106000...	<compound-pre...	<predicate op="...	0.10203419173...	0.64084267753...	⊞	NODE_DISTRIBUTION
Number Cars Owned = 2 and Yearly Income >= 58000 and < 106000...	<compound-pre...	<predicate op="...	0.00676260549...	0.04247366632...	⊞	NODE_DISTRIBUTION
Number Cars Owned = 2 and Yearly Income >= 58000 and < 106000...	<compound-pre...	<predicate op="...	0.02429127894...	0.15256540944...	⊞	NODE_DISTRIBUTION

Analysis

This Content query too returns a nested table column called NODE_DISTRIBUTION. You may have to scroll across in order to see it. If you expand it, there are no demographic attributes, only the predictable Bike Buyer attribute.

Decision Tree Node Types

You've met NODE_TYPE for clusters. Decision tree models also have a node type, although the meanings of the node types are different. NODE_TYPE is specified in the Where clause of this query.

Syntax

```
-- node type = 3 or 4
select * from [TM Decision Tree].content
where node_type = 3 or node_type = 4
```

Result

MODEL_CATAL...	MODEL_SCHEMA	MODEL_NAME	ATTRIBUTE_N...	NODE_NAME	NODE_UNIQUE...	NODE_TYPE	NODE_GUID	NODE_CAPTION	CHILDREN
Adventure Wor...		TM Decision Tree	Bike Buyer	00000000100	00000000100	3		Number Cars O...	3
Adventure Wor...		TM Decision Tree	Bike Buyer	00000000101	00000000101	3		Number Cars O...	3
Adventure Wor...		TM Decision Tree	Bike Buyer	00000000102	00000000102	3		Number Cars O...	2
Adventure Wor...		TM Decision Tree	Bike Buyer	00000000103	00000000103	3		Number Cars O...	2
Adventure Wor...		TM Decision Tree	Bike Buyer	00000000104	00000000104	3		Number Cars O...	4
Adventure Wor...		TM Decision Tree	Bike Buyer	0000000010400	0000000010400	3		Yearly Income <...	2
Adventure Wor...		TM Decision Tree	Bike Buyer	0000000010401	0000000010401	3		Yearly Income >...	2
Adventure Wor...		TM Decision Tree	Bike Buyer	0000000010402	0000000010402	3		Yearly Income >...	6
Adventure Wor...		TM Decision Tree	Bike Buyer	0000000010403	0000000010403	3		Yearly Income >...	2
Adventure Wor...		TM Decision Tree	Bike Buyer	000000001040...	000000001040...	4		Region = 'Europe'	0
Adventure Wor...		TM Decision Tree	Bike Buyer	000000001040...	000000001040...	3		Region not = 'E...	2
Adventure Wor...		TM Decision Tree	Bike Buyer	000000001040...	000000001040...	4		Total Children = 2	0
Adventure Wor...		TM Decision Tree	Bike Buyer	000000001040...	000000001040...	4		Total Children n...	0
Adventure Wor...		TM Decision Tree	Bike Buyer	000000001040...	000000001040...	3		Number Childre...	2
Adventure Wor...		TM Decision Tree	Bike Buyer	000000001040...	000000001040...	3		Number Childre...	2
Adventure Wor...		TM Decision Tree	Bike Buyer	000000001040...	000000001040...	3		Number Childre...	2
Adventure Wor...		TM Decision Tree	Bike Buyer	000000001040...	000000001040...	4		Number Childre...	0
Adventure Wor...		TM Decision Tree	Bike Buyer	000000001040...	000000001040...	3		Number Childre...	2

Analysis

When you browse a decision tree graphically, you can see a root node at the base of the tree. This is followed by splits that lead to other nodes. Some of these subsequent nodes split again leading to yet more nodes. Nodes that split (excluding the root node) have a NODE_TYPE of 3 and are known as *intermediate nodes*. Eventually splitting stops and the tree stops growing. Nodes that don't split any further have a NODE_TYPE of 4, and are called *leaf nodes*. This query shows all of the intermediate and leaf nodes in the decision tree.

Decision Tree Content Columns

Our aim is to establish which customers are likely to buy a bike. With this in mind, let's concentrate on some relevant columns.

Syntax

```
-- sub set of columns
select node_description as Demographics, node_distribution
from [TM Decision Tree].content
where node_type = 3 or node_type = 4
```

Result

Demographics	node_distribution
Number Cars Owned = 0	⊞ node_distribution
Number Cars Owned = 3	⊞ node_distribution
Number Cars Owned = 1	⊞ node_distribution
Number Cars Owned = 4	⊞ node_distribution
Number Cars Owned = 2	⊞ node_distribution
Number Cars Owned = 2 and Yearly Income < 26000	⊞ node_distribution
Number Cars Owned = 2 and Yearly Income >= 26000 and < 58000	⊞ node_distribution
Number Cars Owned = 2 and Yearly Income >= 58000 and < 106000	⊞ node_distribution
Number Cars Owned = 2 and Yearly Income >= 106000	⊞ node_distribution
Number Cars Owned = 2 and Yearly Income >= 106000 and Region = 'Europe'	⊞ node_distribution
Number Cars Owned = 2 and Yearly Income >= 106000 and Region not = 'Europe'	⊞ node_distribution
Number Cars Owned = 2 and Yearly Income >= 106000 and Region not = 'Europe' and Total Children = 2	⊞ node_distribution
Number Cars Owned = 2 and Yearly Income >= 106000 and Region not = 'Europe' and Total Children not = 2	⊞ node_distribution
Number Cars Owned = 2 and Yearly Income >= 58000 and < 106000 and Number Children At Home = 0	⊞ node_distribution
Number Cars Owned = 2 and Yearly Income >= 58000 and < 106000 and Number Children At Home = 3	⊞ node_distribution
Number Cars Owned = 2 and Yearly Income >= 58000 and < 106000 and Number Children At Home = 1	⊞ node_distribution
Number Cars Owned = 2 and Yearly Income >= 58000 and < 106000 and Number Children At Home = 4	⊞ node_distribution
Number Cars Owned = 2 and Yearly Income >= 58000 and < 106000 and Number Children At Home = 2	⊞ node_distribution
Number Cars Owned = 2 and Yearly Income >= 58000 and < 106000 and Number Children At Home = 5	⊞ node_distribution

Analysis

If you expand the NODE_DISTRIBUTION column, it's different from that of a cluster model. Here it contains only the predictable column and no demographic breakdown or profiling. All of the demographics are in the NODE_DESCRIPTION column.

Flattened Column

To make the content easier to read, let's flatten the NODE_DISTRIBUTION column.

Syntax

```
-- flattening node_distribution
select flattened node_description as Demographics, node_distribution
from [TM Decision Tree].content
where node_type = 3 or node_type = 4
```

Result

Demographics	node_distribution.ATTRIBUTE_NAME	node_distribution.ATTRIBUTE_VALUE	node_distribution.SUPPORT	node_distribution.PROBABILITY
Number Cars Owned = 0	Bike Buyer	Missing	0	0
Number Cars Owned = 0	Bike Buyer	0	1551	0.366058795786826
Number Cars Owned = 0	Bike Buyer	1	2687	0.633941204213174
Number Cars Owned = 3	Bike Buyer	Missing	0	0
Number Cars Owned = 3	Bike Buyer	0	951	0.577989075460247
Number Cars Owned = 3	Bike Buyer	1	694	0.422010924539753
Number Cars Owned = 1	Bike Buyer	Missing	0	0
Number Cars Owned = 1	Bike Buyer	0	2187	0.447908849014123
Number Cars Owned = 1	Bike Buyer	1	2696	0.552091150985877
Number Cars Owned = 4	Bike Buyer	Missing	0	0
Number Cars Owned = 4	Bike Buyer	0	795	0.630176734370878
Number Cars Owned = 4	Bike Buyer	1	466	0.369823265629122
Number Cars Owned = 2	Bike Buyer	Missing	0	0
Number Cars Owned = 2	Bike Buyer	0	3868	0.598998916352753
Number Cars Owned = 2	Bike Buyer	1	2589	0.401001083647247
Number Cars Owned = 2 and Yearly Income < 260...	Bike Buyer	Missing	0	0
Number Cars Owned = 2 and Yearly Income < 260...	Bike Buyer	0	852	0.749311133259073
Number Cars Owned = 2 and Yearly Income < 260...	Bike Buyer	1	285	0.250688866740927

Analysis

Each individual intermediate or leaf node now has three rows for the three states of the Bike Buyer attribute.

Honing the Result

If you need to concentrate on specific columns from the nested table column, you'll want a subquery again.

Syntax

```
-- sub set of columns from nested table
select flattened node_description as Demographics,
(select [attribute_name], [attribute_value], [Support],
[Probability] * 100 as [Probability] from node_distribution)
from [TM Decision Tree].content
where node_type = 3 or node_type = 4
```

Result

Demographics	Expression.attribute_name	Expression.attribute_value	Expression.Support	Expression.Probability
Number Cars Owned = 0	Bike Buyer	Missing	0	0
Number Cars Owned = 0	Bike Buyer	0	1551	36.6058795786826
Number Cars Owned = 0	Bike Buyer	1	2687	63.3941204213174
Number Cars Owned = 3	Bike Buyer	Missing	0	0
Number Cars Owned = 3	Bike Buyer	0	951	57.7989075460247
Number Cars Owned = 3	Bike Buyer	1	694	42.2010924539753
Number Cars Owned = 1	Bike Buyer	Missing	0	0
Number Cars Owned = 1	Bike Buyer	0	2187	44.7908849014123
Number Cars Owned = 1	Bike Buyer	1	2696	55.2091150985877
Number Cars Owned = 4	Bike Buyer	Missing	0	0
Number Cars Owned = 4	Bike Buyer	0	795	63.0176734370878
Number Cars Owned = 4	Bike Buyer	1	466	36.9823265629122
Number Cars Owned = 2	Bike Buyer	Missing	0	0
Number Cars Owned = 2	Bike Buyer	0	3868	59.8998916352753
Number Cars Owned = 2	Bike Buyer	1	2589	40.1001083647247
Number Cars Owned = 2 and Yearly Income < 26000	Bike Buyer	Missing	0	0
Number Cars Owned = 2 and Yearly Income < 26000	Bike Buyer	0	852	74.9311133259072
Number Cars Owned = 2 and Yearly Income < 26000	Bike Buyer	1	285	25.0688866740927
Number Cars Owned = 2 and Yearly Income >= 260...	Bike Buyer	Missing	0	0

Analysis

We're starting to get interesting results. For example, customers without a car are about 63 percent likely to buy a bike. Customers with four cars are only about 37 percent likely to do so.

Just the Bike Buyers

Here there is a Where clause in the subquery. It limits the rows to only those for bike buyers.

Syntax

```
-- just those who buy bikes
select flattened node_description as Demographics, (select [attribute_
name], [attribute_value], [Support], [Probability] * 100 as [Probability]
from node_distribution where [attribute_value] = '1') from [TM Decision
Tree].content
where node_type = 3 or node_type = 4
```

Result

Demographics	Expression.attribute_name	Expression.attribute_value	Expression.Support	Expression.Probability
Number Cars Owned = 0	Bike Buyer	1	2687	63.3941204213174
Number Cars Owned = 3	Bike Buyer	1	694	42.2010924539753
Number Cars Owned = 1	Bike Buyer	1	2696	55.2091150985877
Number Cars Owned = 4	Bike Buyer	1	466	36.9823265629122
Number Cars Owned = 2	Bike Buyer	1	2589	40.1001083647247
Number Cars Owned = 2 and Yearly Income < 26000	Bike Buyer	1	285	25.0688866740927
Number Cars Owned = 2 and Yearly Income >= 26000 and < 58...	Bike Buyer	1	745	34.8475400636029
Number Cars Owned = 2 and Yearly Income >= 58000 and < 10...	Bike Buyer	1	1391	47.2650676088877
Number Cars Owned = 2 and Yearly Income >= 106000	Bike Buyer	1	168	70.2477038686335
Number Cars Owned = 2 and Yearly Income >= 106000 and Re...	Bike Buyer	1	93	88.5225110970196
Number Cars Owned = 2 and Yearly Income >= 106000 and Re...	Bike Buyer	1	75	55.952380952381
Number Cars Owned = 2 and Yearly Income >= 106000 and Re...	Bike Buyer	1	6	15.0499286733238
Number Cars Owned = 2 and Yearly Income >= 106000 and Re...	Bike Buyer	1	69	73.3192004845548
Number Cars Owned = 2 and Yearly Income >= 58000 and < 10...	Bike Buyer	1	933	49.4697933709023
Number Cars Owned = 2 and Yearly Income >= 58000 and < 10...	Bike Buyer	1	20	16.0155357550834
Number Cars Owned = 2 and Yearly Income >= 58000 and < 10...	Bike Buyer	1	215	47.8844563211809
Number Cars Owned = 2 and Yearly Income >= 58000 and < 10...	Bike Buyer	1	9	6.99579366836396
Number Cars Owned = 2 and Yearly Income >= 58000 and < 10...	Bike Buyer	1	187	72.4756421612046
Number Cars Owned = 2 and Yearly Income >= 58000 and < 10...	Bike Buyer	1	27	28.1380130874479

Analysis

There are a lot of nodes in this tree. You may have to scroll down some way to see them all. As you scroll, often the demographics become ever more complex.

Tidying Up

A couple of the columns from the previous query are probably superfluous. They have been removed here.

Syntax

```
-- removing more columns
select flattened node_description as Demographics, (select [Support],
[Probability] * 100 as [Probability] from node_distribution where
[attribute_value] = '1') from [TM Decision Tree].content
where node_type = 3 or node_type = 4
```

Result

Demographics	Expression.Support	Expression.Probability
Number Cars Owned = 0	2687	63.3941204213174
Number Cars Owned = 3	694	42.2010924539753
Number Cars Owned = 1	2696	55.2091150985877
Number Cars Owned = 4	466	36.9823265629122
Number Cars Owned = 2	2589	40.1001083647247
Number Cars Owned = 2 and Yearly Income < 26000	285	25.0688866740927
Number Cars Owned = 2 and Yearly Income >= 26000 and < 58000	745	34.8475400636029
Number Cars Owned = 2 and Yearly Income >= 58000 and < 106000	1391	47.2650676088877
Number Cars Owned = 2 and Yearly Income >= 106000	168	70.2477038686335
Number Cars Owned = 2 and Yearly Income >= 106000 and Region = 'Europe'	93	88.5225110970196
Number Cars Owned = 2 and Yearly Income >= 106000 and Region not = 'Europe'	75	55.952380952381
Number Cars Owned = 2 and Yearly Income >= 106000 and Region not = 'Europe' and Total Children = 2	6	15.0499286733238
Number Cars Owned = 2 and Yearly Income >= 106000 and Region not = 'Europe' and Total Children not = 2	69	73.3192004845548
Number Cars Owned = 2 and Yearly Income >= 58000 and < 106000 and Number Children At Home = 0	933	49.4697933709023
Number Cars Owned = 2 and Yearly Income >= 58000 and < 106000 and Number Children At Home = 3	20	16.0155357550834
Number Cars Owned = 2 and Yearly Income >= 58000 and < 106000 and Number Children At Home = 1	215	47.8844563211809
Number Cars Owned = 2 and Yearly Income >= 58000 and < 106000 and Number Children At Home = 4	9	6.99579366836396
Number Cars Owned = 2 and Yearly Income >= 58000 and < 106000 and Number Children At Home = 2	187	72.4756421612046
Number Cars Owned = 2 and Yearly Income >= 58000 and < 106000 and Number Children At Home = 5	27	28.1380130874479

Analysis

There is only one predictable column (Bike Buyer), and the inner Where clause asks for only those rows where this is true. You can probably eliminate the corresponding columns from your query.

VBA in DMX

DMX supports a subset of VBA and Excel functions. If you examine the Assemblies folder under your SSAS in Object Explorer in SSMS, you will see that their libraries are registered.

Syntax

```
-- formatting with VBA, you can also use Excel!
select flattened node_description as Demographics,
```

```
(select [Support], vba!format([Probability],'Percent') as [Probability]
from node_distribution where [attribute_value] = '1')
from [TM Decision Tree].content
where node_type = 3 or node_type = 4
```

Result

Demographics	Expression.Support	Expression.Probability
Number Cars Owned = 0	2687	63.39%
Number Cars Owned = 3	694	42.20%
Number Cars Owned = 1	2696	55.21%
Number Cars Owned = 4	466	36.98%
Number Cars Owned = 2	2589	40.10%
Number Cars Owned = 2 and Yearly Income < 26000	285	25.07%
Number Cars Owned = 2 and Yearly Income >= 26000 and < 58000	745	34.85%
Number Cars Owned = 2 and Yearly Income >= 58000 and < 106000	1391	47.27%
Number Cars Owned = 2 and Yearly Income >= 106000	168	70.25%
Number Cars Owned = 2 and Yearly Income >= 106000 and Region = 'Europe'	93	88.52%
Number Cars Owned = 2 and Yearly Income >= 106000 and Region not = 'Europe'	75	55.95%
Number Cars Owned = 2 and Yearly Income >= 106000 and Region not = 'Europe' and Total Children = 2	6	15.05%
Number Cars Owned = 2 and Yearly Income >= 106000 and Region not = 'Europe' and Total Children not = 2	69	73.32%
Number Cars Owned = 2 and Yearly Income >= 58000 and < 106000 and Number Children At Home = 0	933	49.47%
Number Cars Owned = 2 and Yearly Income >= 58000 and < 106000 and Number Children At Home = 3	20	16.02%
Number Cars Owned = 2 and Yearly Income >= 58000 and < 106000 and Number Children At Home = 1	215	47.88%
Number Cars Owned = 2 and Yearly Income >= 58000 and < 106000 and Number Children At Home = 4	9	7.00%
Number Cars Owned = 2 and Yearly Income >= 58000 and < 106000 and Number Children At Home = 2	187	72.48%
Number Cars Owned = 2 and Yearly Income >= 58000 and < 106000 and Number Children At Home = 5	27	28.14%

Analysis

This query is using the VBA Format function to make our results look better. The syntax is VBA! followed by the VBA function name. Should you wish to exploit Excel functions, then it's Excel! followed by the Excel function name. You should be aware that a large number of common VBA and Excel functions are supported, but not all of them.

Association Content

Subcategory Associations in the Customer Mining structure is a model based on the Association mining algorithm. This type of model can also be fruitfully interrogated by a Content query.

Syntax

```
-- then from other models (association),
-- not using the node_distribution this time
select * from [Subcategory Associations].content
```

Result

NODE_DESCRIPTION	NODE_RULE	MARGINAL_RU...	NODE_PROBA...	MARGINAL_PR...	NODE_DISTRIBUTION
Association Rules Model; ITEMSET_COUNT=457; RULE_COUNT=...			0	0	⊞ NODE_DISTRIBUTION
Tires and Tubes = Existing			0.45931616533...	0.45931616533...	⊞ NODE_DISTRIBUTION
Road Bikes = Existing			0.34608309889...	0.34608309889...	⊞ NODE_DISTRIBUTION
Helmets = Existing			0.32244103008...	0.32244103008...	⊞ NODE_DISTRIBUTION
Bottles and Cages = Existing			0.24605063838...	0.24605063838...	⊞ NODE_DISTRIBUTION
Mountain Bikes = Existing			0.22121835100...	0.22121835100...	⊞ NODE_DISTRIBUTION
Jerseys = Existing			0.17268989396...	0.17268989396...	⊞ NODE_DISTRIBUTION
Helmets = Existing, Tires and Tubes = Existing			0.15802856524...	0.15802856524...	⊞ NODE_DISTRIBUTION
Touring Bikes = Existing			0.11593810863...	0.11593810863...	⊞ NODE_DISTRIBUTION
Caps = Existing			0.11534299935...	0.11534299935...	⊞ NODE_DISTRIBUTION
Fenders = Existing			0.11415278078...	0.11415278078...	⊞ NODE_DISTRIBUTION
Mountain Bikes = Existing, Road Bikes = Existing			0.11106903267...	0.11106903267...	⊞ NODE_DISTRIBUTION
Helmets = Existing, Road Bikes = Existing			0.11096083098...	0.11096083098...	⊞ NODE_DISTRIBUTION
Bottles and Cages = Existing, Road Bikes = Existing			0.08602034191...	0.08602034191...	⊞ NODE_DISTRIBUTION
Bottles and Cages = Existing, Helmets = Existing			0.07860852629...	0.07860852629...	⊞ NODE_DISTRIBUTION
Road Bikes = Existing, Tires and Tubes = Existing			0.07844622376...	0.07844622376...	⊞ NODE_DISTRIBUTION
Mountain Bikes = Existing, Helmets = Existing			0.07509197143...	0.07509197143...	⊞ NODE_DISTRIBUTION
Gloves = Existing			0.07444276130...	0.07444276130...	⊞ NODE_DISTRIBUTION

Analysis

This time, the NODE_DISTRIBUTION nested table column is less interesting. The
real information lies in the NODE_DESCRIPTION column. You may have to scroll
across to see the result shown.

Market Basket Analysis

This query extends the previous query. What you have here is market basket analysis.
Welcome to the world of cross-selling!

Syntax

```
-- sub set
select node_description as Associations,
node_probability * 100 as [Probability], node_support as [Support]
from [Subcategory Associations].content
where node_type <> 1 and node_support > 50
order by node_probability desc
```

Result

Associations	Probability	Support
Fenders = Existing, Road Bikes = Existing -> Mountain Bikes = Existing	100	493
Shorts = Existing, Road Bikes = Existing -> Mountain Bikes = Existing	100	129
Fenders = Existing, Touring Bikes = Existing -> Mountain Bikes = Existing	100	218
Cleaners = Existing, Caps = Existing -> Tires and Tubes = Existing	89.8305084745763	53
Cleaners = Existing, Jerseys = Existing -> Tires and Tubes = Existing	89.7435897435898	70
Gloves = Existing, Caps = Existing -> Tires and Tubes = Existing	89.5348837209302	77
Bike Stands = Existing -> Tires and Tubes = Existing	87.6543209876543	213
Cleaners = Existing, Gloves = Existing -> Tires and Tubes = Existing	86.1538461538462	56
Gloves = Existing, Caps = Existing -> Helmets = Existing	83.7209302325581	72
Shorts = Existing, Helmets = Existing -> Tires and Tubes = Existing	83.3333333333333	85
Cleaners = Existing, Helmets = Existing -> Tires and Tubes = Existing	82.258064516129	102
Hydration Packs = Existing, Touring Bikes = Existing -> Mountain Bikes = Existing	81.8181818181818	108
Touring Bikes = Existing, Tires and Tubes = Existing -> Mountain Bikes = Existing	75.992438563327	402
Shorts = Existing, Mountain Bikes = Existing -> Road Bikes = Existing	75.8823529411765	129
Cleaners = Existing, Touring Bikes = Existing -> Mountain Bikes = Existing	75	66
Gloves = Existing, Touring Bikes = Existing -> Mountain Bikes = Existing	73.8095238095238	124
Touring Bikes = Existing, Bottles and Cages = Existing -> Mountain Bikes = Existing	70.2564102564102	548
Socks = Existing, Touring Bikes = Existing -> Mountain Bikes = Existing	69.7247706422018	76
Vests = Existing, Helmets = Existing -> Tires and Tubes = Existing	69.0476190476191	87

Analysis

The result is pretty powerful stuff. You can see the combinations of purchases by customers. If Joe buys X, will he also buy Y, and what is the probability of that happening? The Where clause is worth a look. NODE_TYPE <> 1 eliminates the model itself from the output. NODE_SUPPORT > 50 eliminates those combinations of purchases that did not happen too often. You want your result to be statistically viable.

Naïve Bayes Content

Now it's time to give Naïve Bayes a workout. The last few queries in this chapter on Content queries examine the content of a Naïve Bayes model, TM Naïve Bayes.

Syntax

```
-- now from (naive bayes)
select * from [TM Naive Bayes].content
```

Result

MODEL_CATAL...	MODEL_SCHEMA	MODEL_NAME	ATTRIBUTE_N...	NODE_NAME	NODE_UNIQUE...	NODE_TYPE	NODE_GUID	NODE_CAPTION	CHILDREN
Adventure Wor...		TM Naive Bayes		0	0	1			2
Adventure Wor...		TM Naive Bayes		101z141z3	101z141z3	26			0
Adventure Wor...		TM Naive Bayes	Bike Buyer	100000000	100000000	9		Bike Buyer	9
Adventure Wor...		TM Naive Bayes	Commute Distan...	200000000000...	200000000000...	10		Bike Buyer -> C...	6
Adventure Wor...		TM Naive Bayes	Education	200000000000...	200000000000...	10		Bike Buyer -> E...	6
Adventure Wor...		TM Naive Bayes	Occupation	200000000000...	200000000000...	10		Bike Buyer -> O...	6
Adventure Wor...		TM Naive Bayes	Marital Status	200000000000...	200000000000...	10		Bike Buyer -> M...	3
Adventure Wor...		TM Naive Bayes	Number Cars O...	200000000000...	200000000000...	10		Bike Buyer -> N...	6
Adventure Wor...		TM Naive Bayes	Number Childre...	200000000000...	200000000000...	10		Bike Buyer -> N...	7
Adventure Wor...		TM Naive Bayes	Region	200000000000...	200000000000...	10		Bike Buyer -> R...	4
Adventure Wor...		TM Naive Bayes	Total Children	200000000000...	200000000000...	10		Bike Buyer -> T...	7
Adventure Wor...		TM Naive Bayes	Age	200000000000...	200000000000...	10		Bike Buyer -> Age	11
Adventure Wor...		TM Naive Bayes	Age	300000000000...	300000000000...	11		Bike Buyer -> A...	0
Adventure Wor...		TM Naive Bayes	Age	300000000000...	300000000000...	11		Bike Buyer -> A...	0
Adventure Wor...		TM Naive Bayes	Age	300000000000...	300000000000...	11		Bike Buyer -> A...	0
Adventure Wor...		TM Naive Bayes	Age	300000000000...	300000000000...	11		Bike Buyer -> A...	0
Adventure Wor...		TM Naive Bayes	Age	300000000000...	300000000000...	11		Bike Buyer -> A...	0
Adventure Wor...		TM Naive Bayes	Age	300000000000...	300000000000...	11		Bike Buyer -> A...	0

Analysis

Naïve Bayes is a simpler algorithm than Decision Trees. Both analyze correlations between input columns and a predictable output (Decision Trees can do much more than this). Naïve Bayes does so with one input at a time. Decision Trees can correlate multiple inputs simultaneously. If you are new to data mining, that may sound suitably obscure! Let's take an example. Suppose you have two inputs or demographics, gender and marital status, and your predictable column is whether or not a bike is bought. Naïve Bayes can see how gender relates to bike buying. It can also examine how marital status affects bike buying. What it can't do (which Decision Trees can) is see how both gender *and* marital status together in differing combinations influence bike buying.

In addition, Naïve Bayes can only handle discrete or discretized values—it can't work with continuous variables. You may be forgiven for thinking, "why bother with Naïve Bayes?" Yet, it's very popular. It's precisely because of its simplicity that it's useful. It's very fast to train. It's very easy to decipher in a Content query. It's often used to identify those inputs that might be valid for a subsequent, more complex, Decision Tree model.

Naïve Bayes Node Type

In this query we add a Where clause to display the rows that are most interesting to us.

Syntax

```
-- node_type = 11 and node_probability to get rid of missing
select node_description as Demographics, node_distribution
from [TM Naive Bayes].content
where node_type = 11 and node_probability > 0 and node_support > 500
```

Result

Demographics	node_distribution
Bike Buyer -> Age < 36	⊞ node_distribution
Bike Buyer -> Age = 36 - 41	⊞ node_distribution
Bike Buyer -> Age = 41 - 48	⊞ node_distribution
Bike Buyer -> Age = 48 - 53	⊞ node_distribution
Bike Buyer -> Age = 53 - 59	⊞ node_distribution
Bike Buyer -> Age = 59 - 64	⊞ node_distribution
Bike Buyer -> Age = 64 - 71	⊞ node_distribution
Bike Buyer -> Total Children = 0	⊞ node_distribution
Bike Buyer -> Total Children = 3	⊞ node_distribution
Bike Buyer -> Total Children = 1	⊞ node_distribution
Bike Buyer -> Total Children = 4	⊞ node_distribution
Bike Buyer -> Total Children = 2	⊞ node_distribution
Bike Buyer -> Total Children = 5	⊞ node_distribution
Bike Buyer -> Region = North America	⊞ node_distribution
Bike Buyer -> Region = Pacific	⊞ node_distribution
Bike Buyer -> Region = Europe	⊞ node_distribution
Bike Buyer -> Number Children At Home = 0	⊞ node_distribution
Bike Buyer -> Number Children At Home = 3	⊞ node_distribution
Bike Buyer -> Number Children At Home = 1	⊞ node_distribution

Analysis

NODE_TYPE of 11 gives us the most interesting rows. NODE_PROBABILITY is used to eliminate missing values. NODE_SUPPORT eliminates rows that may not be statistically viable.

Flattening Naïve Bayes Content

You've seen the Flattened key word a few times now. Is DMX getting easier?

Syntax

```
-- flattening
select flattened node_description as Demographics, node_distribution
from [TM Naive Bayes].content
where node_type = 11 and node_probability > 0 and node_support > 500
```

Result

Demographics	node_distribution.ATTRIBUTE_NAME	node_distribution.ATTRIBUTE_VALUE	node_distribution.SUPPORT	node_distribution.PROBABILITY
Bike Buyer -> Age < 36	Bike Buyer	Missing	0	0
Bike Buyer -> Age < 36	Bike Buyer	0	1749	0.587899159663866
Bike Buyer -> Age < 36	Bike Buyer	1	1226	0.412100840336134
Bike Buyer -> Age = 36 - 41	Bike Buyer	Missing	0	0
Bike Buyer -> Age = 36 - 41	Bike Buyer	0	1060	0.352159468438538
Bike Buyer -> Age = 36 - 41	Bike Buyer	1	1950	0.647840531561462
Bike Buyer -> Age = 41 - 48	Bike Buyer	Missing	0	0
Bike Buyer -> Age = 41 - 48	Bike Buyer	0	2058	0.466772510773418
Bike Buyer -> Age = 41 - 48	Bike Buyer	1	2351	0.533227489226582
Bike Buyer -> Age = 48 - 53	Bike Buyer	Missing	0	0
Bike Buyer -> Age = 48 - 53	Bike Buyer	0	1272	0.49055148476668
Bike Buyer -> Age = 48 - 53	Bike Buyer	1	1321	0.50944851523332
Bike Buyer -> Age = 53 - 59	Bike Buyer	Missing	0	0
Bike Buyer -> Age = 53 - 59	Bike Buyer	0	1174	0.500853242320819
Bike Buyer -> Age = 53 - 59	Bike Buyer	1	1170	0.499146757679181
Bike Buyer -> Age = 59 - 64	Bike Buyer	Missing	0	0
Bike Buyer -> Age = 59 - 64	Bike Buyer	0	878	0.624022743425729
Bike Buyer -> Age = 59 - 64	Bike Buyer	1	529	0.375977256574272

Analysis

There is nothing new syntactically here—but our result looks better.

Naïve Bayes Content Subquery 1/2

Here you have a subquery to extract the most interesting columns. You are looking at bike buyers.

Syntax

```
-- interesting columns using subquery and where clause for bike buyers
select flattened node_description as Demographics,
(select [Probability] * 100 as [Probability], [Support]
from node_distribution where [attribute_value] = '1')
from [TM Naive Bayes].content
where node_type = 11 and node_probability > 0 and node_support > 500
```

Result

Demographics	Expression.Probability	Expression.Support
Bike Buyer -> Age < 36	41.2100840336134	1226
Bike Buyer -> Age = 36 - 41	64.7840531561462	1950
Bike Buyer -> Age = 41 - 48	53.3227489226582	2351
Bike Buyer -> Age = 48 - 53	50.944851523332	1321
Bike Buyer -> Age = 53 - 59	49.9146757679181	1170
Bike Buyer -> Age = 59 - 64	37.5977256574271	529
Bike Buyer -> Age = 64 - 71	39.1925988225399	466
Bike Buyer -> Total Children = 0	51.2681510164569	2648
Bike Buyer -> Total Children = 3	48.359161349134	1061
Bike Buyer -> Total Children = 1	60.0165791655153	2172
Bike Buyer -> Total Children = 4	37.9939209726444	875
Bike Buyer -> Total Children = 2	51.0452500661551	1929
Bike Buyer -> Total Children = 5	31.3904494382022	447
Bike Buyer -> Region = North America	44.9946751863685	4225
Bike Buyer -> Region = Pacific	60.0111389585074	2155
Bike Buyer -> Region = Europe	50.0090859531165	2752
Bike Buyer -> Number Children At Home = 0	51.5383231378194	5729
Bike Buyer -> Number Children At Home = 3	35.0498338870432	422
Bike Buyer -> Number Children At Home = 1	49.7154471544715	1223

Analysis

Customers aged younger than 36 years are about 41 percent likely to buy a bike. Customers from the Pacific region are about 60 percent likely to do the same.

Naïve Bayes Content Subquery 2/2

You are looking at non-bike buyers.

Syntax

```
-- interesting columns using subquery and where clause for non bike
-- buyers
select flattened node_description as Demographics,
(select [Probability] * 100 as [Probability], [Support]
from node_distribution where [attribute_value] = '0')
from [TM Naive Bayes].content
where node_type = 11 and node_probability > 0 and node_support > 500
```

Result

Demographics	Expression.Probability	Expression.Support
Bike Buyer -> Age < 36	58.7899159663866	1749
Bike Buyer -> Age = 36 - 41	35.2159468438538	1060
Bike Buyer -> Age = 41 - 48	46.6772510773418	2058
Bike Buyer -> Age = 48 - 53	49.055148476668	1272
Bike Buyer -> Age = 53 - 59	50.0853242320819	1174
Bike Buyer -> Age = 59 - 64	62.4022743425729	878
Bike Buyer -> Age = 64 - 71	60.8074011774601	723
Bike Buyer -> Total Children = 0	48.7318489835431	2517
Bike Buyer -> Total Children = 3	51.640838650866	1133
Bike Buyer -> Total Children = 1	39.9834208344847	1447
Bike Buyer -> Total Children = 4	62.0060790273556	1428
Bike Buyer -> Total Children = 2	48.9547499338449	1850
Bike Buyer -> Total Children = 5	68.6095505617977	977
Bike Buyer -> Region = North America	55.0053248136315	5165
Bike Buyer -> Region = Pacific	39.9888610414926	1436
Bike Buyer -> Region = Europe	49.9909140468835	2751
Bike Buyer -> Number Children At Home = 0	48.4616768621806	5387
Bike Buyer -> Number Children At Home = 3	64.9501661129568	782
Bike Buyer -> Number Children At Home = 1	50.2845528455285	1237

Analysis

Customers aged younger than 36 years are about 59 percent likely not to buy a bike. Customers from the Pacific region are about 40 percent likely to do the same.

Chapter 3

Prediction Queries
with Decision Trees

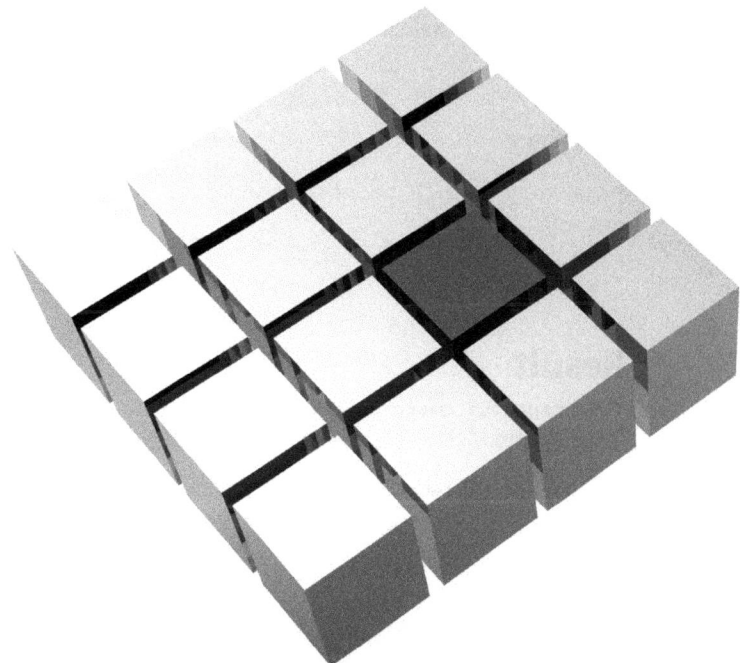

Thischapter demonstrates how to perform DMX Prediction queries with mining models based on the Decision Trees algorithm. Cases queries reveal the original source data for the model. Content queries show the result of training the model and the patterns and clusters and correlations discovered. Both Cases and Content queries are based on existing data. Prediction queries, on the other hand, work on new data (one exception to this rule is the Time Series algorithm, which usually makes predictions based on existing data). They do so by comparing the new data with the results discovered during model training. For example, a Prediction query might show the possibility and probability of a new customer's being a bike buyer. Although this chapter focuses on the Decision Trees algorithm, the techniques learned are generally applicable to all the data mining algorithms.

- ▶ **Key concepts**   Prediction queries, Decision Trees, predictable columns, input columns, data sources
- ▶ **Keywords**   Prediction join, natural prediction join, singleton prediction join, Openquery(), Predict(), PredictHistogram(), PredictProbability(), TopCount(), BottomCount()

Select on Mining Model 1/6

In Chapter 1, you worked with Cases queries. Chapter 2 was largely concerned with Content queries. In this chapter, most of the queries are directly on the data mining model (with no .cases or .content). Many of these queries will be Prediction queries. Here's a simple Select on a model to get you started—only it fails (yes, it's a learning experience)!

Syntax

```
-- a very simple select on a model
select
from
[TM Decision Tree]
```

Result

```
Executing the query ...
The TM Decision Tree cube either does not exist or has not been processed.

Execution complete
```

Analysis

The error message indicates the query is looking for an SSAS cube, yet the code references a data mining model and it's done in the DMX query editor. You may have noticed cube errors in DMX queries before or even data mining errors in MDX queries. The SSAS query parser looks at your code and tries to decide if you are writing DMX or MDX and responds appropriately. Our query looks like MDX, not DMX, and is treated as such—only there is no cube called TM Decision Tree. If you want to, you can write your DMX queries in the MDX query editor. Conversely, as here, you can write MDX queries in the DMX query editor.

Select on Mining Model 2/6

This is an MDX query. It should work, even though you are in the DMX query editor.

Syntax

```
-- MDX works!
select
from
[Adventure Works]
```

Result

```
$80,450,596.98
```

Analysis

I think this is worth knowing. If your Select statement contains a column or comma-separated column list or an asterisk(*) for all columns, it's treated as DMX. If your Select has no column list or it includes the key words On Columns, it is deemed to be MDX. Incidentally, SQL does not work in the DMX query editor.

Select on Mining Model 3/6

This is definitely a DMX query. It's a query directly against a mining model.

Syntax

```
select *
from
[TM Decision Tree]
```

Result

Bike Buyer
0

Analysis

Because of the asterisk (*) representing all columns, the parser identifies this as a DMX query. The result is not particularly illuminating. The next couple of queries will make sense of the result. It is actually a very primitive (implicit) Prediction query.

Select on Mining Model 4/6

This is also an implicit Prediction query. It includes a column in the Select statement.

Syntax

```
-- empty implicit prediction
select [Bike Buyer]
from
[TM Decision Tree]
```

Result

Bike Buyer
0

Analysis

This query returns the same result as the previous query. Bike Buyer is a predictable column. It's an implicit Prediction query as there is no explicit reference to any prediction function.

Select on Mining Model 5/6

Here, the Prediction query is explicit. It contains the Predict() function operating on the Bike Buyer predictable column.

Syntax

```
-- empty explicit prediction
select Predict([Bike Buyer]) as [Bike Buyer]
from
[TM Decision Tree]
```

Result

Bike Buyer

0

Analysis

If you omit the Predict() function, it's assumed. If you also leave out the predictable column name, it's assumed. Should you exclude the column name and include the Predict() function by itself, an error will be generated. It's better to be totally explicit and have both the function *and* the column as here. That's all well and good, but what does it mean?

Bike Buyer is a predictable column in the TM Decision Tree model (based on the Decision Trees algorithm). Predict() is a function that returns a prediction on the referenced column. Here, it's predicting Bike Buyer. The result is 0—which means not likely to buy a bike (a result of 1 would mean likely to buy a bike). Normally, when making predictions, you ask for predictions based on new data (a prediction join query). Here, there is no new data being input. Consequently, the prediction is operating on existing data. The existing data is all of the cases used to train the model. Now, maybe, we can decipher the result. Looking at all of the existing customers, it is most likely that they are not bike buyers. Of course, some may well be bike buyers. However, over 50 percent are not bike buyers. If over 50 percent had been bike buyers, then the result would have been 1, not 0. Prediction queries are not trivial! We have lots of queries soon that, hopefully, will help you unravel the complexities.

Select on Mining Model 6/6

Here we've gone back to an implicit Prediction query—there is no Predict() function. The column has been changed from Bike Buyer to Region.

Syntax

```
-- non-predictable column
select [Region]
from
[TM Decision Tree]
```

Result

```
Executing the query ...
Error (Data mining): Only a predictable column (or a column that is related to a predictable column) can be referenced
...
Execution complete
```

Analysis

The error message indicates that predictions can only be done against predictable columns. Bike Buyer is predictable. If you look at the Bike Buyer column in the TM Decision Tree model in the Targeted Mailing structure within BIDS, you'll notice that its Usage property is set to Predict (PredictOnly is also a valid setting). On the other hand, the usage property for the Region column is set to Input. Region is not a predictable column, that's why the query fails—the Predict() function on the column is assumed.

Prediction Query

The syntax has just gotten more difficult! This is a full and potentially sophisticated Prediction query. It's known as a *prediction join*. This is the type of query (after we've done a little more work) that delivers real business intelligence.

Syntax

```
-- *** EXISTING CUSTOMERS ***
-- prediction join from table/view with matching names
select TM.[Age], TM.[Gender], TM.[Region],
Predict([Bike Buyer]),PredictProbability([Bike Buyer])
from
[TM Decision Tree]
prediction join
openquery
([Adventure Works DW],
'select Age, Gender, Region from vTargetMail') as TM
on [TM Decision Tree].[Age] = TM.[Age] and
[TM Decision Tree].[Gender] = TM.[Gender] and
[TM Decision Tree].[Region] = TM.[Region]
```

Result

Age	Gender	Region	Expression	Expression
43	M	Pacific	0	0.50594594594...
44	M	Pacific	0	0.50594594594...
44	M	Pacific	0	0.50594594594...
41	F	Pacific	0	0.50594594594...
41	F	Pacific	0	0.50594594594...
44	M	Pacific	0	0.50594594594...
43	F	Pacific	0	0.50594594594...
45	M	Pacific	0	0.50594594594...
45	F	Pacific	0	0.50594594594...
45	M	Pacific	0	0.50594594594...
45	F	Pacific	0	0.50594594594...
45	M	Pacific	0	0.50594594594...
41	F	North America	0	0.50594594594...
41	M	North America	0	0.50594594594...
41	F	North America	0	0.50594594594...
30	F	North America	0	0.50594594594...
30	M	North America	0	0.50594594594...
65	F	Pacific	0	0.50594594594...
64	M	Pacific	0	0.50594594594...

Analysis

There's quite a bit of analysis to do! Let's start with the Select statement. It has Age, Gender, and Region as the first three columns. Earlier we saw that Region failed. However, this is not the same Region. It's not from the model, but from a view called vTargetMail, which is aliased as TM. vTargetMail is referenced in a separate Select. vTargetMail is a view in an SQL Server relational database (AdventureWorksDW2008). In fact, it's the same view as that used to provide the cases for the mining structure and to train the model itself in the first place. As such, the view and the model share column names like Region. Next is a Predict() function on Bike Buyer, which will return 1 (bike buyer) or 0 (not a bike buyer). Then there is a PredictProbability() function on Bike Buyer. This shows the probability of the Predict() function result being true.

The From clause joins the model back to the view. It's a prediction join on three columns (Age, Gender, and Region). However, the view has to be referenced in SQL, not DMX, and that is why there is an Openquery. The first parameter for Openquery is a data source that points back to the SQL Server relational database. You can check the data source name under the Data Sources folder in Object Explorer in SSMS. The folder is under your SSAS database (Adventure Works DW 2008). Normally, the data source would have been created graphically in BIDS (or in script from XMLA/ASSL). You can't use DMX or SSMS to do so directly, although you can from a Common Language Runtime (CLR) stored procedure. The data source reference is followed by an SQL Select query and the join columns.

There are two important provisos. Firstly, the prediction is being made against the source data itself (vTargetMail). In reality, you'll want new data—you want to know how new (not existing) customers are likely to behave. You'll see how to do this shortly. Secondly, the predictions look strange. The first Expression column is the result of the Predict() function. It seems that all of our existing customers are not bike buyers. But, if you run a Cases query you'll see that some of them are. The Predict() function is not interested in historical data—it works out what is likely to happen, not what has happened. It has examined the Age, Gender, and Region of all customers and decided that none of them would buy a bike (even if they had already done so). This can be a little confusing. Does it mean that the mining model has gotten it wrong? Fortunately not. It simply means that we don't have enough data (that is, not enough columns or demographics) to differentiate individual customers—we'll fix this shortly. The second Expression is from PredictProbability(). We can apply similar reasoning to understand why it's always just over 0.50 (50 percent).

Aliases and Formatting

Judicious use of aliases and formatting can make the results of a Prediction query so much easier to read.

Syntax

```
-- same with * and aliases and VBA formatting
select TM.* , Predict([Bike Buyer]) as [Bike Buyer],
vba!format(PredictProbability([Bike Buyer]),'Percent') as [Probability]
from
[TM Decision Tree]
prediction join
openquery
([Adventure Works DW],
'select Age, Gender, Region from vTargetMail') as TM
on [TM Decision Tree].[Age] = TM.[Age] and
[TM Decision Tree].[Gender] = TM.[Gender] and
[TM Decision Tree].[Region] = TM.[Region]
```

Result

Age	Gender	Region	Bike Buyer	Probability
43	M	Pacific	0	50.59%
44	M	Pacific	0	50.59%
44	M	Pacific	0	50.59%
41	F	Pacific	0	50.59%
41	F	Pacific	0	50.59%
44	M	Pacific	0	50.59%
43	F	Pacific	0	50.59%
45	M	Pacific	0	50.59%
45	F	Pacific	0	50.59%
45	M	Pacific	0	50.59%
45	F	Pacific	0	50.59%
45	M	Pacific	0	50.59%
41	F	North America	0	50.59%
41	M	North America	0	50.59%
41	F	North America	0	50.59%
30	F	North America	0	50.59%
30	M	North America	0	50.59%
65	F	Pacific	0	50.59%
64	M	Pacific	0	50.59%

Analysis

The three columns from the relational view are now represented by an asterisk (*). The VBA Format function is used to display percentages for the probability.

Natural Prediction Join

This query gives the same result as the last query. Suddenly, the syntax got a bit simpler.

Syntax

```
-- natural prediction with matching names
select TM.* , Predict([Bike Buyer]) as [Bike Buyer],
vba!format(PredictProbability([Bike Buyer]),'Percent') as [Probability]
from
[TM Decision Tree]
natural prediction join
openquery
([Adventure Works DW],
'select Age, Gender, Region from vTargetMail') as TM
```

Result

Age	Gender	Region	Bike Buyer	Probability
43	M	Pacific	0	50.59%
44	M	Pacific	0	50.59%
44	M	Pacific	0	50.59%
41	F	Pacific	0	50.59%
41	F	Pacific	0	50.59%
44	M	Pacific	0	50.59%
43	F	Pacific	0	50.59%
45	M	Pacific	0	50.59%
45	F	Pacific	0	50.59%
45	M	Pacific	0	50.59%
45	F	Pacific	0	50.59%
45	M	Pacific	0	50.59%
41	F	North America	0	50.59%
41	M	North America	0	50.59%
41	F	North America	0	50.59%
30	F	North America	0	50.59%
30	M	North America	0	50.59%
65	F	Pacific	0	50.59%
64	M	Pacific	0	50.59%

Analysis

The three joins between the three model columns and the three view columns have gone. The prediction join is now a natural prediction join. A natural prediction join assumes the column names are the same in the view and in the model. It's worth noting that you can use a relational table as well as a relational view.

More Demographics

One more column has been added. It shows the number of cars owned for each customer. Now we have bike buyers and the probabilities are different!

Syntax

```
-- prediction join with non-matching names
-- now we have bike buyers!
select TM.* , Predict([Bike Buyer]) as [Bike Buyer],
vba!format(PredictProbability([Bike Buyer]),'Percent') as [Probability]
from
[TM Decision Tree]
prediction join
openquery
([Adventure Works DW],
```

```
'select Age, Gender, Region, NumberCarsOwned from vTargetMail') as TM
on [TM Decision Tree].[Age] = TM.[Age] and
[TM Decision Tree].[Gender] = TM.[Gender] and
[TM Decision Tree].[Region] = TM.[Region] and
[TM Decision Tree].[Number Cars Owned] = TM.[NumberCarsOwned]
```

Result

Age	Gender	Region	NumberCarsOwn...	Bike Buyer	Probability
43	M	Pacific	0	1	91.68%
44	M	Pacific	1	1	59.85%
44	M	Pacific	1	1	59.85%
41	F	Pacific	1	1	59.85%
41	F	Pacific	4	0	69.03%
44	M	Pacific	1	1	59.85%
43	F	Pacific	1	1	59.85%
45	M	Pacific	2	0	59.90%
45	F	Pacific	3	0	57.80%
45	M	Pacific	1	1	59.85%
45	F	Pacific	1	1	59.85%
45	M	Pacific	4	0	69.03%
41	F	North America	2	0	59.90%
41	M	North America	3	0	57.80%
41	F	North America	3	0	57.80%
30	F	North America	1	0	71.26%
30	M	North America	1	0	71.26%
65	F	Pacific	2	0	59.90%
64	M	Pacific	2	0	59.90%

Analysis

This is a prediction join, not a natural prediction join. A natural prediction join is not possible because of the new column. In the view it's called NumberCarsOwned. The equivalent in the model contains spaces—BIDS automatically adds spaces for you. The names for the column do not match.

The result shows both bike buyers and non-bike buyers. Also, the probabilities are now varied. That's because we have more inputs or demographics. The model is working after all. On the basis of Age, Gender, and Region, it was unable to discriminate between customers. Adding NumberCarsOwned makes all the difference. In statistical terms, there is no correlation between Age—Gender—Region and Bike Buyer. However, there is a correlation between Age—Gender—Region—NumberCarsOwned and Bike Buyer. Indeed, the correlation is pretty strong given the wide range of probabilities returned.

Natural Prediction Join Broken

You might be tempted to save some typing by trying a natural prediction join. You will get results, but they are different from the last query.

Syntax

```
-- natural prediction with non-matching names
-- seems to work but NumberCarsOwned has been ignored
select TM.* , Predict([Bike Buyer]) as [Bike Buyer],
vba!format(PredictProbability([Bike Buyer]),'Percent') as [Probability]
from
[TM Decision Tree]
natural prediction join
openquery
([Adventure Works DW],
'select Age, Gender, Region, NumberCarsOwned from vTargetMail') as TM
```

Result

Age	Gender	Region	NumberCarsOwned	Bike Buyer	Probability
43	M	Pacific	0	0	50.59%
44	M	Pacific	1	0	50.59%
44	M	Pacific	1	0	50.59%
41	F	Pacific	1	0	50.59%
41	F	Pacific	4	0	50.59%
44	M	Pacific	1	0	50.59%
43	F	Pacific	1	0	50.59%
45	M	Pacific	2	0	50.59%
45	F	Pacific	3	0	50.59%
45	M	Pacific	1	0	50.59%
45	F	Pacific	1	0	50.59%
45	M	Pacific	4	0	50.59%
41	F	North America	2	0	50.59%
41	M	North America	3	0	50.59%
41	F	North America	3	0	50.59%
30	F	North America	1	0	50.59%
30	M	North America	1	0	50.59%
65	F	Pacific	2	0	50.59%
64	M	Pacific	2	0	50.59%

Analysis

We are back to all non-bike buyers all with the same probability. In effect, NumberCarsOwned has been ignored (and there is no error message to tell you). That's because we attempted a natural prediction join and missed out on the join columns.

A natural prediction join only works on those columns where the column name is identical in the model and the relational source. Otherwise, the column is ignored completely in the prediction even if it still displays as part of the first Select list.

Natural Prediction Join Fixed

This is still a natural prediction join. The change is quite subtle. There is an alias on the unmatched column name in the second (relational) Select.

Syntax

```
-- natural prediction with non-matching names and aliases
select TM.* , Predict([Bike Buyer]) as [Bike Buyer],
vba!format(PredictProbability([Bike Buyer]),'Percent') as [Probability]
from
[TM Decision Tree]
natural prediction join
openquery
([Adventure Works DW],
'select Age, Gender, Region, NumberCarsOwned as [Number Cars Owned]
from vTargetMail') as TM
```

Result

Age	Gender	Region	Number Cars Owned	Bike Buyer	Probability
43	M	Pacific	0	1	91.68%
44	M	Pacific	1	1	59.85%
44	M	Pacific	1	1	59.85%
41	F	Pacific	1	1	59.85%
41	F	Pacific	4	0	69.03%
44	M	Pacific	1	1	59.85%
43	F	Pacific	1	1	59.85%
45	M	Pacific	2	0	59.90%
45	F	Pacific	3	0	57.80%
45	M	Pacific	1	1	59.85%
45	F	Pacific	1	1	59.85%
45	M	Pacific	4	0	69.03%
41	F	North America	2	0	59.90%
41	M	North America	3	0	57.80%
41	F	North America	3	0	57.80%
30	F	North America	1	0	71.26%
30	M	North America	1	0	71.26%
65	F	Pacific	2	0	59.90%
64	M	Pacific	2	0	59.90%

Analysis

This is looking good again. If you use aliasing correctly, it's possible to have a natural prediction join (and save typing) even when column names do not match.

Nonmodel Columns

Maybe you would like to know potential bike buyers by their name (or email or address). Here the names of the customers are added to the query.

Syntax

```
-- which customers?
select TM.* , Predict([Bike Buyer]) as [Bike Buyer],
vba!format(PredictProbability([Bike Buyer]),'Percent') as [Probability]
from
[TM Decision Tree]
natural prediction join
openquery
([Adventure Works DW],
'select FirstName, LastName, Age, Gender, Region, NumberCarsOwned
as [Number Cars Owned] from vTargetMail') as TM
```

Result

FirstName	LastName	Age	Gender	Region	Number Cars Owned	Bike Buyer	Probability
Jon	Yang	43	M	Pacific	0	1	91.68%
Eugene	Huang	44	M	Pacific	1	1	59.85%
Ruben	Torres	44	M	Pacific	1	1	59.85%
Christy	Zhu	41	F	Pacific	1	1	59.85%
Elizabeth	Johnson	41	F	Pacific	4	0	69.03%
Julio	Ruiz	44	M	Pacific	1	1	59.85%
Janet	Alvarez	43	F	Pacific	1	1	59.85%
Marco	Mehta	45	M	Pacific	2	0	59.90%
Rob	Verhoff	45	F	Pacific	3	0	57.80%
Shannon	Carlson	45	M	Pacific	1	1	59.85%
Jacquelyn	Suarez	45	F	Pacific	1	1	59.85%
Curtis	Lu	45	M	Pacific	4	0	69.03%
Lauren	Walker	41	F	North America	2	0	59.90%
Ian	Jenkins	41	M	North America	3	0	57.80%
Sydney	Bennett	41	F	North America	3	0	57.80%
Chloe	Young	30	F	North America	1	0	71.26%
Wyatt	Hill	30	M	North America	1	0	71.26%
Shannon	Wang	65	F	Pacific	2	0	59.90%
Clarence	Rai	64	M	Pacific	2	0	59.90%

Analysis

If we had been using new customers, rather than existing ones, you would now know who they are. FirstName and LastName are not columns in the model. They are not relevant to predictions, and they don't alter the results for bike buyers—but they can provide you with vital information for a mail-shot.

Ranking Probabilities

Here, there is a new Order By clause.

Syntax

```
-- descending sort on probability
select TM.* , Predict([Bike Buyer]) as [Bike Buyer],
vba!format(PredictProbability([Bike Buyer]),'Percent') as [Probability]
from
[TM Decision Tree]
natural prediction join
openquery
([Adventure Works DW],
'select FirstName, LastName, Age, Gender, Region, NumberCarsOwned
as [Number Cars Owned] from vTargetMail') as TM
order by PredictProbability([Bike Buyer]) desc
```

Result

FirstName	LastName	Age	Gender	Region	Number Cars Owned	Bike Buyer	Probability
Candace	Madan	30	F	Pacific	0	1	91.68%
Wendy	Romero	31	F	Pacific	0	1	91.68%
George	Lopez	32	M	Pacific	0	1	91.68%
Tracy	Deng	42	F	Pacific	0	1	91.68%
Casey	Pal	30	F	Pacific	0	1	91.68%
Janet	Ortega	39	F	Pacific	0	1	91.68%
Bruce	Hernandez	31	M	Pacific	0	1	91.68%
Erik	Gomez	40	M	Pacific	0	1	91.68%
Mitchell	Xie	30	M	Pacific	0	1	91.68%
Robyn	Blanco	32	F	Pacific	0	1	91.68%
Dylan	Jai	49	M	Pacific	0	1	91.68%
Lucas	Hughes	40	M	Pacific	0	1	91.68%
Wendy	Carlson	40	F	Pacific	0	1	91.68%
Andre	Sanchez	43	M	Pacific	0	1	91.68%
Shawna	Lal	31	F	Pacific	0	1	91.68%
Bryant	Perez	32	M	Pacific	0	1	91.68%
Bonnie	Sharma	29	F	Pacific	0	1	91.68%
Jenny	Sun	32	F	Pacific	0	1	91.68%
Savannah	Gonzalez	30	F	Pacific	0	1	91.68%

Analysis

The highest probabilities appear first. You will have to scroll down to see the probabilities change. Again, your result may differ.

Predicted Versus Actual

One more column, Bike Buyer, has been added and aliased in the second (relational) Select.

Syntax

```
-- with original Bike Buyer data
select TM.* , Predict([Bike Buyer]) as [Bike Buyer],
vba!format(PredictProbability([Bike Buyer]),'Percent') as [Probability]
from
[TM Decision Tree]
natural prediction join
openquery
([Adventure Works DW],
'select FirstName, LastName, Age, Gender, Region, NumberCarsOwned
as [Number Cars Owned], BikeBuyer as [Original Data] from vTargetMail')
as TM order by PredictProbability([Bike Buyer]) desc
```

Result

FirstName	LastName	Age	Gender	Region	Number Cars Owned	Original Data	Bike Buyer	Probability
Candace	Madan	30	F	Pacific	0	1	1	91.68%
Wendy	Romero	31	F	Pacific	0	1	1	91.68%
George	Lopez	32	M	Pacific	0	1	1	91.68%
Tracy	Deng	42	F	Pacific	0	0	1	91.68%
Casey	Pal	30	F	Pacific	0	1	1	91.68%
Janet	Ortega	39	F	Pacific	0	1	1	91.68%
Bruce	Hernandez	31	M	Pacific	0	1	1	91.68%
Erik	Gomez	40	M	Pacific	0	1	1	91.68%
Mitchell	Xie	30	M	Pacific	0	1	1	91.68%
Robyn	Blanco	32	F	Pacific	0	1	1	91.68%
Dylan	Jai	49	M	Pacific	0	0	1	91.68%
Lucas	Hughes	40	M	Pacific	0	1	1	91.68%
Wendy	Carlson	40	F	Pacific	0	1	1	91.68%
Andre	Sanchez	43	M	Pacific	0	1	1	91.68%
Shawna	Lal	31	F	Pacific	0	1	1	91.68%
Bryant	Perez	32	M	Pacific	0	1	1	91.68%
Bonnie	Sharma	29	F	Pacific	0	1	1	91.68%
Jenny	Sun	32	F	Pacific	0	1	1	91.68%
Savannah	Gonzalez	30	F	Pacific	0	1	1	91.68%

Analysis

There are two columns for bike buyer. Bike Buyer is the result of the Predict() function. Original Data is based on historical, recorded fact. This leads to some interesting results. I found a customer named Maurice Andersen who didn't buy a bike, yet the model thinks he is the type of customer that would. Allen Rana is the opposite. He did buy a bike, but this time the model thinks he's a type that wouldn't. There are a lot of customers to scroll. Have a look at customers with Original Data of 0 and Bike Buyer of 1 and those with Original Data of 1 and Bike Buyer of 0. It's also important to notice those customers with value pairs 1-1 and 0-0. If there are many of these, then the algorithm has done a good job—it's pretty accurate.

Bike Buyers Only

Quite possibly, you would only want to target mail on those customers who are likely to buy a bike. Here, a Where clause eliminates the potential non-bike buyers.

Syntax

```
-- Bike Buyers only
select TM.* , Predict([Bike Buyer]) as [Bike Buyer],
vba!format(PredictProbability([Bike Buyer]),'Percent') as [Probability]
from
[TM Decision Tree]
natural prediction join
openquery
([Adventure Works DW],
'select FirstName, LastName, Age, Gender, Region, NumberCarsOwned
as [Number Cars Owned], BikeBuyer as [Original Data] from vTargetMail')
as TM
where Predict([Bike Buyer]) = 1
order by PredictProbability([Bike Buyer]) desc
```

Result

FirstName	LastName	Age	Gender	Region	Number Cars Owned	Original Data	Bike Buyer	Probability
Misty	Raji	32	F	Pacific	0	1	1	91.68%
Derek	Goel	40	M	Pacific	0	1	1	91.68%
Natalie	Moore	41	F	Pacific	0	1	1	91.68%
Whitney	Rana	43	F	Pacific	0	1	1	91.68%
Kelvin	Chander	32	M	Pacific	0	1	1	91.68%
Ruth	Arun	43	F	Pacific	0	1	1	91.68%
Aimee	Zhang	39	F	Pacific	0	1	1	91.68%
Carrie	Gutierrez	51	F	Pacific	0	0	1	91.68%
Jamie	Gao	40	F	Pacific	0	1	1	91.68%
Brett	Raman	41	M	Pacific	0	1	1	91.68%
Monica	Martinez	29	F	Pacific	0	1	1	91.68%
Rebekah	Serrano	30	F	Pacific	0	1	1	91.68%
Amy	Huang	28	F	Pacific	0	0	1	91.68%
Tara	Raje	33	F	Pacific	0	1	1	91.68%
Victor	Sanz	43	M	Pacific	0	1	1	91.68%
Erica	Sun	42	F	Pacific	0	1	1	91.68%
Mallory	Blanco	39	F	Pacific	0	1	1	91.68%
Larry	Martin	42	M	Pacific	0	1	1	91.68%
Meghan	Gutierrez	40	F	Pacific	0	1	1	91.68%

Analysis

Well done, you are getting there. This is cool DMX and real data mining. Now you know who to try and sell to—an unofficial phrase for data mining is "maximize profits." There is just one catch; these are our existing customers, many of whom already have a bike. Later in the chapter, we get to look at new customers who may not already have bikes, both individually and in batches.

More Demographics

In general, the more inputs the model analyzes, the more accurate the prediction results. One more column is added here.

Syntax

```
-- with Yearly Income
select TM.* , Predict([Bike Buyer]) as [Bike Buyer],
vba!format(PredictProbability([Bike Buyer]),'Percent') as [Probability]
from
[TM Decision Tree]
natural prediction join
openquery
([Adventure Works DW],
'select FirstName, LastName, Age, Gender, Region, NumberCarsOwned
```

```
as [Number Cars Owned], YearlyIncome as [Yearly Income], BikeBuyer
as [Original Data] from vTargetMail') as TM
where Predict([Bike Buyer]) = 1
order by PredictProbability([Bike Buyer]) desc
```

Result

FirstName	LastName	Age	Gender	Region	Number Cars Ow...	Yearly Income	Original Data	Bike Buyer	Probability
Gregory	Nara	39	M	Pacific	0	80000	1	1	91.68%
Byron	Carlson	39	M	Pacific	0	90000	1	1	91.68%
Jessie	Rubio	32	F	Pacific	0	10000	1	1	91.68%
Javier	Hernandez	39	M	Pacific	0	90000	1	1	91.68%
Misty	Raji	32	F	Pacific	0	10000	1	1	91.68%
Candace	Subram	39	F	Pacific	0	90000	1	1	91.68%
Phillip	Kapoor	39	M	Pacific	0	80000	1	1	91.68%
George	Garcia	30	M	Pacific	0	20000	1	1	91.68%
Felicia	Moreno	40	F	Pacific	0	90000	1	1	91.68%
Autumn	Liu	29	F	Pacific	0	20000	1	1	91.68%
Kathleen	Gomez	40	F	Pacific	0	100000	1	1	91.68%
Diana	Dominguez	42	F	Pacific	0	90000	1	1	91.68%
Barry	Lopez	40	M	Pacific	0	100000	1	1	91.68%
Troy	Sanchez	28	M	Pacific	0	20000	1	1	91.68%
Cedric	Chen	43	M	Pacific	0	100000	1	1	91.68%
Rebekah	Chandra	30	F	Pacific	0	20000	1	1	91.68%
Danny	Suarez	30	M	Pacific	0	20000	1	1	91.68%
Willie	Deng	32	M	Pacific	0	10000	1	1	91.68%

Analysis

The new column is YearlyIncome. This is going to influence the result. A few customers who were predicted to be bike buyers are now predicted not to be, and vice versa. Often, the more inputs or demographics available to the model, the more accurate the predictions will be. That's not to say you should have hundreds of input columns and matching model columns. If the color of a customer's hair has nothing to do with bike-buying potential, then you might want to exclude it. Too many inputs can complicate the structure and the model. In addition, you will prejudice processing time and Prediction query execution times. How do you know what to exclude? It might just be possible that hair color is an important factor. Many data miners first try Naïve Bayes many times to determine which columns have a correlation to the predictable column and to include only those columns in a more sophisticated algorithm such as Decision Trees. Even then, there is a note of caution. Suppose hair color as a single input makes no difference according to Naïve Bayes. Suppose star sign makes no difference. However, maybe Capricorn brunettes are more likely to buy a bike than blonde Aries! Naïve Bayes will not tell you this, whereas Decision Trees will.

Choosing Inputs 1/3

Let's continue our discussion on how to choose inputs (demographics in this model) in order to arrive at the most accurate Prediction queries. YearlyIncome has been removed. The Where clause artificially limits the prediction to one customer to help us in our analysis.

Syntax

```
-- Probabilities change - no Yearly Income data
select TM.* , Predict([Bike Buyer]) as [Bike Buyer],
vba!format(PredictProbability([Bike Buyer]),'Percent') as [Probability]
from
[TM Decision Tree]
natural prediction join
openquery
([Adventure Works DW],
'select FirstName, LastName, Age, Gender, Region, NumberCarsOwned
as [Number Cars Owned], BikeBuyer as [Original Data] from vTargetMail')
as TM
where Predict([Bike Buyer]) = 1 and FirstName = 'Phillip'
and LastName = 'Sai'
order by PredictProbability([Bike Buyer]) desc
```

Result

FirstName	LastName	Age	Gender	Region	Number Cars Owned	Original Data	Bike Buyer	Probability
Phillip	Sai	40	M	Europe	0	1	1	66.61%

Analysis

On the basis of these inputs, Phillip Sai is about 67 percent likely to buy a bike. Maybe not such a good prospect (assume for now that he's a new customer).

Choosing Inputs 2/3

This query reintroduces YearlyIncome as an input to the prediction.

Syntax

```
-- again with Yearly Income
select TM.* , Predict([Bike Buyer]) as [Bike Buyer],
vba!format(PredictProbability([Bike Buyer]),'Percent') as [Probability]
```

```
from
[TM Decision Tree]
natural prediction join
openquery
([Adventure Works DW],
'select FirstName, LastName, Age, Gender, Region, NumberCarsOwned
as [Number Cars Owned], YearlyIncome as [Yearly Income], BikeBuyer
as [Original Data] from vTargetMail') as TM
where Predict([Bike Buyer]) = 1 and FirstName = 'Phillip'
and LastName = 'Sai'
order by PredictProbability([Bike Buyer]) desc
```

Result

FirstName	LastName	Age	Gender	Region	Number Cars Ow...	Yearly Income	Original Data	Bike Buyer	Probability
Phillip	Sai	40	M	Europe	0	50000	1	1	82.15%

Analysis

Maybe he's better than we thought. According to this query, Phillip Sai is about 82 percent likely to buy a bike—worth a mail shot?

Choosing Inputs 3/3

Here we add as many inputs as there are input columns defined for the model in BIDS.

Syntax

```
-- all inputs
select TM.* , Predict([Bike Buyer]) as [Bike Buyer],
vba!format(PredictProbability([Bike Buyer]),'Percent') as [Probability]
from
[TM Decision Tree]
natural prediction join
openquery
([Adventure Works DW],
'select FirstName, LastName, Age, CommuteDistance as [Commute Distance],
EnglishEducation as Education, Gender, HouseOwnerFlag as [House Owner
Flag],
MaritalStatus as [Marital Status], NumberChildrenAtHome
as [Number Children At Home], EnglishOccupation as Occupation,
TotalChildren as [Total Children], Region, NumberCarsOwned
as [Number Cars Owned], YearlyIncome as [Yearly Income],
```

```
BikeBuyer as [Original Data] from vTargetMail') as TM
where Predict([Bike Buyer]) = 1 and FirstName = 'Phillip'
and LastName = 'Sai'
order by PredictProbability([Bike Buyer]) desc
```

Result

FirstN...	LastNa...	Age	Commute Di...	Educ...	Gender	Hou...	Marital ...	Number Chi...	Occup...	Total Ch...	Region	Numbe...	Yearly In...	Original ...	Bike Bu...	Probability
Phillip	Sai	40	0-1 Miles	Grad...	M	0	M	0	Skille...	0	Europe	0	50000	1	1	85.25%

Analysis

Let's send him an email right away! Phillip Sai is now about 85 percent likely to buy a bike. By gradually increasing the inputs, he has gone from 67 percent to 82 percent to 85 percent likely to buy a bike. In general, the more inputs you have, the more accurate the results. You eventually see the emergence of good customers (who might at first sight have appeared not so good) and vice versa for bad customers. There is a trade-off. If you have many inputs and lots of customers, your Prediction queries will take longer to execute.

All Inputs and All Customers

The Where clause has gone. This query examines all inputs and returns probabilities for all customers.

Syntax

```
-- all existing customers
select TM.* , Predict([Bike Buyer]) as [Bike Buyer],
vba!format(PredictProbability([Bike Buyer]),'Percent') as [Probability]
from
[TM Decision Tree]
natural prediction join
openquery
([Adventure Works DW],
'select FirstName, LastName, Age, CommuteDistance as [Commute Distance],
EnglishEducation as Education, Gender, HouseOwnerFlag
as [House Owner Flag], MaritalStatus as [Marital Status],
NumberChildrenAtHome as [Number Children At Home],
EnglishOccupation as Occupation, TotalChildren as [Total Children],
Region, NumberCarsOwned as [Number Cars Owned], YearlyIncome
as [Yearly Income], BikeBuyer as [Original Data] from vTargetMail')
as TM
-- where Predict([Bike Buyer]) = 1
order by PredictProbability([Bike Buyer]) desc
```

Result

FirstName	LastName	Age	Commute...	Education	Gen...	Hou...	Marital...	Num...	Occupat...	Total Ch...	Region	Number ...	Yearly I...	Origi...	Bike Buyer	Probability
Ian	Anderson	43	0-1 Miles	Graduate ...	M	0	M	0	Professi...	0	North A...	0	60000	0	0	100.00%
Katelyn	Lopez	42	0-1 Miles	Graduate ...	F	1	M	0	Professi...	0	North A...	0	60000	0	0	100.00%
Hailey	Campbell	42	0-1 Miles	Graduate ...	F	1	M	0	Professi...	0	North A...	0	60000	0	0	100.00%
Hannah	Brown	42	0-1 Miles	Graduate ...	F	0	S	0	Professi...	0	North A...	0	60000	0	0	100.00%
Ian	Roberts	43	0-1 Miles	Graduate ...	M	0	S	0	Professi...	0	North A...	0	70000	0	0	100.00%
Jessica	Thomps...	43	0-1 Miles	Graduate ...	F	1	M	0	Professi...	0	North A...	0	60000	0	0	100.00%
Alan	Hu	43	0-1 Miles	Graduate ...	M	1	M	0	Professi...	0	North A...	0	80000	0	0	100.00%
Caleb	Foster	43	0-1 Miles	Graduate ...	M	0	S	0	Professi...	0	North A...	0	60000	0	0	100.00%
John	Lewis	43	0-1 Miles	Graduate ...	M	1	M	0	Professi...	0	North A...	0	60000	0	0	100.00%
Savannah	Rivera	42	0-1 Miles	Graduate ...	F	0	M	0	Professi...	0	North A...	0	60000	0	0	100.00%
Julian	Bryant	43	0-1 Miles	Graduate ...	M	0	S	0	Professi...	0	North A...	0	60000	0	0	100.00%
Jeremiah	Sanchez	42	0-1 Miles	Graduate ...	M	0	M	0	Professi...	0	North A...	0	70000	0	0	100.00%
Eduardo	Smith	44	0-1 Miles	Graduate ...	M	1	M	0	Professi...	0	North A...	0	60000	0	0	100.00%
Jeremy	Rivera	43	0-1 Miles	Graduate ...	M	1	M	0	Professi...	0	North A...	0	60000	0	0	100.00%
Vanessa	Hughes	42	0-1 Miles	Graduate ...	F	0	S	0	Professi...	0	North A...	0	60000	0	0	100.00%
Olivia	Cook	43	0-1 Miles	Graduate ...	F	0	S	0	Professi...	0	North A...	0	60000	0	0	100.00%
Ethan	Patterson	44	0-1 Miles	Graduate ...	M	0	M	0	Professi...	0	North A...	0	60000	0	0	100.00%
Brandon	Lewis	42	0-1 Miles	Graduate ...	M	0	M	0	Professi...	0	North A...	0	60000	0	0	100.00%

Analysis

In the real world, such a query can take a while to run—maybe you have 50 input columns and a table/view containing 100,000 potential new customers. Interestingly, some customers are 100 percent likely to buy a bike and some are 100 percent likely not to.

Singletons 1/6

Often, you might want to concentrate on individual customers. Maybe they are interesting. Maybe you are prototyping your DMX and want Prediction queries to run quickly by only using one customer—when your DMX is honed, then you can switch to working with many customers. When you work with individual customers (or products or shares or whatever), they are called *singletons*. Here, we start a series of queries that work with singletons. First of all, how do you reference a singleton? Let's try SQL first.

Syntax

```
-- only one Phillip Sai
-- SQL does not work!
select * from AdventureWorksDW2008.dbo.vTargetMail
where LastName = 'Sai' and FirstName = 'Phillip'
```

Result

```
Executing the query ...
The dbo cube either does not exist or has not been processed.

Execution complete
```

Analysis

DMX (naturally) and MDX might work in the DMX query editor, but SQL generally does not.

Singletons 2/6

Maybe we can find a singleton in the model cases with a Cases query? In the previous query, we tried SQL—here we are trying DMX.

Syntax

```
-- model does not have the columns
select * from [TM Decision Tree].cases
where LastName = 'Sai' and FirstName = 'Phillip'
```

Result

```
Executing the query ...
Error (Data mining): The specified DMX column was not found in the context at line 3, column 7.

Execution complete
```

Analysis

Phillip Sai is not in the model cases—there is no LastName or FirstName column. Yet we used him in an earlier query to make predictions.

Singletons 3/6

Maybe we should try both DMX and SQL. The SQL is embedded inside the Openquery construct. This is a repeat of an earlier query.

Syntax

```
-- singleton - Phillip Sai
-- repeat of earlier query
select TM.* , Predict([Bike Buyer]) as [Bike Buyer],
vba!format(PredictProbability([Bike Buyer]),'Percent') as [Probability]
from
[TM Decision Tree]
natural prediction join
openquery
([Adventure Works DW],
```

```
'select FirstName, LastName, Age, Gender, Region, NumberCarsOwned
as [Number Cars Owned], BikeBuyer as [Original Data] from vTargetMail')
as TM
where Predict([Bike Buyer]) = 1 and FirstName = 'Phillip'
and LastName = 'Sai'
order by PredictProbability([Bike Buyer]) desc
```

Result

FirstName	LastName	Age	Gender	Region	Number Cars Ow...	Original Data	Bike Buyer	Probability
Phillip	Sai	40	M	Europe	0	1	1	66.61%

Analysis

Now we have results for an individual customer. Phillip Sai, according to the inputs we have chosen, is about 67 percent likely to buy a bike. Unfortunately, this is not enough. Firstly, we had to identify an individual by using an SQL Where clause—how did we know Phillip Sai existed? Secondly, he's an existing customer—we should ideally be analyzing a new customer. Thirdly, the new customer may not have a FirstName and LastName, maybe just an email address. Fourthly, it's highly unlikely that a new customer would be called Phillip Sai. What's important about Phillip is *not* his name but his demographics. He is 40, male, lives in Europe, and doesn't own a car.

Singletons 4/6

Our analysis of the last query determined that Phillip Sai is 40, male, lives in Europe, and doesn't own a car. Take a quick look at the second Select statement after the natural prediction join.

Syntax

```
-- singleton - Phillip Sai-like customer
-- no openquery no from no datasource no single quotes around select
select TM.* , Predict([Bike Buyer]) as [Bike Buyer],
vba!format(PredictProbability([Bike Buyer]),'Percent') as [Probability]
from
[TM Decision Tree]
natural prediction join
(select '40' as Age, 'M' as Gender, 'Europe' as Region, '0'
as NumberCarsOwned as [Number Cars Owned]) as TM
```

Result

Age	Gender	Region	Number Cars Ow...	Bike Buyer	Probability
40	M	Europe	0	1	66.61%

Analysis

This is a singleton Prediction query—extremely powerful stuff, as we'll see in the next two queries. This customer may or may not be Phillip Sai. Just like Phillip, he (the gender is male) is about 67 percent likely to buy a bike given the inputs provided. He has the same demographics. In fact, this is a generic, anonymous customer who is 40, male, lives in Europe, and has no car—an abstract Phillip Sai if you will.

The syntax for a singleton query is different. There's no Openquery, no From for the second Select, no data source, and no single quotes around the second Select.

Singletons 5/6

Here the inputs (demographics) are slightly different.

Syntax

```
-- singleton new customers
select TM.* , Predict([Bike Buyer]) as [Bike Buyer],
vba!format(PredictProbability([Bike Buyer]),'Percent') as [Probability]
from
[TM Decision Tree]
natural prediction join
(select '39' as Age, 'M' as Gender, 'Pacific' as Region, '0'
as NumberCarsOwned as [Number Cars Owned]) as TM
```

Result

Age	Gender	Region	Number Cars Ow...	Bike Buyer	Probability
39	M	Pacific	0	1	91.68%

Analysis

This customer is 39 rather than 40 and he (the gender is male) lives in the Pacific region, not Europe. If this is a new customer, he has real interest for our Adventure Works company. He's about 92 percent likely to buy a bike. Let's get him on the phone straightaway! But that could prove difficult. There's no phone number and no name (it would be nice to greet him by first name when our marketing people call him).

Singletons 6/6

Again the inputs (demographics) have been altered.

Syntax

```
--
select TM.* , Predict([Bike Buyer]) as [Bike Buyer],
vba!format(PredictProbability([Bike Buyer]),'Percent') as [Probability]
from
[TM Decision Tree]
natural prediction join
(select '44' as Age, 'F' as Gender, 'Europe' as Region,
'4' as NumberCarsOwned as [Number Cars Owned]) as TM
```

Result

Age	Gender	Region	Number Cars Ow...	Bike Buyer	Probability
44	F	Europe	4	0	69.03%

Analysis

She (the gender is female) is about 69 percent likely not to buy a bike (only 31 percent likely to). She's kind of marginal—needs some work. Maybe we should call her instead in order to make a sale. After all, the last customer (92 percent likely to buy a bike) will probably buy a bike without the need for a phone call or email or mail shot—shall we spend our limited marketing budget on the marginal customers only? Maybe she's not too interested in bikes as she has four cars and drives everywhere? Maybe we could offer her a free bike rack for one of her cars if she buys a bike, then she can still drive (with the bike in the rack on the back of the car) and park, but maybe cycle the last couple of miles? Maybe we ought to highlight the health benefits of cycling rather than driving?

However, we don't know who she is—she's anonymous. If we had her name (and maybe phone number) from some source data (see the next query), then we could add the necessary columns to the second Select statement. That would work up to a point. It's impractical to write a separate DMX singleton query for every new customer, especially if there are thousands. There are two classic solutions to this problem. One is to batch up the data (including names and phone numbers and emails) for new customers and forget about singleton queries—this is the approach adopted in the next query. Another solution is to automate the generation of multiple, maybe thousands of, singleton queries. When a new customer calls your call center, you enter the data into an SQL Server relational database including name, phone number, and demographics such as age and gender. You can have an SQL Insert trigger that fires and runs the DMX singleton query automatically from within the SQL code using the SQL Openquery construct. The Prediction query will return its results to the SQL trigger. From there, it can be displayed on the call center screen or maybe saved into a table for the marketing people.

Writing SQL triggers and the SQL Openquery construct are beyond the scope of this book. You might find some help at www.sqlserverdatamining.com.

Singleton queries have many other uses. For example, you may simply need to run Prediction queries on an ad hoc basis if you are researching correlations or you have only a few infrequent new records to analyze.

New Customers

This is a fundamental Prediction query. It uses new data rather than existing data. The view (vTargetMail) previously used in the second relational Select has been replaced by another table/view (a table called ProspectiveBuyer) that contains new customers only. Please note that this new table/view must be added to the data source view in BIDS.

Syntax

```
-- all new customers - remove Original Data -- new table/view
select TM.* , Predict([Bike Buyer]) as [Bike Buyer],
vba!format(PredictProbability([Bike Buyer]),'Percent') as [Probability]
from
[TM Decision Tree]
natural prediction join
openquery
([Adventure Works DW],
'select FirstName, LastName, DateDiff(yy,BirthDate,GetDate()) as Age,
Education, Gender, HouseOwnerFlag as [House Owner Flag],
MaritalStatus as [Marital Status], NumberChildrenAtHome
as [Number Children At Home], Occupation, TotalChildren as [Total
Children],
NumberCarsOwned as [Number Cars Owned], YearlyIncome as [Yearly Income]
from ProspectiveBuyer') as TM
order by PredictProbability([Bike Buyer]) desc
```

Result

FirstName	LastName	Age	Educ...	Ge...	Hous...	Mari...	Numbe...	Occupation	Total Children	Number Cars Ow...	Yearly Income	Bike Buyer	Probability
Felicia	Alvarez	49	Parti...	F	0	S	3	Professio...	0	2	100000	0	94.11%
Melissa	Ross	45	Bach...	F	1	M	3	Professio...	3	2	60000	0	94.11%
Fernando	Young	49	Parti...	M	1	M	3	Professio...	0	2	100000	0	94.11%
Carmen	Fernandez	49	Parti...	F	1	S	3	Professio...	0	2	100000	0	94.11%
Andres	Yuan	45	Bach...	M	1	M	3	Professio...	3	2	60000	0	94.11%
Olivia	Diaz	46	Parti...	F	1	M	3	Professio...	4	2	80000	0	94.11%
Nancy	Malhotra	45	Bach...	F	0	S	3	Professio...	3	2	60000	0	94.11%
Bruce	Romero	49	Parti...	M	0	S	3	Professio...	0	2	100000	0	94.11%
Damien	Nath	46	Parti...	M	1	S	3	Professio...	4	2	80000	0	94.11%
Eric	Hernandez	46	Parti...	M	0	S	3	Professio...	4	2	80000	0	94.11%
Mallory	Ruiz	46	Parti...	F	1	M	3	Professio...	4	2	80000	0	94.11%
Marissa	Alexander	45	Bach...	F	0	M	3	Professio...	3	2	60000	0	94.11%
Shannon	Ramos	49	Parti...	M	1	S	3	Professio...	0	2	100000	0	94.11%
Steve	She	41	Parti...	M	1	M	4	Skilled M...	4	2	90000	0	93.00%
Hannah	Miller	41	Parti...	F	1	M	4	Skilled M...	4	2	90000	0	93.00%
Ricardo	Xu	47	Parti...	M	1	M	4	Skilled M...	5	2	70000	0	93.00%
Jennifer	Gray	41	Parti...	F	1	M	4	Skilled M...	4	2	90000	0	93.00%
Alexander	Clark	41	Parti...	M	0	S	4	Skilled M...	4	2	90000	0	93.00%

Analysis

This new data contains names as well as demographics. It also contains contact information, which you might like to add to the second Select. The table is in the SQL Server AdventureWorksDW2008 relational database. Importantly, it does not include a Bike Buyer column.

New Bike-Buying Customers

Here we've added a Where clause to identify the potential bike buyers.

Syntax

```
-- just potential buyers
select TM.* , Predict([Bike Buyer]) as [Bike Buyer],
vba!format(PredictProbability([Bike Buyer]),'Percent') as [Probability]
from
[TM Decision Tree]
natural prediction join
openquery
([Adventure Works DW],
'select FirstName, LastName, DateDiff(yy,BirthDate,GetDate()) as Age,
Education, Gender, HouseOwnerFlag as [House Owner Flag],
MaritalStatus as [Marital Status], NumberChildrenAtHome
as [Number Children At Home], Occupation, TotalChildren as [Total
Children],
```

```
NumberCarsOwned as [Number Cars Owned], YearlyIncome as [Yearly Income]
from ProspectiveBuyer') as TM
where Predict([Bike Buyer]) = 1
order by PredictProbability([Bike Buyer]) desc
```

Result

FirstNa...	LastN...	Age	Educati...	Gen...	House ...	Marital Sta...	Number Ch...	Occupation	Total Chi...	Number Cars Ow...	Yearly Income	Bike Buyer	Probability
Carly	Pal	46	Bachel...	F	0	M	2	Professional	3	2	60000	1	84.39%
Ana	Hughes	58	Partial Hi	F	1	M	2	Skilled Ma...	5	2	70000	1	84.39%
Barbara	Shan	46	Bachel...	F	0	S	2	Professional	3	2	60000	1	84.39%
Cara	Zhu	58	Partial Hi	F	1	M	2	Skilled Ma...	5	2	70000	1	84.39%
Gina	Ramos	57	Partial Hi	F	1	M	2	Skilled Ma...	5	2	70000	1	84.39%
Melvin	Lal	57	Partial Hi	M	1	S	2	Skilled Ma...	5	2	70000	1	84.39%
Riley	Morris	57	Partial ...	F	1	M	2	Professional	5	2	70000	1	84.39%
Lydia	Madan	58	Partial Hi	F	0	S	2	Skilled Ma...	5	2	70000	1	84.39%
Tanya	Ortega	57	Partial ...	F	0	S	2	Professional	5	2	70000	1	84.39%
Seth	Martin...	67	Bachel...	M	0	S	3	Managem...	1	3	160000	1	76.08%
Jesus	Jimenez	52	Partial ...	M	1	S	4	Professional	3	3	130000	1	76.08%
Latoya	Xie	72	Bachel...	F	0	S	3	Managem...	1	3	160000	1	76.08%
Abigail	Davis	54	Partial ...	F	0	S	4	Professional	3	3	130000	1	76.08%
Rebek...	Rodri...	52	Partial ...	F	1	S	4	Professional	3	3	130000	1	76.08%
Tony	Goel	72	Bachel...	M	0	S	3	Managem...	2	3	130000	1	76.08%
Zachary	Brown	52	Partial ...	M	1	M	4	Professional	3	3	130000	1	76.08%
Connor	Carter	54	Partial ...	M	1	S	4	Professional	3	3	130000	1	76.08%
Melody	Serrano	39	Partial Hi	F	1	M	5	Professional	0	4	120000	1	70.95%

Analysis

You can paste this code into SSRS and generate a DMX-based report in Report Manager or SharePoint Report Center for your marketing department. We know who might buy a bike.

A Cosmetic Touch

This query shows how to concatenate columns.

Syntax

```
-- concatenate names? two single quotes not one!
select TM.* , Predict([Bike Buyer]) as [Bike Buyer],
vba!format(PredictProbability([Bike Buyer]),'Percent') as [Probability]
from
[TM Decision Tree]
natural prediction join
openquery
([Adventure Works DW],
'select FirstName + '' '' + LastName as FullName,
DateDiff(yy,BirthDate,GetDate()) as Age, Education, Gender,
```

```
HouseOwnerFlag as [House Owner Flag], MaritalStatus as [Marital Status],
NumberChildrenAtHome as [Number Children At Home], Occupation,
TotalChildren as [Total Children], NumberCarsOwned as [Number Cars
Owned],
YearlyIncome as [Yearly Income] from ProspectiveBuyer') as TM
where Predict([Bike Buyer]) = 1
order by PredictProbability([Bike Buyer]) desc
```

Result

FullName	Age	Education	Gender	House Owner Flag	Marital Status	Number Children...	Occupation	Total Children	Number Car
Carly Pal	46	Bachelors	F	0	M	2	Professional	3	2
Ana Hughes	58	Partial Hi	F	1	M	2	Skilled Manual	5	2
Barbara Shan	46	Bachelors	F	0	S	2	Professional	3	2
Cara Zhu	58	Partial Hi	F	1	M	2	Skilled Manual	5	2
Gina Ramos	57	Partial Hi	F	1	M	2	Skilled Manual	5	2
Melvin Lal	57	Partial Hi	M	1	S	2	Skilled Manual	5	2
Riley Morris	57	Partial Co	F	1	M	2	Professional	5	2
Lydia Madan	58	Partial Hi	F	0	S	2	Skilled Manual	5	2
Tanya Ortega	57	Partial Co	F	0	S	2	Professional	5	2
Seth Martinez	67	Bachelors	M	0	S	3	Management	1	3
Jesus Jimenez	52	Partial Co	M	1	S	4	Professional	3	3
Latoya Xie	72	Bachelors	F	0	S	3	Management	1	3
Abigail Davis	54	Partial Co	F	0	S	4	Professional	3	3
Rebekah Rodri...	52	Partial Co	F	1	S	4	Professional	3	3
Tony Goel	72	Bachelors	M	0	S	3	Management	2	3
Zachary Brown	52	Partial Co	M	1	M	4	Professional	3	3
Connor Carter	54	Partial Co	M	1	S	4	Professional	3	3
Melody Serrano	39	Partial Hi	F	1	M	5	Professional	0	4

Analysis

You now have FullName, a concatenation of FirstName and LastName with an embedded space. The language in the second Select is SQL. Because it's enclosed within single quotes, you can't use single quotes to delineate a space or any other string as you would normally do in SQL. You have to replace your single quotes with two single quotes (not double quotes).

PredictHistogram() 1/2

This is an introduction to the PredictHistogram() function for Prediction queries. It returns a small nested table—a non-graphical histogram. The query also incorporates a BottomCount() function.

Syntax

```
-- predicthistogram 1/2
select
[TM Decision Tree].[Bike Buyer],
```

```
BottomCount(PredictHistogram([Bike Buyer]),$Probability,2)
From
[TM Decision Tree]
natural prediction join
(select 28 AS [Age],
'2-5 Miles' AS [Commute Distance],
'Graduate Degree' AS [Education],
0 AS [Number Cars Owned],
0 AS [Number Children At Home]) AS t
```

Result

Bike Buyer	Expression
1	⊞ Expression

Analysis

There are quite a few new things in this query. PredictHistogram() returns a small nested table. Among other things, it shows probabilities for the possible states (or values) of Bike Buyer. These states are bike buyer (1), non-bike buyer (0), and a missing value. This customer is about 37 percent likely not to buy a bicycle. But it does not show that the customer is about 63 percent likely to buy a bike. BottomCount() with the parameters of $Probability and 2, is only going to return the two states (missing and non-bike buyer) with the lowest probabilities (0 percent for missing and 37 percent for non-bike buyer). This is more useful when there are more states for a predictable column. For example, you might have possible outcomes for missing, non-bike buyer, buys one bike, buys two bikes, and so on.

PredictHistogram() 2/2

This is our last query in this chapter on Prediction queries with the Decision Trees algorithm. It uses a TopCount() function and does not include the singleton natural prediction join we saw in the last query.

Syntax

```
-- predicthistogram 2/2
select flattened (select [Bike Buyer], $Probability from
topcount(PredictHistogram([Bike Buyer]), $Probability,1))
from
[TM Decision Tree]
```

Result

Expression.Bike Buyer	Expression.$PROBABILITY
0	0.505945945945946

Analysis

Here we have flattened the results and used a subquery to reference the columns from the previously nested histogram. There is no prediction join, so it's acting against all of the existing cases in the model. TopCount() has the parameters $PROBABILITY and 1. This means only return the state of bike buyer with the highest probability. In the TM Decision Tree model, this happens to be for a non-bike buyer with a probability of about 50.6 percent. In other words, a customer is more likely not to buy a bike—just over half of existing customers have not bought a bike.

Chapter 4

Prediction Queries
with Time Series

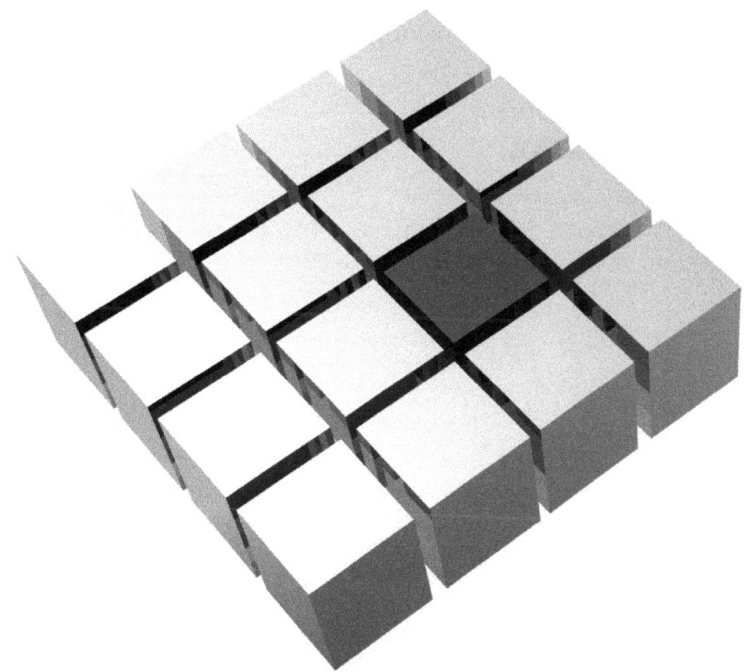

D ata mining models based on the Time Series algorithm also support Prediction queries. Most mining algorithms use new data (through a prediction join) to make predictions. The Time Series algorithm is an exception—its predictions (that is, forecasting future trends) are based on existing data and not on new data. Therefore, a prediction join is not required to analyze new data against existing content data. The predictions are generally extrapolations of existing figures and trends. There are two minor exceptions to this rule—EXTEND_MODEL_CASES and REPLACE_MODEL_CASES (these are not available in SSAS 2005), which can be used to simulate new data. This chapter concentrates on DMX Prediction queries with models based on the Time Series algorithm.

▶   **Key concepts**   Prediction queries, Time Series, looking at existing data, looking at existing data from specific categories, looking at existing data from specific time periods, forecasting by time period, forecasting by time period by category, forecasting by time period by category by measure, forecasting with standard deviations, what-if analysis

▶   **Keywords**   .cases, lag(), Predict(), PredictTimeSeries(), $TIME, VBA!Format, PredictStDev(), EXTEND_MODEL_CASES

Analyzing All Existing Sales

The Forecasting data mining model is based on sales quantities and sales amounts by product model by region over a period of time. The mining model has the same name as the mining structure. This query looks at the mining model cases to show quantity sold in existing cases.

Syntax

```
-- existing sales
select [Model Region], [Time Index], [Quantity]
from [Forecasting].cases
```

Result

Model Region	Time Index	Quantity
M200 Europe	200107	6
M200 North Am...	200107	6
M200 Pacific	200107	19
R250 Europe	200107	25
R250 North Am...	200107	35
R250 Pacific	200107	40
R750 Europe	200107	5
R750 North Am...	200107	7
R750 Pacific	200107	3
R750 Pacific	200108	6
R750 North Am...	200108	5
R750 Europe	200108	5
R250 Pacific	200108	44
R250 North Am...	200108	40
R250 Europe	200108	25
M200 Pacific	200108	18
M200 North Am...	200108	7
M200 Europe	200108	6
M200 Europe	200109	5

Analysis

The result shown is partial. R250 Pacific quantities have increased from 40 to 44 as we move from 200107 to 200108. You can only see the cases if the CacheMode property of the structure is set to KeepTrainingCases in BIDS. Quantity is a measure or fact. There is another measure called Amount, which is not used in this query. Both Quantity and Amount are Predict columns. Model Region is the Key column. Time Index is a Key Time column. The source data is a relational view called vTimeSeries in the SQL Server AdventureWorksDW2008 database. You could, of course, have used an SQL Select statement to return the same data. That's assuming you still have access to the original source data. A Predict column can be used as *both* a prediction column and an input column. A PredictOnly column can only be used as a prediction column and not as an input column.

Analyzing Existing Sales by Category

Often, you are not interested in sales of everything, but wish to concentrate on particular categories (Model Region). This query shows the existing sales quantities for the T1000 model in the North America region.

Syntax

```
-- existing sales for T1000 North America
select [Model Region], [Time Index], [Quantity]
from [Forecasting].cases
where [Model Region] = 'T1000 North America'
```

Result

Model Region	Time Index	Quantity
T1000 North America	200307	17
T1000 North America	200308	17
T1000 North America	200309	15
T1000 North America	200310	26
T1000 North America	200311	34
T1000 North America	200312	57
T1000 North America	200401	49
T1000 North America	200402	58
T1000 North America	200403	56
T1000 North America	200404	62
T1000 North America	200405	61
T1000 North America	200406	68

Analysis

This query consists of a simple Where clause that restricts the records returned. They should be in Time Index order, but you can guarantee this by using an Order By clause. Or, you might want to sort on Quantity—either ascending or descending. The Order By syntax is the same as in SQL—however, in DMX you can sort on only one column at a time. A descending sort on Quantity would show you the year and month when you sold the most (in terms of quantity) at the top of the result set.

Analyzing Existing Sales by Specific Periods—Lag() 1/3

Maybe the objective is to check on an individual time period. For example, you might want to view the sales quantity three months ago. Or rather, you might want to see the data as it was three months before the last time period used in your training cases.

Syntax

```
-- existing sales for T1000 North America 3 months ago
select [Model Region], [Time Index], [Quantity]
from [Forecasting].cases
where [Model Region] = 'T1000 North America' and lag() = 3
```

Result

Model Region	Time Index	Quantity
T1000 North America	200403	56

Analysis

Lag() = 3 takes you back three periods from the last date in your data. A negative number does not take you into the future (it actually returns a blank)! The DMX Lag() is different from the MDX .lag(). To move into the future to see projections or forecasts, you have to use a Prediction query. This is covered shortly.

Analyzing Existing Sales by Specific Periods—Lag() 2/3

Suppose you want a range of periods, not just a specific date. Here's a query returning the last four months' worth of data.

Syntax

```
-- existing sales for T1000 North America last 4 months
select [Model Region], [Time Index], [Quantity]
from [Forecasting].cases
where [Model Region] = 'T1000 North America' and lag() < 4
```

Result

Model Region	Time Index	Quantity
T1000 North America	200403	56
T1000 North America	200404	62
T1000 North America	200405	61
T1000 North America	200406	68

Analysis

Lag() < 4 shows the last four time periods starting from (and including) the very last time period. Here we have March 2004 through June 2004.

Analyzing Existing Sales by Specific Periods—Lag() 3/3

This is our last query looking into the past—three months and six months before our last date.

Syntax

```
-- existing sales for T1000 North America 3 and 6 months ago
select [Model Region], [Time Index], [Quantity]
from [Forecasting].cases
where [Model Region] = 'T1000 North America' and (lag() = 3 or lag() = 6)
```

Result

Model Region	Time Index	Quantity
T1000 North America	200312	57
T1000 North America	200403	56

Analysis

Six and three time periods back from our last recorded date. Sales quantity declined slightly from December 2003 to March 2004. It's time to look into the future for a change.

PredictTimeSeries() 1/11

Now, let's consider projections into the future. The Time Series algorithm can extrapolate data, so you can forecast how measures might change. The DMX function used is PredictTimeSeries().

Syntax

```
-- forecasting, no prediction join
select [Model Region], PredictTimeSeries([Quantity],3)
from [Forecasting]
```

Result

Model Region	Expression
M200 Europe	⊞ Expression
M200 North America	⊞ Expression
M200 Pacific	⊞ Expression
R250 Europe	⊞ Expression
R250 North America	⊞ Expression
R250 Pacific	⊞ Expression
R750 Europe	⊞ Expression
R750 North America	⊞ Expression
R750 Pacific	⊞ Expression
T1000 Europe	⊞ Expression
T1000 North America	⊞ Expression
T1000 Pacific	⊞ Expression

Analysis

Unlike predictions on many of the other data mining algorithms, PredictTimeSeries() does not require a prediction join. Predictions are normally based on new data. But there is no data yet for future time periods! The only time when you need a prediction join for PredictTimeSeries() is when you are doing a what-if analysis. That topic is covered at the end of this chapter.

The first parameter for PredictTimeSeries() is the measure you want to extrapolate. The second parameter is the number of time periods for the extrapolation. Here we are asking for sales quantities for the next three months after our last date period in the existing data. The result set includes a nested table called Expression. You may want to expand the nested table to examine its contents.

PredictTimeSeries() 2/11

Here is a very minor change to the previous query. PredictTimeSeries() has been replaced by Predict().

Syntax

```
-- polymorphic predict
select [Model Region], Predict([Quantity],3)
from [Forecasting]
```

Result

Model Region	Expression
M200 Europe	⊞ Expression
M200 North America	⊞ Expression
M200 Pacific	⊞ Expression
R250 Europe	⊞ Expression
R250 North America	⊞ Expression
R250 Pacific	⊞ Expression
R750 Europe	⊞ Expression
R750 North America	⊞ Expression
R750 Pacific	⊞ Expression
T1000 Europe	⊞ Expression
T1000 North America	⊞ Expression
T1000 Pacific	⊞ Expression

Analysis

If you look at the nested table contents, you will notice that it's the same as in the previous query. Here we are simply demonstrating the polymorphic behavior of the Predict() function. When used with a time series model, it defaults to PredictTimeSeries().

PredictTimeSeries() 3/11

This query has an elementary cosmetic change using an alias.

Syntax

```
-- alias
select [Model Region], PredictTimeSeries([Quantity],3) as [Future]
from [Forecasting]
```

Result

Model Region	Future
M200 Europe	⊞ Future
M200 North America	⊞ Future
M200 Pacific	⊞ Future
R250 Europe	⊞ Future
R250 North America	⊞ Future
R250 Pacific	⊞ Future
R750 Europe	⊞ Future
R750 North America	⊞ Future
R750 Pacific	⊞ Future
T1000 Europe	⊞ Future
T1000 North America	⊞ Future
T1000 Pacific	⊞ Future

Analysis

The default nested table name, Expression, has been changed to Future. It makes the result look a little better.

PredictTimeSeries() 4/11

Now to flatten out the nested table so its columns and rows are readily visible.

Syntax

```
-- flattened
select flattened [Model Region], PredictTimeSeries([Quantity],3)
as [Future]
from [Forecasting]
```

Result

Model Region	Future.$TIME	Future.Quantity
M200 Europe	200407	121
M200 Europe	200408	142
M200 Europe	200409	152
M200 North America	200407	163
M200 North America	200408	178
M200 North America	200409	156
M200 Pacific	200407	46
M200 Pacific	200408	45
M200 Pacific	200409	43
R250 Europe	200407	13
R250 Europe	200408	24
R250 Europe	200409	26
R250 North America	200407	8
R250 North America	200408	9
R250 North America	200409	14
R250 Pacific	200407	23
R250 Pacific	200408	26
R250 Pacific	200409	31
R750 Europe	200407	55

Analysis

This is much clearer. For each Model Region we have the projected sales quantity for three months after the last time period in our existing data. Notice that M200 North America goes up then down—it's a bit more than a simple extrapolation. If you're interested, the algorithms used are ARTXP or ARIMA or both—seasonal fluctuations in the existing data (periodicities) are accommodated. In addition, the Enterprise Edition of SSAS also looks at how trends in one Model Region might influence trends in another Model Region—this functionality is provided by the ARTXP algorithm.

PredictTimeSeries() 5/11

Let's zoom in on a particular Model Region—T1000 North America.

Syntax

```
-- T1000 North America
select flattened [Model Region], PredictTimeSeries([Quantity],3)
as [Future]
from [Forecasting]
where [Model Region] = 'T1000 North America'
```

Result

Model Region	Future.$TIME	Future.Quantity
T1000 North America	200407	82
T1000 North America	200408	78
T1000 North America	200409	78

Analysis

We have a simple Where clause—very useful when you have lots of categories in your results.

PredictTimeSeries() 6/11

This is the same as the previous query, except it includes a subquery.

Syntax

```
-- as a subquery
select flattened [Model Region], (select $Time, Quantity
from PredictTimeSeries([Quantity],3)) as [Future]
from [Forecasting]
where [Model Region] = 'T1000 North America'
```

Result

Model Region	Future.$TIME	Future.Quantity
T1000 North America	200407	82
T1000 North America	200408	78
T1000 North America	200409	78

Analysis

Exactly the same results—but here we have a Select within a Select (a subquery). Notice the Time Index column is referenced using $Time. $Time returns the Key Time column from within the original nested table.

PredictTimeSeries() 7/11

A cosmetic touch—$Time has been aliased.

Syntax

```
-- with aliases
select flattened [Model Region], (select $Time as [Year Month], Quantity
```

```
from PredictTimeSeries([Quantity],3)) as [Future]
from [Forecasting]
where [Model Region] = 'T1000 North America'
```

Result

Model Region	Future.Year Month	Future.Quantity
T1000 North America	200407	82
T1000 North America	200408	78
T1000 North America	200409	78

Analysis

As you might have seen elsewhere in the book, subqueries allow us to alias columns in nested tables. The more work you do up front, the less you will have to do later—for example, your SSRS reports based on your models will look better for end users.

PredictTimeSeries() 8/11

Here we are adding T1000 Europe to the output.

Syntax

```
-- two Model Regions
select flattened [Model Region], (select $Time as [Year Month], Quantity
from PredictTimeSeries([Quantity],3)) as [Future]
from [Forecasting]
where [Model Region] = 'T1000 North America'
or [Model Region] = 'T1000 Europe'
```

Result

Model Region	Future.Year Month	Future.Quantity
T1000 Europe	200407	42
T1000 Europe	200408	41
T1000 Europe	200409	43
T1000 North America	200407	82
T1000 North America	200408	78
T1000 North America	200409	78

Analysis

The Where clause has been extended. If you wanted to see all regions for the T1000 model, you might use VBA!Left([Model Region],4) = 'T1000'. If you wanted to see all models for the Pacific region, you might try VBA!InStr([Model Region],'Pacific') > 0.

PredictTimeSeries() 9/11

Suppose you wish to see sales amounts as well as sales quantities forecasts. Here there are two subqueries within the outer flattened Select.

Syntax

```
-- two measures
select flattened [Model Region], (select $Time as [Year Month], Quantity
from PredictTimeSeries([Quantity],3)) as [FutureQ],
(select $Time as [Year Month], Amount from PredictTimeSeries([Amount],3))
as [FutureA]
from [Forecasting]
where [Model Region] = 'T1000 North America'
or [Model Region] = 'T1000 Europe'
```

Result

Model Region	FutureQ.Year Month	FutureQ.Quantity	FutureA.Year Month	FutureA.Amount
T1000 Europe	200407	42		
T1000 Europe	200408	41		
T1000 Europe	200409	43		
T1000 Europe			200407	99878.3621589...
T1000 Europe			200408	98102.2943702...
T1000 Europe			200409	103196.108117...
T1000 North America	200407	82		
T1000 North America	200408	78		
T1000 North America	200409	78		
T1000 North America			200407	194454.918987...
T1000 North America			200408	186423.835218...
T1000 North America			200409	185842.002713...

Analysis

The two measures (Quantity and Amount) are on separate rows. The aliasing helps you to decipher the result.

PredictTimeSeries() 10/11

We can extend the syntax to produce customized solutions. This query demonstrates differing projection periods for the two measures.

Syntax

```
-- different periods
select flattened [Model Region], (select $Time as [Year Month],
Quantity from PredictTimeSeries([Quantity],5)) as [FutureQ],
(select $Time as [Year Month], Amount from PredictTimeSeries([Amount],3))
as [FutureA]
from [Forecasting]
where [Model Region] = 'T1000 North America'
or [Model Region] = 'T1000 Europe'
```

Result

Model Region	FutureQ.Year Month	FutureQ.Quantity	FutureA.Year Month	FutureA.Amount
T1000 Europe	200407	42		
T1000 Europe	200408	41		
T1000 Europe	200409	43		
T1000 Europe	200410	42		
T1000 Europe	200411	43		
T1000 Europe			200407	99878.3621589848
T1000 Europe			200408	98102.2943702707
T1000 Europe			200409	103196.108117117
T1000 North America	200407	82		
T1000 North America	200408	78		
T1000 North America	200409	78		
T1000 North America	200410	83		
T1000 North America	200411	83		
T1000 North America			200407	194454.918987671
T1000 North America			200408	186423.835218412
T1000 North America			200409	185842.002713549

Analysis

One interesting point to note here is the figures for T1000 North America for 200408 and 200409. The quantity sold is forecast to be the same for both time periods, yet the sales amount is projected to fall slightly—the algorithm works on each measure separately.

PredictTimeSeries() 11/11

Here's some VBA to tidy up the amount column.

Syntax

```
-- sub query for formatting
select flattened [Model Region], (select $Time as [Year Month],
```

```
Quantity from PredictTimeSeries([Quantity],5)) as [FutureQ],
(select $Time as [Year Month], vba!format(Amount,'Currency') as [Amount]
from PredictTimeSeries([Amount],3)) as [FutureA]
from [Forecasting]
where [Model Region] = 'T1000 North America' or [Model Region] = 'T1000
Europe'
```

Result

Model Region	FutureQ.Year Month	FutureQ.Quantity	FutureA.Year Month	FutureA.Amount
T1000 Europe	200407	42		
T1000 Europe	200408	41		
T1000 Europe	200409	43		
T1000 Europe	200410	42		
T1000 Europe	200411	43		
T1000 Europe			200407	£99,878.36
T1000 Europe			200408	£98,102.29
T1000 Europe			200409	£103,196.11
T1000 North America	200407	82		
T1000 North America	200408	78		
T1000 North America	200409	78		
T1000 North America	200410	83		
T1000 North America	200411	83		
T1000 North America			200407	£194,454.92
T1000 North America			200408	£186,423.84
T1000 North America			200409	£185,842.00

Analysis

The second parameter for the VBA!Format function is 'Currency'. My result is showing UK sterling—it's picking up on my Control Panel Regional Settings. You can, of course, hard-code the formatting to override any regional settings—VBA!Format(Amount,'$#,###.00') or VBA!Format(Amount,'#,###.00€').

PredictStDev()

How accurate are the results of time prediction queries? It's a good idea to check out the standard deviation of the forecasts.

Syntax

```
-- standard deviation
select flattened [Model Region], (select $Time as [Year Month],
Quantity, PredictStDev(Quantity) as [SD] from
PredictTimeSeries([Quantity],5)) as [FutureQ],
```

```
(select $Time as [Year Month], vba!format(Amount,'Currency')
as [Amount], PredictStDev(Amount) as [SD]
from PredictTimeSeries([Amount],3)) as [FutureA]
from [Forecasting]
where [Model Region] = 'T1000 North America'
or [Model Region] = 'T1000 Europe'
```

Result

Model Region	FutureQ.Year Month	FutureQ.Quantity	FutureQ.SD	FutureA.Year Month	FutureA.Amount	FutureA.SD
T1000 Europe	200407	42	2.09382791970...			
T1000 Europe	200408	41	2.41064003371...			
T1000 Europe	200409	43	2.42484126779...			
T1000 Europe	200410	42	2.72597345542...			
T1000 Europe	200411	43	2.73735388885...			
T1000 Europe				200407	£99,878.36	4991.83190805...
T1000 Europe				200408	£98,102.29	5747.13434705...
T1000 Europe				200409	£103,196.11	5780.991113187
T1000 North America	200407	82	2.32143518820...			
T1000 North America	200408	78	3.99191338903...			
T1000 North America	200409	78	4.44334002519...			
T1000 North America	200410	83	4.28411763829...			
T1000 North America	200411	83	4.60424142314...			
T1000 North America				200407	£194,454.92	5534.46361517...
T1000 North America				200408	£186,423.84	9517.00028708...
T1000 North America				200409	£185,842.00	10593.2331091...

Analysis

PredictStDev() gives you an idea of the accuracy of the forecast—it returns the standard deviation. In general, the smaller the standard deviation, the greater confidence you can have in the projected figures. A serious word of caution—the time series algorithm works best when it finds established trends that are likely to continue or regular cycles (maybe for sales or inventory levels); it does not work (for example, on share prices) where trends can reverse suddenly and unpredictably and cycles can break unexpectedly. Also, the further you go into the future, the less reliable are the results as forecasts begin to be based on forecasted results!

What-If 1/3

You might also like to try some what-if analysis. Maybe you have some idea about sales this coming month and even the next month. Naturally, this data is not recorded yet and your "hunch" figures have not been used to train the model. But they might have a profound effect on future projections. Perhaps you are expecting a sudden rise or dip in sales over the next few weeks. How will these changes affect sales further into the future? Here is a base query to get you started on what-if analysis.

Syntax

```
-- existing
select [Model Region], [Time Index], [Quantity]
from [Forecasting].cases
where [Model Region] = 'R250 North America'
```

Result

Model Region	Time Index	Quantity
R250 North America	200107	35
R250 North America	200108	40
R250 North America	200109	44
R250 North America	200110	45
R250 North America	200111	55
R250 North America	200112	78
R250 North America	200201	62
R250 North America	200202	63
R250 North America	200203	66
R250 North America	200204	75
R250 North America	200205	76
R250 North America	200206	79
R250 North America	200207	83
R250 North America	200208	84
R250 North America	200209	17
R250 North America	200210	18
R250 North America	200211	14
R250 North America	200212	18
R250 North America	200301	13

Analysis

These are partial results. If you scroll down, you will notice that the last time period for which we have existing data in the training cases is 200406.

What-If 2/3

Now we predict three time periods into the future.

Syntax

```
-- projection based on existing
select flattened [Model Region], PredictTimeSeries([Quantity],3)
as [Future]
from [Forecasting]
where [Model Region] = 'R250 North America'
or [Model Region] = 'R750 North America'
```

Result

Model Region	Future.$TIME	Future.Quantity
R250 North America	200407	8
R250 North America	200408	9
R250 North America	200409	14
R750 North America	200407	74
R750 North America	200408	82
R750 North America	200409	98

Analysis

The $Time column displays 200407, 200408, and 200409. The projected quantity for 200409 for R250 North America is 14. The quantities for 200407 and 200408 are 8 and 9, respectively.

What-If 3/3

But the sales we are expecting are going to be higher for 200407 and 200408 for R250 North America. How is this going to influence the sales quantity for 200409?

Syntax

```
-- projection based on what-if?
-- uses a prediction join
select flattened [Model Region], PredictTimeSeries([Quantity],1,3,
EXTEND_MODEL_CASES) as [Future]
from [Forecasting]
natural prediction join
(
select 200407 as [Time Index], 10 as [Quantity], 'R250 North America'
as [Model Region]
union
select 200408 as [Time Index], 12 as [Quantity], 'R250 North America'
) as X
where [Model Region] = 'R250 North America'
or [Model Region] = 'R750 North America'
```

Result

Model Region	Future.$TIME	Future.Quantity
R250 North America	200407	10
R250 North America	200408	12
R250 North America	200409	10
R750 North America	200407	74
R750 North America	200408	82
R750 North America	200409	98

Analysis

EXTEND_MODEL_CASES allows you to replace the algorithm forecasts with your own (possibly more enlightened) projections. These, in turn, will change the algorithm projections further down the line. EXTEND_MODEL_CASES is the fourth parameter to PredictTimeSeries(). The second parameter is the start position—a value of 1 means include your first change as part of the forecast. The second parameter is the number of periods to show. Despite increasing the algorithm projections for 200407 and 200408 for R250 North America, the new forecast for 200409 has gone down—from 14 to 10! The three figures for R750 are unchanged. If you have the Standard Edition of SSAS, they will be unchanged. If you have the Enterprise Edition, they might change—that is, if the R250 sales influence the R750 sales.

There is also a REPLACE_MODEL_CASES parameter. This is similar to EXTEND_MODEL_CASES, except that, rather than replacing projected data, it replaces existing data within the training cases.

Chapter 5

Prediction and Cluster Queries with Clustering

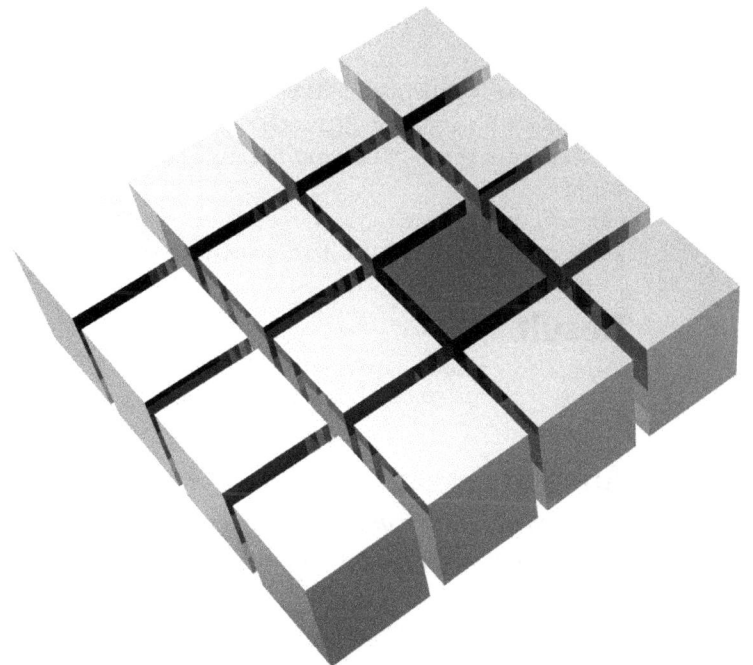

M ining models based on the Clustering algorithm may or may not have a predictable column—both varieties of models are explored in this chapter. A cluster model with a predictable column (for example, Bike Buyer) supports Prediction queries (for example, using the Predict() function). All cluster models support a range of functions that are specific to clusters (for example, the Cluster() function)—I have called these Cluster queries to distinguish them from Prediction queries. This chapter shows you how to perform Prediction and Cluster queries against models based on the Clustering algorithm. Cluster queries are useful for profiling and anomaly detection. Prediction queries are useful for indicating potential future behavior.

▶ **Key concepts**   Prediction queries, cluster queries, clusters, Clustering, anomaly and fraud detection

▶ **Keywords**   Prediction join, Cluster(), ClusterDistance(), ClusterProbability(), CLUSTERING_METHOD, Predict(), PredictCaseLikelihood(), NORMALIZED, PredictProbability(), Union, NODE_CAPTION

Cluster Membership 1/3

Customer Clusters is a model based on the Clustering algorithm. It's part of the Customer Mining structure. The model contains no predictable columns as such—but cluster membership is predictable. Our first query is a singleton natural prediction join, even though there is no Predict() function.

Syntax

```
-- cluster without predict column
select Cluster() as [Cluster], ClusterProbability() * 100
as [Probability],ClusterDistance() as Distance, x.* from[Customer
Clusters]
natural prediction join
(select 'Clerical' as Occupation,'Graduate' as Education) as x
```

Result

Cluster	Probability	Distance	Occupation	Education
Cluster 8	30.8173509151...	0.69182649084...	Clerical	Graduate

Analysis

As a reminder, in this and other queries, your results may be different. When you train and retrain models, the various algorithms can produce slightly different outcomes. They are non-deterministic, but in general the results should be similar, if not identical. *Please bear this in mind as you work through the book.* The Cluster() function predicts the most likely cluster for the customer. ClusterProbability() returns the probability that this is so. ClusterDistance() shows the distance from the center of the cluster. The latter is an advanced topic and is beyond the scope of this book. If you are a statistician, ClusterDistance() operates differently on EM and K-Means clusters—you are referred to SQL Server Books Online (BOL). If you are not a statistician, then rest assured it is nowhere near as important as Cluster() or ClusterProbability().

If we have a new customer who is a graduate and works as a clerk, he or she is most likely to belong to Cluster 8. But that is only about 30 percent likely. This is a low percentage; it's quite possible that he or she might fit into another cluster.

Cluster Membership 2/3

Here the demographics have changed slightly.

Syntax

```
--
select Cluster() as [Cluster], ClusterProbability() * 100
as [Probability],ClusterDistance() as Distance, x.* from
[Customer Clusters]
natural prediction join
(select 'Manual' as Occupation,'Graduate' as Education) as x
```

Result

Cluster	Probability	Distance	Occupation	Education
Cluster 4	51.4685637941...	0.48531436205...	Manual	Graduate

Analysis

The probability is around 51 percent for Cluster 4. This time we can have a little more confidence in the result.

Cluster Membership 3/3

Once again, this query has a small change to the demographics.

Syntax

```
--
select Cluster() as [Cluster], ClusterProbability() * 100
as [Probability],ClusterDistance() as Distance, x.* from
[Customer Clusters]
natural prediction join
(select 'Manual' as Occupation,'Partial High School' as Education) as x
```

Result

Cluster	Probability	Distance	Occupation	Education
Cluster 8	55.1764543110...	0.44823545688...	Manual	Partial High School

Analysis

Cluster 8 with around 55 percent probability.

ClusterProbability() 1/2

This is almost identical to the previous query, except a parameter has been supplied for ClusterProbability() and ClusterDistance(). The parameter supplied (Cluster 8) is based on the result of the previous query—you may have to adapt the syntax.

Syntax

```
--
select Cluster() as [Cluster], ClusterProbability('Cluster 8') * 100
as [Probability],ClusterDistance('Cluster 8') as Distance, x.* from
[Customer Clusters]
natural prediction join
(select 'Manual' as Occupation,'Partial High School' as Education) as x
```

Result

Cluster	Probability	Distance	Occupation	Education
Cluster 8	55.1764543110...	0.44823545688...	Manual	Partial High School

Analysis

Cluster 8 with around 55 percent probability. ClusterProbability() returns the probability of membership in the most likely cluster. ClusterProbability('Cluster 8') returns the probability of membership in Cluster 8. In this example, Cluster 8 is the most likely; therefore, ClusterProbability() and ClusterProbability('Cluster 8') produce the same answer.

ClusterProbability() 2/2

We have a few ClusterProbability() functions. This is quite a handy query for profiling new customers.

Syntax

```
--
select Cluster() as [Cluster], ClusterProbability('Cluster 8') * 100
as [Probability8], ClusterProbability('Cluster 4') * 100
as [Probability4], ClusterProbability('Cluster 9') * 100 as
[Probability9],
 x.* from
[Customer Clusters]
natural prediction join
(select 'Manual' as Occupation,'Partial High School' as Education) as x
```

Result

Cluster	Probability8	Probability4	Probability9	Occupation	Education
Cluster 8	55.1764543110211	43.9371111584287	0	Manual	Partial High School

Analysis

A customer with a partial high school education and working in a manual job is probably a candidate for Cluster 8, possibly so for Cluster 4, and definitely not for Cluster 9. Once again, you may have to adapt the clusters.

Clustering Parameters

Every algorithm has parameters that affect its behavior. These parameters can be set in BIDS or programmatically in a DMX query that defines the model. For example, Clustering has a CLUSTERING_METHOD parameter.

Syntax

```
-- clustering method
select MINING_PARAMETERS
from $system.DMSCHEMA_MINING_MODELS
where MODEL_NAME = 'Customer Clusters'
```

Result

MINING_PARAMETERS

CLUSTER_COUNT=10,CLUSTER_SEED=0,CLUSTERING_METHOD=1,MAXIMUM_INPUT_ATTRIBUTES=255,MAXIMUM_STATES=100,MINIMUM_SUPPORT=1,MODELLING_CARDINALITY=10...

Analysis

This is a Schema query. You may have to widen the returned column to see the CLUSTERING_METHOD parameter setting. If you are statistically inclined, once you know the value of this parameter, you can include ClusterDistance() in your query and understand its meaning. I guess this is for very advanced users only—1 is Scalable EM, 2 is Non-scalable EM, 3 is Scalable K-means, and 4 is Non-scalable K-means.

Another ClusterProbability

This query probably shows how *not* to write a cluster membership query. Your attempt to profile new customers may be inaccurate.

Syntax

```
--
select Cluster() as [Cluster], ClusterProbability('Cluster 8') * 100
as [Probability8], ClusterProbability('Cluster 4') * 100 as [Probability4],
x.* from
[Customer Clusters]
natural prediction join
(select 'Manual' as Occupation) as x
```

Result

Cluster	Probability8	Probability4	Occupation
Cluster 4	39.4473026036...	51.4685637941...	Manual

Analysis

The most likely cluster is Cluster 4 with a 51 percent probability. However, there is a 39 percent chance of it being Cluster 8. These two percentages are pretty close together. Is it Cluster 4 or Cluster 8 for this customer? The problem arises because we only have one input or demographic. We are probably not feeding enough information into the model—it's finding it hard to discriminate between clusters. You should, ideally, add more input columns.

Cluster Content 1/2

Another way of looking at cluster membership is to write a Content query.

Syntax

```
--
select flattened node_caption as [Cluster],
(select attribute_value as [Occupation], vba!format([Probability],'Percent')
as [Probability] from node_distribution where attribute_name = 'Occupation'
and attribute_value = 'Manual')
as [Occupation]
from [Customer Clusters].content
```

Result

Cluster	Occupation.Occupation	Occupation.Probability
Cluster Model	Manual	12.90%
Cluster 1	Manual	10.22%
Cluster 2	Manual	0.00%
Non Graduates	Manual	1.73%
Cluster 4	Manual	67.74%
Cluster 5	Manual	0.00%
Graduates	Manual	0.00%
Cluster 7	Manual	0.00%
Cluster 8	Manual	51.92%
Cluster 9	Manual	0.00%
Cluster 10	Manual	0.00%

Analysis

Manual workers make up about 68 percent of Cluster 4. Our last query indicated that a Manual worker is about 51 percent likely to belong to Cluster 4. The two figures are different as they mean completely different things. This query shows the proportion of all customers in Cluster 4 who are manual workers—it's an intra-cluster measure. The last query showed the possibility of a manual worker belonging to Cluster 4, as opposed to other clusters—it's an inter-cluster measure.

Cluster Content 2/2

Here, a Where clause has been added to the previous query.

Syntax

```
--
select flattened node_caption as [Cluster],
(select attribute_value as [Occupation], vba!format([Probability],'Percent')
as [Probability] from node_distribution where attribute_name = 'Occupation'
and attribute_value = 'Manual')
as [Occupation]
from [Customer Clusters].content
where (node_caption = 'Cluster 8' or node_caption = 'Cluster 4')
```

Result

Cluster	Occupation.Occupation	Occupation.Probability
Cluster 4	Manual	67.74%
Cluster 8	Manual	51.92%

Analysis

This syntax allows you to concentrate on just one or two clusters. Both Cluster 4 and Cluster 8 have a majority of members who are manual workers.

PredictCaseLikelihood() 1/3

Perhaps you have a new customer and you want to know how similar this customer is to your existing customers in the clusters. This query demonstrates the PredictCaseLikelihood() function with a singleton natural prediction join.

Syntax

```
-- case likelihood
select PredictCaseLikelihood() from
[Customer Clusters]
natural prediction join
(select 'Manual' as Occupation, 'M' as Gender, 'M' as [Marital Status], 2
as [Total Children], 1 as [Number of Cars Owned], 1
as [Number of Children At Home]) as x
```

Result

Expression
7.29782892084...

Analysis

The answer is fairly difficult to understand—unless you are a statistician! In general, the nearer to 1, the more likely the customer is going to fit into an existing cluster—the nearer to 0, the less likely. Rather than try to decipher the number, try varying the inputs and see how the values compare relatively. We'll do this shortly.

PredictCaseLikelihood() 2/3

This is a repeat of the last query with the addition of the NORMALIZED parameter to the PredictCaseLikelihood() function.

Syntax

```
-- also NONNORMALIZED
select PredictCaseLikelihood(NORMALIZED) from
[Customer Clusters]
natural prediction join
(select 'Manual' as Occupation, 'M' as Gender, 'M' as [Marital Status], 2
as [Total Children], 1 as [Number of Cars Owned], 1
as [Number of Children At Home]) as x
```

Result

Expression

7.29782892084...

Analysis

You should get exactly the same result. By default, the function is normalized. This means the result will be between 0 and 1, using logarithmic values. There is an alternative nondefault parameter—NONNORMALIZED. If you are interested in the equation, highlight the function name and press F1 to open SQL Server Books Online (BOL).

PredictCaseLikelihood() 3/3

The number of cars has been increased from 1 to 10. Do we have any customers with 10 cars?

Syntax

```
-- 10 cars
select PredictCaseLikelihood(NORMALIZED) from
[Customer Clusters]
natural prediction join
(select 'Manual' as Occupation, 'M' as Gender, 'M' as [Marital Status], 2
as [Total Children], 10 as [Number of Cars Owned], 1
as [Number of Children At Home]) as x
```

Result

Expression

2.34183667565...

Analysis

This time, the answer is much lower (the number is in exponential format or scientific notation). It's getting close to zero—suggesting this customer is less likely to fit in with existing customers. You may have to widen the column in the result to see the exponent.

Anomaly Detection

I guess this customer is pretty affluent—100 cars.

Syntax

```
-- 100 cars, anomaly detection
select PredictCaseLikelihood(NORMALIZED) from
[Customer Clusters]
natural prediction join
(select 'Manual' as Occupation, 'M' as Gender, 'M' as [Marital Status], 2
as [Total Children], 100 as [Number of Cars Owned], 1
as [Number of Children At Home]) as x
```

Result

Expression

0

Analysis

Here's an interesting result of zero. Such a result is worth investigating. This customer just does not fit. Either the customer is very, very unusual (an outlier) or there's been a typo—or maybe it's a deliberately fraudulent entry. This technique is very useful for both anomaly and fraud detection.

Cluster with Predictable Column 1/3

We are changing from the Customer Clusters model to the TM Clustering model. Both are based on the Clustering algorithm. Customer Clusters is a pure cluster with no predictable column. TM Clustering has the Bike Buyer predictable column.

Syntax

```
-- cluster with predict column
-- TM Clustering not Customer Clusters
select
TM.*, [Bike Buyer], vba!format(PredictProbability([Bike
Buyer]),'Percent')
from
[TM Clustering]
natural prediction join
(select 'Pacific' as [Region],
'M' as [Gender], 44 as [Age]) as TM
```

Result

Region	Gender	Age	Bike Buyer	Expression
Pacific	M	44	1	58.45%

Analysis

This singleton Prediction query shows that the customer is about 58 percent likely to buy a bike.

Cluster with Predictable Column 2/3

We've simply altered the input data.

Syntax

```
-- more
select
TM.*, [Bike Buyer], vba!format(PredictProbability([Bike Buyer]),
'Percent')from
[TM Clustering]
natural prediction join
(select 'North America' as [Region],
'F' as [Gender], 75 as [Age]) as TM
```

Result

Region	Gender	Age	Bike Buyer	Expression
North America	F	75	0	66.28%

Analysis

Here's a not-so-promising customer. She is around 66 percent likely not to buy a bike.

Cluster with Predictable Column 3/3

So far, in this book, you've seen batch prediction joins (using Openquery on a table or view) and singleton queries. Here we have two singletons together.

Syntax

```
--
select
TM.*, [Bike Buyer], vba!format(PredictProbability([Bike Buyer]),
'Percent')
from
[TM Clustering]
natural prediction join
(select 'Europe' as [Region],
'F' as [Gender], 25 as [Age]
union
select 'North America' as [Region],
'M' as [Gender], 55 as [Age]
) as TM
```

Result

Region	Gender	Age	Bike Buyer	Expression
Europe	F	25	0	65.57%
North America	M	55	0	58.62%

Analysis

Notice the use of Union to put the two singletons together. Another Union would allow a third singleton, and so on.

Clusters and Predictions

This is the final query in this chapter on clustering and predicting. It ties together a number of the techniques you've seen.

Syntax

```
--
select
Cluster() as [Cluster], TM.*, [Bike Buyer],
vba!format(PredictProbability([Bike Buyer]),'Percent')
from
[TM Clustering]
natural prediction join
(select 'Pacific' as [Region],
'F' as [Gender], 45 as [Age]
union
select 'North America' as [Region],
'M' as [Gender], 55 as [Age]
) as TM
```

Result

Cluster	Region	Gender	Age	Bike Buyer	Expression
Cluster 4	Pacific	F	45	1	59.00%
Cluster 6	North America	M	55	0	58.62%

Analysis

A query like this is really going to be of interest to your marketing colleagues. All you have to do now is learn SSRS and paste in the DMX to produce informative and useful reports.

Chapter 6

Prediction Queries with Association and Sequence Clustering

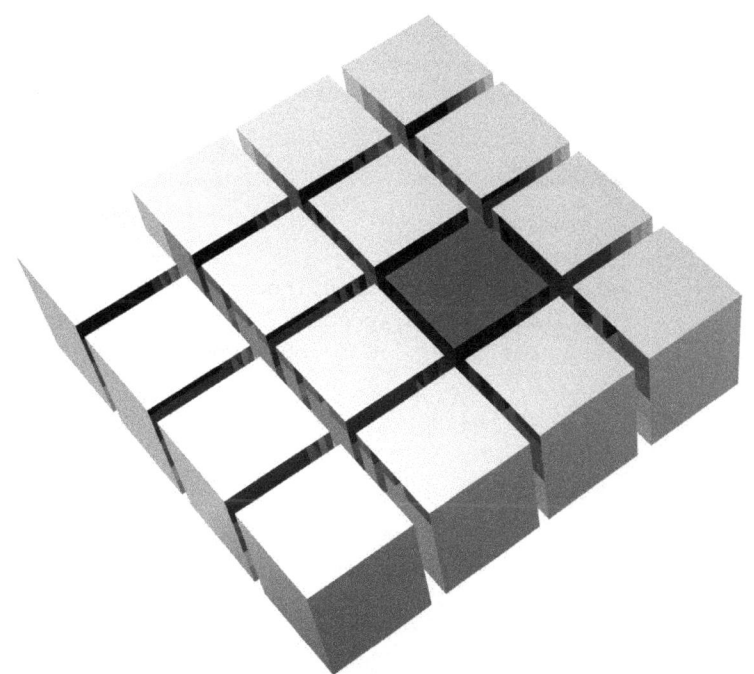

This chapter contains yet more Prediction queries. The DMX queries this time are written against mining models based on two algorithms, Association and Sequence Clustering. Both algorithms appear in the same chapter as they share a lot of common characteristics. Although every mining algorithm has lots of uses, these two algorithms are typically used in market basket analysis. Market basket analysis is the focus of this chapter; there are quite a few Prediction queries devoted to identifying cross-selling opportunities. However, it's important to realize they can be used in other applications—for example, Sequence Clustering can be used to analyze click-stream data on web sites. The main difference between the two algorithms is quite subtle. Association, for example, can show purchasing combinations for all customers—it's generic. Sequence Clustering, by contrast, can show purchasing combinations for individual groups (clusters) of customers—it's specific. These groups are not the same as the demographic clusters we saw earlier for the Clustering algorithm. If you are a mathematician, these Sequence Clustering clusters are derived from a Markov Chain.

▶ **Key concepts**   Prediction queries, Association, Sequence Clustering, market basket analysis, cross selling, sequencing

▶ **Keywords**   Prediction join, Predict(), PredictAssociation(), PredictSequence(), Top, INCLUDE_STATISTICS, $NODEID, $PROBABILITY, $SEQUENCE

Association Content—Item Sets

The Association model in the Market Basket structure is based on the Association algorithm. This is the classic cross-selling algorithm. Item sets show the combinations of purchases.

Syntax

```
-- association
-- item sets
select node_description, node_support
from [Association].content
where node_type = 1 or node_type = 7
```

Result

node_description	node_support
Association Rules Model; ITEMSET_COUNT=116; RULE_COU...	21255
Sport-100 = Existing	6171
Water Bottle = Existing	4076
Patch kit = Existing	3010
Mountain Tire Tube = Existing	2908
Mountain-200 = Existing	2477
Road Tire Tube = Existing	2216
Cycling Cap = Existing	2095
Fender Set - Mountain = Existing	2014
Mountain Bottle Cage = Existing	1941
Road Bottle Cage = Existing	1702
Long-Sleeve Logo Jersey = Existing	1642
Mountain Bottle Cage = Existing, Water Bottle = Existing	1623
Short-Sleeve Classic Jersey = Existing	1537
Road Bottle Cage = Existing, Water Bottle = Existing	1513
Road-750 = Existing	1443
Touring Tire Tube = Existing	1397
Half-Finger Gloves = Existing	1363
HL Mountain Tire = Existing	1331

Analysis

NODE_TYPE of 7 indicates item sets. NODE_TYPE of 1 is the model itself. The result shows items (product models, in this example) bought as sets, and how often those sets occurred (NODE_SUPPORT).

Association Content—Rules

Rules are subtly different from item sets. Item sets show purchase combinations, including products bought individually and not in combination with others. Rules show the relationships between item sets and purchases—how likely it was that a product model had been bought at the same time as a particular item set. This is a Content query dealing with existing purchases. A Prediction query would show possible projected purchases.

Syntax

```
-- rules
select node_description, node_support
from [Association].content
where node_type = 8
```

Result

node_description	node_support
Touring Tire = Existing, Sport-100 = Existing -> Touring Tire Tube = Existing	236
ML Road Tire = Existing, Sport-100 = Existing -> Road Tire Tube = Existing	221
Mountain-200 = Existing, Mountain Tire Tube = Existing -> HL Mountain Tire = Existing	331
Touring-1000 = Existing, Water Bottle = Existing -> Road Bottle Cage = Existing	309
Mountain-200 = Existing, Water Bottle = Existing -> Mountain Bottle Cage = Existing	589
Road Bottle Cage = Existing, Cycling Cap = Existing -> Water Bottle = Existing	222
Fender Set - Mountain = Existing, Water Bottle = Existing -> Mountain Bottle Cage = Existing	307
Road Bottle Cage = Existing, Sport-100 = Existing -> Water Bottle = Existing	376
Road-750 = Existing, Water Bottle = Existing -> Road Bottle Cage = Existing	485
ML Mountain Tire = Existing, Sport-100 = Existing -> Mountain Tire Tube = Existing	333
Mountain Bottle Cage = Existing, Cycling Cap = Existing -> Water Bottle = Existing	229
Touring-1000 = Existing, Road Bottle Cage = Existing -> Water Bottle = Existing	309
HL Mountain Tire = Existing, Sport-100 = Existing -> Mountain Tire Tube = Existing	383
Road Bottle Cage = Existing -> Water Bottle = Existing	1513
Road-750 = Existing, Road Bottle Cage = Existing -> Water Bottle = Existing	485
Touring Tire = Existing -> Touring Tire Tube = Existing	758
Mountain Bottle Cage = Existing, Sport-100 = Existing -> Water Bottle = Existing	446
Mountain Bottle Cage = Existing -> Water Bottle = Existing	1623
Mountain Bottle Cage = Existing, Fender Set - Mountain = Existing -> Water Bottle = Existing	307

Analysis

NODE_TYPE 8 constrains the query to return only the rules and not the item sets. The purchase of a Touring Tire and a Sport-100 together also resulted in the purchase of a Touring Tire Tube 236 times. This is classic market basket analysis.

Important Rules

Maybe you would like to see the most important purchase combinations first. Here's the addition of an Order By clause.

Syntax

```
-- sorting
select node_description, node_support
from [Association].content
where node_type = 8
order by node_support desc
```

Result

node_description	node_support
Mountain Bottle Cage = Existing -> Water Bottle = Existing	1623
Water Bottle = Existing -> Mountain Bottle Cage = Existing	1623
Water Bottle = Existing -> Road Bottle Cage = Existing	1513
Road Bottle Cage = Existing -> Water Bottle = Existing	1513
Mountain Tire Tube = Existing -> Sport-100 = Existing	1240
Sport-100 = Existing -> Mountain Tire Tube = Existing	1240
Water Bottle = Existing -> Sport-100 = Existing	1056
Sport-100 = Existing -> Water Bottle = Existing	1056
HL Mountain Tire = Existing -> Mountain Tire Tube = Existing	915
Mountain Tire Tube = Existing -> HL Mountain Tire = Existing	915
Sport-100 = Existing -> Road Tire Tube = Existing	815
Road Tire Tube = Existing -> Sport-100 = Existing	815
Touring Tire = Existing -> Touring Tire Tube = Existing	758
Touring Tire Tube = Existing -> Touring Tire = Existing	758
Patch kit = Existing -> Mountain Tire Tube = Existing	737
Mountain Tire Tube = Existing -> Patch kit = Existing	737
Fender Set - Mountain = Existing -> Mountain-200 = Existing	730
Mountain-200 = Existing -> Fender Set - Mountain = Existing	730
ML Mountain Tire = Existing -> Mountain Tire Tube = Existing	727

Analysis

Mountain Bottle Cage and Water Bottle go together well!

Twenty Most Important Rules

To pursue our cross-selling, we are going to concentrate on the top 20 purchase combinations.

Syntax

```
-- top 20
select top 20 node_description, node_support
from [Association].content
where node_type = 8
order by node_support desc
```

Result

node_description	node_support
Water Bottle = Existing -> Mountain Bottle Cage = Existing	1623
Mountain Bottle Cage = Existing -> Water Bottle = Existing	1623
Road Bottle Cage = Existing -> Water Bottle = Existing	1513
Water Bottle = Existing -> Road Bottle Cage = Existing	1513
Sport-100 = Existing -> Mountain Tire Tube = Existing	1240
Mountain Tire Tube = Existing -> Sport-100 = Existing	1240
Water Bottle = Existing -> Sport-100 = Existing	1056
Sport-100 = Existing -> Water Bottle = Existing	1056
HL Mountain Tire = Existing -> Mountain Tire Tube = Existing	915
Mountain Tire Tube = Existing -> HL Mountain Tire = Existing	915
Road Tire Tube = Existing -> Sport-100 = Existing	815
Sport-100 = Existing -> Road Tire Tube = Existing	815
Touring Tire Tube = Existing -> Touring Tire = Existing	758
Touring Tire = Existing -> Touring Tire Tube = Existing	758
Mountain Tire Tube = Existing -> Patch kit = Existing	737
Patch kit = Existing -> Mountain Tire Tube = Existing	737
Mountain-200 = Existing -> Fender Set - Mountain = Existing	730
Fender Set - Mountain = Existing -> Mountain-200 = Existing	730
Mountain Tire Tube = Existing -> ML Mountain Tire = Existing	727

Analysis

Our query has Top 20. Maybe if a new customer asks for a Road Bottle Cage, we should offer them a Water Bottle, and vice versa? The top 20 are sorted in descending order by support. Support shows how often the combination of purchases occurred. We are looking at the most important in terms of frequency. However, combinations with low support may be even more interesting—these often show combinations we are not expecting. You may want to try this query without the Top 20 and also include and sort on the node_probability column. This can give even more interesting and unexpected results.

Particular Product Models

We can narrow it down by looking at particular product model names (or partial names as in this example).

Syntax

```
-- particular product model
select node_description, node_support
from [Association].content
where node_type = 8 and vba!left(node_description,5) = 'Water'
```

Result

node_description	node_support
Water Bottle = Existing, Sport-100 = Existing -> Mountain Bottle Cage = Existing	446
Water Bottle = Existing -> Mountain Bottle Cage = Existing	1623
Water Bottle = Existing -> Road Bottle Cage = Existing	1513
Water Bottle = Existing, Sport-100 = Existing -> Road Bottle Cage = Existing	376
Water Bottle = Existing -> Sport-100 = Existing	1056
Water Bottle = Existing -> Cycling Cap = Existing	599
Water Bottle = Existing -> Mountain-200 = Existing	589
Water Bottle = Existing -> Road-750 = Existing	485

Analysis

The VBA Left function helps us to display only those product models beginning with 'Water' and its associated rules. Water Bottle seems to be bought in combination with lots of other product models.

Another Product Model

This is a simple variation on the previous query.

Syntax

```
-- one way rule
select node_description, node_support
from [Association].content
where node_type = 8 and vba!left(node_description,9) = 'Hydration'
```

Result

node_description	node_support
Hydration Pack = Existing -> Water Bottle = Existing	283

Analysis

I guess Hydration Pack is not such an exciting purchase. It promises to present far fewer opportunities for future cross-selling.

Nested Table

As so often occurs in Content queries, there is a nested table column.

Syntax

```
-- name of nested table (also in metadata)
select flattened top 1 node_support, (select [attribute_name]
from node_distribution) from [Association].content
where node_type = 7
```

Result

node_support	Expression.attribute_name
6171	v Assoc Seq Line Items(Sport-100)

Analysis

As usual, the nested table column is called NODE_DISTRIBUTION. Here it's flattened and a subquery is used to select just one of the inner columns.

PredictAssociation()

PredictAssociation() is used to see which product models are most likely to be bought together with other product models.

Syntax

```
-- 2 most likely together
select
PredictAssociation([Association].[v Assoc Seq Line Items],2)
From
[Association]
```

Result

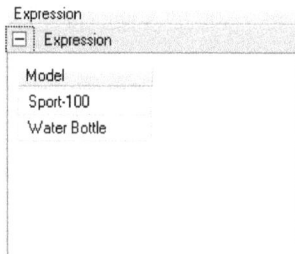

Analysis

The PredictAssociation() has two parameters here. The first parameter is the name of the nested case table. The last query returned its name as part of the second column. You could also check this out in BIDS. Often in an Association model, the case is an order header and the nested case is composed of the order line items for each order. The second parameter is a numeric one. Here, the parameter is 2—show me the two product models that are most frequently purchased in combination with other product models. Both Sport-100 and Water Bottle offer significant cross-selling opportunities.

Cross-Selling Prediction 1/7

As market basket analysis and identifying cross-selling opportunities are so popular, coming up are seven queries concentrating on just that. If a customer buys a Water Bottle, what else should we offer him?

Syntax

```
-- simpler
select flattened
(
select [Model] from Predict([v Assoc Seq Line Items],5)
)
from [Association]
natural prediction join
(select
(select 'Water Bottle' as [Model]) as [v Assoc Seq Line Items]) as Y
```

Result

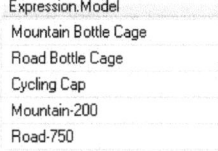

Expression.Model
Mountain Bottle Cage
Road Bottle Cage
Cycling Cap
Mountain-200
Road-750

Analysis

This is a singleton natural prediction join. You are asking for the five most likely product models that a customer who buys Water Bottle might also buy. Notice that the second Select is composed on two Selects—that's because we are joining to a nested case table.

Cross-Selling Prediction 2/7

This time we are looking at Hydration Pack. What are the five most popular product models that go with Hydration Pack? What support and likelihood do we have for this? This time we've added INCLUDE_STATISTICS.

Syntax

```
-- and again
select Predict([v Assoc Seq Line Items],5,include_statistics)
from [Association]
natural prediction join
(select
(select 'Hydration Pack' as [Model]) as [v Assoc Seq Line Items]) as Y
```

Result

Model	$SUPPORT	$PROBABILITY
Water Bottle	4076	0.40084985835...
Sport-100	6171	0.29033168666...
Patch kit	3010	0.14161373794...
Mountain Tire Tube	2908	0.13681486709...
Mountain-200	2477	0.11653728534...

Analysis

Perhaps we should mention Water Bottle to Hydration Pack buyers. Of our existing customers, 4076 bought Water Bottle with Hydration Pack—and they were about 40 percent of all those who bought Hydration Pack. Please note that the possibility of buying Patch Kit is 14 percent.

Cross-Selling Prediction 3/7

Or maybe a new customer wants Hydration Pack and Bike Wash. What else might they be interested in?

Syntax

```
-- hydration pack to water bottle to mountain-200 to patch kit
-- union
-- bike wash to patch kit
select Predict([v Assoc Seq Line Items],5,include_statistics)
from [Association]
```

```
natural prediction join
(select
(select 'Hydration Pack' as [Model] union select 'Bike Wash' as [Model])
as [v Assoc Seq Line Items]) as Y
```

Result

Model	$SUPPORT	$PROBABILITY
Water Bottle	4076	0.40084985835...
Patch kit	3010	0.30671296296...
Sport-100	6171	0.29033168666...
Mountain Tire Tube	2908	0.13681486709...
Mountain-200	2477	0.11653728534...

Analysis

Again, there are two Selects in the second Select. The two singletons are combined with Union. Interestingly, Patch Kit is now 30 percent compared to 14 percent in our last query. If someone buys Hydration Pack, they are 14 percent likely to buy Patch Kit. On the other hand, if they buy Hydration Pack *and* Bike Wash, they are 30 percent likely to buy Patch Kit.

Cross-Selling Prediction 4/7

So we've concluded that customers who buy Hydration Pack also are reasonably likely to buy Patch Kit. But is there a direct link between the two product models?

Syntax

```
-- use nested table in prediction
-- cross-selling up-selling based on products
select flattened (select [Model], $Probability
from PredictAssociation([v Assoc Seq Line Items],
include_node_id,include_statistics) where $nodeid <> '')
from [Association]
natural prediction join
(select
(select 'Hydration Pack' as [Model]) as [v Assoc Seq Line Items]
) as Y
```

Result

Expression.Model	Expression.$PROBABILITY
Water Bottle	0.400849858356941

Analysis

Water Bottle but no Patch Kit! Indirect links do not have a value for $NODEID. Notice the inclusion of INCLUDE_NODE_ID and the Where clause on $NODEID. In plain English, this means Hydration Pack might directly result in Water Bottle. Hydration Pack might only indirectly result in Patch Kit. If you view the model graphically, you can see the links on the Dependency Network tab. If you're interested, the route is Hydration Pack to Water Bottle to Mountain-200 to Patch Kit.

Cross-Selling Prediction 5/7

Water Bottle to Mountain-200.

Syntax

```
select flattened (select [Model], $Probability
from PredictAssociation([v Assoc Seq Line Items],
include_node_id,include_statistics) where $nodeid <> '')
from [Association]
natural prediction join
(select
(select 'Water Bottle' as [Model]) as [v Assoc Seq Line Items]
) as Y
```

Result

Expression.Model	Expression.$PROBABILITY
Sport-100	0.259077526987242
Road-750	0.118989205103042
Road Bottle Cage	0.371197252208047
Mountain-200	0.14450441609421
Mountain Bottle Cage	0.398184494602552
Cycling Cap	0.146957801766438

Analysis

Again we are using $NODEID to show direct relationships.

Cross-Selling Prediction 6/7

Here's another example—we're interested in direct cross-purchase links to Cycling Cap.

Syntax

```
select flattened (select [Model], $Probability
from PredictAssociation([v Assoc Seq Line Items],
include_node_id,include_statistics) where $nodeid <> '')
from [Association]
natural prediction join
(select
(select 'Cycling Cap' as [Model]) as [v Assoc Seq Line Items]
) as Y
```

Result

Expression.Model	Expression.$PROBABILITY
Water Bottle	0.285918854415274
Sport-100	0.222434367541766
Short-Sleeve Classic Jersey	0.157517899761337
Road Bottle Cage	0.105966587112172
Mountain Bottle Cage	0.115990453460621
Long-Sleeve Logo Jersey	0.122195704057279

Analysis

There's nothing new here, simply a change of product model.

Cross-Selling Prediction 7/7

Finally, on the subject of Prediction queries for Association models, we'll do a little formatting with the VBA Format function.

Syntax

```
-- tidying up and polymorphic
select flattened
(
select [Model], vba!format($Probability,'Percent') as [Probability]
from Predict([v Assoc Seq Line Items],include_node_id,include_statistics)
where $nodeid <> ''
) as [CrossSell]
from [Association]
```

```
natural prediction join
(select
(select 'Water Bottle' as [Model]) as [v Assoc Seq Line Items]) as Y
```

Result

CrossSell.Model	CrossSell.Probability
Sport-100	25.91%
Road-750	11.90%
Road Bottle Cage	37.12%
Mountain-200	14.45%
Mountain Bottle Cage	39.82%
Cycling Cap	14.70%

Analysis

I think we should sell Road Bottle Cage and Mountain Bottle Cage.

Sequence Clustering Prediction 1/3

A Sequence Clustering model concerned with product model purchases is different from an Association model. The latter shows what is bought with what and in what order, for *all* cases. Sequence Clustering, on the other hand, shows not only what is bought with what, but also the *sequence* in which they were bought by members of different clusters. Did one cluster buy Water Bottle, then Mountain Bottle Cage second, or Mountain Bottle Cage followed by Water Bottle? And what did they buy as a third product model? Did another cluster demonstrate different purchase sequence patterns?

Syntax

```
-- sequences
select flattened PredictSequence([v Assoc Seq Line Items],100)
from [Sequence Clustering]
natural prediction join
(select (select 1 as [Line Number], 'Mountain Bottle Cage' as [Model])
as [v Assoc Seq Line Items]) as x
```

Result

Expression.$SEQUENCE	Expression.Line ...	Expression.Model
1		Water Bottle
2		Sport-100
3		Half-Finger Gloves
4		Cycling Cap
5		Sport-100
6		Half-Finger Gloves
7		Half-Finger Gloves
8		Short-Sleeve Classic Jersey
9		All-Purpose Bike Stand
10		All-Purpose Bike Stand
11		All-Purpose Bike Stand
12		All-Purpose Bike Stand
13		All-Purpose Bike Stand
14		All-Purpose Bike Stand
15		All-Purpose Bike Stand
16		All-Purpose Bike Stand
17		All-Purpose Bike Stand
18		All-Purpose Bike Stand
19		All-Purpose Bike Stand

Analysis

The PredictSequence() function is used here to see the next 100 purchases in order after Mountain Bottle Cage. It looks as if people buy Water Bottle, then Sport-100. When an entry begins to repeat, as in All-Purpose Bike Stand, it means the sequence has reached an end.

Sequence Clustering Prediction 2/3

PredictSequence() is now Predict().

Syntax

```
--
select flattened Predict([v Assoc Seq Line Items],100)
from [Sequence Clustering]
natural prediction join
(select (select 1 as [Line Number], 'Mountain Bottle Cage' as [Model])
as [v Assoc Seq Line Items]) as x
```

Result

Expression.$SE...	Expression.Line Number	Expression.Model
1		Water Bottle
2		Sport-100
3		Half-Finger Glov...
4		Cycling Cap
5		Sport-100
6		Half-Finger Glov...
7		Half-Finger Glov...
8		Short-Sleeve Cl...
9		All-Purpose Bike...
10		All-Purpose Bike...
11		All-Purpose Bike...
12		All-Purpose Bike...
13		All-Purpose Bike...
14		All-Purpose Bike...
15		All-Purpose Bike...
16		All-Purpose Bike...
17		All-Purpose Bike...
18		All-Purpose Bike...
19		All-Purpose Bike...

Analysis

Here's an almost identical repeat of the previous query. It is simply demonstrating the polymorphic nature of Predict().

Sequence Clustering Prediction 3/3

Often, you'll want to see only the next few entries in a sequence.

Syntax

```
--
select flattened bottomcount(Predict([v Assoc Seq Line
Items],100),$SEQUENCE,5)
from [Sequence Clustering]
natural prediction join
(select (select 1 as [Line Number], 'Mountain Bottle Cage' as [Model])
as [v Assoc Seq Line Items]) as x
```

Result

Expression.$SEQUENCE	Expression.Line Number	Expression.Model
1		Water Bottle
2		Sport-100
3		Half-Finger Gloves
4		Cycling Cap
5		Sport-100

Analysis

We end with a BottomCount(). It's showing the next five in the series of purchases. The second parameter for BottomCount() is $SEQUENCE—this returns the lowest sequence numbers. The third parameter is 5, showing the lowest five sequences.

Chapter 7

Data Definition Language (DDL) Queries

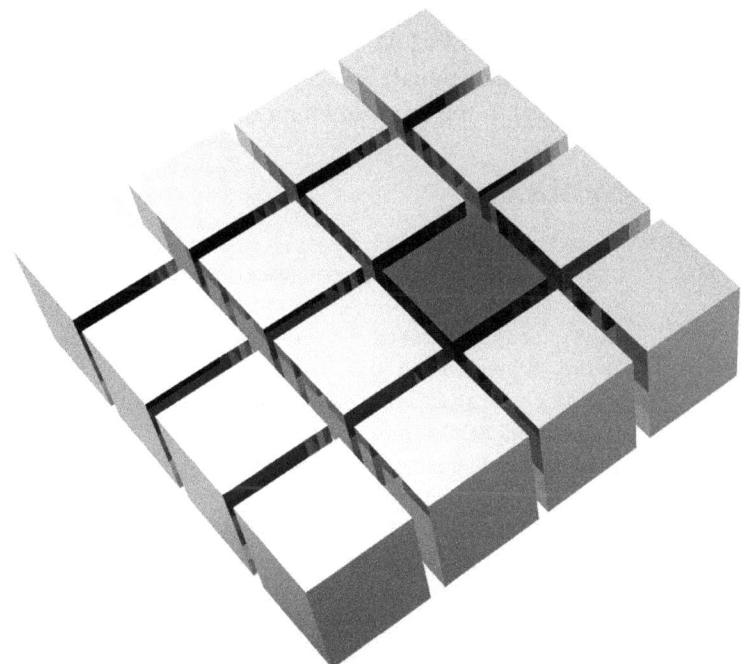

D MX DDL queries are used to create, alter, drop, back up, and restore data mining objects. In addition, they are used to train the mining models. The source data used for cases and model training in this chapter is both relational (using embedded SQL) and multidimensional (using embedded MDX). You will learn how to specify the usage and content of structure and model columns as well as build all the mining objects you will ever need.

▶ **Key concepts**   Creating mining structures, creating mining models, training models, cases, nested case tables, relational source data, multidimensional (cube) source data, filters, drill-through, hold out, algorithm parameters, backup and restore, deleting structures and models, input columns, key columns, predictable columns, table columns

▶ **Keywords**   Create, Alter, Add, Using, Insert, key, discrete, discretized, continuous, predict, predict_only, With Drillthrough, With Filter, With Holdout, Openquery(), SKIP, Shape, Append, Relate, Rename, Delete, Drop, Export, Import

Creating a Mining Structure

In the previous chapters, you've been working with existing data mining objects from the Microsoft sample SSAS database, Adventure Works DW 2008. Now it's time to create your own data mining objects. We start with the DMX DDL (Data Definition Language) syntax to create a mining structure. Make sure the database context is Adventure Works DW 2008—you probably don't want to start adding objects to other (possibly operational) SSAS databases. The current database context can be changed (if necessary) in the drop-down on the toolbar.

Syntax

```
-- create structure
create mining structure [Mail Shot]
(
[Age] long discretized(automatic,10),
[Bike Buyer] long discrete,
[Commute Distance] text discrete,
[Customer Key] long key,
[Education] text discrete,
[Gender] text discrete,
[House Owner Flag] text discrete,
[Marital Status] text discrete,
[Number Cars Owned] long discrete,
```

```
[Number Children At Home] long discrete,
[Occupation] text discrete,
[Region] text discrete,
[Total Children] long discrete,
[Yearly Income] double continuous
)
```

Result

```
Executing the query ...
Execution complete
```

Analysis

You can verify the creation of the structure by right-clicking the Mining Structures folder in Object Explorer in SSMS and choosing Refresh. If you attempt to run the query a second time, you'll receive an error message saying the structure already exists.

The syntax specifies the name of the new structure, Mail Shot. Inside the parentheses is a comma-separated list of column names. The square brackets are obligatory if a column name contains spaces. Each column is followed by an appropriate data type (these data types are not the same as SQL Server or SSAS cube data types)—this is the Type property in BIDS. Of course, we are in a DMX query window in SSMS and not in the graphical BIDS environment. If you wish to view your new mining objects in BIDS, click File | New | Project and choose Import Analysis Services 2008 Database.

There's also a setting for the content of the values in each column. This corresponds to the Content property in BIDS. Here we've set Customer Key to Key, which means it's the case key (similar to a relational primary key). A column like Occupation is set to Discrete—it will contain a limited number of clearly delineated distinct values (for example, Professional). The Yearly Income is Continuous—it will contain a large range of values that do not fit easily into delineated distinct values. Age is discretized. The source data for the column is continuous (maybe too many values for easy analysis), so it's going to be made discrete in a process called *discretization*. It will be split into ten distinct discrete ranges (or buckets). The discretization method will be Automatic (meaning either EqualAreas or Clusters, whichever is the most appropriate for the data). In BIDS there are two corresponding properties, DiscretizationBucketCount and DiscretizationMethod.

If you wanted to use a column like Yearly Income in a Naïve Bayes mining model, you must discretize it first—Naïve Bayes does not support continuous values. Our model is going to a decision tree, which can cope with continuous values—in fact, it's a type of decision tree that uses regression. The Age column has been discretized merely as a convenience to make analysis easier.

Creating a Mining Model

Once a mining structure is in place, you can start to add one or more mining models to the structure. Here, a model based on the Decision Trees algorithm is being added. There are alternative approaches. For example, you can create a model and have it create the containing structure automatically on the fly. Or you can create temporary (session) mining models that disappear as soon as you disconnect. These alternative methods are beyond the scope of this book.

Syntax

```
-- Create model (alter/add)
alter mining structure [Mail Shot]
add mining model [Mail Shot Decision Tree]
(
[Age],
[Bike Buyer] predict,
[Commute Distance],
[Customer Key],
[Education],
[Gender],
[House Owner Flag],
[Marital Status],
[Number Cars Owned],
[Number Children At Home],
[Occupation],
[Region],
[Total Children],
[Yearly Income]
)
using microsoft_decision_trees
```

Result

```
Executing the query ...
Execution complete
```

Analysis

To create a data mining model, you add the model to the structure by altering the structure. You also specify the algorithm for the model in the Using clause. Please note that the Bike Buyer column has the Predict qualifier. This designates it as a predictable column. All of the other columns (the demographics, in this case) are the input columns. These correspond to the Predict and Input settings for the Usage property in BIDS. The key column, Customer Key, will have its Usage property set automatically to Key. There is one other possible Usage property, Predict_Only—which could have been chosen here in the DMX instead of Predict. Predict and Predict_Only (called PredictOnly in BIDS) have different semantics. Predict means that the column can function as an input as well as a predictable column. Thus, the fact that a customer is a bike buyer already can be used to help determine if that customer will be a bike buyer again in the future (probably in a Prediction query). PredictOnly means that any other previous bike purchases are ignored.

The case key (defined in the structure in the last query) automatically and implicitly has a usage of key. Any columns not defined with a Predict or Predict_Only usage automatically and implicitly have a usage of input.

You don't have to include all of the columns from the mining structure in the mining model (although you must include the case key).

Training a Mining Model

If you look under the structure (Mail Shot) in Object Explorer in SSMS, you'll see your new model (Mail Shot Decision Tree)—you might need to right-click and choose Refresh first. However, you can't browse the model just yet (or write DMX Cases, Content, or Prediction queries). First of all, you must train or process the model. You train a model from DMX by writing an Insert query. The Insert query is written against the structure (not the model) to provide the cases for the structure. Once the structure is populated with all of the cases, it then automatically trains the model. If the structure contains more than one model, it will train all of the models.

Syntax

```
-- Train (insert) you can browse. may take a while
insert into mining structure [Mail Shot]
(
[Age],
[Bike Buyer],
[Commute Distance],
[Customer Key],
[Education],
[Gender],
[House Owner Flag],
[Marital Status],
[Number Cars Owned],
[Number Children At Home],
```

```
[Occupation],
[Region],
[Total Children],
[Yearly Income]
)
openquery
(
[Adventure Works DW],
'select
[Age],
[BikeBuyer] as [Bike Buyer],
[CommuteDistance] as [Commute Distance],
[CustomerKey] as [Customer Key],
[EnglishEducation] as [Education],
[Gender],
[HouseOwnerFlag] as [House Owner Flag],
[MaritalStatus] as [Marital Status],
[NumberCarsOwned] as [Number Cars Owned],
[NumberChildrenAtHome] as [Number Children At Home],
[EnglishOccupation] as [Occupation],
[Region],
[TotalChildren] as [Total Children],
[YearlyIncome] as [Yearly Income]
from vTargetMail'
)
```

Result

```
Executing the query ...
Execution complete
```

Analysis

The query begins with an Insert. The Openquery construct requires a data source name. You can check the name of the data source in BIDS or under the Data Sources folder in Object Explorer. It also requires a Select query against the original source data enclosed within single quotes. If you have nonmatching column names, then you must use aliases appropriately. The original source data is a view called vTargetMail in the SQL Server AdventureWorksDW2008 relational database. The SQL Server server name and database name are held in the data source.

With large amounts of data, this query can take quite a while to run. Also, if we had first added some more models to the same structure, this would further increase the time taken for training. When the query completes, you can browse your decision tree graphically in SSMS or BIDS or Excel 2007. You can also begin to write DMX Cases or Content or Prediction queries against the model. You can also write Cases queries against the containing structure.

If you retrospectively add models to the structure, there is no need to repopulate the structure with cases and retrain existing models (by deleting the cases and repeating this query). You can simply insert the cases directly into the model from the structure and therefore train it. The syntax would look like this:

```
insert into mining model [new model name]
```

Structure Cases

This is a simple test to verify that the structure is now populated with cases data.

Syntax

```
-- Cases (select) on structure
select * from mining structure [Mail Shot].cases
```

Result

Age	Bike Buyer	Commute Distance	Customer Key	Education	Gender	House Owner Flag	Marital Status	Number Cars Ow...	Number Chil
45	1	1-2 Miles	11000	Bachelors	M	1	M	0	0
45	1	0-1 Miles	11001	Bachelors	M	0	S	1	3
45	1	2-5 Miles	11002	Bachelors	M	1	M	1	3
39	1	5-10 Miles	11003	Bachelors	F	0	S	1	0
39	1	1-2 Miles	11004	Bachelors	F	1	S	4	5
45	1	5-10 Miles	11005	Bachelors	M	1	S	1	0
45	1	5-10 Miles	11006	Bachelors	F	1	S	1	0
45	1	0-1 Miles	11007	Bachelors	M	1	M	2	3
45	1	10+ Miles	11008	Bachelors	F	1	S	3	4
45	1	5-10 Miles	11009	Bachelors	M	0	S	1	0
45	1	5-10 Miles	11010	Bachelors	F	0	S	1	0
45	1	10+ Miles	11011	Bachelors	M	1	M	4	4
39	0	1-2 Miles	11012	Bachelors	F	1	M	2	0
39	0	0-1 Miles	11013	Bachelors	M	1	M	3	0
39	0	1-2 Miles	11014	Bachelors	F	0	S	3	0
32	1	5-10 Miles	11015	Partial College	F	0	S	1	0
32	1	5-10 Miles	11016	Partial College	M	1	M	1	0
65	1	5-10 Miles	11017	High School	F	1	S	2	0

Analysis

You should see lots of cases. Each case record contains the case key (Customer Key), the predictable column (Bike Buyer), and quite a few input (demographic) columns.

Model Cases

This is a test to see if the structure cases have in turn populated the model cases.

Syntax

```
-- Cases (select) on model
select * from [Mail Shot Decision Tree].cases
```

Result

```
Executing the query ...
Error (Data mining): Drillthrough (SELECT ... FROM model.CASES) is not enabled for the 'Mail Shot Decision Tree' model.

Execution complete
```

Analysis

Well, not quite. The cases may or may not be in the model. The problem is that drill-through on a model is not enabled by default. We are not allowed to view the cases, even if they are there. Later in the chapter you'll learn how to enable drill-through directly from your DMX.

Model Content

Let's try a Content query rather than a Cases query.

Syntax

```
-- Content (select)
select * from [Mail Shot Decision Tree].content
```

Result

MODEL_CATAL...	MODEL_SCHEMA	MODEL_NAME	ATTRIBUTE_N...	NODE_NAME	NODE_UNIQUE...	NODE_TYPE	NODE_GUID	NODE_CAPTION	CHILDREN
Adventure Wor...		Mail Shot Decisi...		0	0	1			1
Adventure Wor...		Mail Shot Decisi...	Bike Buyer	000000001	000000001	2		All	5
Adventure Wor...		Mail Shot Decisi...	Bike Buyer	00000000100	00000000100	3		Number Cars O...	3
Adventure Wor...		Mail Shot Decisi...	Bike Buyer	00000000101	00000000101	3		Number Cars O...	2
Adventure Wor...		Mail Shot Decisi...	Bike Buyer	00000000102	00000000102	3		Number Cars O...	2
Adventure Wor...		Mail Shot Decisi...	Bike Buyer	00000000103	00000000103	3		Number Cars O...	4
Adventure Wor...		Mail Shot Decisi...	Bike Buyer	00000000104	00000000104	3		Number Cars O...	3
Adventure Wor...		Mail Shot Decisi...	Bike Buyer	0000000010400	0000000010400	3		Yearly Income <...	2
Adventure Wor...		Mail Shot Decisi...	Bike Buyer	0000000010401	0000000010401	3		Yearly Income >...	2
Adventure Wor...		Mail Shot Decisi...	Bike Buyer	0000000010402	0000000010402	3		Yearly Income >...	2
Adventure Wor...		Mail Shot Decisi...	Bike Buyer	000000001040...	000000001040...	3		Commute Distan...	0
Adventure Wor...		Mail Shot Decisi...	Bike Buyer	000000001040...	000000001040...	3		Commute Distan...	2
Adventure Wor...		Mail Shot Decisi...	Bike Buyer	000000001040...	000000001040...	4		Commute Distan...	0
Adventure Wor...		Mail Shot Decisi...	Bike Buyer	000000001040...	000000001040...	4		Commute Distan...	0
Adventure Wor...		Mail Shot Decisi...	Bike Buyer	000000001040...	000000001040...	4		Total Children = 0	0
Adventure Wor...		Mail Shot Decisi...	Bike Buyer	000000001040...	000000001040...	3		Total Children n...	2
Adventure Wor...		Mail Shot Decisi...	Bike Buyer	000000001040...	000000001040...	4		Commute Distan...	0
Adventure Wor...		Mail Shot Decisi...	Bike Buyer	000000001040...	000000001040...	3		Commute Distan...	2

Analysis

This time, there are results. The fact that a Content query works indicates that the model has been trained. The ability to run a Content query is not affected by the ability (or not) to drill through to cases with a Cases query.

Model Predict

This Prediction query includes PredictProbability(). The new model is already producing useful results.

Syntax

```
-- Predict (select) with Prospective Buyer
select
[Mail Shot Decision Tree].[Bike Buyer],
TM.[FirstName] + ' ' + TM.[LastName],
PredictProbability([Bike Buyer]) as [Mail Merge]
from
[Mail Shot Decision Tree]
prediction join
openquery
(
[Adventure Works DW],
'select
[FirstName],
[LastName],
[Age],
[CommuteDistance],
[EnglishEducation],
[Gender],
[HouseOwnerFlag],
[MaritalStatus],
[NumberCarsOwned],
[NumberChildrenAtHome],
[EnglishOccupation],
[Region],
[TotalChildren] ,
[YearlyIncome]
from vTargetMail'
)
as TM
on
```

```
[Mail Shot Decision Tree].[Age] = TM.[Age] and
[Mail Shot Decision Tree].[Commute Distance] = TM.[CommuteDistance] and
[Mail Shot Decision Tree].[Education] = TM.[EnglishEducation] and
[Mail Shot Decision Tree].[Gender] = TM.[Gender] and
[Mail Shot Decision Tree].[House Owner Flag] = TM.[HouseOwnerFlag] and
[Mail Shot Decision Tree].[Marital Status] = TM.[MaritalStatus] and
[Mail Shot Decision Tree].[Number Cars Owned] = TM.[NumberCarsOwned] and
[Mail Shot Decision Tree].[Number Children At Home] =
TM.[NumberChildrenAtHome] and
[Mail Shot Decision Tree].[Occupation] = TM.[EnglishOccupation] and
[Mail Shot Decision Tree].[Region] = TM.[Region] and
[Mail Shot Decision Tree].[Total Children] = TM.[TotalChildren] and
[Mail Shot Decision Tree].[Yearly Income] = TM.[YearlyIncome]
```

Result

Bike Buyer	Expression	Mail Merge
1	Jon Yang	0.94374009508...
1	Eugene Huang	0.63202038924...
0	Ruben Torres	0.90319387276...
0	Christy Zhu	0.75884853168...
0	Elizabeth Johnson	0.81132075471...
1	Julio Ruiz	0.84867097019...
1	Janet Alvarez	0.84867097019...
0	Marco Mehta	0.94113528148...
0	Rob Verhoff	0.78835489833...
0	Shannon Carlson	0.75884853168...
0	Jacquelyn Suarez	0.75884853168...
0	Curtis Lu	0.87564179104...
1	Lauren Walker	0.54672795918...
0	Ian Jenkins	0.65904500865...
0	Sydney Bennett	0.92038072216...
0	Chloe Young	0.88397384632...
0	Wyatt Hill	0.88397384632...
0	Shannon Wang	0.64200799740...
1	Clarence Rai	0.68235518292...

Analysis

Jon Yang is about 94 percent likely to buy a bike. He's an existing customer from the original cases. He may or may not have originally bought a bike. Rather, the result shows that a customer with the same inputs as Jon Yang (first and last names are not inputs or structure columns) is 94 percent likely to be a bike buyer. You may want to alias the concatenated name column as well.

Specifying Structure Holdout

This is a new structure. It includes a With Holdout clause to split the cases into training and testing cases.

Syntax

```
-- create structure with holdout (2008 only)
create mining structure [Mail Shot Holdout]
(
[Age] long discretized(automatic,10),
[Bike Buyer] long discrete,
[Commute Distance] text discrete,
[Customer Key] long key,
[Education] text discrete,
[Gender] text discrete,
[House Owner Flag] text discrete,
[Marital Status] text discrete,
[Number Cars Owned] long discrete,
[Number Children At Home] long discrete,
[Occupation] text discrete,
[Region] text discrete,
[Total Children] long discrete,
[Yearly Income] double continuous
)
with holdout (30 percent)
```

Result

```
Executing the query ...
Execution complete
```

Analysis

The structure will train any enclosed models with 70 percent of the cases data. The rest of the cases (30 percent) will be held back for retrospective testing and validation of any models in the structure. This testing can be done in SSMS or BIDS, maybe by viewing a lift chart. Testing on holdout data is very useful for validating (or not validating) the results of the original training.

Specifying Model Parameter

All of the mining algorithms, on which your models are based, have a number of parameter settings. These parameters control how the model is trained and influence the subsequent content results. This query sets the MINIMUM_SUPPORT parameter for a model based on the Decision Trees algorithm.

Syntax

```
-- create model with algorithm parameter settings
alter mining structure [Mail Shot Holdout]
add mining model [Mail Shot Decision Tree Parameter]
(
[Age],
[Bike Buyer] predict,
[Commute Distance],
[Customer Key],
[Education],
[Gender],
[House Owner Flag],
[Marital Status],
[Number Cars Owned],
[Number Children At Home],
[Occupation],
[Region],
[Total Children],
[Yearly Income]
)
using microsoft_decision_trees
(MINIMUM_SUPPORT = 15)
```

Result

```
Executing the query ...
Execution complete
```

Analysis

The default for MINIMUM_SUPPORT is 10. Here it's been changed to 15. This means that a node will not be created in the decision tree unless it contains a minimum of 15 cases. Setting too low a figure for MINIMUM_SUPPORT can result in an over-large tree with too many nodes, splits, and branches.

Specifying Model Filter

Please note the With Filter clause. Only female customers will be used to train the model—male customers (even they exist in the structure cases) are simply ignored.

Syntax

```
-- create model with filter
alter mining structure [Mail Shot Holdout]
add mining model [Mail Shot Decision Tree Filter]
(
[Age],
[Bike Buyer] predict,
[Commute Distance],
[Customer Key],
[Education],
[Gender],
[House Owner Flag],
[Marital Status],
[Number Cars Owned],
[Number Children At Home],
[Occupation],
[Region],
[Total Children],
[Yearly Income]
)
using microsoft_decision_trees
with filter (Gender = 'F')
```

Result

```
Executing the query ...
Execution complete
```

Analysis

If the structure has male customer cases, then the model will contain fewer cases than the structure itself. Only female customers are used to train the model. All the cases in the model are for females only. The content of the model is based on female customers only. This filtering (starting with SSAS 2008) can be quite useful. Maybe you want to build a series of identical models, with each one dedicated to a subset of the structure cases data.

Specifying Model Drill-through

Earlier in the chapter, you saw a Cases query on a model fail. That's because drill-through on a model is disabled by default. Please note the addition of a With Drillthrough clause.

Syntax

```
-- create model with drillthrough
alter mining structure [Mail Shot Holdout]
add mining model [Mail Shot Decision Tree Drillthrough]
(
[Age],
[Bike Buyer] predict,
[Commute Distance],
[Customer Key],
[Education],
[Gender],
[House Owner Flag],
[Marital Status],
[Number Cars Owned],
[Number Children At Home],
[Occupation],
[Region],
[Total Children],
[Yearly Income]
)
using microsoft_decision_trees
with drillthrough
```

Result

```
Executing the query ...
Execution complete
```

Analysis

This is the DMX equivalent of setting the AllowDrillThrough property to True in BIDS. Now, you'll be able to issue Cases queries directly against the model.

Training the New Models

Our latest structure, Mail Shot Holdout, now contains a few models. There are no cases in the structure and, consequently, none of the models have been trained. This query trains all of the models in the Mail Shot Holdout structure.

Syntax

```
-- train model to test drillthrough
insert into [Mail Shot Holdout]
(
[Age],
[Bike Buyer],
[Commute Distance],
[Customer Key],
[Education],
[Gender],
[House Owner Flag],
[Marital Status],
[Number Cars Owned],
[Number Children At Home],
[Occupation],
[Region],
[Total Children],
[Yearly Income]
)
openquery
(
[Adventure Works DW],
'select
[Age],
[BikeBuyer] as [Bike Buyer],
[CommuteDistance] as [Commute Distance],
[CustomerKey] as [Customer Key],
[EnglishEducation] as [Education],
[Gender],
[HouseOwnerFlag] as [House Owner Flag],
[MaritalStatus] as [Marital Status],
[NumberCarsOwned] as [Number Cars Owned],
[NumberChildrenAtHome] as [Number Children At Home],
[EnglishOccupation] as [Occupation],
[Region],
```

```
[TotalChildren] as [Total Children],
[YearlyIncome] as [Yearly Income]
from vTargetMail'
)
```

Result

```
Executing the query ...
Execution complete
```

Analysis

Inserting data into a structure processes or trains all of the models in the structure.

Cases—with No Drill-through

The Mail Shot Decision Tree Filter model was added without the With Drillthrough clause.

Syntax

```
-- Cases (select) on model without drillthrough
select * from [Mail Shot Decision Tree Filter].cases
```

Result

```
Executing the query ...
Error (Data mining): Drillthrough (SELECT ... FROM model.CASES) is not enabled for the 'Mail Shot Decision Tree Filter' model.
Execution complete
```

Analysis

The Cases query fails.

Cases—with Drill-through

The Mail Shot Decision Tree Drillthrough model was added with the With Drillthrough clause.

Syntax

```
-- Cases (select) on model with drillthrough
select * from [Mail Shot Decision Tree Drillthrough].cases
```

Result

Age	Bike Buyer	Commute Distance	Customer Key	Education	Gender	House Owner Flag	Marital Status	Number Cars Ow...	Number Chil
45	1	1-2 Miles	11000	Bachelors	M	1	M	0	0
45	1	0-1 Miles	11001	Bachelors	M	0	S	1	3
45	1	2-5 Miles	11002	Bachelors	M	1	M	1	3
39	1	5-10 Miles	11003	Bachelors	F	0	S	1	0
39	1	1-2 Miles	11004	Bachelors	F	1	S	4	5
45	1	5-10 Miles	11005	Bachelors	M	1	S	1	0
45	1	5-10 Miles	11006	Bachelors	F	1	S	1	0
45	1	0-1 Miles	11007	Bachelors	M	1	M	2	3
45	1	10+ Miles	11008	Bachelors	F	1	S	3	4
45	1	5-10 Miles	11009	Bachelors	M	0	S	1	0
45	1	5-10 Miles	11010	Bachelors	F	0	S	1	0
45	1	10+ Miles	11011	Bachelors	M	1	M	4	4
39	0	1-2 Miles	11012	Bachelors	F	1	M	2	0
39	0	0-1 Miles	11013	Bachelors	M	1	M	3	0
39	0	1-2 Miles	11014	Bachelors	F	0	S	3	0
32	1	5-10 Miles	11015	Partial College	F	0	S	1	0
32	1	5-10 Miles	11016	Partial College	M	1	M	1	0
65	1	5-10 Miles	11017	High School	F	1	S	2	0

Analysis

The Cases query works.

Structure with Holdout

This time we have a Cases query on the structure rather than on individual models.

Syntax

```
-- Cases (select) on structure with holdout
select * from mining structure [Mail Shot Holdout].cases
```

Result

Age	Bike Buyer	Commute Distance	Customer Key	Education	Gender	House Owner Flag	Marital Status	Number Cars Ow...	Number Chil
45	1	1-2 Miles	11000	Bachelors	M	1	M	0	0
45	1	0-1 Miles	11001	Bachelors	M	0	S	1	3
45	1	2-5 Miles	11002	Bachelors	M	1	M	1	3
39	1	5-10 Miles	11003	Bachelors	F	0	S	1	0
39	1	1-2 Miles	11004	Bachelors	F	1	S	4	5
45	1	5-10 Miles	11005	Bachelors	M	1	S	1	0
45	1	5-10 Miles	11006	Bachelors	F	1	S	1	0
45	1	0-1 Miles	11007	Bachelors	M	1	M	2	3
45	1	10+ Miles	11008	Bachelors	F	1	S	3	4
45	1	5-10 Miles	11009	Bachelors	M	0	S	1	0
45	1	5-10 Miles	11010	Bachelors	F	0	S	1	0
45	1	10+ Miles	11011	Bachelors	M	1	M	4	4
39	0	1-2 Miles	11012	Bachelors	F	1	M	2	0
39	0	0-1 Miles	11013	Bachelors	M	1	M	3	0
39	0	1-2 Miles	11014	Bachelors	F	0	S	3	0
32	1	5-10 Miles	11015	Partial College	F	0	S	1	0
32	1	5-10 Miles	11016	Partial College	M	1	M	1	0
65	1	5-10 Miles	11017	High School	F	1	S	2	0

Analysis

When we created this structure, a few queries back, it included a With Holdout clause. This query shows *all* of the cases in the structure. If you wish to see only those used in training (70 percent), try a Where clause with IsTrainingCase(). To see the test cases held back, try IsTestCase(). If you try these, you will see two separate groups of case records (take a look at the Customer Key column).

Specifying Model Parameter, Filter, and Drill-through

This DMX demonstrates how to combine a parameter and a filter with drill-through.

Syntax

```
-- model with parameter, filter, and drillthrough
alter mining structure [Mail Shot Holdout]
add mining model [Mail Shot Decision Tree With]
(
[Age],
[Bike Buyer] predict,
[Commute Distance],
[Customer Key],
[Education],
[Gender],
[House Owner Flag],
[Marital Status],
[Number Cars Owned],
[Number Children At Home],
[Occupation],
[Region],
[Total Children],
[Yearly Income]
)
using microsoft_decision_trees (MINIMUM_SUPPORT = 20)
with drillthrough, filter (Gender = 'F')
```

Result

```
Executing the query ...
Execution complete
```

Analysis

The important things to notice are the Using clause and the With clause.

Training New Model

Our last model was added after the initial processing of the structure and the training of the original models. Maybe we ought to reprocess the structure to train our latest model.

Syntax

```
-- process
insert into [Mail Shot Holdout]
(
[Age],
[Bike Buyer],
[Commute Distance],
[Customer Key],
[Education],
[Gender],
[House Owner Flag],
[Marital Status],
[Number Cars Owned],
[Number Children At Home],
[Occupation],
[Region],
[Total Children],
[Yearly Income]
)
openquery
(
[Adventure Works DW],
'select
[Age],
[BikeBuyer] as [Bike Buyer],
[CommuteDistance] as [Commute Distance],
[CustomerKey] as [Customer Key],
[EnglishEducation] as [Education],
[Gender],
[HouseOwnerFlag] as [House Owner Flag],
[MaritalStatus] as [Marital Status],
[NumberCarsOwned] as [Number Cars Owned],
```

```
[NumberChildrenAtHome] as [Number Children At Home],
[EnglishOccupation] as [Occupation],
[Region],
[TotalChildren] as [Total Children],
[YearlyIncome] as [Yearly Income]
from vTargetMail'
)
```

Result

```
Executing the query ...
Error (Data mining): The mining structure , Mail Shot Holdout is already trained and does not support incremental updates. Before using the
Execution complete
```

Analysis

The error message indicates that you can't reprocess a structure that's already been processed. First you must "unprocess" the structure. You do so by deleting all of the cases it contains.

Unprocessing a Structure

To reset the structure (so we can process it all again), you use Delete From.

Syntax

```
-- clear out structure cases and models
-- redo the previous insert
delete from mining structure [Mail Shot Holdout]
```

Result

```
Executing the query ...
Execution complete
```

Analysis

This looks a little like SQL again. However, unlike in SQL, you must use the full Delete From; you can't use the Delete shortcut.

Model Cases with Filter and Drill-through

Please reprocess the Mail Shot Holdout structure—that's the query before the last one. This will train the original models and our latest model, which has a parameter, a filter, and a drill-through defined.

Syntax

```
-- Cases (select) on model with drillthrough and filter
select * from [Mail Shot Decision Tree With].cases
```

Result

Age	Bike Buyer	Commute Distance	Customer Key	Education	Gender	House Owner Flag	Marital Status	Number Cars Ow...	Number Chil
39	1	5-10 Miles	11003	Bachelors	F	0	S	1	0
39	1	1-2 Miles	11004	Bachelors	F	1	S	4	5
45	1	5-10 Miles	11006	Bachelors	F	1	S	1	0
45	1	10+ Miles	11008	Bachelors	F	1	S	3	4
45	1	5-10 Miles	11010	Bachelors	F	0	S	1	0
39	0	1-2 Miles	11012	Bachelors	F	1	M	2	0
39	0	1-2 Miles	11014	Bachelors	F	0	S	3	0
32	1	5-10 Miles	11015	Partial College	F	0	S	1	0
65	1	5-10 Miles	11017	High School	F	1	S	2	0
32	1	1-2 Miles	11021	Partial College	F	0	S	1	0
65	1	1-2 Miles	11028	Partial College	F	1	M	2	0
65	1	1-2 Miles	11030	Partial High Sch...	F	1	M	2	1
65	1	1-2 Miles	11031	High School	F	1	M	2	0
65	1	1-2 Miles	11032	High School	F	1	M	2	0
65	1	5-10 Miles	11034	High School	F	1	M	2	0
65	1	1-2 Miles	11035	Partial High Sch...	F	1	M	2	1
32	1	1-2 Miles	11036	Partial College	F	1	M	2	0
32	1	5-10 Miles	11037	Partial High Sch...	F	0	S	2	0

Analysis

If you receive an error about the model not being processed, please reprocess the Mail Shot Holdout structure (the query before the last one), as we just deleted all the cases (the last query).

If you receive a drill-through error, please make sure you are querying the correct model (Mail Shot Decision Tree With).

If you scroll down the result, you'll see that only female cases are visible. That's because of the filter we set on the model. The fact that we are able to view the cases at all is because we enabled drill-through.

Clearing Out Cases

Let's try deleting the cases again and then running a Cases query on a model.

Syntax

```
-- clear out structure cases only (not the models)
delete from mining structure [Mail Shot Holdout].cases
select * from [Mail Shot Decision Tree With].cases
```

Result

Executing the query ...
Error (Data mining): The 'Mail Shot Holdout' object does not contain any cases. The drillthrough store is empty either because the Process1

Execution complete

Analysis

The Delete From statement removes all the cases from the structure and from the models. It "untrains" the models. However, it does not remove the models from the structure.

Removing Models

To remove a model from a structure, you'll need Drop.

Syntax

```
-- drop a model
drop mining model [Mail Shot Decision Tree With]
select * from [Mail Shot Decision Tree With].cases
```

Result

Executing the query ...
Error (Data mining): Either the user, ART\Art, does not have permission to access the referenced mining model or structure, Mail Shot Decis

Execution complete

Analysis

This is a little like SQL too. Delete From removes data only. Drop removes objects including any data they might contain.

Removing Structures

Again, Drop is used to remove objects, this time a structure.

Syntax

```
-- drop a structure
drop mining structure [Mail Shot Holdout]
select * from mining structure [Mail Shot Holdout].cases
```

Result

```
Executing the query ...
Error (Data mining): Either the user, ART\Art, does not have permission to access the referenced mining structure, Mail Shot Holdout, or th
Execution complete
```

Analysis

If you drop a structure, it disappears along with any models it might contain. Not only are all the cases deleted, but the containing structure and models go too.

Renaming a Model

The syntax to rename a model is straightforward. Please make sure you run those two queries separately.

Syntax

```
-- rename a model
rename mining model [Mail Shot Decision Tree] to [DT Model]
select * from [DT Model].content
```

Result

MODEL_CATAL...	MODEL_SCHEMA	MODEL_NAME	ATTRIBUTE_N...	NODE_NAME	NODE_UNIQUE...	NODE_TYPE	NODE_GUID	NODE_CAPTION	CHILDREN_
Adventure Wor...		DT Model		0	0	1			1
Adventure Wor...		DT Model	Bike Buyer	000000001	000000001	2		All	5
Adventure Wor...		DT Model	Bike Buyer	00000000100	00000000100	3		Number Cars O...	3
Adventure Wor...		DT Model	Bike Buyer	00000000101	00000000101	3		Number Cars O...	2
Adventure Wor...		DT Model	Bike Buyer	00000000102	00000000102	3		Number Cars O...	2
Adventure Wor...		DT Model	Bike Buyer	00000000103	00000000103	3		Number Cars O...	4
Adventure Wor...		DT Model	Bike Buyer	00000000104	00000000104	3		Number Cars O...	3
Adventure Wor...		DT Model	Bike Buyer	0000000010400	0000000010400	3		Yearly Income <...	2
Adventure Wor...		DT Model	Bike Buyer	0000000010401	0000000010401	3		Yearly Income >...	2
Adventure Wor...		DT Model	Bike Buyer	0000000010402	0000000010402	3		Yearly Income >...	2
Adventure Wor...		DT Model	Bike Buyer	000000001040...	000000001040...	4		Commute Distan...	0
Adventure Wor...		DT Model	Bike Buyer	000000001040...	000000001040...	3		Commute Distan...	2
Adventure Wor...		DT Model	Bike Buyer	000000001040...	000000001040...	4		Commute Distan...	0
Adventure Wor...		DT Model	Bike Buyer	000000001040...	000000001040...	4		Commute Distan...	0
Adventure Wor...		DT Model	Bike Buyer	000000001040...	000000001040...	4		Total Children = 0	0
Adventure Wor...		DT Model	Bike Buyer	000000001040...	000000001040...	3		Total Children n...	2
Adventure Wor...		DT Model	Bike Buyer	000000001040...	000000001040...	4		Commute Distan...	0
Adventure Wor...		DT Model	Bike Buyer	000000001040...	000000001040...	3		Commute Distan...	2

Analysis

This query assumes you created the Mail Shot Decision Tree model in the Mail Shot structure earlier.

Renaming a Structure

Please run the queries separately.

Syntax

```
-- rename a structure
rename mining structure [Mail Shot] to [Mail Structure]
select * from mining structure [Mail Structure].cases
```

Result

Age	Bike Buyer	Commute Distance	Customer Key	Education	Gender	House Owner Flag	Marital Status	Number Cars Ow...	Number Chil
45	1	1-2 Miles	11000	Bachelors	M	1	M	0	0
45	1	0-1 Miles	11001	Bachelors	M	0	S	1	3
45	1	2-5 Miles	11002	Bachelors	M	1	M	1	3
39	1	5-10 Miles	11003	Bachelors	F	0	S	1	0
39	1	1-2 Miles	11004	Bachelors	F	1	S	4	5
45	1	5-10 Miles	11005	Bachelors	M	1	S	1	0
45	1	5-10 Miles	11006	Bachelors	F	1	S	1	0
45	1	0-1 Miles	11007	Bachelors	M	1	M	2	3
45	1	10+ Miles	11008	Bachelors	F	1	S	3	4
45	1	5-10 Miles	11009	Bachelors	M	0	S	1	0
45	1	5-10 Miles	11010	Bachelors	F	0	S	1	0
45	1	10+ Miles	11011	Bachelors	M	1	M	4	4
39	0	1-2 Miles	11012	Bachelors	F	1	M	2	0
39	0	0-1 Miles	11013	Bachelors	M	1	M	3	0
39	0	1-2 Miles	11014	Bachelors	F	0	S	3	0
32	1	5-10 Miles	11015	Partial College	F	0	S	1	0
32	1	5-10 Miles	11016	Partial College	M	1	M	1	0
65	1	5-10 Miles	11017	High School	F	1	S	2	0

Analysis

This query assumes you still have the Mail Shot structure created earlier in the chapter.

Making Backups

The Export Mining Structure command is used to back up a data mining structure. You can back up data mining objects separately from the containing SSAS database—you can't do this for SSAS cubes.

Syntax

```
-- export the structure and models, optional password
export mining structure [Mail Structure] to 'c:\mail.abf'
```

Result

```
Executing the query ...
Execution complete
```

Analysis

The convention is to have an .abf (analysis services backup file) file extension. You may want to create a dedicated folder for backups and not use the root as I have done here. Many versions of Windows disable writing files to the root by default—it's considered bad practice in a production environment.

Removing the Backed-up Structure

Hopefully, you have a backup! Please run the two queries separately.

Syntax

```
-- drop the structure and models
drop mining structure [Mail Structure]
select * from mining structure [Mail Structure].cases
```

Result

```
Executing the query ...
Error (Data mining): Either the user, ART\Art, does not have permission to access the referenced mining structure, Mail Structure, or the c

Execution complete
```

Analysis

Everything has gone!

Restoring a Backup

The syntax to restore a backup is Import From.

Syntax

```
-- import the structure and models
import from 'c:\mail.abf'
select * from mining structure [Mail Structure].cases
select * from [DT Model].content
```

Result

MODEL_CATAL...	MODEL_SCHEMA	MODEL_NAME	ATTRIBUTE_N...	NODE_NAME	NODE_UNIQUE...	NODE_TYPE	NODE_GUID	NODE_CAPTION	CHILDREN
Adventure Wor...		DT Model		0	0	1			1
Adventure Wor...		DT Model	Bike Buyer	000000001	000000001	2		All	5
Adventure Wor...		DT Model	Bike Buyer	00000000100	00000000100	3		Number Cars O...	3
Adventure Wor...		DT Model	Bike Buyer	00000000101	00000000101	3		Number Cars O...	2
Adventure Wor...		DT Model	Bike Buyer	00000000102	00000000102	3		Number Cars O...	2
Adventure Wor...		DT Model	Bike Buyer	00000000103	00000000103	3		Number Cars O...	4
Adventure Wor...		DT Model	Bike Buyer	00000000104	00000000104	3		Number Cars O...	3
Adventure Wor...		DT Model	Bike Buyer	0000000010400	0000000010400	3		Yearly Income <...	2
Adventure Wor...		DT Model	Bike Buyer	0000000010401	0000000010401	3		Yearly Income >...	2
Adventure Wor...		DT Model	Bike Buyer	0000000010402	0000000010402	3		Yearly Income >...	2
Adventure Wor...		DT Model	Bike Buyer	000000001040...	000000001040...	4		Commute Distan...	0
Adventure Wor...		DT Model	Bike Buyer	000000001040...	000000001040...	3		Commute Distan...	2
Adventure Wor...		DT Model	Bike Buyer	000000001040...	000000001040...	4		Commute Distan...	0
Adventure Wor...		DT Model	Bike Buyer	000000001040...	000000001040...	4		Commute Distan...	0
Adventure Wor...		DT Model	Bike Buyer	000000001040...	000000001040...	4		Total Children = 0	0
Adventure Wor...		DT Model	Bike Buyer	000000001040...	000000001040...	3		Total Children n...	2
Adventure Wor...		DT Model	Bike Buyer	000000001040...	000000001040...	4		Commute Distan...	0
Adventure Wor...		DT Model	Bike Buyer	000000001040...	000000001040...	3		Commute Distan...	2

Analysis

After the Import completes, try the structure Cases query and the model Content query. Hopefully, you got everything back.

Structure with Nested Case Table

This structure is different from the previous ones in this chapter. The Purchases column is a table—a nested table. It's a case within a case—often referred to as a *nested case table*. This type of structure is commonly used with Association, Sequence Clustering, and Clustering (if there's a predictable column) models. It is analogous to a one-to-many relationship in a relational database. A customer, when placing an order, may buy many product models on that particular order.

Syntax

```
-- nested structure
create mining structure [Sales Analysis]
(
OrderNumber text key,
Purchases table
(
[Model] text key
)
)
```

Result

```
Executing the query ...
Execution complete
```

Analysis

The Purchases column is of type Table. It, in turn, contains a Model column—its type is Key. If you think in relational terms, each order has a unique OrderNumber—that's the primary key of a parent table. Each order will include one or more line items (child table) that is joined via a foreign key (OrderNumber) back to the parent table. However, the foreign key is not the primary key of the order line items child table. The primary key is actually the product model bought (we are assuming the same product model does not appear more than once). Thus, the Model column has a Content property of Key. It's not necessary to show the foreign key in the nested table. Please note the inner set of parentheses.

In plain English, this structure shows product models bought on an order-by-order basis. This is market basket analysis—which product models were purchased together in each shopping basket or order.

Model Using Nested Case Table

The model is based on the Association algorithm. It's called Cross Sell and is being added to the Sales Analysis structure that we built in the last query.

Syntax

```
-- model
alter mining structure [Sales Analysis]
add mining model [Cross Sell]
(
OrderNumber,
Purchases predict
(
[Model]
)
)
using Microsoft_Association_Rules
```

Result

```
Executing the query ...
Execution complete
```

Analysis

The nested table column (Purchases) has its Usage property set to Predict. Shortly, we are going to predict which product model is likely to be bought with another product model. The product model is represented by the Model column within the nested table column. Please notice, once again, the inner set of parentheses, which ensures that the Model column in the models maps to the Model column in the structure.

Model Training with Nested Case Table

The source data for the structure/model cases and for the model training is from two relational views (they could just as easily be tables). The two views are from the SQL Server AdventureWorksDW2008 relational database. The parent view (table) is vAssocSeqOrders—it's an order header view. The child view (table) is vAssocSeqLineItems—it's an order details view. The primary key to foreign key relationship is on the OrderNumber column.

Syntax

```
insert into mining structure [Sales Analysis]
(
OrderNumber,
Purchases
(
SKIP,
[Model]
)
)
shape -- braces
{
openquery
(
[Adventure Works DW],
'select
OrderNumber
from vAssocSeqOrders'
)
}
append -- parentheses and braces
(
{
openquery
```

```
(
[Adventure Works DW],
'select
OrderNumber,
Model
from vAssocSeqLineItems'
)
}
relate OrderNumber to OrderNumber
)
as Purchases
```

Result

```
Executing the query ...
Execution complete
```

Analysis

Wow, some syntax! The DMX is a little complex as the source data is from two views. These have to be joined to extract all of the data needed by the cases and the nested case tables.

The key word Shape is for the parent view. It requires the use of braces around the Openquery construct, and it's extracting the OrderNumber column for the structure cases. The key word Append is for the child view. It too has braces around its separate Openquery construct. It's returning the OrderNumber and Model columns. Now, we have the OrderNumber column twice. The first is used to populate the case column OrderNumber. The second OrderNumber column is *not* used to populate any column in the nested case table—there is only a Model column in the nested table. That's why the nested table has a Skip keyword. The second OrderNumber column does have a use. It's used with the key word Relate—this is analogous to an Inner Join in a relational query. Relate is part of the Append construct, which is why you have an extra pair of parentheses outside the braces in the Append construct.

This is not the easiest syntax in the world to remember. It's a good idea to keep this as a template and copy and paste for your own DMX training queries. Of course, you'll have to change column names and view/table names.

Prediction Queries with Nested Cases 1/2

Maybe it's time to test the model. This is a Prediction query to help us identify cross-selling opportunities.

Syntax

```
-- prediction water bottle no hydration pack
select flattened
(
select [Model] from Predict([Purchases],5)
)
from [Cross Sell]
natural prediction join
(select
(select 'Water Bottle' as [Model]) as [Purchases]) as Y
```

Result

Expression.Model
Sport-100
Patch kit
Mountain Tire Tube
Mountain-200
Road Tire Tube

Analysis

This Prediction query is flattened and incorporates a subquery. It is showing the five product models most likely to be bought alongside Water Bottle. The upper Select is a double Select. The matching lower Select is also a double Select. Please note that buying Water Bottle does not lead to Hydration Pack.

You can also view this result graphically, as a Dependency Network, for example, in SSMS or BIDS or Excel 2007 (you need to download and install the data mining add-in for Excel). If you wish to do so in BIDS, you need to import the SSAS database (File | New | Project | Import Analysis Services 2008 Database) or open it directly (File | Open | Analysis Services Database). The former is called *disconnected mode*; the latter, *connected mode*. Please be careful if working in connected mode—any changes you make in BIDS immediately update the live SSAS database. Changes you make in disconnected mode in BIDS have no effect on the live SSAS database unless you explicitly deploy and process the changes.

Prediction Queries with Nested Cases 2/2

Water Bottle has been changed to Hydration Pack.

Syntax

```
-- prediction hydration pack leads to water bottle
select flattened
(
select [Model] from Predict([Purchases],5)
)
from [Cross Sell]
natural prediction join
(select
(select 'Hydration Pack' as [Model]) as [Purchases]) as Y
```

Result

Expression.Model
Water Bottle
Sport-100
Patch kit
Mountain Tire Tube
Mountain-200

Analysis

It seems that buying Hydration Pack does result in the purchase of Water Bottle. In the previous query, Water Bottle did not lead to Hydration Pack. In this query, Hydration Pack does lead to Water Bottle. It's a one-way relationship. You can confirm this graphically by observing the color-coding in the Dependency Network viewer in SSMS or Excel 2007 or BIDS.

Cube—Mining Structure

All of our data mining structures so far have used relational source data for the structure cases. The next few queries show how to work with multidimensional data. We are going to populate the structure and train a mining model using data from an SSAS cube rather than an SQL Server relational database. Our containing structure is called Profiles. There is no nested case table this time.

Syntax

```
-- Cluster (non predict) and MDX
create mining structure [Profiles]
(
[Name] text discrete,
```

```
[Commute Distance] text discrete,
[Customer Key] long key,
[Education] text discrete,
[Gender] text discrete,
[House Owner Flag] text discrete,
[Marital Status] text discrete
-- etc
)
```

Result

```
Executing the query ...
Execution complete
```

Analysis

The case key is Customer Key. All of the other columns are going to be input columns. All of these potential input columns are Discrete—there are no Continuous or Discretized columns. This structure is no different from a structure based on a relational source.

Cube—Mining Model

We are adding a mining model called Customers to the Profiles structure. The model is based on the Clustering algorithm. It's pure clustering; there is no column or nested table column with a Usage of Predict.

Syntax

```
-- Create model (alter/add)
alter mining structure [Profiles]
add mining model [Customers]
(
[Name],
[Commute Distance],
[Customer Key],
[Education],
[Gender],
[House Owner Flag],
[Marital Status]
-- etc
)
using microsoft_clustering
```

Result

```
Executing the query ...
Execution complete
```

Analysis

Any column that is not Key in the structure or flagged as Predict (or Predict_Only) in the model is an input column. This model is no different from a model based on a relational source.

Cube—Model Training

The source data for the cases is coming from an SSAS cube. It is multidimensional data, not relational. As such, it's accessed in a different way. There is no Openquery (nor a data source) construct for multidimensional data.

Syntax

```
-- Train (insert) you can browse - France
insert into [Profiles]
(
[Name],
[Commute Distance],
[Customer Key],
[Education],
[Gender],
[House Owner Flag],
[Marital Status]
-- etc
)
with
member [Measures].[Commute Distance] as
[Customer].[Customer].Properties("Commute Distance")
member [Measures].[Customer Key] as
[Customer].[Customer].currentmember.member_key
member [Measures].[Education] as [Customer].[Customer].Properties("Education")
member [Measures].[Gender] as [Customer].[Customer].Properties("Gender")
member [Measures].[House Owner Flag] as
[Customer].[Customer].Properties("Home Owner")
member [Measures].[Marital Status] as
[Customer].[Customer].Properties("Marital Status")
select
{[Measures].[Commute Distance],[Measures].[Customer Key],
[Measures].[Education],[Measures].[Gender],
```

```
[Measures].[House Owner Flag],[Measures].[Marital Status]}
on columns,
[Customer].[Customer].[Customer]
on rows
from
[Adventure Works]
where [Customer].[Customer Geography].[Country].[France]
```

Result

```
Executing the query ...
Execution complete
```

Analysis

You can now browse the Customers model graphically. Try the Cluster Profiles tab.

The Select statement incorporates a With construct and a Where clause. If you examine the Where clause, you can see that this is not SQL! The language is MDX, the query language for cubes. The Where clause is called a *slicer* and is restricting the clustering to French customers. The originating cube is called Adventure Works and it's in the same SSAS database (Adventure Works DW 2008) as our new mining structure and model.

It's conventional in MDX to make heavy use of square brackets, even if they are not always obligatory. MDX returns data organized on columns and rows. The With constructs are converting dimension attribute hierarchy member properties into measures. MDX queries are beyond the scope of a DMX query book!

In effect, you have assembled a few thousand customers into only ten clusters. If you are conversant with BIDS, it's also possible to create a new customer dimension based on these clusters and to add this cluster dimension to your cube. Then, you can browse your measures (say, sales) by customer cluster. This is an advanced (but powerful) topic—you need to understand cubes as well as data mining. If you do it, you are mining a cube and then putting the mining results back into the cube.

Cube—Structure Cases

This is a Cases query on the Profiles structure.

Syntax

```
-- Cases (select) on structure
select * from mining structure [Profiles].cases
```

Result

Name	Commute Distance	Customer Key	Education	Gender	House Owner Flag	Marital Status
Aaron L. Wright	5-10 Miles	12650	High School	Male	Yes	Married
Abby P. Gonzalez	0-1 Miles	22480	Bachelors	Female	Yes	Married
Abby P. Rana	0-1 Miles	14534	Bachelors	Female	Yes	Single
Abby Perez	1-2 Miles	16195	High School	Female	No	Married
Abby Sandberg	0-1 Miles	12494	Partial College	Female	No	Married
Abigail A. Griffin	0-1 Miles	19256	Bachelors	Female	Yes	Married
Abigail D. Rivera	1-2 Miles	14717	Partial College	Female	Yes	Single
Abigail G. Diaz	2-5 Miles	22641	Partial College	Female	Yes	Single
Abigail Ross	0-1 Miles	20855	Bachelors	Female	Yes	Married
Adam A. Hall	2-5 Miles	13681	High School	Male	Yes	Single
Adam A. Shan	2-5 Miles	28496	High School	Male	Yes	Single
Adam Baker	0-1 Miles	12849	Partial College	Male	Yes	Single
Adam Hayes	2-5 Miles	24028	Partial College	Male	No	Single
Adriana L. Gonzalez	10+ Miles	12300	Partial College	Female	Yes	Single
Adriana Rana	0-1 Miles	21675	Partial High Sch...	Female	No	Single
Adriana W. Prasad	2-5 Miles	20050	High School	Female	No	Single
Adrienne M. Blanco	5-10 Miles	18132	Partial College	Female	Yes	Married
Adrienne Suarez	2-5 Miles	24559	Partial College	Female	Yes	Married
Aidan Washington	2-5 Miles	23444	Partial College	Male	No	Single

Analysis

You are looking at the attributes and attribute values from the cube's Customer dimension. If you are familiar with MDX, you are actually looking at the attribute values (members) of the Customer attribute hierarchy in the Customer dimension and the member properties of that Customer attribute hierarchy.

Cube—Model Content

This is a Content query on the Customers model.

Syntax

```
-- Content (select)
select * from [Customers].content
```

Result

MODEL_CATAL...	MODEL_SCHEMA	MODEL_NAME	ATTRIBUTE_N...	NODE_NAME	NODE_UNIQUE...	NODE_TYPE	NODE_GUID	NODE_CAPTION	CHILDREN_CA
Adventure Wor...		Customers		000	000	1		Cluster Model	10
Adventure Wor...		Customers		001	001	5		Cluster 1	0
Adventure Wor...		Customers		002	002	5		Cluster 2	0
Adventure Wor...		Customers		003	003	5		Cluster 3	0
Adventure Wor...		Customers		004	004	5		Cluster 4	0
Adventure Wor...		Customers		005	005	5		Cluster 5	0
Adventure Wor...		Customers		006	006	5		Cluster 6	0
Adventure Wor...		Customers		007	007	5		Cluster 7	0
Adventure Wor...		Customers		008	008	5		Cluster 8	0
Adventure Wor...		Customers		009	009	5		Cluster 9	0
Adventure Wor...		Customers		010	010	5		Cluster 10	0

Analysis

The results from data mining are independent of the nature of the source data. SSAS data mining works equally well with both relational and multidimensional source data. But, if your multidimensional cubes are designed well, multidimensional data sources are often more convenient. Your data is quite possibly a "better fit" to your structure cases. Presumably, cube data has gone through a lengthy ETL (extract, transform, load) procedure. It's clean, consistent, and often in a structure that maps directly onto the structure of your structure cases. Relational sources often involve lots of inner joins, resulting in fairly complex relational views.

The demographics for each cluster here are in the NODE_DISTRIBUTION nested table column.

Cube—Model Prediction

This is a Prediction query (using Cluster() rather than Predict()) on the Customers model. The model was trained using French customers. The clusters are based on the characteristics of French customers only. Let's see how our German customers fit into those clusters. The language for the query to look at new German customers is MDX. The Where slicer clause points to Germany.

Syntax

```
-- Predict (select) - Germany
select
MDX.[[Measures]].[Customer Name]]], Cluster()
from
[Customers]
prediction join
(
with
```

```
member [Measures].[Commute Distance] as
[Customer].[Customer].Properties("Commute Distance")
member [Measures].[Customer Key] as
[Customer].[Customer].currentmember.member_key
member [Measures].[Customer Name] as
[Customer].[Customer].currentmember.member_name
member [Measures].[Education] as
[Customer].[Customer].Properties("Education")
member [Measures].[Gender] as [Customer].[Customer].Properties("Gender")
member [Measures].[House Owner Flag] as
[Customer].[Customer].Properties("Home Owner")
member [Measures].[Marital Status] as
[Customer].[Customer].Properties("Marital Status")
select
{[Measures].[Commute Distance],[Measures].[Customer Key],
[Measures].[Education],[Measures].[Gender],
[Measures].[House Owner Flag],[Measures].[Marital Status],
[Measures].[Customer Name]}
on columns,
[Customer].[Customer].[Customer]
on rows
from
[Adventure Works]
where [Customer].[Customer Geography].[Country].[Germany]
) as MDX
on
[Customers].[Commute Distance] = MDX.[[Measures]].[Commute Distance]]]
and
[Customers].[Marital Status] = MDX.[[Measures]].[Marital Status]]]
-- etc
```

Result

[Measures].[Customer Name]	$CLUSTER
Abby A. Garcia	Cluster 6
Abby Arthur	Cluster 1
Abby E. Chandra	Cluster 6
Abby Madan	Cluster 3
Abby Subram	Cluster 4
Abigail H. Russell	Cluster 5
Abigail R. Henderson	Cluster 1
Adam D. Perez	Cluster 5
Adam H. Diaz	Cluster 4
Adrian F. Morris	Cluster 5
Adrian Sanders	Cluster 1
Adriana C. Raman	Cluster 4
Adriana Chandra	Cluster 5
Adriana J. Arthur	Cluster 4
Adriana Kapoor	Cluster 6
Adriana L. Patel	Cluster 1
Adriana Madan	Cluster 6
Adriana Mehta	Cluster 6
Adriana Rodriguez	Cluster 1

Analysis

The German customer Abby A. Garcia is most likely to fit into Cluster 6.

This is a non-singleton (batch) prediction join. It's not a natural prediction join. If you are sure the column (attribute) names are identical, then a natural prediction join is better. Then you can miss the On clause. I've included it here (though all the names match) to show some of the intricacies involved in an On clause that uses MDX rather than SQL. Please notice some of the square brackets have been doubled—and, in two places, the square brackets have been trebled. These are necessary to escape the square brackets.

Now that you have completed this chapter, you might want to delete any structures and models that have been created—this will reset your SSAS Adventure Works to its original form.

Chapter 8

Schema and Column Queries

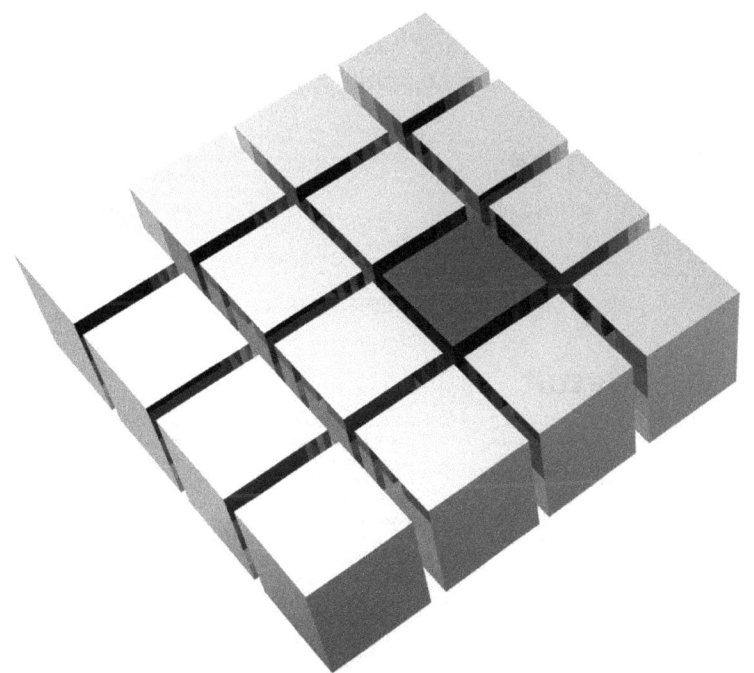

This chapter focuses on two main areas, Schema queries and Column queries. Schema queries are all about *metadata* (data about data). For example, you can list all of the algorithms available, all of your mining structures, all of your mining models, all of your structure or model columns, and more. DMSCHEMA_MINING_SERVICE_PARAMETERS is very useful for showing the various parameters for each algorithm and what they mean. Column queries are used to examine the values (or states) of all your discrete, discretized, and continuous structure columns.

► **Key concepts** Discrete columns, discretized columns, continuous columns, Range() functions, DMSHEMA_MINING schema tables

► **Keywords** Distinct, RangeMax(), RangeMid(), RangeMin(), DMSCHEMA_MINING_SERVICES, DMSCHEMA_MINING_SERVICE_PARAMETERS, DMSCHEMA_MINING_MODELS, DMSCHEMA_MINING_COLUMNS, DMSCHEMA_MINING_MODEL_CONTENT, DMSCHEMA_MINING_FUNCTIONS, DMSCHEMA_MINING_STRUCTURES, DMSCHEMA_MINING_STRUCTURE_COLUMNS, DMSCHEMA_MINING_MODEL_XML, DMSCHEMA_MINING_MODEL_PMML

DMSCHEMA_MINING_SERVICES 1/2

Queries that return metadata are often called Schema queries. This one examines the mining services (algorithms) available to you.

Syntax

```
-- schemas
-- mining services
select *
from $system.DMSCHEMA_MINING_SERVICES
```

Result

SERVICE_NAME	SE...	SERVICE_DISPLAY_NAME	SE...	DESCRIPTION
Microsoft_Association_Rules	1	Microsoft Association Rules	8e...	The Microsoft Association Rules algorithm builds rules describing which items are most likely to be appear together...
Microsoft_Clustering	2	Microsoft Clustering	fe8...	The Microsoft Clustering algorithm uses iterative techniques to group records from a dataset into clusters containin...
Microsoft_Decision_Trees	1	Microsoft Decision Trees	f39...	The Microsoft Decision Trees algorithm is a classification algorithm that works well for predictive modeling. The alg...
Microsoft_Naive_Bayes	1	Microsoft Naive Bayes	e8...	The Microsoft Naive Bayes algorithm is a classification algorithm that is quick to build, and works well for predictiv...
Microsoft_Neural_Network	1	Microsoft Neural Network	07...	The Microsoft Neural Network algorithm uses a gradient method to optimize parameters of multilayer networks to pr...
Microsoft_Sequence_Clustering	18	Microsoft Sequence Clustering	02f...	The Microsoft Sequence Clustering algorithm is a combination of sequence analysis and clustering, which identifie...
Microsoft_Time_Series	17	Microsoft Time Series	d5...	The Microsoft Time Series algorithm uses a combination of ARIMA analysis and linear regression based on decisio...
Microsoft_Linear_Regression	1	Microsoft Linear Regression	4e...	The Microsoft Linear Regression algorithm is a regression algorithm that works well for regression modeling. This al...
Microsoft_Logistic_Regression	1	Microsoft Logistic Regression	2a...	The Microsoft Logistic Regression algorithm is a regression algorithm that works well for regression modeling. This ...

Analysis

The schema we are looking at is DMSCHEMA_MINING_SERVICES. It's preceded by the $System namespace. It returns a list of all the data mining algorithms supplied by Microsoft with SSAS. You should have nine of them. In fact, there are really only seven! Linear Regression is a variant of Decision Trees, and Logistic Regression is a variant of Neural Networks.

DMSCHEMA_MINING_SERVICES 2/2

Here we've specified just a few columns—possibly the most interesting columns.

Syntax

```
-- interesting columns
select service_name, [description], supported_input_content_types,
supported_prediction_content_types
from $system.DMSCHEMA_MINING_SERVICES
```

Result

service_name	description	supported_input_content_types
Microsoft_Asso...	The Microsoft Association Rules algorithm builds rules describing which items are most likely to be appe...	Cyclical,Discrete,Discretized,Key,Table,Ordered
Microsoft_Clust...	The Microsoft Clustering algorithm uses iterative techniques to group records from a dataset into clusters...	Continuous,Cyclical,Discrete,Discretized,Key,Table,Ordered
Microsoft_Decis...	The Microsoft Decision Trees algorithm is a classification algorithm that works well for predictive modelin...	Continuous,Cyclical,Discrete,Discretized,Key,Table,Ordered
Microsoft_Naive...	The Microsoft Naive Bayes algorithm is a classification algorithm that is quick to build, and works well for...	Cyclical,Discrete,Discretized,Key,Table,Ordered
Microsoft_Neur...	The Microsoft Neural Network algorithm uses a gradient method to optimize parameters of multilayer net...	Continuous,Cyclical,Discrete,Discretized,Key,Table,Ordered
Microsoft_Sequ...	The Microsoft Sequence Clustering algorithm is a combination of sequence analysis and clustering, whi...	Continuous,Cyclical,Discrete,Discretized,Key,Key Sequence,Table,Ordered
Microsoft_Time...	The Microsoft Time Series algorithm uses a combination of ARIMA analysis and linear regression based ...	Continuous,Key,Key Time,Table
Microsoft_Linea...	The Microsoft Linear Regression algorithm is a regression algorithm that works well for regression modeli...	Continuous,Cyclical,Key,Table,Ordered
Microsoft_Logist...	The Microsoft Logistic Regression algorithm is a regression algorithm that works well for regression mode...	Continuous,Cyclical,Discrete,Discretized,Key,Table,Ordered

Analysis

The Description column explains the purpose of each algorithm—you may have to widen the column to view its contents. Or you could right-click, choose Copy, and then paste into Notepad to make viewing easier. The Supported_Input_Content_Types column might prove useful. For example, you can see that the Naïve Bayes algorithm does not support inputs with continuous data.

DMSCHEMA_MINING_SERVICE_PARAMETERS 1/2

This is a query that lists every single algorithm parameter for every algorithm. Many of these parameters are advanced settings and often (but not always) function best with their default values. If you are interested in detailed explanations, you are referred to SQL Server Books Online (BOL).

Syntax

```
-- mining service parameters
select *
from $system.DMSCHEMA_MINING_SERVICE_PARAMETERS
```

Result

SERVICE_NAME	PARAMETER_NAME	PARAMETER_T...	IS_REQUIRED	PARAMETER_F...	DESCRIPTION	DEFAULT_VAL.
Microsoft_Association_Rules	MAXIMUM_ITEMSET_COUNT	DBTYPE_I4	False	1	Specifies the maximum number of items...	200000
Microsoft_Association_Rules	MAXIMUM_ITEMSET_SIZE	DBTYPE_I4	False	1	Specifies the maximum number of items...	3
Microsoft_Association_Rules	MAXIMUM_SUPPORT	DBTYPE_R8	False	1	Specifies the maximum number of cases...	1.0
Microsoft_Association_Rules	MINIMUM_SUPPORT	DBTYPE_R8	False	1	Specifies the minimum number of cases...	0.0
Microsoft_Association_Rules	MINIMUM_IMPORTANCE	DBTYPE_R8	False	1	Specifies the importance threshold for ...	-999999999
Microsoft_Association_Rules	MINIMUM_ITEMSET_SIZE	DBTYPE_I4	False	1	Specifies the minimum number of items ...	1
Microsoft_Association_Rules	MINIMUM_PROBABILITY	DBTYPE_R8	False	1	Specifies the minimum probability that a...	0.4
Microsoft_Clustering	CLUSTER_COUNT	DBTYPE_I4	False	1	Specifies the approximate number of cl...	10
Microsoft_Clustering	CLUSTER_SEED	DBTYPE_I4	False	1	Specifies the seed number used to ran...	0
Microsoft_Clustering	CLUSTERING_METHOD	DBTYPE_I4	False	1	The clustering method the algorithm us...	1
Microsoft_Clustering	MAXIMUM_INPUT_ATTRIBUTES	DBTYPE_I4	False	1	Specifies the maximum number of input...	255
Microsoft_Clustering	MAXIMUM_STATES	DBTYPE_I4	False	1	Specifies the maximum number of attrib...	100
Microsoft_Clustering	MINIMUM_SUPPORT	DBTYPE_I4	False	1	This parameter specifies the minimum n...	1
Microsoft_Clustering	MODELLING_CARDINALITY	DBTYPE_I4	False	1	This parameter specifies the number of ...	10
Microsoft_Clustering	SAMPLE_SIZE	DBTYPE_I4	False	1	Specifies the number of cases that the ...	50000
Microsoft_Clustering	STOPPING_TOLERANCE	DBTYPE_I4	False	1	Specifies the value used to determine ...	10
Microsoft_Decision_Trees	COMPLEXITY_PENALTY	DBTYPE_R8	False	1	Inhibits the growth of the decision tree. ...	
Microsoft_Decision_Trees	MAXIMUM_INPUT_ATTRIBUTES	DBTYPE_I4	False	1	Specifies the maximum number of input...	255

Analysis

Let's examine just one of the many entries. The Clustering algorithm (Microsoft_Clustering) has a PARAMETER_NAME of CLUSTER_COUNT and its DEFAULT_VALUE is 10. This means the algorithm will attempt (as far as possible) to divide your data into ten clusters.

DMSCHEMA_MINING_SERVICE_PARAMETERS 2/2

This is the previous query with a few interesting columns specified.

Syntax

```
-- interesting columns
select service_name, parameter_name, [description]
from $system.DMSCHEMA_MINING_SERVICE_PARAMETERS
```

Result

service_name	parameter_name	description
Microsoft_Association_Rules	MAXIMUM_ITEMSET_COUNT	Specifies the maximum number of itemsets to produce. If no number is specified, the algorithm generates all possible itemsets.
Microsoft_Association_Rules	MAXIMUM_ITEMSET_SIZE	Specifies the maximum number of items allowed in an itemset. Setting this value to 0 specifies that there is no limit to the size of the
Microsoft_Association_Rules	MAXIMUM_SUPPORT	Specifies the maximum number of cases in which an itemset can have support. If this value is less than one, it represents a percent
Microsoft_Association_Rules	MINIMUM_SUPPORT	Specifies the minimum number of cases that must contain the itemset before generating a rule. Setting this value to less than 1 spec
Microsoft_Association_Rules	MINIMUM_IMPORTANCE	Specifies the importance threshold for association rules. Rules with importance less than this value are filtered out. [Enterprise Editic
Microsoft_Association_Rules	MINIMUM_ITEMSET_SIZE	Specifies the minimum number of items allowed in an itemset. [Enterprise Edition]
Microsoft_Association_Rules	MINIMUM_PROBABILITY	Specifies the minimum probability that a rule is true. For example, setting this value to 0.5 specifies that no rule with less than 50% pr
Microsoft_Clustering	CLUSTER_COUNT	Specifies the approximate number of clusters to be built by the algorithm. If the approximate number of clusters cannot be built from
Microsoft_Clustering	CLUSTER_SEED	Specifies the seed number used to randomly generate clusters for the initial stage of model building. [Enterprise Edition]
Microsoft_Clustering	CLUSTERING_METHOD	The clustering method the algorithm uses can be either: Scalable EM (1), Non-scalable EM (2), Scalable K-means (3), or Non-scalal
Microsoft_Clustering	MAXIMUM_INPUT_ATTRIBUTES	Specifies the maximum number of input attributes that the algorithm can handle before invoking feature selection. Setting this value
Microsoft_Clustering	MAXIMUM_STATES	Specifies the maximum number of attribute states that the algorithm supports. If the number of states that an attribute has is greater t
Microsoft_Clustering	MINIMUM_SUPPORT	This parameter specifies the minimum number of cases in each cluster.
Microsoft_Clustering	MODELLING_CARDINALITY	This parameter specifies the number of sample models constructed during the clustering process.
Microsoft_Clustering	SAMPLE_SIZE	Specifies the number of cases that the algorithm uses on each pass if the CLUSTERING_METHOD parameter is set to one of the s
Microsoft_Clustering	STOPPING_TOLERANCE	Specifies the value used to determine when convergence is reached and the algorithm is finished building the model. Convergence
Microsoft_Decision_Trees	COMPLEXITY_PENALTY	Inhibits the growth of the decision tree. Decreasing the value increases the likelihood of a split, while increasing the value decrease
Microsoft_Decision_Trees	MAXIMUM_INPUT_ATTRIBUTES	Specifies the maximum number of input attributes that the algorithm can handle before invoking feature selection. Setting this value

Analysis

The Description column is probably worth studying. It's a brief synopsis of the information available in SQL Server Books Online (BOL). Please note the square brackets around the column name in the query—these are obligatory as Description is a reserved word.

DMSCHEMA_MINING_MODELS 1/3

This time you'll get a list of all the mining models in the current SSAS database.

Syntax

```
-- mining models
select *
from $system.DMSCHEMA_MINING_MODELS
```

Result

MODEL_CATAL...	MODEL_SCHEMA	MODEL_NAME	MODEL_TYPE	MODEL_GUID	DESCRIPTION	MODEL_PROPID	DATE_CREATED	DATE_MODIFIED	SERV
Adventure Wor...		Customer Clusters		9da76ce2-55ac...			11/08/2009 18:...	11/08/2009 18:...	2
Adventure Wor...		Subcategory Associations		e8f9fff2-8750-4...			11/08/2009 18:...	11/08/2009 18:...	1
Adventure Wor...		Forecasting		05f21b5d-6841-...			11/08/2009 18:...	11/08/2009 18:...	17
Adventure Wor...		DT Model		6d1cf0f9-75d2-...			21/08/2009 20:...	21/08/2009 20:...	1
Adventure Wor...		Association		f8265fe0-b819-...			11/08/2009 18:...	11/08/2009 18:...	1
Adventure Wor...		Customers		90219b77-07e2...			22/08/2009 21:...	22/08/2009 21:...	2
Adventure Wor...		Cross Sell		707965ed-bde4...			22/08/2009 21:...	22/08/2009 21:...	1
Adventure Wor...		Sequence Clustering		e1637f8b-333f-...			11/08/2009 18:...	11/08/2009 18:...	18
Adventure Wor...		TM Clustering		d56ce8c6-c38e...			11/08/2009 18:...	11/08/2009 18:...	2
Adventure Wor...		TM Decision Tree		b4c5aa99-0af2-...			11/08/2009 18:...	11/08/2009 18:...	1
Adventure Wor...		TM Naive Bayes		d3bac7e5-e5e1...			11/08/2009 18:...	11/08/2009 18:...	1
Adventure Wor...		TM Neural Net		5d74146d-5f26-...			11/08/2009 18:...	11/08/2009 18:...	1

Analysis

As a reminder, the current database can easily be changed by using the drop-down on the toolbar.

DMSCHEMA_MINING_MODELS 2/3

Here are some of the more useful columns from the previous query.

Syntax

```
-- interesting columns
select model_name, service_name, is_populated, prediction_entity, mining_
parameters, mining_structure, last_processed
from $system.DMSCHEMA_MINING_MODELS
```

Result

model_name	service_name	is_populated	prediction_entity	mining_parameters	mining_structure	last_processed
Customer Clusters	Microsoft_Clustering	True		CLUSTER_COUNT=10,CLUSTER...	Customer Mining	11/08/2009 18:...
Subcategory Associations	Microsoft_Association_Rules	True	Subcategories	MAXIMUM_ITEMSET_COUNT=20...	Customer Mining	11/08/2009 18:...
Forecasting	Microsoft_Time_Series	True	Amount,Quantity	COMPLEXITY_PENALTY=0.1,MIN...	Forecasting	11/08/2009 18:...
DT Model	Microsoft_Decision_Trees	True	Bike Buyer	COMPLEXITY_PENALTY=0.9,MA...	Mail Structure	21/08/2009 20:...
Association	Microsoft_Association_Rules	True	v Assoc Seq Line Items	MAXIMUM_ITEMSET_COUNT=20...	Market Basket	11/08/2009 18:...
Customers	Microsoft_Clustering	True		CLUSTER_COUNT=10,CLUSTER...	Profiles	22/08/2009 21:...
Cross Sell	Microsoft_Association_Rules	True	Purchases	MAXIMUM_ITEMSET_COUNT=20...	Sales Analysis	22/08/2009 21:...
Sequence Clustering	Microsoft_Sequence_Clustering	True	v Assoc Seq Line Items,v ...	CLUSTER_COUNT=15,MINIMUM...	Sequence Clustering	11/08/2009 18:...
TM Clustering	Microsoft_Clustering	True	Bike Buyer	CLUSTER_COUNT=10,CLUSTER...	Targeted Mailing	11/08/2009 18:...
TM Decision Tree	Microsoft_Decision_Trees	True	Bike Buyer	COMPLEXITY_PENALTY=0.9,MA...	Targeted Mailing	11/08/2009 18:...
TM Naive Bayes	Microsoft_Naive_Bayes	True	Bike Buyer	MAXIMUM_INPUT_ATTRIBUTES...	Targeted Mailing	11/08/2009 18:...
TM Neural Net	Microsoft_Neural_Network	True	Bike Buyer	HOLDOUT_PERCENTAGE=30,HO...	Targeted Mailing	11/08/2009 18:...

Analysis

As well as the mining model name, this query shows the algorithm used and the name of the containing mining structure.

DMSCHEMA_MINING_MODELS 3/3

Now we are narrowing down to examine a single model, TM Decision Tree.

Syntax

```
-- a particular mining model
select service_name, is_populated, prediction_entity, mining_parameters,
mining_structure, last_processed
from $system.DMSCHEMA_MINING_MODELS
where MODEL_NAME = 'TM Decision Tree'
```

Result

service_name	is_populated	prediction_entity	mining_parameters	mining_structure	last_processed
Microsoft_Decision_Trees	True	Bike Buyer	COMPLEXITY_PENALTY=0.9,MAXIMUM_INPUT_ATTRIBUTES=255,MAXIMU...	Targeted Mailing	11/08/2009 18:...

Analysis

The Is_Populated column lets you know that this model has been trained using the parent structure cases. The Prediction_Entity column shows the predictable column (here it's Bike Buyer) of the model.

DMSCHEMA_MINING_COLUMNS 1/3

This time, our query is listing all of the columns in all of our mining models.

Syntax

```
-- mining columns
select *
from $system.DMSCHEMA_MINING_COLUMNS
```

Result

MODEL_CATAL...	MODEL_SCHEMA	MODEL_NAME	COLUMN_NAME	COLUMN_GUID	COLUMN_PRO...	ORDINAL_POSI...	COLUMN_HAS_...	COLUMN_DEFA...
Adventure Wor...		Customer Clusters	Commute Distance			1	False	
Adventure Wor...		Customer Clusters	Customer Counts 1			2	False	
Adventure Wor...		Customer Clusters	Education			3	False	
Adventure Wor...		Customer Clusters	Gender			4	False	
Adventure Wor...		Customer Clusters	Home Owner			5	False	
Adventure Wor...		Customer Clusters	Marital Status			6	False	
Adventure Wor...		Customer Clusters	Number of Cars Owned			7	False	
Adventure Wor...		Customer Clusters	Number of Children At Home			8	False	
Adventure Wor...		Customer Clusters	Occupation			9	False	
Adventure Wor...		Customer Clusters	Total Children			10	False	
Adventure Wor...		Customer Clusters	Yearly Income			11	False	
Adventure Wor...		Subcategory As...	Customer Counts 1			1	False	
Adventure Wor...		Subcategory As...	Subcategories			2	False	
Adventure Wor...		Subcategory As...	Subcategory			3	False	
Adventure Wor...		Forecasting	Amount			1	False	
Adventure Wor...		Forecasting	Model Region			2	False	
Adventure Wor...		Forecasting	Quantity			3	False	
Adventure Wor...		Forecasting	Time Index			4	False	

Analysis

These are the mining model columns. If two models belong to the same structure and both use the same structure column, the column will appear twice. For example, the Bike Buyer column is shown for both TM Decision Tree and TM Naïve Bayes models—both models belong to the Targeted Mailing structure.

DMSCHEMA_MINING_COLUMNS 2/3

Here's a look at some of the columns from the last query.

Syntax

```
-- interesting columns
select model_name, column_name, content_type, is_input, is_predictable,
prediction_scalar_functions, prediction_table_functions
from $system.DMSCHEMA_MINING_COLUMNS
```

Result

model_name	column_name	content_type	is_input	is_predictable	prediction_scalar...	prediction_table_...
Customer Clusters	Commute Distance	DISCRETE	True	False		
Customer Clusters	Customer Counts 1	KEY	True	False		
Customer Clusters	Education	DISCRETE	True	False		
Customer Clusters	Gender	DISCRETE	True	False		
Customer Clusters	Home Owner	DISCRETE	True	False		
Customer Clusters	Marital Status	DISCRETE	True	False		
Customer Clusters	Number of Cars Owned	CONTINUOUS	True	False		
Customer Clusters	Number of Children At Home	CONTINUOUS	True	False		
Customer Clusters	Occupation	DISCRETE	True	False		
Customer Clusters	Total Children	CONTINUOUS	True	False		
Customer Clusters	Yearly Income	DISCRETIZED()	True	False	RangeMax,Ran...	
Subcategory Associations	Customer Counts 1	KEY	True	False		
Subcategory Associations	Subcategories		True	True		BottomCount,Bo...
Subcategory Associations	Subcategory	KEY	True	False		
Forecasting	Amount	CONTINUOUS	True	True	Predict,PredictA...	PredictHistogram
Forecasting	Model Region	KEY	True	False		
Forecasting	Quantity	CONTINUOUS	True	True	Predict,PredictA...	PredictHistogram
Forecasting	Time Index	KEY TIME	False	False		
DT Model	Age	DISCRETIZED(...	True	False	RangeMax,Ran...	

Analysis

Three columns particularly worth noting are Content_Type, Is_Input, and Is_Predictable.

DMSCHEMA_MINING_COLUMNS 3/3

Our query here concentrates on the columns of just one mining model.

Syntax

```
-- a particular mining model
select column_name, content_type, is_input, is_predictable, prediction_
```

```
scalar_functions, prediction_table_functions
from $system.DMSCHEMA_MINING_COLUMNS
where MODEL_NAME = 'TM Decision Tree'
```

Result

column_name	content_type	is_input	is_predictable	prediction_scalar...	prediction_table_...
Age	DISCRETIZED(AUTOMATIC,10)	True	False	RangeMax,Ran...	
Bike Buyer	DISCRETE	True	True	Predict,PredictA...	PredictHistogram
Commute Distance	DISCRETE	True	False		
Customer Key	KEY	True	False		
Education	DISCRETE	True	False		
Gender	DISCRETE	True	False		
House Owner Flag	DISCRETE	True	False		
Marital Status	DISCRETE	True	False		
Number Cars Owned	DISCRETE	True	False		
Number Children At Home	DISCRETE	True	False		
Occupation	DISCRETE	True	False		
Region	DISCRETE	True	False		
Total Children	DISCRETE	True	False		
Yearly Income	CONTINUOUS	True	False		

Analysis

A query like this can return lots of helpful information. It's probably quicker than opening BIDS and searching windows and tabs and property windows! Age is a discretized column, Occupation is discrete, Customer Key is the key, and Yearly Income is continuous. You can also see that Bike Buyer is a predictable column.

DMSCHEMA_MINING_MODEL_CONTENT 1/5

This is another Schema query, but it's asking for content.

Syntax

```
-- mining model content
select *
from $system.DMSCHEMA_MINING_MODEL_CONTENT
```

Result

MODEL_CATAL...	MODEL_SCHEMA	MODEL_NAME	ATTRIBUTE_N...	NODE_NAME	NODE_UNIQUE...	NODE_TYPE	NODE_GUID	NODE_CAPTION	CHILDREN_
Adventure Wor...		Customer Clusters		000	000	1		Cluster Model	10
Adventure Wor...		Customer Clusters		001	001	5		Cluster 1	0
Adventure Wor...		Customer Clusters		002	002	5		Cluster 2	0
Adventure Wor...		Customer Clusters		003	003	5		Non Graduates	0
Adventure Wor...		Customer Clusters		004	004	5		Cluster 4	0
Adventure Wor...		Customer Clusters		005	005	5		Cluster 5	0
Adventure Wor...		Customer Clusters		006	006	5		Graduates	0
Adventure Wor...		Customer Clusters		007	007	5		Cluster 7	0
Adventure Wor...		Customer Clusters		008	008	5		Cluster 8	0
Adventure Wor...		Customer Clusters		009	009	5		Cluster 9	0
Adventure Wor...		Customer Clusters		010	010	5		Cluster 10	0
Adventure Wor...		Subcategory As...		0	0	1		Association Rul...	661
Adventure Wor...		Subcategory As...		17	17	7		Tires and Tubes...	0
Adventure Wor...		Subcategory As...		16	16	7		Road Bikes = E...	0
Adventure Wor...		Subcategory As...		15	15	7		Helmets = Existing	0
Adventure Wor...		Subcategory As...		14	14	7		Bottles and Cag...	0
Adventure Wor...		Subcategory As...		13	13	7		Mountain Bikes ...	0
Adventure Wor...		Subcategory As...		12	12	7		Jerseys = Existing	0

Analysis

In effect, you have a Content query—or rather, you have a Content query for every single model. The result set can get quite large.

DMSCHEMA_MINING_MODEL_CONTENT 2/5

We have narrowed it down to three columns.

Syntax

```
-- interesting columns
select model_name, node_description, node_distribution
from $system.DMSCHEMA_MINING_MODEL_CONTENT
```

Result

model_name	node_description	node_distribution
Customer Clusters	All	⊞ node_distribution
Customer Clusters	Number of Cars Owned =0 , Education=Graduate Degree , Number of Children At Home =0 , Commute Distance=0-1 Miles , Occupation...	⊞ node_distribution
Customer Clusters	0 <=Number of Children At Home <=3 , Yearly Income=40000 - 70000 , 0 <=Number of Cars Owned <=3 , Education=Bachelors , Occu...	⊞ node_distribution
Customer Clusters	Number of Cars Owned =2 , Commute Distance=5-10 Miles , Education=High School , Number of Children At Home =0 , Occupation=S...	⊞ node_distribution
Customer Clusters	0 <=Number of Children At Home <=1 , Occupation=Manual , Yearly Income=10000 - 30000 , 0 <=Total Children <=2 , 0 <=Number of C...	⊞ node_distribution
Customer Clusters	Occupation=Management , Number of Children At Home =0 , Yearly Income=80000 - 90000 , Commute Distance=10+ Miles , Education...	⊞ node_distribution
Customer Clusters	Yearly Income=130000 - 170000 , Yearly Income=100000 - 120000 , Occupation=Management , 1 <=Number of Children At Home <=5 ...	⊞ node_distribution
Customer Clusters	Number of Cars Owned =1 , Yearly Income=40000 - 70000 , Number of Children At Home =0 , 0 <=Total Children <=2 , Education=Parti...	⊞ node_distribution
Customer Clusters	Yearly Income=10000 - 30000 , Occupation=Manual , Education=Partial High School , 0 <=Number of Children At Home <=4 , Commute...	⊞ node_distribution
Customer Clusters	Yearly Income=80000 - 90000 , Total Children >5 , 0 <=Number of Children At Home <=5 , Occupation=Professional , 0 <=Number of Ca...	⊞ node_distribution
Customer Clusters	4 <=Total Children <=5 , 4 <=Number of Children At Home <=5 , Occupation=Professional , 1 <=Number of Cars Owned <=4 , Commute ...	⊞ node_distribution
Subcategory Associations	Association Rules Model; ITEMSET_COUNT=457; RULE_COUNT=204; MIN_SUPPORT=18; MAX_SUPPORT=8490; MIN_ITEMSET...	⊞ node_distribution
Subcategory Associations	Tires and Tubes = Existing	⊞ node_distribution
Subcategory Associations	Road Bikes = Existing	⊞ node_distribution
Subcategory Associations	Helmets = Existing	⊞ node_distribution
Subcategory Associations	Bottles and Cages = Existing	⊞ node_distribution
Subcategory Associations	Mountain Bikes = Existing	⊞ node_distribution
Subcategory Associations	Jerseys = Existing	⊞ node_distribution

Analysis

NODE_DISTRIBUTION is a nested table, which you can expand.

DMSCHEMA_MINING_MODEL_CONTENT 3/5

The key word Flattened is used to "flatten" the nested table.

Syntax

```
-- interesting columns flattened
select flattened model_name, node_description, node_distribution
from $system.DMSCHEMA_MINING_MODEL_CONTENT
```

Result

model_name	node_description	node_distribution.ATTRIBUTE_NAME	node_distribution.ATTRIBUTE_VALUE	node_distribution...	node_distribution...	node_distribution...	node_d
Customer Clusters	All	Commute Distance	Missing	0	0	0	1
Customer Clusters	All	Commute Distance	10+ Miles	2494	0.13492750486...	0	4
Customer Clusters	All	Commute Distance	0-1 Miles	6310	0.34137632547...	0	4
Customer Clusters	All	Commute Distance	2-5 Miles	3234	0.17496212940...	0	4
Customer Clusters	All	Commute Distance	5-10 Miles	3214	0.17388011252...	0	4
Customer Clusters	All	Commute Distance	1-2 Miles	3232	0.17485392772...	0	4
Customer Clusters	All	Education	Missing	0	0	0	1
Customer Clusters	All	Education	Partial High School	1581	0.08553343432...	0	4
Customer Clusters	All	Education	High School	3294	0.17820818004...	0	4
Customer Clusters	All	Education	Bachelors	5356	0.28976412032...	0	4
Customer Clusters	All	Education	Graduate Degree	3189	0.17252759143...	0	4
Customer Clusters	All	Education	Partial College	5064	0.27396667388...	0	4
Customer Clusters	All	Gender	Missing	0	0	0	1
Customer Clusters	All	Gender	Female	9133	0.49410300800...	0	4
Customer Clusters	All	Gender	Male	9351	0.50589699199...	0	4
Customer Clusters	All	Home Owner	Missing	0	0	0	1
Customer Clusters	All	Home Owner	No	5982	0.32363124864...	0	4
Customer Clusters	All	Home Owner	Yes	12502	0.67636875135...	0	4

Analysis

This is going to give even more rows.

DMSCHEMA_MINING_MODEL_CONTENT 4/5

This time, we've introduced a subquery to select only a few columns from the now flattened NODE_DISTRIBUTION nested table.

Syntax

```
-- specific columns in sub query
select flattened model_name, node_description, (select [attribute_name],
[attribute_value], [Probability] from node_distribution)
from $system.DMSCHEMA_MINING_MODEL_CONTENT
```

Result

model_name	node_description	Expression.attribute_name	Expression.attribute_value	Expression.Probability
Customer Clusters	All	Commute Distance	Missing	0
Customer Clusters	All	Commute Distance	10+ Miles	0.134927504869076
Customer Clusters	All	Commute Distance	0-1 Miles	0.341376325470677
Customer Clusters	All	Commute Distance	2-5 Miles	0.174962129409219
Customer Clusters	All	Commute Distance	5-10 Miles	0.173880112529755
Customer Clusters	All	Commute Distance	1-2 Miles	0.174853927721272
Customer Clusters	All	Education	Missing	0
Customer Clusters	All	Education	Partial High School	0.0855334343215754
Customer Clusters	All	Education	High School	0.178208180047609
Customer Clusters	All	Education	Bachelors	0.289764120320277
Customer Clusters	All	Education	Graduate Degree	0.172527591430426
Customer Clusters	All	Education	Partial College	0.273966673880113
Customer Clusters	All	Gender	Missing	0
Customer Clusters	All	Gender	Female	0.494103008006925
Customer Clusters	All	Gender	Male	0.505896991993075
Customer Clusters	All	Home Owner	Missing	0
Customer Clusters	All	Home Owner	No	0.323631248647479
Customer Clusters	All	Home Owner	Yes	0.676368751352521
Customer Clusters	All	Marital Status	Missing	0

Analysis

There are probably far too many rows in the result. The next query presents a subset.

DMSCHEMA_MINING_MODEL_CONTENT 5/5

Note the addition of a Where clause. This is a Schema query on the model content of one model.

Syntax

```
-- a particular mining model
select flattened model_name, node_description, (select [attribute_name],
[attribute_value], [Probability] from node_distribution)
from $system.DMSCHEMA_MINING_MODEL_CONTENT
where model_name = 'TM Naive Bayes' and node_type = 11
```

Result

model_name	node_description	Expression.attribute_name	Expression.attribute_value	Expression.Probability
TM Naive Bayes	Bike Buyer -> Age = Missing	Bike Buyer	Missing	0
TM Naive Bayes	Bike Buyer -> Age = Missing	Bike Buyer	0	0
TM Naive Bayes	Bike Buyer -> Age = Missing	Bike Buyer	1	0
TM Naive Bayes	Bike Buyer -> Age < 36	Bike Buyer	Missing	0
TM Naive Bayes	Bike Buyer -> Age < 36	Bike Buyer	0	0.587899159663866
TM Naive Bayes	Bike Buyer -> Age < 36	Bike Buyer	1	0.412100840336134
TM Naive Bayes	Bike Buyer -> Age = 36 - 41	Bike Buyer	Missing	0
TM Naive Bayes	Bike Buyer -> Age = 36 - 41	Bike Buyer	0	0.352159468438538
TM Naive Bayes	Bike Buyer -> Age = 36 - 41	Bike Buyer	1	0.647840531561462
TM Naive Bayes	Bike Buyer -> Age = 41 - 48	Bike Buyer	Missing	0
TM Naive Bayes	Bike Buyer -> Age = 41 - 48	Bike Buyer	0	0.466772510773418
TM Naive Bayes	Bike Buyer -> Age = 41 - 48	Bike Buyer	1	0.533227489226582
TM Naive Bayes	Bike Buyer -> Age = 48 - 53	Bike Buyer	Missing	0
TM Naive Bayes	Bike Buyer -> Age = 48 - 53	Bike Buyer	0	0.49055148476668
TM Naive Bayes	Bike Buyer -> Age = 48 - 53	Bike Buyer	1	0.50944851523332
TM Naive Bayes	Bike Buyer -> Age = 53 - 59	Bike Buyer	Missing	0
TM Naive Bayes	Bike Buyer -> Age = 53 - 59	Bike Buyer	0	0.500853242320819
TM Naive Bayes	Bike Buyer -> Age = 53 - 59	Bike Buyer	1	0.499146757679181
TM Naive Bayes	Bike Buyer -> Age = 59 - 64	Bike Buyer	Missing	0

Analysis

In fact, this Schema query is pretty similar to a Content query. Naïve Bayes is a good way to extract information quickly and easily. For example, those customers aged from 36 to 41 are 64 percent likely to buy a bike. If you worked through Chapter 2 on Content queries, then you could have used a Content query directly:

```
select flattened model_name, node_description, (select [attribute_name],
[attribute_value], [Probability] from node_distribution)
from [TM Naive Bayes].content
where node_type = 11
```

DMSCHEMA_MINING_FUNCTIONS 1/3

Our query here is going to list the main DMX functions. Many of these functions have been used throughout this book in Cases, Content, and Predict queries.

Syntax

```
-- mining functions
select *
from $system.DMSCHEMA_MINING_FUNCTIONS
```

Result

SERVICE_NAME	FUNCTION_NAME	FUNCTION_SIGNATURE	RETURNS_TAB...	DESCRIPTION
Microsoft_Association_Rules	IsInNode	IsInNode(<node id>)	False	The IsInNode fu...
Microsoft_Association_Rules	Predict	Predict(<Scalar column reference>[, EXCLUDE_NULL|INCLUDE_NULL][, INCLUDE_NO...	False	The ScalarPredi...
Microsoft_Association_Rules	Predict	Predict(<Table column reference> [, INCLUSIVE|EXCLUSIVE|INPUT_ONLY][, INCLUDE...	True	The TablePredi...
Microsoft_Association_Rules	PredictAdjustedProbability	PredictAdjustedProbability(<Scalar column reference> [, EXCLUDE_NULL|INCLUDE_NU...	False	The PredictAdju...
Microsoft_Association_Rules	PredictAssociation	PredictAssociation(<Table column reference> [, INCLUSIVE|EXCLUSIVE|INPUT_ONLY][...	True	The PredictAss...
Microsoft_Association_Rules	PredictHistogram	PredictHistogram(<Scalar column reference>)	True	The PredictHist...
Microsoft_Association_Rules	PredictNodeId	PredictNodeId(<Scalar column reference>)	False	The PredictNod...
Microsoft_Association_Rules	PredictProbability	PredictProbability(<Scalar column reference> [, EXCLUDE_NULL|INCLUDE_NULL][<valu...	False	The PredictProb...
Microsoft_Association_Rules	PredictSupport	PredictSupport(<Scalar column reference>[, EXCLUDE_NULL|INCLUDE_NULL[<value>]])	False	The PredictSup...
Microsoft_Association_Rules	$AdjustedProbability	$AdjustedProbability	False	$AdjustedProba...
Microsoft_Association_Rules	$NodeId	$NodeId	False	$NodeId is a sel...
Microsoft_Association_Rules	$Probability	$Probability	False	$Probability is a ...
Microsoft_Association_Rules	$Support	$Support	False	$Support is a se...
Microsoft_Association_Rules	BottomCount	BottomCount(<Table expression>, <Rank column reference>, <n-items>)	True	The BottomCou...
Microsoft_Association_Rules	BottomPercent	BottomPercent(<Table expression>, <Rank column reference>, <percentage>)	True	The BottomPerc...
Microsoft_Association_Rules	BottomSum	BottomSum(<Table expression>, <Rank column reference>, <sum>)	True	The BottomSum...
Microsoft_Association_Rules	IsDescendent	IsDescendent(<node id>)	False	The IsDescend...
Microsoft_Association_Rules	RangeMax	RangeMax(<Scalar column reference>)	False	The RangeMax ...

Analysis

Not all algorithms support the same set of functions. Some functions, like Predict(), are generic and apply to all algorithms. Some, like Cluster, are specific to particular algorithms only—in this case, to Clustering and Sequence Clustering only.

DMSCHEMA_MINING_FUNCTIONS 2/3

This time, we are asking for a few columns only.

Syntax

```
-- interesting columns
select service_name, function_name, function_signature, returns_table,
[description]
from $system.DMSCHEMA_MINING_FUNCTIONS
```

Result

service_name	function_name	function_signature	returns_table	description
Microsoft_Association_Rules	IsInNode	IsInNode(<node...	False	The IsInNode function returns a value of true if the input case is considered in the specified node.
Microsoft_Association_Rules	Predict	Predict(<Scalar ...	False	The ScalarPredict function returns the most likely value for the specified column.
Microsoft_Association_Rules	Predict	Predict(<Table ...	True	The TablePredict function returns the most likely set of values for the specified column.
Microsoft_Association_Rules	PredictAdjusted...	PredictAdjusted...	False	The PredictAdjustedProbability function returns the adjusted probability value for either the most likel...
Microsoft_Association_Rules	PredictAssociati...	PredictAssociati...	True	The PredictAssociation function returns a set of rows that are associated with the input case.
Microsoft_Association_Rules	PredictHistogram	PredictHistogra...	True	The PredictHistogram function returns a table that contains the statistics for all states of a predictabl...
Microsoft_Association_Rules	PredictNodeId	PredictNodeId(<...	False	The PredictNodeId function returns a node ID that the algorithm uses in performing a prediction.
Microsoft_Association_Rules	PredictProbability	PredictProbabilit...	False	The PredictProbability function returns the probability value for either the most likely or specified val...
Microsoft_Association_Rules	PredictSupport	PredictSupport(...	False	The PredictSupport function returns the support value for either the most likely value or the specified...
Microsoft_Association_Rules	$AdjustedProba...	$AdjustedProba...	False	$AdjustedProbability is a selectable column from PredictHistogram or Predict(...,INCLUDE_STATIST...
Microsoft_Association_Rules	$NodeId	$NodeId	False	$NodeId is a selectable column from PredictHistogram or Predict(...,INCLUDE_STATISTICS).
Microsoft_Association_Rules	$Probability	$Probability	False	$Probability is a selectable column from PredictHistogram or Predict(...,INCLUDE_STATISTICS).
Microsoft_Association_Rules	$Support	$Support	False	$Support is a selectable column from PredictHistogram or Predict(...,INCLUDE_STATISTICS).
Microsoft_Association_Rules	BottomCount	BottomCount(<T...	True	The BottomCount function returns the last n-item rows of the table expression, ordered in ascending ...
Microsoft_Association_Rules	BottomPercent	BottomPercent(...	True	The BottomPercent function returns the smallest number of rows in increasing order such that the su...
Microsoft_Association_Rules	BottomSum	BottomSum(<Ta...	True	The BottomSum function returns the smallest number of rows in increasing order such that the sum o...
Microsoft_Association_Rules	IsDescendent	IsDescendent(<...	False	The IsDescendent function returns a value of true if the input case is considered to be a descendan...
Microsoft_Association_Rules	RangeMax	RangeMax(<Sc...	False	The RangeMax function returns either the upper bound of a continuous column or the specified buc...

Analysis

The Description column is very helpful. For example, take a look at the PredictTimeSeries() function for the Time Series algorithm (Microsoft_Time_Series)—you may have to scroll down a fair way to see it.

DMSCHEMA_MINING_FUNCTIONS 3/3

This is exactly the same query with the addition of a Where clause specifying a particular algorithm.

Syntax

```
-- a particular service/algorithm
select function_name, function_signature, returns_table, [description]
from $system.DMSCHEMA_MINING_FUNCTIONS
where service_name = 'microsoft_neural_network'
```

Result

function_name	function_signature	returns_table	description
Predict	Predict(<Scalar ...	False	The ScalarPredict function returns the most likely value for the specified column.
PredictAdjustedProbability	PredictAdjusted...	False	The PredictAdjustedProbability function returns the adjusted probability value for either the most likely or specified value.
PredictHistogram	PredictHistogra...	True	The PredictHistogram function returns a table that contains the statistics for all states of a predictable column. The table contains t...
PredictProbability	PredictProbabilit...	False	The PredictProbability function returns the probability value for either the most likely or specified value.
PredictStdev	PredictStdev(<S...	False	The PredictStdev function returns the standard deviation value of the specified column.
PredictSupport	PredictSupport(...	False	The PredictSupport function returns the support value for either the most likely value or the specified value.
PredictVariance	PredictVariance...	False	The PredictVariance function returns the variance value of the specified column.
$AdjustedProbability	$AdjustedProba...	False	$AdjustedProbability is a selectable column from PredictHistogram or Predict(...,INCLUDE_STATISTICS).
$NodeId	$NodeId	False	$NodeId is a selectable column from PredictHistogram or Predict(...,INCLUDE_STATISTICS).
$Probability	$Probability	False	$Probability is a selectable column from PredictHistogram or Predict(...,INCLUDE_STATISTICS).
$Stdev	$Stdev	False	$Stdev is a selectable column from PredictHistogram or Predict(...,INCLUDE_STATISTICS).
$Support	$Support	False	$Support is a selectable column from PredictHistogram or Predict(...,INCLUDE_STATISTICS).
$Variance	$Variance	False	$Variance is a selectable column from PredictHistogram or Predict(...,INCLUDE_STATISTICS).
BottomCount	BottomCount(<T...	True	The BottomCount function returns the last n-item rows of the table expression, ordered in ascending order by the rank expression.
BottomPercent	BottomPercent(...	True	The BottomPercent function returns the smallest number of rows in increasing order such that the sum of the rank expression valu...
BottomSum	BottomSum(<Ta...	True	The BottomSum function returns the smallest number of rows in increasing order such that the sum of the rank expression values i...
IsDescendent	IsDescendent(<...	False	The IsDescendant function returns a value of true if the input case is considered to be a descendent of the specified node.
RangeMax	RangeMax(<Sc...	False	The RangeMax function returns either the upper bound of a continuous column or the specified bucket of a discretized column.

Analysis

The result shows only those functions that apply to the Neural Networks algorithm (microsoft_neural_network).

DMSCHEMA_MINING_STRUCTURES 1/2

Maybe you would like a quick list of the mining structures in the current database.

Syntax

```
-- mining structures
select *
from $system.DMSCHEMA_MINING_STRUCTURES
```

Result

STRUCTURE_CATALOG	STRUCTURE_S...	STRUCTURE_NAME	STRUCTURE_...	DESCRIPTION	STRUCTURE_P...	DATE_CREATED	DATE_MODIFIED	CREATION_
Adventure Works DW 2008		Customer Mining	8e56c3be-1f02-...			11/08/2009 18:...	11/08/2009 18:...	
Adventure Works DW 2008		Forecasting	f942ca75-5c48-...			11/08/2009 18:...	11/08/2009 18:...	
Adventure Works DW 2008		Mail Structure	ddd5ecae-1f37-...			21/08/2009 20:...	21/08/2009 20:...	
Adventure Works DW 2008		Market Basket	7336e50e-cc78...			11/08/2009 18:...	11/08/2009 18:...	
Adventure Works DW 2008		Profiles	fb1f03f6-41d3-4...			22/08/2009 21:...	22/08/2009 21:...	
Adventure Works DW 2008		Sales Analysis	1cd1771f-aae0-...			22/08/2009 21:...	22/08/2009 21:...	
Adventure Works DW 2008		Sequence Clustering	a6ffc6fc-b7ce-4...			11/08/2009 18:...	11/08/2009 18:...	
Adventure Works DW 2008		Targeted Mailing	bc261743-eeb4...			11/08/2009 18:...	11/08/2009 18:...	

Analysis

Your result may differ from the one shown here. My result includes the five structures provided by Microsoft for Adventure Works. The others in my list are Mail Structure, Profiles, and Sales Analysis. If you worked all the way through the last chapter on structure and model creation, you may have these (unless you cleaned up as mentioned)—otherwise, they won't appear in your list.

DMSCHEMA_MINING_STRUCTURES 2/2

Here's a subset of the available columns from the last query.

Syntax

```
-- interesting columns
select structure_name, is_populated, last_processed, holdout_actual_size
from $system.DMSCHEMA_MINING_STRUCTURES
```

Result

structure_name	is_populated	last_processed	holdout_actual_size
Customer Mining	True	11/08/2009 18:11:19	0
Forecasting	True	11/08/2009 18:09:22	0
Mail Structure	True	21/08/2009 20:33:21	0
Market Basket	True	11/08/2009 18:09:58	0
Profiles	True	22/08/2009 21:18:09	0
Sales Analysis	True	22/08/2009 21:07:49	0
Sequence Clustering	True	11/08/2009 18:09:40	0
Targeted Mailing	True	11/08/2009 18:10:18	0

Analysis

Last_Processed could be an interesting column. Maybe you last processed the structure and populated the cases (and therefore last trained the enclosed models) some time ago—and you've gathered lots of fresh data since then!

DMSCHEMA_MINING_STRUCTURE_COLUMNS 1/3

This query uses DMSCHEMA_MINING_STRUCTURE_COLUMNS and not DMSCHEMA_MINING_COLUMNS (this was in an earlier query).

Syntax

```
-- mining structure columns
select *
from $system.DMSCHEMA_MINING_STRUCTURE_COLUMNS
```

Result

STRUCTURE_C...	STRUCTURE_S...	STRUCTURE_NAME	COLUMN_NAME	COLUMN_GUID	COLUMN_PRO...	ORDINAL_POSI...	COLUMN_HAS...	COLUMN_D
Adventure Wor...		Customer Mining	Commute Distance			1	False	
Adventure Wor...		Customer Mining	Customer Counts			2	False	
Adventure Wor...		Customer Mining	Education			3	False	
Adventure Wor...		Customer Mining	Gender			4	False	
Adventure Wor...		Customer Mining	Home Owner			5	False	
Adventure Wor...		Customer Mining	Marital Status			6	False	
Adventure Wor...		Customer Mining	Number of Cars Owned			7	False	
Adventure Wor...		Customer Mining	Number of Children At Home			8	False	
Adventure Wor...		Customer Mining	Occupation			9	False	
Adventure Wor...		Customer Mining	Subcategories			10	False	
Adventure Wor...		Customer Mining	Internet Sales Amount			11	False	
Adventure Wor...		Customer Mining	Subcategory			12	False	
Adventure Wor...		Customer Mining	Total Children			14	False	
Adventure Wor...		Customer Mining	Yearly Income			15	False	
Adventure Wor...		Forecasting	Amount			1	False	
Adventure Wor...		Forecasting	Model Region			2	False	
Adventure Wor...		Forecasting	Quantity			3	False	
Adventure Wor...		Forecasting	Time Index			4	False	

Analysis

This returns the structure columns and not the columns of the models within the structures. Structure and model columns are not always the same. For example, a model may not use all of the available columns in the structure. TM Naïve Bayes, which is in the Targeted Mailing structure, does not use the structure's Yearly Income column. This makes sense as Yearly Income is continuous and Naïve Bayes does not support continuous value inputs.

DMSCHEMA_MINING_STRUCTURE_COLUMNS 2/3

Once again, we are looking at some of the more useful columns.

Syntax

```
-- interesting columns
select structure_name, column_name, content_type
from $system.DMSCHEMA_MINING_STRUCTURE_COLUMNS
```

Result

structure_name	column_name	content_type
Customer Mining	Commute Distance	DISCRETE
Customer Mining	Customer Counts	KEY
Customer Mining	Education	DISCRETE
Customer Mining	Gender	DISCRETE
Customer Mining	Home Owner	DISCRETE
Customer Mining	Marital Status	DISCRETE
Customer Mining	Number of Cars Owned	CONTINUOUS
Customer Mining	Number of Children At Home	CONTINUOUS
Customer Mining	Occupation	DISCRETE
Customer Mining	Subcategories	
Customer Mining	Internet Sales Amount	CONTINUOUS
Customer Mining	Subcategory	KEY
Customer Mining	Total Children	CONTINUOUS
Customer Mining	Yearly Income	DISCRETIZED()
Forecasting	Amount	CONTINUOUS
Forecasting	Model Region	KEY
Forecasting	Quantity	CONTINUOUS
Forecasting	Time Index	KEY TIME
Mail Structure	Age	DISCRETIZED(AUTOMATIC,10)

Analysis

The Content_Type for Subcategories in the Customer Mining structure is blank—this indicates it's a nested case table.

DMSCHEMA_MINING_STRUCTURE_COLUMNS 3/3

The query here looks at one particular mining structure, Targeted Mailing.

Syntax

```
-- a particular structure
select column_name, content_type
from $system.DMSCHEMA_MINING_STRUCTURE_COLUMNS
where structure_name = 'Targeted Mailing'
```

Result

column_name	content_type
Age	DISCRETIZED(AUTOMATIC,10)
Bike Buyer	DISCRETE
Commute Distance	DISCRETE
Customer Key	KEY
Education	DISCRETE
Gender	DISCRETE
House Owner Flag	DISCRETE
Marital Status	DISCRETE
Number Cars Owned	DISCRETE
Number Children At Home	DISCRETE
Occupation	DISCRETE
Region	DISCRETE
Total Children	DISCRETE
Yearly Income	CONTINUOUS

Analysis

Again, this can be a lot quicker than opening BIDS.

DMSCHEMA_MINING_MODEL_XML 1/2

If you are an XML person, you might like to see a model definition as an XML file.

Syntax

```
-- mining model xml
select *
from $system.DMSCHEMA_MINING_MODEL_XML
where model_name = 'Customer Clusters'
```

Result

MODEL_CATAL...	MODEL_SCHEMA	MODEL_NAME	MODEL_TYPE	MODEL_GUID	MODEL_PMML	SIZE	LOCATION
Adventure Wor...		Customer Clusters		9da76ce2-55ac...	<PMML version="2.1" xmlns="http://www.dmg.org/P...	35434	

Analysis

All SSAS objects can be represented as XML files—there is a language called XMLA (and a related language called ASSL) that can create/represent objects using an XML-based syntax. XMLA is beyond the scope of a DMX book.

DMSCHEMA_MINING_MODEL_CONTENT_PMML

This query returns the same result as the previous query. However, it uses DMSCHEMA_MINING_MODEL_PMML and not DMSCHEMA_MINING_MODEL_XML. The former is for backward compatibility only.

Syntax

```
-- or for backward compatibility
select *
from $system.DMSCHEMA_MINING_MODEL_CONTENT_PMML
where model_name = 'Customer Clusters'
```

Result

MODEL_CATAL...	MODEL_SCHEMA	MODEL_NAME	MODEL_TYPE	MODEL_GUID	MODEL_PMML	SIZE	LOCATION
Adventure Wor...		Customer Clusters		9da76ce2-55ac...	<PMML version="2.1" xmlns="http://www.dmg.org/PM...	35434	

Analysis

This query is using legacy syntax and is provided for completeness only.

DMSCHEMA_MINING_MODEL_XML 2/2

This is our last Schema query.

Syntax

```
-- interesting column, select all then copy
select model_pmml
from $system.DMSCHEMA_MINING_MODEL_XML
where model_name = 'Customer Clusters'
```

Result

model_pmml

<PMML version="2.1" xmlns="http://www.dmg.org/PMML-2_1" xmlns:xsd="http://www.w3.org/2001/XMLSchema"><Header copyright="Copyright (c) 2003 Microsoft Corporation, All Rights Reserved"><...

Analysis

If you are interested in the XML behind a model, right-click, click Select All, and then right-click and click Copy. Then paste into your favorite XML editor.

Discrete Model Columns 1/5

Earlier in this chapter, you used the Schema query, DMSCHEMA_MINING_
COLUMNS, to examine the columns in a mining model. But, especially if you have an
SQL background, you might be tempted to try a query just like the one here to view
columns.

Syntax

```
-- select model
select * from [Customer Clusters]
```

Result

```
Executing the query ...
Error (Data mining): A * is not allowed in the context at line 2, column 1.

Execution complete
```

Analysis

Unfortunately, it doesn't work!

Discrete Model Columns 2/5

Our last query failed. Maybe if we tried just one column?

Syntax

```
-- select column
select Occupation from [Customer Clusters]
```

Result

```
Executing the query ...
Error (Data mining): Only a predictable column (or a column that is related to a predictable column) can be referenced from the mining mode

Execution complete
```

Analysis

The only column you can reference individually in this manner is a predictable column.
Occupation is not a predictable column; it's an input column only.

Discrete Model Columns 3/5

The all-important difference here is the inclusion of the key word Distinct.

Syntax

```
-- select distinct column, discrete
select distinct Occupation from [Customer Clusters]
```

Result

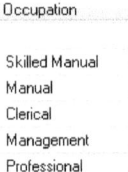

Occupation

Skilled Manual
Manual
Clerical
Management
Professional

Analysis

Now it works. If you use Distinct with a discrete input column, it returns all the possible states (unique values) for that column. The result also includes an empty row signifying a possible missing value. This is neither a Cases query (no .cases), nor a Content query (no .content), nor a Prediction query (no Predict()), nor a Schema query (no $System). It's a query directly on a single column in a model, a Column query.

Discrete Model Columns 4/5

Here, we have the simple addition of an Order By clause.

Syntax

```
-- select distinct column, sorted
select distinct Occupation from [Customer Clusters]
order by occupation
```

Result

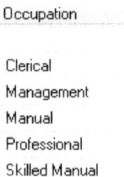

Occupation

Clerical
Management
Manual
Professional
Skilled Manual

Analysis

This is quite a good way to record all the states (values) of all the discrete columns in a model—you have to do so on a column-by-column basis.

Discrete Model Columns 5/5

To retrieve a subset of possible discrete column values, you may want to include Top.

Syntax

```
-- select top distinct column, sorted
select top 3 distinct Occupation from [Customer Clusters]
order by occupation
```

Result

Occupation

Clerical
Management

Analysis

The result shows the first three values for Occupation in alphabetical order. The missing value sorts first.

Discretized Model Column

The approach we just adopted only works on discrete columns. Discretized columns behave differently. Discretized columns do not have single unique values or states. Instead, a range of values is possible for each discretization bucket.

Syntax

```
-- select numeric column, discretized
select distinct [Yearly Income] from [Customer Clusters]
```

Result

Yearly Income

24610.7033
55115.7284
84821.5439
111633.872
147317.3532

Analysis

Yearly Income in the Customer Clusters model is discretized—you can check its Content property in BIDS (by looking at the containing Customer Mining structure), or you can run a DMSCHEMA_MINING_COLUMNS Schema query as you did earlier in this chapter. The result shows five buckets of data and the extra blank missing value. But for each bucket, there is only a single value—there are no start and end values for each bucket.

Discretized Model Column—Minimum

Please note the addition of the RangeMin() function.

Syntax

```
-- select minimum, discretized
select distinct RangeMin([Yearly Income]) from [Customer Clusters]
```

Result

Expression

```
10000
39221.4066
71010.0502
98633.0375
124634.7064
```

Analysis

The result shows the lowest value in each bucket of incomes.

Discretized Model Column—Maximum

Let's try RangeMax().

Syntax

```
-- select maximum, discretized
select distinct RangeMax([Yearly Income]) from [Customer Clusters]
```

Result

Expression

39221.4066
71010.0502
98633.0375
124634.7064
170000

Analysis

As you might expect, RangeMax() returns the highest income in each bucket created by the discretization.

Discretized Model Column—Mid Value

Here it's the turn of RangeMid().

Syntax

```
-- select midpoint, discretized
select distinct RangeMid([Yearly Income]) from [Customer Clusters]
```

Result

Expression

24610.7033
55115.7284
84821.5439
111633.872
147317.3532

Analysis

RangeMid() returns the midpoint between the lowest and highest values of a bucket of incomes.

Discretized Model Column—Range Values

This Column query uses all of the Range family of functions.

Syntax

```
-- select all ranges, discretized
select distinct RangeMin([Yearly Income]) as [Min],
RangeMid([Yearly Income]) as Mid, [Yearly Income],
RangeMax([Yearly Income]) as [Max] from [Customer Clusters]
```

Result

Min	Mid	Yearly Income	Max
10000	24610.7033	24610.7033	39221.4066
39221.4066	55115.7284	55115.7284	71010.0502
71010.0502	84821.5439	84821.5439	98633.0375
98633.0375	111633.872	111633.872	124634.7064
124634.7064	147317.3532	147317.3532	170000

Analysis

RangeMid() is the default and can be omitted.

Discretized Model Column—Spread

Now, it's fairly trivial to ascertain the spread of values in a discretized column's buckets.

Syntax

```
-- select spread, discretized
select distinct RangeMin([Yearly Income]) as [Min],
RangeMid([Yearly Income]) as Mid, [Yearly Income],
RangeMax([Yearly Income]) as [Max],
RangeMax([Yearly Income]) - RangeMin([Yearly Income]) as Spread
from [Customer Clusters]
```

Result

Min	Mid	Yearly Income	Max	Spread
10000	24610.7033	24610.7033	39221.4066	29221.4066
39221.4066	55115.7284	55115.7284	71010.0502	31788.6436
71010.0502	84821.5439	84821.5439	98633.0375	27622.9873
98633.0375	111633.872	111633.872	124634.7064	26001.6689
124634.7064	147317.3532	147317.3532	170000	45365.2936

Analysis

Our last few Column queries have returned interesting information about our discrete and discretized columns. Only the continuous columns remain.

Continuous Model Column—Spread

Our last Column query looks at an input column with a Content property of Continuous.

Syntax

```
-- select spread, continuous
select distinct RangeMin([Yearly Income]) as [Min],
RangeMid([Yearly Income]) as Mid, [Yearly Income],
RangeMax([Yearly Income]) as [Max],
RangeMax([Yearly Income]) - RangeMin([Yearly Income]) as Spread
from [TM Clustering]
```

Result

Min	Mid	Yearly Income	Max	Spread
10000	90000	90000	170000	160000

Analysis

The column, Yearly Income, is the same, but the model is different. Yearly Income in the TM Clustering model is continuous. This time, we don't have the five buckets. Continuous values are not discretized—there is simply a minimum value and a maximum value, with lots of values in between.

Chapter 9

After You Finish

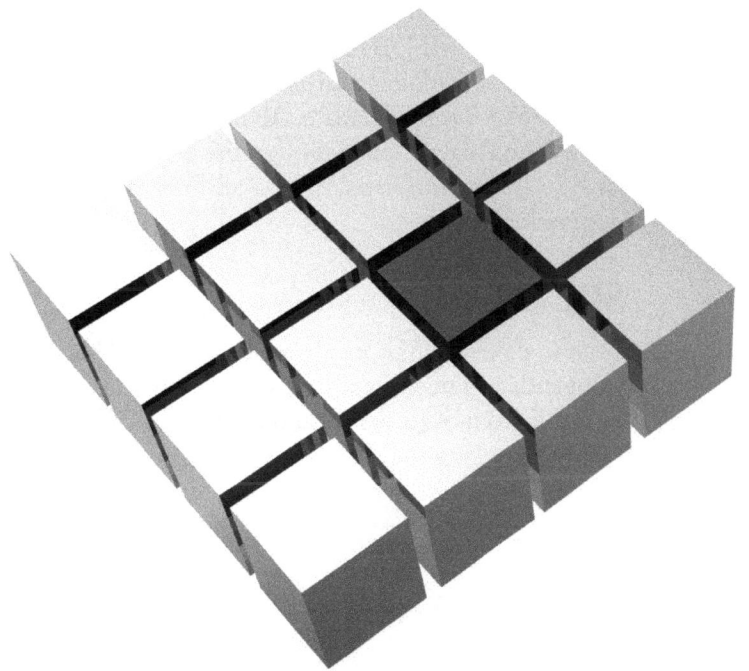

Where to Use DMX

Throughout this book, you've been using SSMS to write your DMX queries and display the results. It's unlikely that your users will have SSMS—indeed, it's not recommended for end users as it's simply too powerful and potentially dangerous. This chapter presents some alternative software and methods for getting DMX query results to the end user.

SSRS

SSRS can generate simple DMX prediction queries for you, but you may want some of the more sophisticated queries (for example, content and cases queries) that you've seen in this book. You will need an SSAS connection to do this. To use your own DMX, click the Command Type DMX, then the Design Mode button on the toolbar, while in Query Designer in SSRS. You are then able to paste in code that you have developed in SSMS.

SSIS

With SSIS you can get the DMX results into a data pipeline using a Data Flow task. It's then quite easy to convert it into a text file, an Excel worksheet, or an SQL Server table. For DMX prediction queries, there is the Data Mining Query transform within the Data Flow task. An alternative is to use the Data Mining Query task in the SSIS Control Flow and configure a suitable Output. For DMX content or Cases queries, you will need an OLE DB or ADO NET source with an SSAS connection. Then change the Data access mode from Table or view to SQL command and paste it in your DMX from SSMS. To issue Create, Alter, Drop, Insert, and Update DMX commands, you can try the Analysis Services Execute DDL task. As if that's not enough, rather than issue an Insert command, the Data Flow task supports a Data Mining Model Training destination.

SQL

You can embed DMX inside an SQL query. This allows you to exploit any SQL Server front ends you may already have. One way to accomplish this is to set up a linked server to SSAS from SQL Server and paste the DMX into an Openquery construct.

XMLA

Your DMX queries can also be nested inside XMLA. To do so, use an <Execute> <Command> <Statement> construct.

Winforms and Webforms

If you are a .NET developer, you can create your own Windows applications (Winforms) or web pages (Webforms) to display the results of your DMX queries. The simplest way to do so is to use a datagrid. Your application will need a reference to Microsoft .AnalysisServices.AdomdClient. The DMX can return the data as a dataset or datareader or as XML. Here's some sample VB.NET code that creates a dataset (you may have to adapt the Data Source and Initial Catalog properties as well as the mining model name in the From clause):

```
Imports Microsoft.AnalysisServices.AdomdClient

Dim con As New AdomdConnection("Data Source=localhost;
Initial Catalog=Adventure Works DW 2008")
con.open()
Dim cmd As New AdomdCommand("select flattened *
from [TM Decision Tree].content", con)
Dim adt As New AdomdDataAdapter(cmd)
Dim dst As New DataSet
adt.Fill(dst)

    'or use a DATAREADER
    'Dim rdr As AdomdDataReader = cmd.ExecuteReader
    'do stuff with reader
    'rdr.Close()

    'or use an XMLREADER
    'Dim xml As System.Xml.XmlReader = cmd.ExecuteXmlReader
    'do stuff with XML

DataGridView1.DataSource = dst.Tables(0)
'for a Webform add .DataBind

con.Close()
```

Third-Party Software

There is an infinite variety of third-party software applications available that allow you to paste in your DMX.

Copy and Paste

Or you can right-click on the Results pane in SSMS and choose Select All. Then right-click again and choose Copy. You can then paste the DMX results (rather than the DMX itself) into an application of your choice.

Appendix A

Graphical
Content Queries

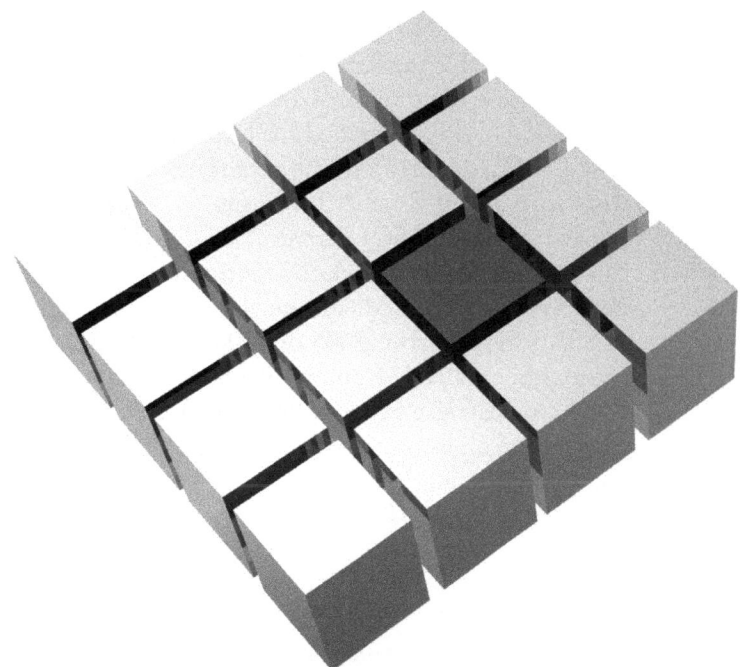

The previous chapters showed the syntax for DMX queries and involved entering the syntax manually in SSMS. However, it is possible to generate the DMX syntax behind the scenes using the graphical user interface. The appendixes show various ways of running DMX queries graphically, without the need to enter any syntax. This first appendix demonstrates how to return data mining model content using graphical tools. In particular, it uses both SSMS and Excel 2007/2010 to generate Content queries graphically and to display the results graphically, too.

▶ **Key concepts** Generating Content queries graphically, viewing the content graphically, capturing generated DMX

Content Queries

In Chapter 2, you saw how to write DMX Content queries. Content queries, in general, show the results of data mining model training. The nature of the content depends upon the type of data mining model and algorithm used. For example, the content returned by a Clustering model will differ from that returned by a Decision Tree model. In Chapter 2, the queries were entered manually in the SSMS query editor and the results displayed as a table, or a table containing a nested table, in the Results pane of the editor. There are other ways of doing this. You have the option to both generate the DMX query graphically and to display the results graphically. You can do so from within SSMS itself. You may also be able to do this from Excel 2007 or 2010—you will need the Microsoft SQL Server Data Mining add-ins for Microsoft Office 2007 first. This is a free download. As of this writing, there were versions available for SSAS 2005, SSAS 2008, and SSAS 2008 R2. Again, as of this writing, these three versions are for Excel 2007 only. It's possible that the SSAS 2008 R2 version may be upgraded for Excel 2010 (probably for 32-bit Excel 2010 and not for 64-bit Excel 2010). In the meantime, you should find that the Excel 2007 editions work with 32-bit Excel 2010. Currently, you can download this Excel add-in from the feature pack of SQL Server 2005, SQL Server 2008, or SQL Server 2008 R2. You can locate the feature packs by visiting www.microsoft.com and searching on SQL Server Feature Pack. Make sure you choose the feature pack that matches your edition of SSAS/SQL Server (2005 or 2008 or 2008 R2). In addition, the 2005 and 2008 versions are available from www.sqlserverdatamining.com. If you are familiar with BIDS, you can also generate and view DMX queries graphically. In this appendix, we concentrate on using SSMS and Excel 2007—there is a small section at the end of the appendix on using BIDS.

Graphical Content Queries in SSMS

This section assumes you have some familiarity with SSMS. Also, in this section and the rest of the three appendixes, we will usually be referring to the Adventure Works DW 2008 SSAS 2008 database (called Adventure Works DW in SSAS 2005). This database contains a number of data mining structures and data mining models that you met earlier in this book. To get started, you need a connection to SSAS in the Object Explorer window in SSMS. If you are not sure how to locate the data mining models, here are a few simple steps to help you:

1. Expand your SSAS server, if necessary, in Object Explorer.
2. Expand the Databases folder, if necessary.
3. Expand the folder for the Adventure Works DW 2008 (Adventure Works DW in SSAS 2005) database, if necessary.
4. Expand the Mining Structures folders, if necessary. You can now see all of the data mining structures in this database.
5. Expand any of these data mining structures. Each of them contains a Mining Models folder. If you recall, a data mining structure can contain zero, one, or more data mining models. The models share all or some of the data defined for the structure. Often, if there is more than one model, they will be based on different data mining algorithms. If they are based on the same algorithm, they will generally have different parameters.
6. Expand the Mining Models folder under any structure to see the models defined for that structure. Figure A-1 shows the result of expanding the Mining Models folder underneath the Customer Mining structure. There are two models shown, Customer Clusters and Subcategory Associations.
7. To generate a Content query graphically, and to display the results graphically, you simply right-click on a model and choose Browse. However, this is only going to work if the data mining model has already been processed or trained. You can process, or train, a model by right-clicking on the model and choosing Process. If you process a data mining structure (right-click on the structure and choose Process), it will also process all of its constituent models. If you process a database (right-click on the database and choose Process), then all of the constituent mining structures and models will also be processed as a result.

No matter on which algorithm the model is based, you always right-click on the model and then click Browse to generate the Content query graphically. However, the graphical results will differ according to the algorithm. Here we examine four of the most popular algorithms: Clustering, Time Series, Association Rules, and Decision Trees. The graphical display is rendered in a data mining model viewer. The viewer

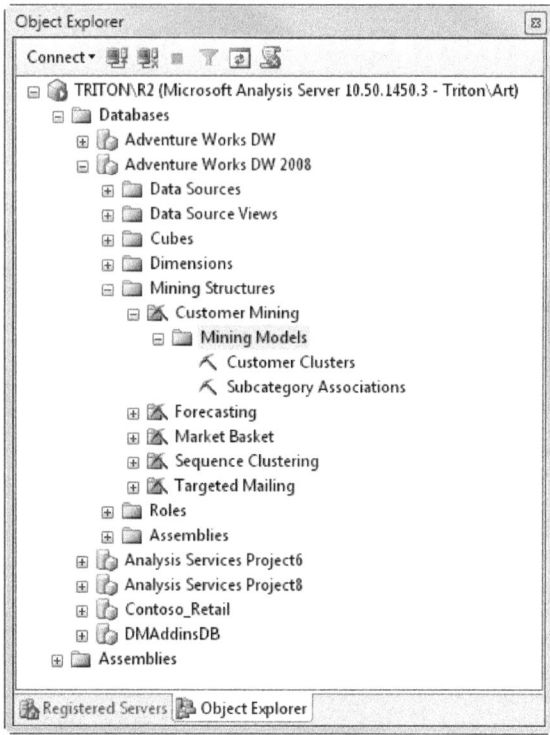

Figure A-1 *Displaying data mining models in SSMS Object Explorer*

is different for most of the algorithms. In addition, each viewer may have multiple tabs presenting different ways of showing the content. Only a few of the tabs within the different viewers are considered here. Feel free to experiment with the algorithm viewers and tabs not illustrated here. The same viewers are also available from the Data Mining ribbon of the Data Mining add-in in Excel—this is covered later in this chapter. If you are a .NET developer, you may like to know that you can add these viewers to your own Windows or Web applications. The viewers are available as controls that can be downloaded from the SQL Server Feature Pack mentioned earlier.

Clustering Model

The viewer for data mining models based on the Clustering algorithm is called the Microsoft Cluster Viewer. It has four tabs: Cluster Diagram, Cluster Profiles, Cluster Characteristics, and Cluster Discrimination.

The model used here is the Customer Clusters model under the Customer Mining structure. To view the model content graphically, right-click on the Customer Clusters model and choose Browse.

Figure A-2 shows the Cluster Diagram tab. Figure A-3 shows the Cluster Profiles tab. The Cluster Diagram tab will, by default, show all the cases (here, they're customers) segmented into ten clusters. Again by default, the density of color of each cluster is an indication of how many customers have been assigned to that cluster. You can look at the Density bar to help decipher the color-coding. The Shading Variable drop-down lets you switch from a view based on population to one based on any of the input variables. If you choose an input variable, the State drop-down is enabled. For discrete variables, the values are shown. Continuous variables are automatically discretized or split into ranges. To the left is a slider. By moving the slider up and down, you can see the strength of the links (or degree of similarity) between clusters. A cluster that has very weak links with other clusters may contain outliers (that is, unusual and interesting customers). If drill-down is enabled on the model, you can right-click on a cluster to drill down and see the individual customers in a cluster (you need to be analyzing

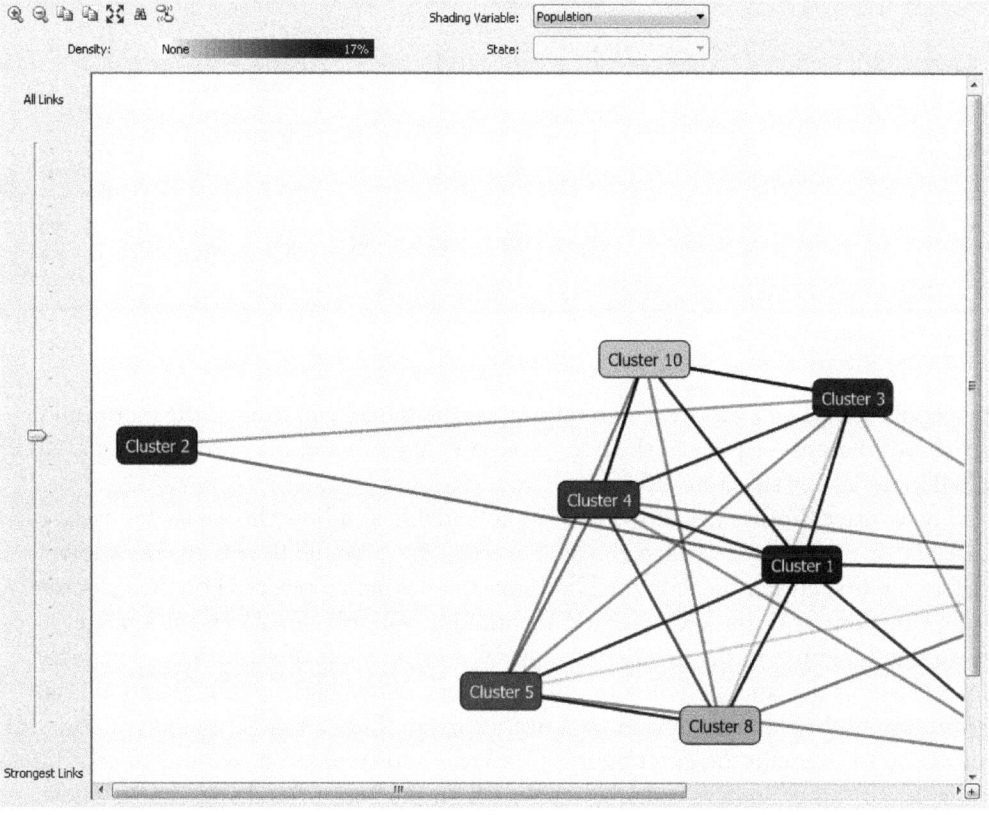

Figure A-2   *Cluster Diagram tab*

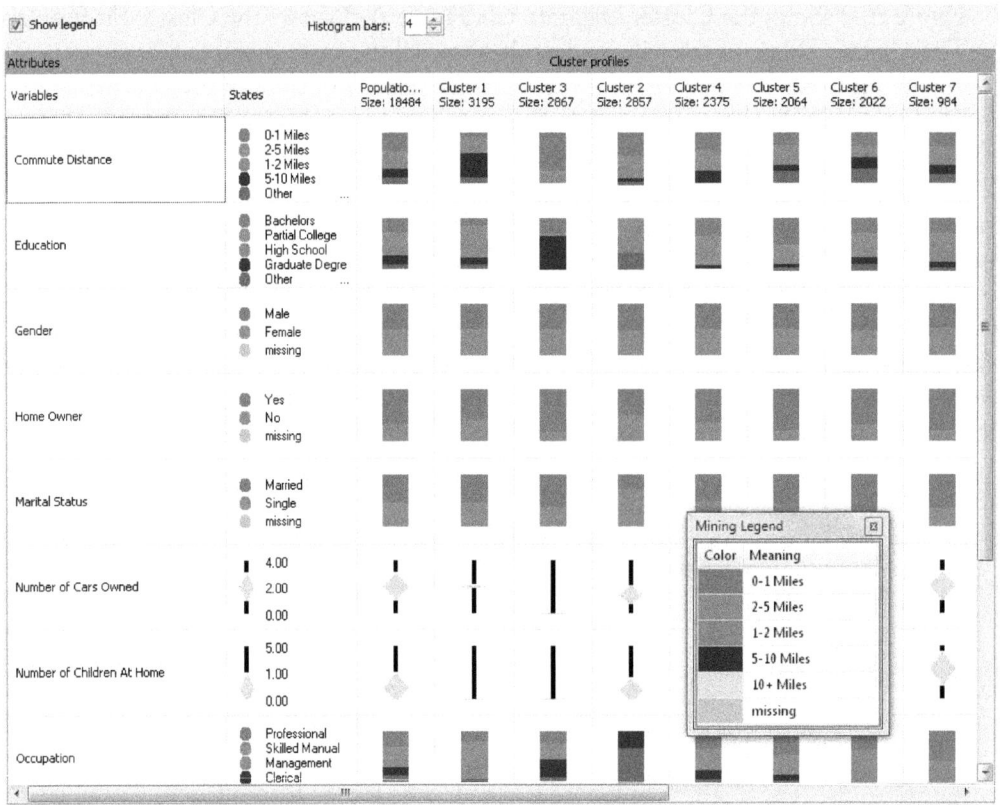

Figure A-3 *Cluster Profiles tab*

by population). The drill-down can return just the model columns or the model and structure columns—earlier in the book, you saw that a model may only contain a subset of all the available structure columns.

The Cluster Profiles tab shows each input variable and how the values for each variable are represented in each cluster—there is also a population-wide breakdown before the first cluster breakdown. Discrete variables are represented by their discrete values and appear as stacked columns. Continuous variables are shown as a range from the minimum to the maximum value. The mean value of a continuous variable for a cluster is the center of the turquoise diamond. The height of the diamond is an indication of the standard deviation about the mean. The Mining Legend window will allow you to ascertain the exact figures for means and standard deviations of continuous variables (if this window is hidden, right-click on the background and choose Show Legend). The Mining Legend window also shows the most likely value for a discrete variable for the cluster with the mouse focus. By examining profiles, you can reach a conclusion about the type of customer in a cluster (for example, high or low income and marital status). The Cluster Characteristics tab and the Cluster Discrimination tab can help you refine this conclusion. You can rename each cluster to give it a more informative name. You saw how to do this by using DMX syntax much earlier in the book. Graphically, you simply right-click on a cluster in the Cluster Diagram tab (make sure that the Shading Variable is Population). If you win new customers, you can then run a DMX Prediction query (either from syntax or graphically) to see which clusters they are likely to fit into.

You can even create an SSAS cube dimension based on these clusters and analyze sales by cluster in a pivot table. SSAS cubes and pivot tables are beyond the scope of this book.

Time Series Model

The viewer for data mining models based on the Time Series algorithm is called the Microsoft Time Series Viewer. It has two tabs: Charts and Model.

The model used here is the Forecasting model (the only one) under the Forecasting structure. To view the model content graphically, right-click on the Forecasting model (not structure) and choose Browse.

Figure A-4 shows the Charts tab.

The Charts tab displays existing sales based on the source cases. These sales are for each value in the case key across time based on the key time attribute. Existing sales are shown as solid colored lines. The forecasted future sales are shown as dotted colored lines. You can determine which lines to display (here, they are for the key, which is a concatenation of the product model and the region in which the model is sold) by using the drop-down list and check boxes to the right of the chart. There is also a check box, labeled Show Deviations, which can be turned on to show the standard deviation of forecasts. The Prediction Steps spin button is used to control how far into the future you wish to go. Of course, the further you go into the future, the more spurious the projections. You can get some help on sales figures (existing and future) by looking at the Mining Legend window. If the window is not displayed, right-click on the gray pane to the right of the chart and choose Show Legend. For a model based on the Time Series algorithm, the viewer shows the results of a Prediction query as well as a Content/Cases query.

Association Rules Model

The viewer for data mining models based on the Association Rules algorithm is called the Microsoft Association Rules Viewer. It has three tabs: Rules, Itemsets, and Dependency Network.

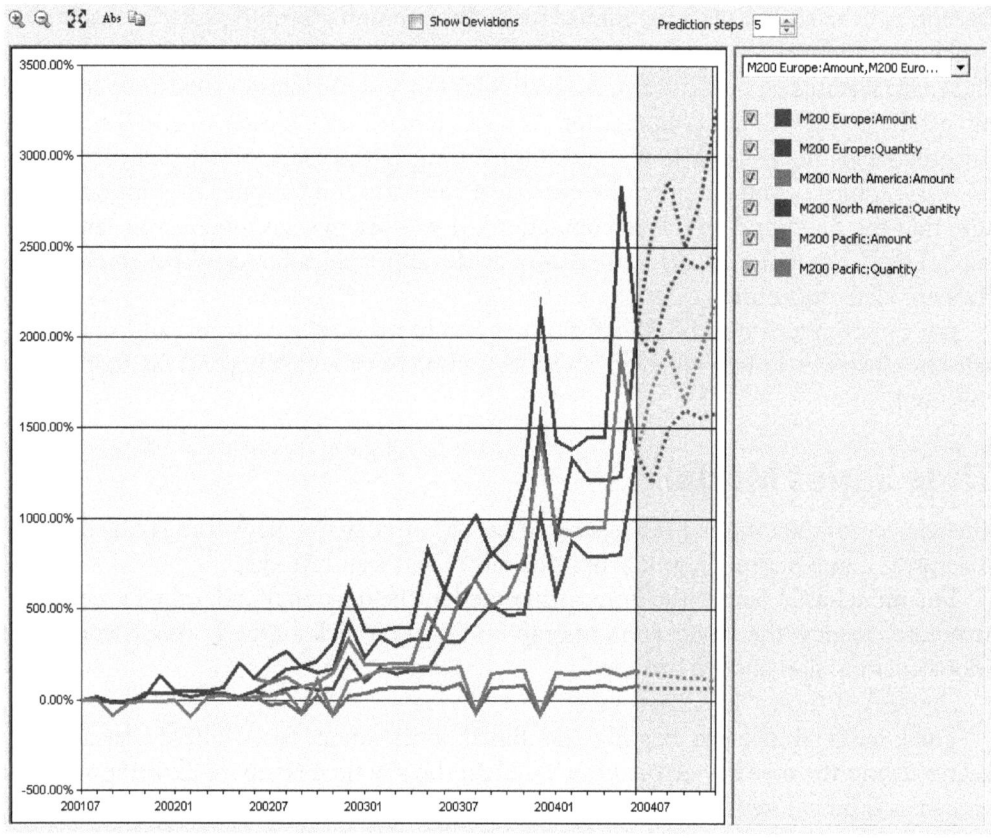

Figure A-4 *Charts tab*

The model used here is the Association one (the only one) under the Market Basket structure. To view the model content graphically, right-click on the Association model and choose Browse.

Figure A-5 shows the Itemsets tab. Figure A-6 shows the Dependency Network tab.

The Itemsets tab is very useful for examining cross-selling and up-selling opportunities. Of particular interest are item sets where the Size is 2 or more. You can filter the results by changing the Minimum Itemset Size property. You may also want to set the Minimum Support property to a reasonably large amount—the fact that two products were bought together only on one occasion, out of thousands of shopping baskets analyzed, is probably not statistically significant. If there are simply too many rows to analyze, you can lower the figure for the Maximum Rows property. Take a look at the Filter Itemset drop-down. There are no entries yet. Try typing in a product name, such as Water Bottle (it's not case-sensitive) and pressing ENTER. This filters the products

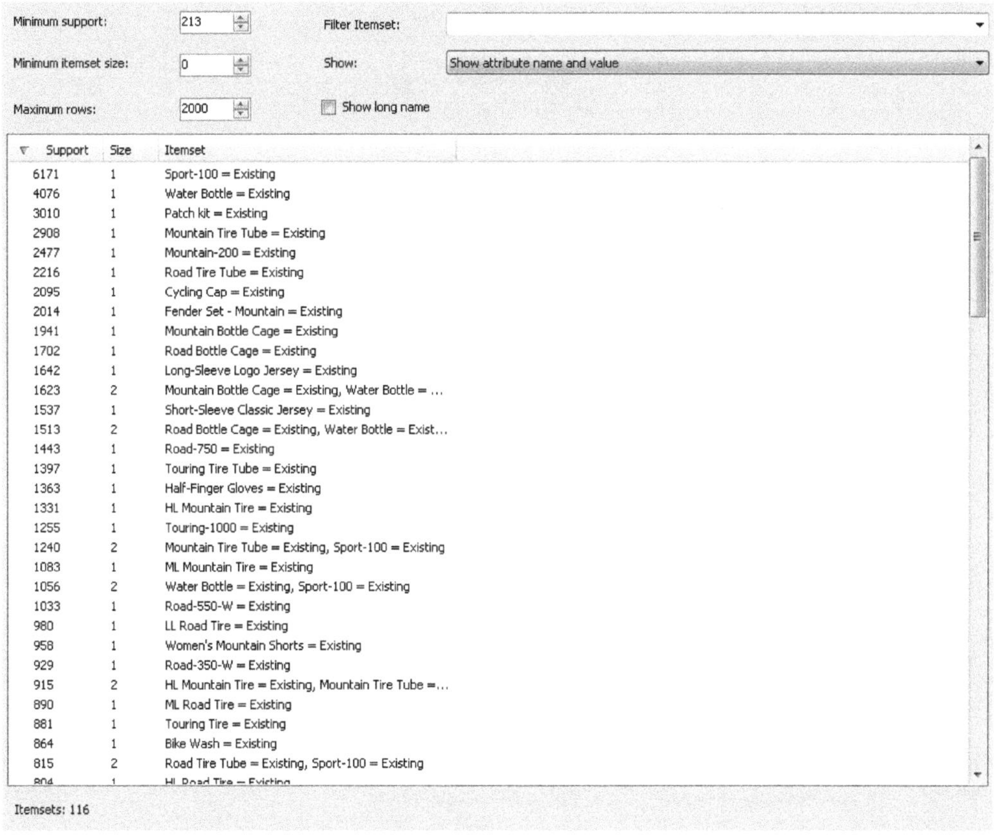

Minimum support:	213		Filter Itemset:		
Minimum itemset size:	0		Show:	Show attribute name and value	
Maximum rows:	2000		☐ Show long name		

▽ Support	Size	Itemset
6171	1	Sport-100 = Existing
4076	1	Water Bottle = Existing
3010	1	Patch kit = Existing
2908	1	Mountain Tire Tube = Existing
2477	1	Mountain-200 = Existing
2216	1	Road Tire Tube = Existing
2095	1	Cycling Cap = Existing
2014	1	Fender Set - Mountain = Existing
1941	1	Mountain Bottle Cage = Existing
1702	1	Road Bottle Cage = Existing
1642	1	Long-Sleeve Logo Jersey = Existing
1623	2	Mountain Bottle Cage = Existing, Water Bottle = ...
1537	1	Short-Sleeve Classic Jersey = Existing
1513	2	Road Bottle Cage = Existing, Water Bottle = Exist...
1443	1	Road-750 = Existing
1397	1	Touring Tire Tube = Existing
1363	1	Half-Finger Gloves = Existing
1331	1	HL Mountain Tire = Existing
1255	1	Touring-1000 = Existing
1240	2	Mountain Tire Tube = Existing, Sport-100 = Existing
1083	1	ML Mountain Tire = Existing
1056	2	Water Bottle = Existing, Sport-100 = Existing
1033	1	Road-550-W = Existing
980	1	LL Road Tire = Existing
958	1	Women's Mountain Shorts = Existing
929	1	Road-350-W = Existing
915	2	HL Mountain Tire = Existing, Mountain Tire Tube = ...
890	1	ML Road Tire = Existing
881	1	Touring Tire = Existing
864	1	Bike Wash = Existing
815	2	Road Tire Tube = Existing, Sport-100 = Existing
804	1	HL Road Tire = Existing

Itemsets: 116

Figure A-5   *Itemsets tab*

shown and adds the entry to the drop-down. To remove a filter on a product name, delete the entry and press ENTER. By clicking column headers, you can sort the item sets by Support or Size or alphabetically by product name.

The Dependency Network tab is also used to see cross-selling and up-selling relationships. It is more graphical than the result in the Itemsets tab. If you click on the oval shape for a particular product, you can see its relationship to other products. The ovals become color-coded—you can see what the colors indicate underneath the network. The arrow between the two product ovals shows whether it is a one-way or two-way relationship between the products. The slider on the left is used to hide (or reveal) weaker relationships or correlations between products. If you drag the slider all the way down, you are left with the strongest product relationship—this may be a pretty good cross-selling opportunity. Sometimes, there may be thousands of products in the dependency network and it's difficult to find the product you want. The last button on the small toolbar at the top lets you search for a particular product.

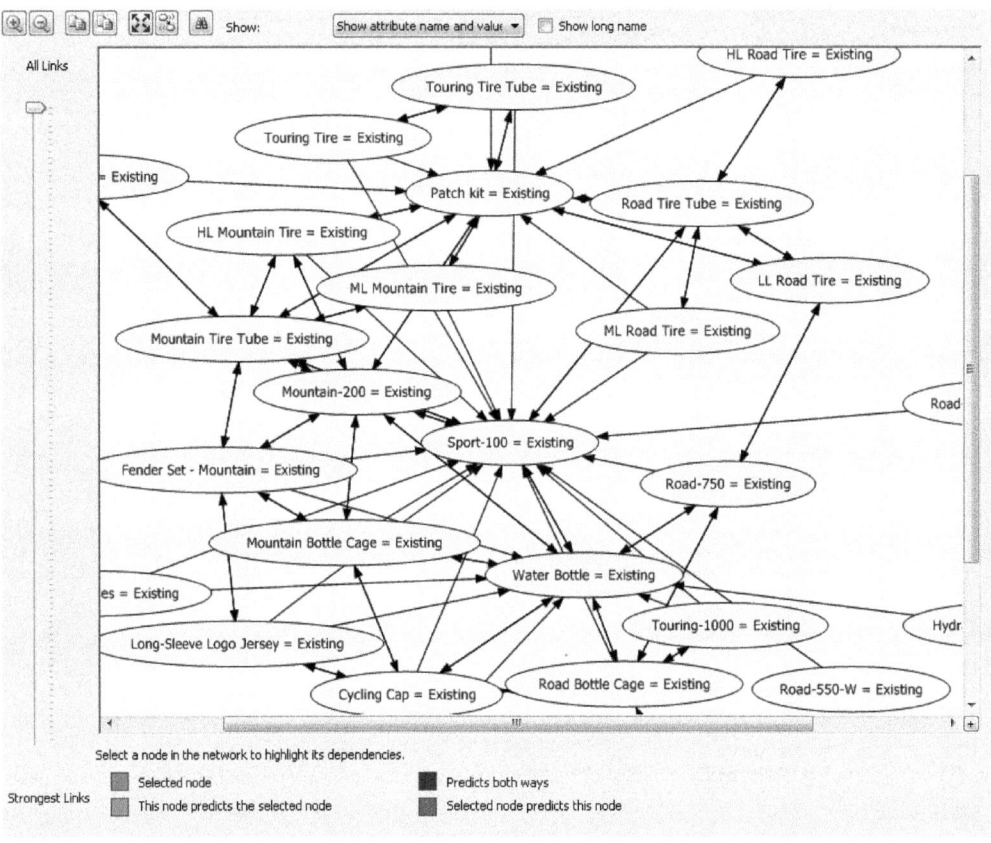

Figure A-6 *Dependency Network tab (Association Rules)*

Decision Trees Model

The viewer for data mining models based on the Decision Trees algorithm is called the Microsoft Tree Viewer. It has two tabs: Decision Tree and Dependency Network.

The model used here is the TM Decision Tree model under the Targeted Mailing structure. To view the model content graphically, right-click on the TM Decision Tree model and choose Browse.

Figure A-7 shows the Decision Tree tab. Figure A-8 shows the Dependency Network tab.

The Decision Tree tab shows a fairly complex decision tree based on the model content. The tree is split into nodes, and you can control how many nodes to view through the Default Expansion drop-down or the Show Level slider. If you display

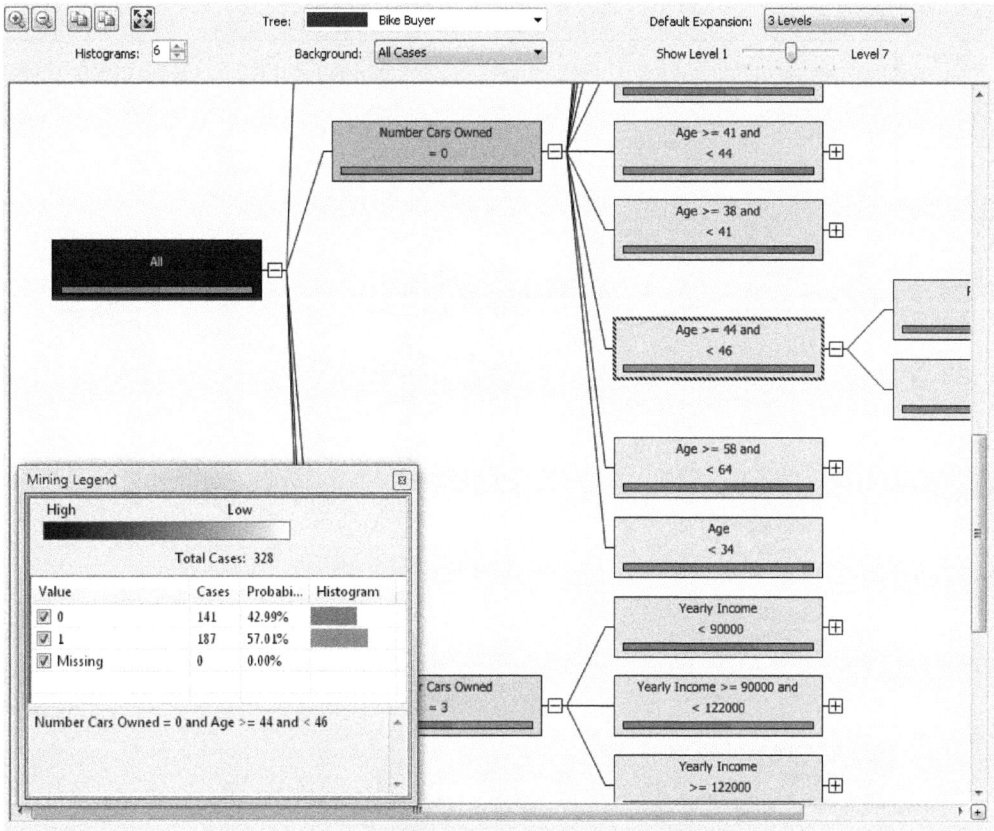

Figure A-7   *Decision Tree tab*

too many nodes, you can zoom out to fit all the nodes into the window without having to scroll. The depth of color in each node is an indication of how many customers are in the node. By using the Background drop-down, you can change the color-coding to reflect the number of customers in each node who bought (or didn't buy) a bike from Adventure Works. The caption of a node is the demographic on which the tree is split further. If drill-down is enabled on the model, you can right-click on a node to see the individual customers in the node. When a particular node is selected, the Mining Legend window shows the probabilities of a bike being bought, or not, for the customers in the node. At the foot of the legend, you can see the demographics of the customers in the node. If the Mining Legend window is not showing, right-click on the background and choose Show Legend.

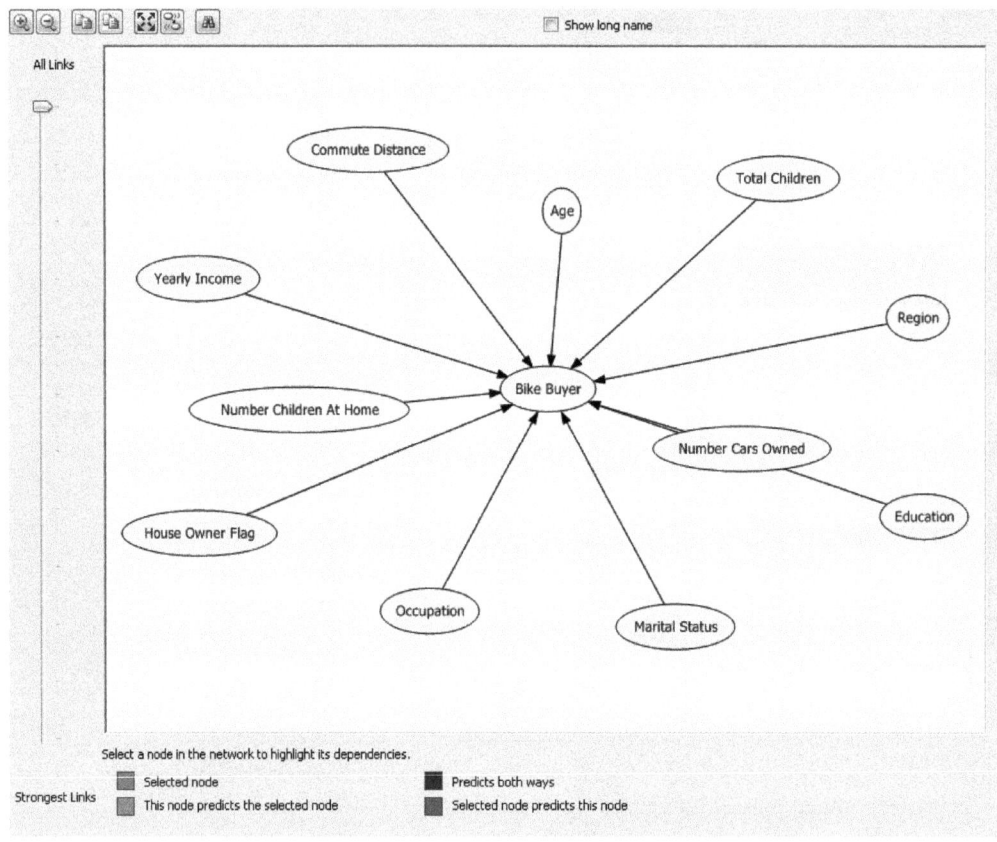

Figure A-8   *Dependency Network tab (Decision Trees)*

The Dependency Network tab in the tree viewer is different from the Dependency Network tab in the Association Rules viewer. The network for a decision tree generally has the predict attribute at the center. The surrounding ovals are the predictors of that attribute. Here, the predictable outcome is Bike Buyer. You can easily see the most important determinants of Bike Buyer (that is, the strongest correlations) by dragging the slider at the left downward.

Graphical Content Queries in Excel 2007

The previous section examined viewing models from within SSMS. You can have the same viewers from within Excel 2007or Excel 2010 (32-bit). As explained earlier, you need to download the Data Mining add-in for Excel. After download and installation, you have to configure SSAS to work with Excel. This configuration is done through the Server Configuration Utility, which is in the new program group that the installation will create. If you are an SSAS administrator, you can also do the configuration manually. The most important configuration is to change the Data Mining \ AllowSessionMiningModels property to true. You can access this property by right-clicking your SSAS server in Object Explorer in SSMS and choosing Properties. This opens the Analysis Server Properties dialog. The dialog is shown in Figure A-9. You can then change the Data Mining \ AllowSessionMiningModels property from its default value of false to true. By doing so, you are giving Excel permission to create temporary data mining models in SSAS and retrieve the content.

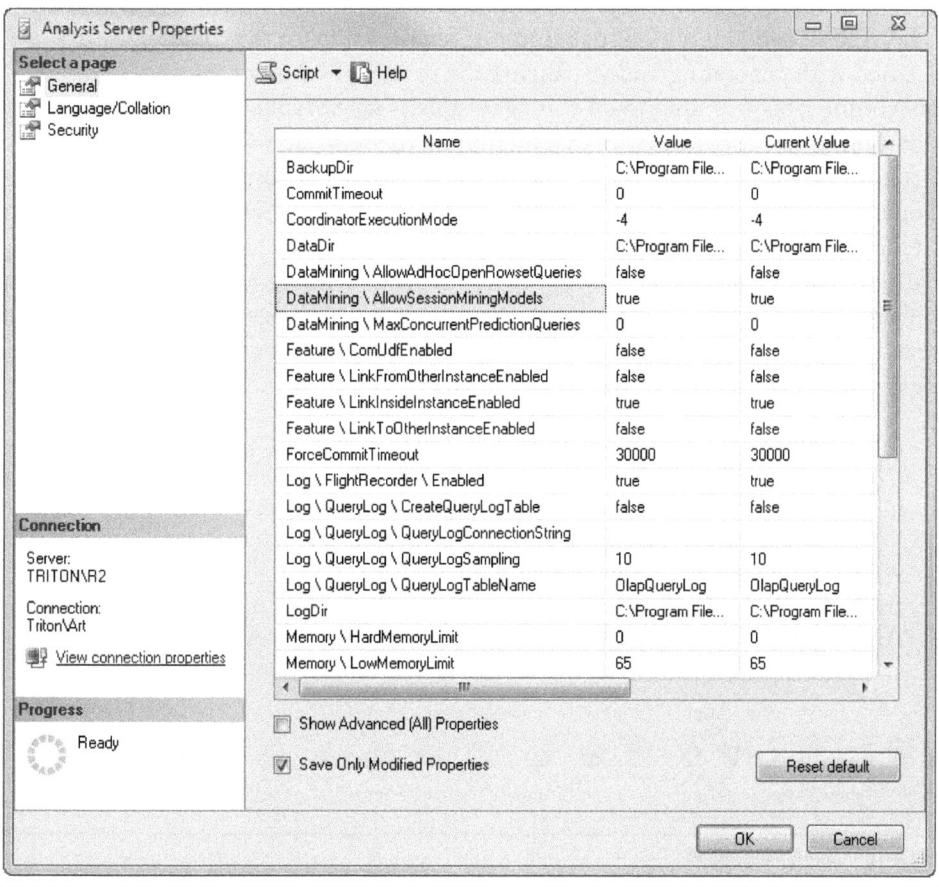

Figure A-9   *Analysis Server Properties dialog*

This is more important for DDL queries generated graphically in Excel, rather than Content queries.

After you have downloaded, installed, and configured the Data Mining add-in, you will see an extra ribbon in Excel—the Data Mining ribbon. There is a second ribbon of interest called the Table Tools/Analyze ribbon. You will not see this second ribbon until you create an Excel table and the table has the focus. The next two sections discuss the two ribbons and their similarities and differences—but both can be used for data mining and for generating DMX queries graphically.

Data Mining Ribbon

The Data Mining ribbon is shown in Figure A-10.

This ribbon contains a lot of data mining functionality. In this chapter, we are concerned with generating and visualizing the results of Content queries. The Data Mining ribbon is used to do this against existing SSAS data mining models. In addition, it can also create SSAS data mining models (either permanently or temporarily)—this is a topic for Appendix C. When model content is visualized, this ribbon uses the SSAS data mining viewers we met in SSMS earlier. The data used to train the model can come from many sources.

To generate a DMX Content query from this Data Mining ribbon, there are a couple of prerequisites. First, you need a connection to your SSAS server. Second, you need to have a data mining model available (deployed and processed or trained) on the server. Here is a step-by-step procedure to get you started:

1. On the Data Mining tab, click the button labeled <No Connection> in the Connection group. This opens the Analysis Services Connections dialog, shown in Figure A-11. If you have been experimenting and already have a connection to the SSAS Adventure Works DW 2008 database, you can skip these initial steps on setting up a connection and jump to step 4.

2. In the Analysis Services Connections dialog, click New to open the Connect to Analysis Services dialog. This dialog is shown in Figure A-12.

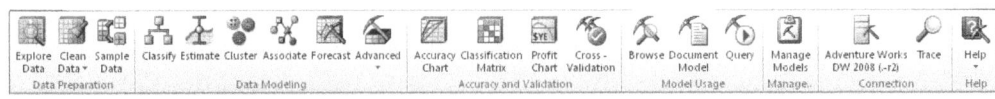

Figure A-10 *Data Mining ribbon*

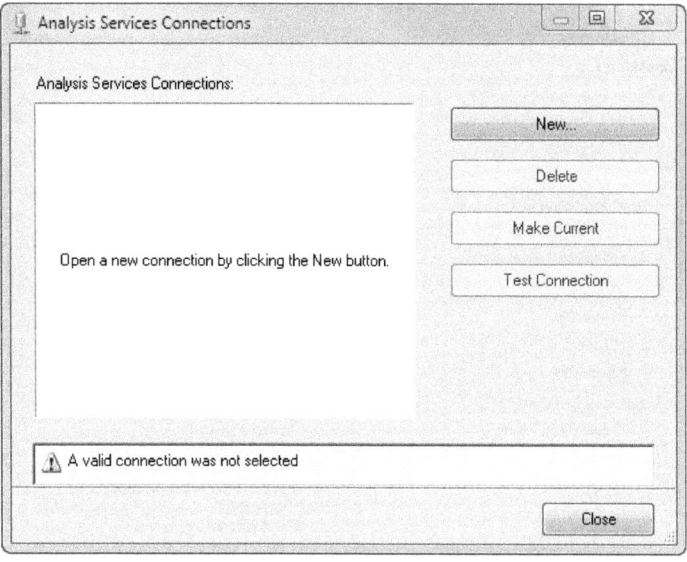

Figure A-11   *Analysis Services Connections dialog*

3. In the Connect to Analysis Services dialog, enter the Server Name for your SSAS server. Select your Adventure Works (names will vary) database from the Catalog Name drop-down, click Test Connection, and, finally, click OK. You are returned to the Analysis Services Connections dialog. In this dialog, click Close. You should now see your connection in the Connection group of the Data Mining ribbon.

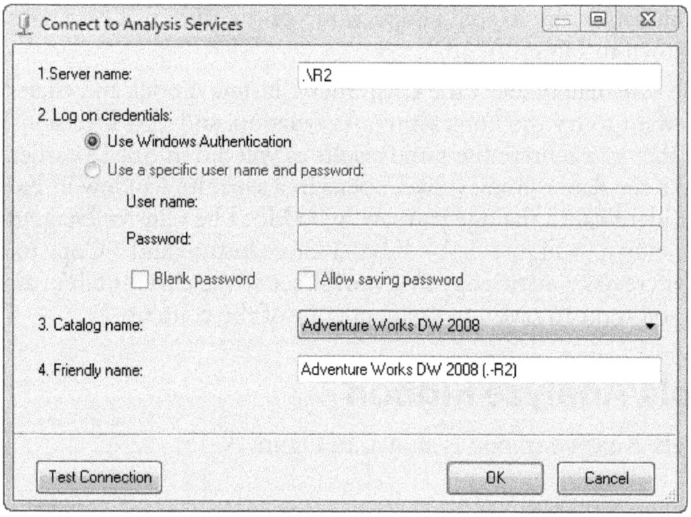

Figure A-12   *Connect to Analysis Services dialog*

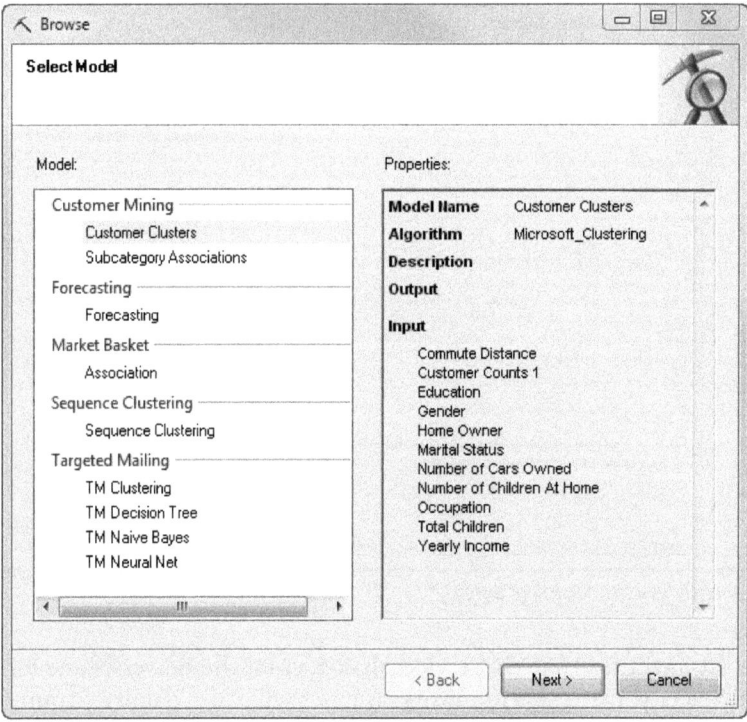

Figure A-13 *Browse dialog*

4. Now you want to generate a Content query and display the results. Click the Browse button in the Model Usage group of the ribbon. This opens the Browse dialog shown in Figure A-13.

5. In the Browse dialog, select the Customer Clusters model, and click Next. Later, you may want to try the Forecasting, Association, and TM Decision Tree models to verify that you achieve the same results as you did in SSMS earlier. After you click Next, the data mining viewer opens in a separate window in Excel. This viewer is almost identical to the one you saw in SSMS. The Cluster Diagram tab of the viewer is shown in Figure A-14. It has a Close button and a Copy to Excel button. The latter creates a static copy in a worksheet of the current tab in a viewer—this is useful if you want to save a permanent copy of the content.

Table Tools/Analyze Ribbon

The Table Tools/Analyze ribbon is shown in Figure A-15.

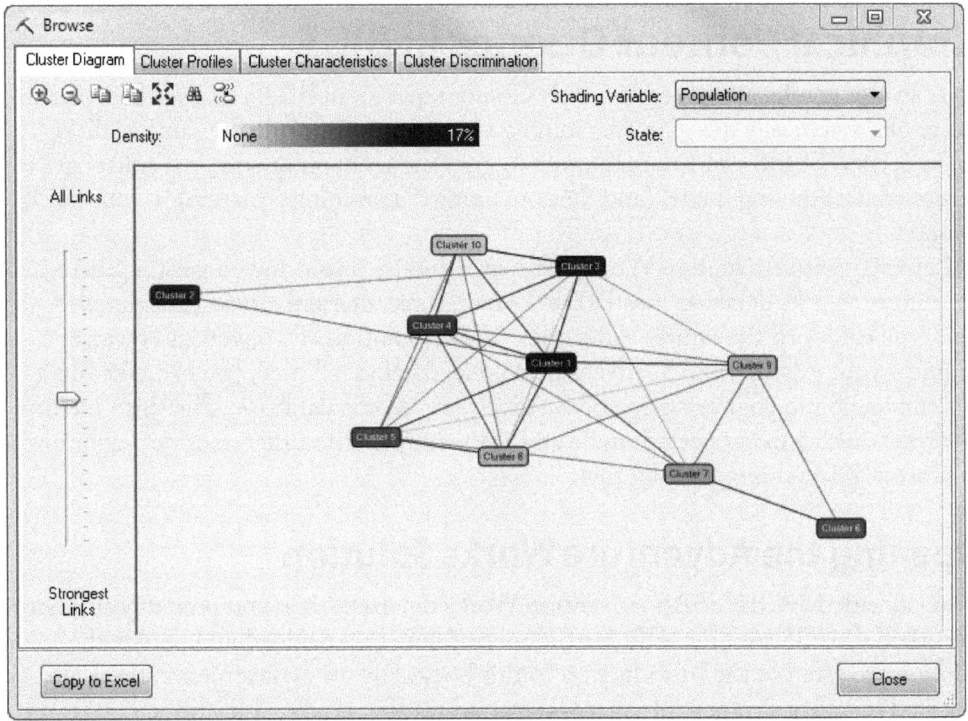

Figure A-14   *Cluster Diagram tab in Excel*

This ribbon also contains data mining functionality. However, it *cannot* be used to generate Content queries against existing SSAS data mining models. It can be used to create temporary SSAS data mining models, but these are not persistent in SSAS. When the content of these temporary models is visualized, the SSAS data mining viewers are not used. Instead, the content is displayed (and optionally saved) within an Excel worksheet, usually as a new Excel table. The data used to train the model must reside in an existing Excel table. This appendix is all about graphically writing DMX queries against established SSAS data mining models—consequently, the Table Tools/Analyze ribbon is not discussed further in this appendix. It's mentioned for completeness and so you can experiment with its functionality at a later date.

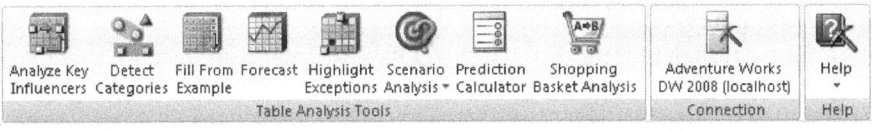

Figure A-15   *Table Tools/Analyze ribbon*

Graphical Content Queries in BIDS

You can also graphically generate DMX Content queries in BIDS, and you can visualize the results graphically too. The data mining viewers are essentially the same as those you've seen in SSMS and Excel. In order to generate Content queries, you must have a processed data mining model (and the containing data mining structure) in your BIDS solution.

Let's stay with Adventure Works. The question is, "How do you get the SSAS Adventure Works database into BIDS?" Here, three alternatives are considered. One, you can open the sample Adventure Works solution. Two, you can reverse-engineer your existing SSAS Adventure Works database. Three, you can take out a live connection to your existing SSAS Adventure Works database. The third method involves working in connected mode and is the only method that does not require you to process a data mining model first.

Opening the Adventure Works Solution

If you already have the SSAS Adventure Works database, then you probably still have the original BIDS solution. Full instructions of how to download and deploy the solution are given in the Introduction to this book. For your convenience, these are repeated here. It's also possible that you started reading the book in this appendix on graphical queries.

You will need two databases. First, the SSAS Adventure Works DW 2008 database (called Adventure Works DW in SSAS 2005), which contains the Adventure Works mining models. Second, the SQL Server AdventureWorksDW2008 database (called AdventureWorksDW in SQL Server 2005), which provides the source data required by the SSAS Adventure Works DW 2008 database.

You can download the required SSAS database (with the Adventure Works mining models) and SQL Server database from www.codeplex.com (both 2008 and 2005 versions). As of this writing, the URL was http://www.codeplex.com/MSFTDBProdSamples/Release/ProjectReleases.aspx?ReleaseID=16040. Choose SQL Server 2008 or SQL Server 2005 from the Releases box. URLs can change—if you have difficulty, search for Adventure Works Samples on www.codeplex.com.

Before you begin the download, you might want to check the two hyperlinks for Database Prerequisites and Installing Databases. For SSAS 2008, download and run SQL2008.AdventureWorks All Databases.x86.msi (there are also 64-bit versions, x64 and ia64). As the installation proceeds, you will have to choose an instance name for your SQL Server. When the installation finishes, you will have some new SQL Server databases including AdventureWorksDW2008 (used to build the SSAS Adventure Works mining models).

For SSAS 2005, the download file is called AdventureWorksBICI.msi (there are also 64-bit versions, x64 and IA64). With 2005 you can also go through Setup or Control Panel to add the samples—this is not possible in 2008. Unlike in 2008, the download and subsequent installation do not result in the new SQL Server source database appearing under SQL Server in SSMS. You have to manually attach the database. You can do this from SSMS (right-click the Databases folder and choose Attach) if you have some DBA knowledge. Or you might ask your SQL Server DBA to do this for you.

Deploying and Processing the Database

You won't be able to see the data mining content, just yet. You must deploy and process the database first. Doing so also deploys and processes all of the data mining models.

1. Navigate to C:\Program Files\Microsoft SQL Server\100\Tools\Samples\ AdventureWorks 2008 Analysis Services Project (C:\Program Files\Microsoft SQL Server\90\Tools\Samples\AdventureWorks Analysis Services Project for 2005).

2. Depending on your edition of SSAS, open the Enterprise or Standard folder.

3. Double-click the Adventure Works.sln file. This will open BIDS.

4. In Solution Explorer, right-click on the Adventure Works project, which is probably in bold. If you can't see Solution Explorer, click View | Solution Explorer. The project will be called Adventure Works DW 2008 (for SSAS 2008 Enterprise Edition) or Adventure Works DW 2008 SE (for SSAS 2008 Standard Edition) or Adventure Works DW (for SSAS 2005 Enterprise Edition) or Adventure Works DW Standard Edition (for SSAS 2005 Standard Edition).

5. Click Deploy (then click Yes if prompted). After a few minutes, you should see a Deploy Succeeded message on the status bar and Deployment Completed Successfully in the Deployment Progress window.

If the deployment fails, try these steps:

1. Right-click on the project and choose Properties. Go to the Deployment page and check that the Server entry points to your SSAS (*not* SQL Server) instance—you might have a named SSAS instance rather than a default instance, or your SSAS may be on a remote server.

2. Right-click on Adventure Works.ds (under the Data Sources folder in Solution Explorer) and choose Open. Click Edit and check that the Server Name entry points to your SQL Server (*not* SSAS) instance—you might have a named SQL Server instance rather than a default instance, or your SQL Server may be on a remote server.

3. Try to deploy again.

If the deployment is successful, you can now browse the Adventure Works data mining models in BIDS (and in SSMS and in Excel).

Reverse-Engineering the Adventure Works Database

Instead of opening the Adventure Works solution, you may wish to use your existing SSAS Adventure Works database. This involves reverse-engineering the database. (I have heard this referred to as "undeployment.") Reverse engineering creates a BIDS solution based on an existing database that has already been deployed to the server and processed. Here are the steps to reverse-engineer Adventure Works:

1. Open BIDS. If you are new to BIDS, its full name is SQL Server Business Intelligence Development Studio, and it can be found in your SQL Server program group.

2. Click File | New | Project to open the New Project dialog. This dialog is shown in Figure A-16.

3. In the New Project dialog, select Import Analysis Services Database and click OK. This starts the Import Analysis Services Database Wizard. Click Next to move on from the welcoming page. You are now on the Source database page, which is shown in Figure A-17.

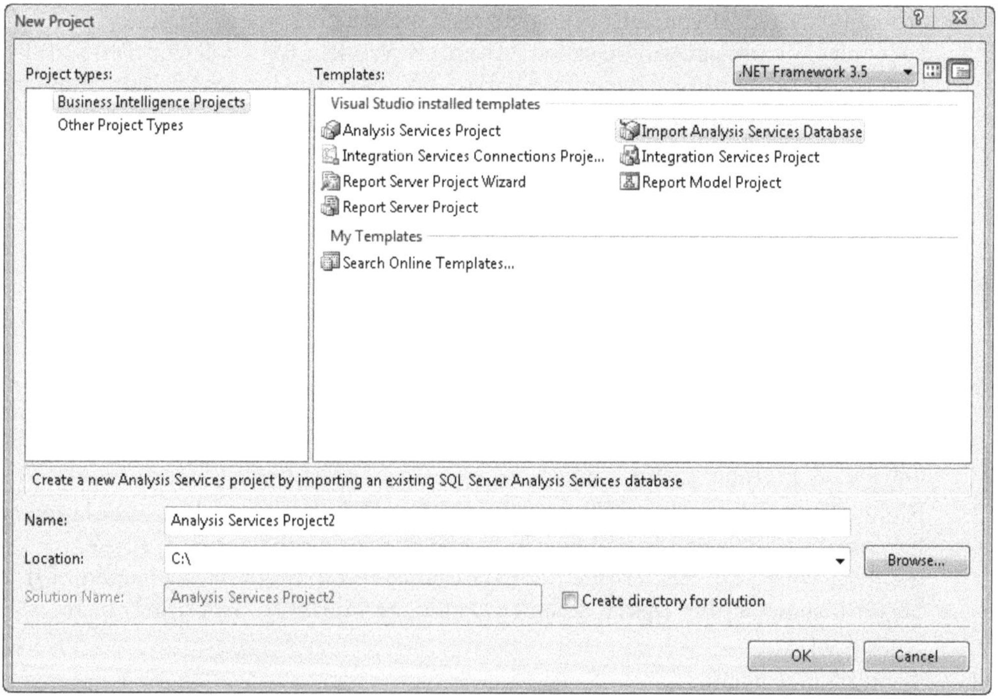

Figure A-16 *New Project dialog*

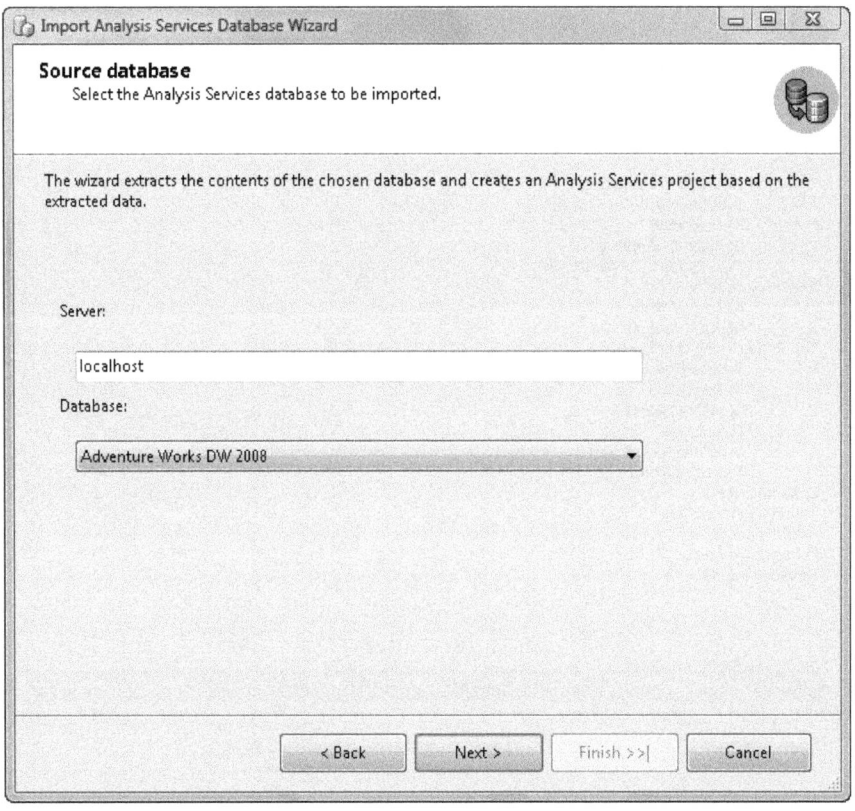

Figure A-17   *Choosing a database to import*

4. On the Source database page, enter a name in the Server field, and from the
    Database drop-down choose your Adventure Works database (this has various
    names depending on your version and edition of SSAS). Click Next to display
    the Completing the Wizard page (shown in Figure A-18). When the reverse
    engineering is complete, the Finish button is enabled. Click Finish.

In the BIDS Solution Explorer window, you will see a few data mining structures.
These have a file extension of .dmm. If the Solution Explorer window is not visible,
click View | Solution Explorer. You won't see a database as such. The SSAS database
is represented by the project, which has a name starting "Analysis Services Project."
This is also the name of the database—the original database name is not imported.
If you deploy and process the database (that is, send it back to the server), a new
SSAS database will be created. If you want to overwrite the original database, it's not

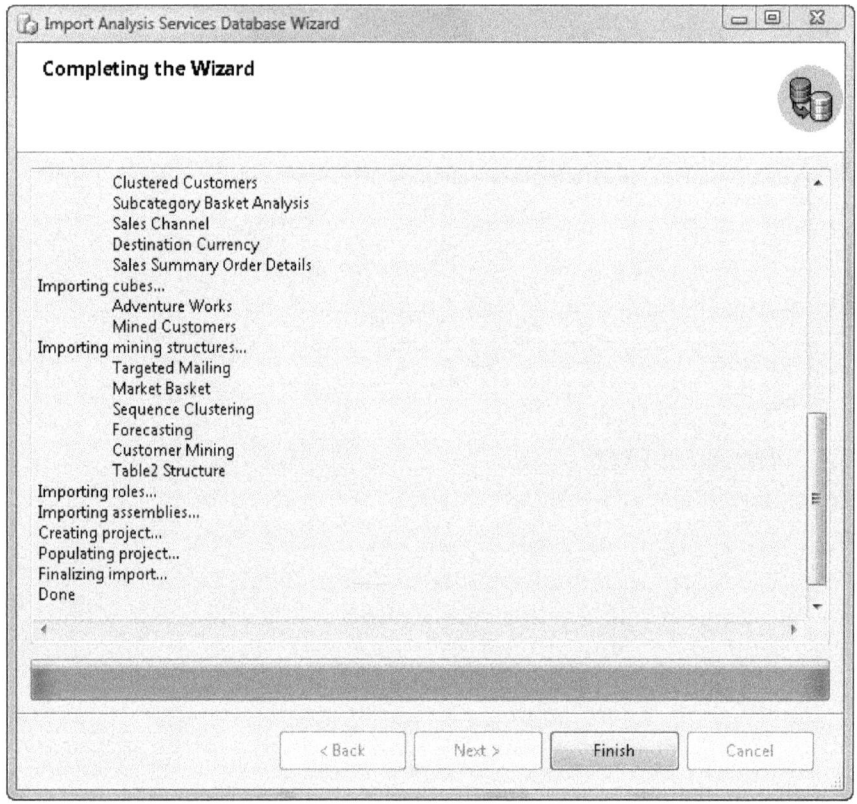

Figure A-18 *Completing the wizard*

sufficient to simply rename the project. You must also right-click the project and choose Properties to open the Property Pages dialog. Then, go to the Deployment page and change the Database name. For our purposes, this is not necessary; we will simply create a new SSAS database—you can always delete it later from SSMS. However, you might want to check the Server name on the Deployment page, especially if your SSAS server is either remote or a named instance. Before you can generate DMX queries, you must process or train the data mining models. The easiest way to do this is to deploy and process the whole database. Deploying the database is a single step:

1. Right-click on the project in Solution Explorer and choose Deploy. You can also choose Process, but that involves an extra step. When you deploy, you are also processing. When you process, you are also deploying.

If the deployment is successful, you can now browse the Adventure Works data mining models in BIDS (and in SSMS and in Excel).

Adventure Works Database in Connected Mode

Rather than deploy and process a database (whether reverse-engineered, or not), you can connect directly to an existing SSAS database from BIDS. This is called working in connected mode. You should be wary of doing this on a production SSAS database as any changes you make in BIDS are reflected on the server, without the need for deployment and processing. If you are happy to try this on the Adventure Works database, here are the steps:

1. Once again, in BIDS, click File | Open | Analysis Services Database. This opens the Connect To Database dialog shown in Figure A-19.
2. In this dialog, enter a name in the Server field and choose the Adventure Works database from the Database drop-down. Then, click OK.

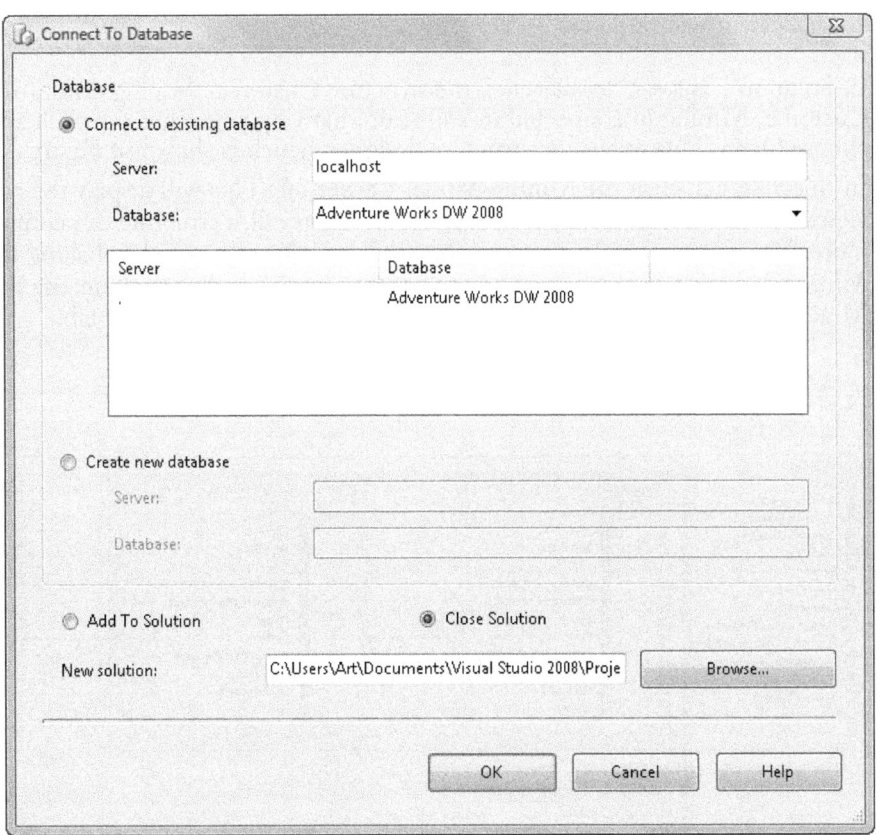

Figure A-19   *Connect To Database dialog*

You can tell you are working in connected mode as the server name appears in the title bar and after the project name in Solution Explorer. This is a live connection to a processed database, so there is no need to deploy and process again to train the data mining models.

Viewing Content

Whether you deployed a new solution, reverse-engineered a database, or took out a live connection to a database, you should see the data mining structures in Solution Explorer. Solution Explorer only shows the structures and not the models. Data mining structures are under the Mining Structures folder. The structures have a file extension of .dmm (unless you are in connected mode, where the extensions are not shown). To see and browse the data mining models, you have to open a structure first. Here are the steps to generate a DMX Content query and visualize the results in BIDS (we'll use Customer Clusters again):

1. In Solution Explorer, double-click the structure Customer Mining.dmm (or just Customer Mining in connected mode)—alternatively, you can right-click and choose Open. This opens the structure designer, which is shown in Figure A-20.

2. In this designer, click the Mining Model Viewer tab. This will display the relevant viewer for the first model in the structure (if you recall, a structure can contain more than one model). You can see the models in the structure by clicking the Mining Models tab. If you wish to see another model in the structure, use the Mining Model drop-down at the top of the Mining Model Viewer tab.

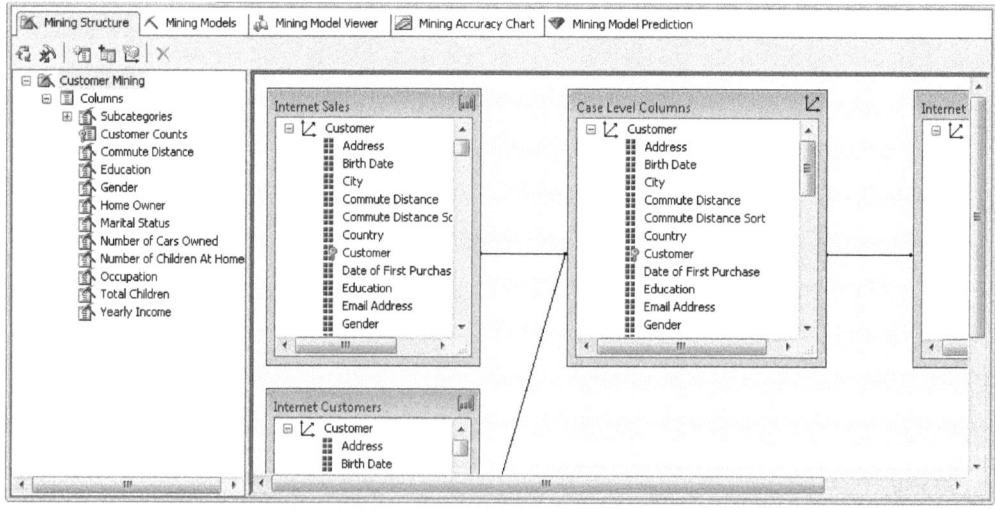

Figure A-20 *Data mining structure designer*

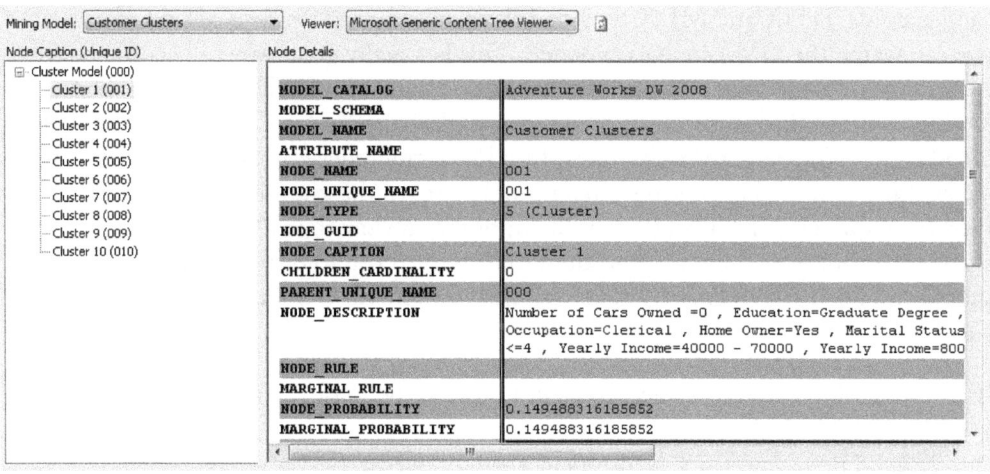

Figure A-21   *Microsoft Generic Content Tree Viewer*

3. The first model in the Customer Mining structure is the Customer Clusters model. The default viewer for a Cluster model is the Microsoft Cluster Viewer. You can see this in the Viewer drop-down at the top of the Mining Model Viewer tab. This viewer was discussed earlier in this appendix, so we won't review its features here. Instead, we'll see a different type of content.

4. From the Viewer drop-down, choose Microsoft Generic Content Tree Viewer. The viewer is shown in Figure A-21. This viewer has a Node Caption pane to the left, which shows the model and the individual clusters in the model. Note that the NODE_TYPE for the model is 1.

5. Click on any cluster in the model in the left-hand pane. Note that the NODE_TYPE for an individual cluster is 5. Have a look at all the other information presented in the Node Details pane.

This is pretty clever stuff. In Chapter 2, you saw some quite intricate DMX syntax to extract the content from a clustering model. Now you've accomplished the same with just a couple of mouse clicks!

Tracing Generated DMX

In a way, this appendix is all about avoiding have to type DMX syntax. However, knowing the DMX syntax gives you total control and allows you to retrieve results into SSRS reports, for example. Whenever you graphically generate DMX queries, the DMX is still there—it's the language that SSAS understands (strictly speaking, SSAS "understands" DMX and MDX provided they are wrapped inside XMLA). Fortunately, you can watch the DMX being generated. This is a really good way to become familiar with DMX. This section examines capturing or tracing the DMX generated. You can use SQL Server Profiler to do so. This is particularly useful for Content queries. You can also use SQL Server Profiler to capture Prediction query (next appendix) and DDL query (third and final appendix) generation. However, the graphical tools for creating Prediction queries generally give you the option to review the DMX.

Here's a short step-by-step procedure to introduce you to SQL Server Profiler (you should still be in BIDS looking at the Microsoft Generic Content Tree Viewer for the Customer Clusters model):

1. Open SQL Server Profiler. You can find it in the Performance Tools subgroup of the main SQL Server program group.

2. Click File | New Trace. This opens the Connect to Server dialog shown in Figure A-22. In the Server Type drop-down, make sure that you select Analysis Services and not Database Engine. In the Server Name drop-down, choose or type the name of your SSAS server. Click Connect.

3. You should now be looking at the Trace Properties dialog. Click on the Events Selection tab. In this tab, turn off all the check boxes under the Events column except Query Begin and Query End, which are in the Query Events section. The Events Selection tab of the Trace Properties dialog is shown in Figure A-23. Then click Run.

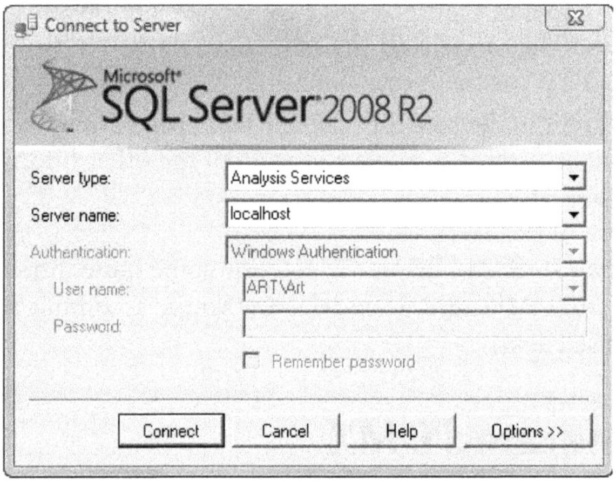

Figure A-22   *Connect to Server dialog*

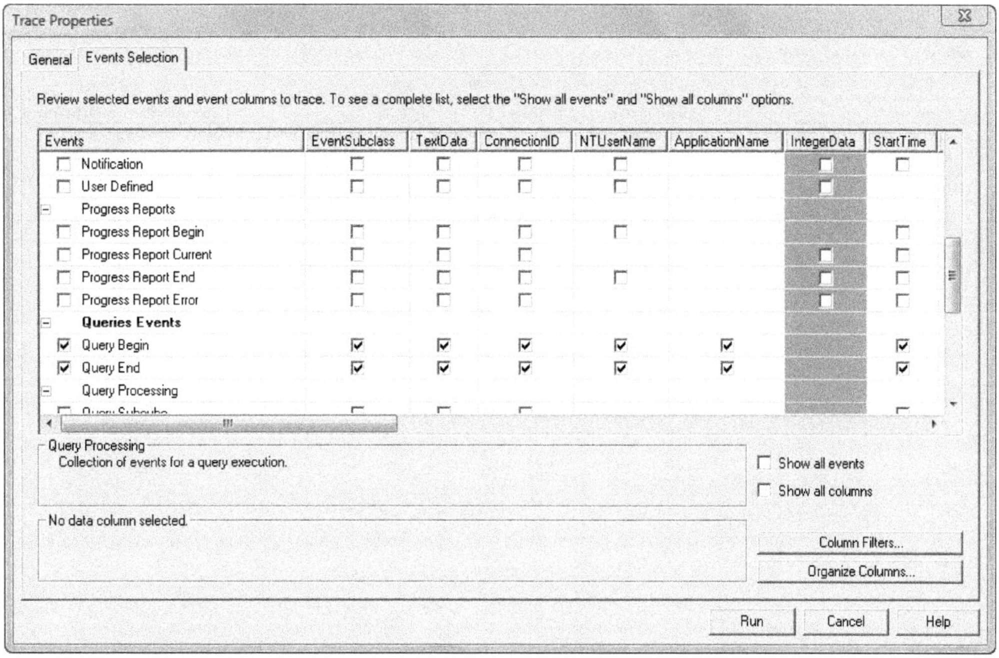

Figure A-23   *Trace Properties dialog*

4.   Switch to BIDS. From the Viewer drop-down on the Mining Model Viewer tab, choose Microsoft Cluster Viewer.

5.   Switch back to SQL Server Profiler and click File | Stop Trace as soon as you can see the DMX query (there should be two entries with an EventSubclass of 1—DMXQuery). This is shown in Figure A-24.

6.   The two entries are for the start and finish of the same query. Select either one and examine the DMX underneath. The syntax should look like the following.

```
SELECT NODE_UNIQUE_NAME, NODE_DESCRIPTION FROM [Customer Clusters].CONTENT
```

7.   Copy and paste the query, and try it out in the DMX query editor in SSMS.

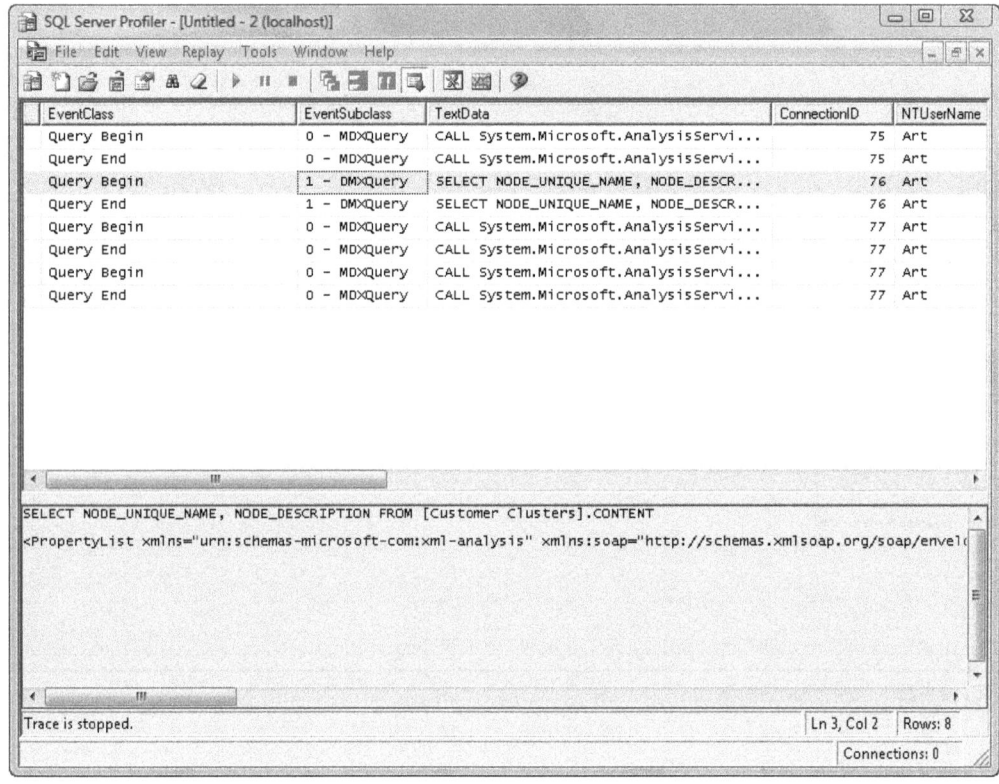

Figure A-24   *SQL Server Profiler trace*

Excel Data Mining Functions

Once you have installed the Data Mining add-in for Excel, you can use the three Excel data mining functions. The one that is relevant to this appendix on Content queries is DMCONTENTQUERY(). Although this is not graphical and involves a fair bit of typing, it does generate a DMX query for you. You can see the DMX generated by the function by tracing in SQL Server Profiler. For this function to work, you will need a data mining connection to SSAS from Excel. This was covered earlier in this appendix—you have to use the <No Connection> button in the Connection group of the Data Mining ribbon. If you set up a connection when we looked at Excel data mining earlier, that will work just fine. This is some sample syntax for DMCONTENTQUERY():

```
=DMCONTENTQUERY("","Customer Clusters","(select [Probability]
from node_distribution where [attribute_name] = 'Education' and
[attribute_value] = 'Graduate Degree')","node_caption = 'Cluster 3'")
```

You enter this in the Excel formula bar for a convenient cell in a worksheet. If you are tracing with SQL Server Profiler, you can view the DMX generated. It looks like this:

```
SELECT FLATTENED (select [Probability] from node_distribution
where [attribute_name] = 'Education' and
[attribute_value] = 'Graduate Degree') FROM [CUSTOMER CLUSTERS].CONTENT
WHERE node_caption = 'Cluster 3'
```

I have kept the capitalization from SQL Server Profiler in this DMX sample. You may want to try this DMX in SSMS. If you do so, you will find that you have the same result as the Excel function returned in the worksheet. If you worked through Chapter 2 on Content queries, you will understand the DMX syntax. It's asking for the probability that a customer in Cluster 3 has a graduate degree for their education. The DMCONTENTQUERY() syntax has four parameters, with the fourth parameter being optional. The first parameter is the name of an SSAS connection—an empty string means the current connection. The second parameter is the name of the data mining model. The third parameter can be outer query column names and/or a subquery for a nested table—here a subquery is being used. The optional fourth parameter generates a Where clause on the outer query. You will notice that the Excel function has automatically flattened the nested table.

That concludes our overview of graphical Content queries. The next appendix takes a look at graphical Prediction queries.

Appendix B

Graphical
Prediction Queries

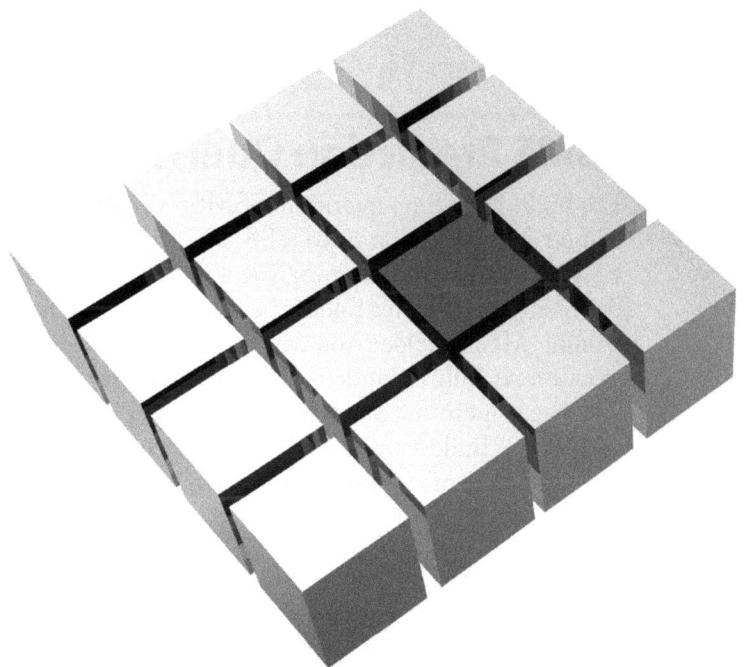

Y ou can also generate Prediction queries graphically. This appendix shows how to do so in SSMS, SSRS, SSIS, SSAS, and Excel 2007/2010.

▶ **Key concepts**   Graphically generating Prediction queries

Prediction Queries

In Chapters 3 through 6, you saw how to write DMX for Prediction queries. You can also generate most of those queries graphically and then view the underlying DMX. This saves on typing and helps eliminate syntax errors. In addition, it's a good way to learn many of the intricacies of DMX syntax for Prediction queries. Nearly all of the graphical tools available use the Prediction Query Builder. This can be found in SSMS, SSRS projects in BIDS, SSIS projects in BIDS (in two places), and SSAS projects in BIDS. The graphical interface available is almost identical in all of those locations— although there are some minor cosmetic differences. Also, the Prediction Query Builder does not always allow you to build singleton queries; in some cases you must use an input table, or view, rather than hard-coded entries for an individual case—of course, you can emulate a singleton query by having only one record in the input table. You can also create Prediction queries from the Data Mining ribbon in Excel (this assumes you have the Data Mining add-in for Excel). The interface in Excel is different from that of the Prediction Query Builder in SSMS, SSRS, SSIS, and SSAS. The Excel alternative is covered toward the end of this appendix.

Before creating some Prediction queries graphically, we examine how to access the Prediction Query Builder.

SSMS Prediction Queries

You build Prediction queries in SSMS from Object Explorer. In Object Explorer you will need a connection to your SSAS server and be able to see a data mining model. To view a model, expand, in turn, your SSAS server, the Databases folder, your database, the Mining Structures folder, the structure containing the data mining model, and the Mining Models folder. You will then be able to see all of the models in the current structure. A fully expanded Object Explorer is shown in Figure B-1.

Once you can see the data mining model of interest, you right-click on the model and choose Build Prediction Query. This opens the Prediction Query Builder. The SSMS version of this builder is shown in Figure B-2.

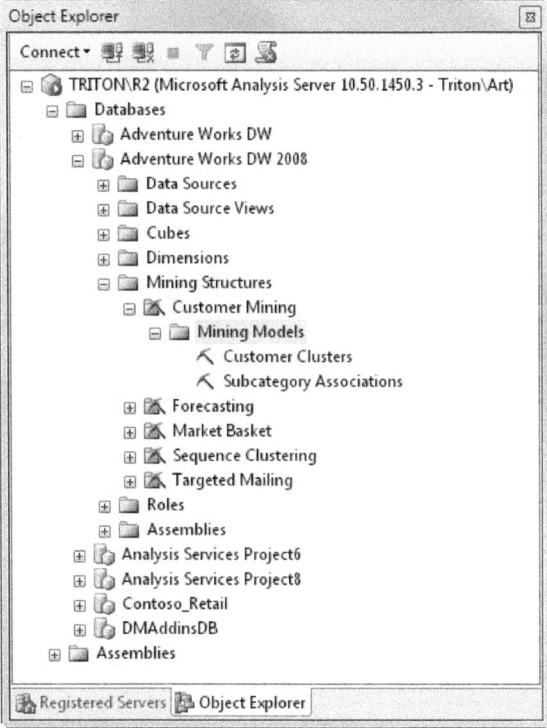

Figure B-1   *Object Explorer*

By default, the query builder is expecting a case table. Also, by default, the mining model is the current one. To change models, you can click the Select Model button—this opens the Select Mining Model dialog shown in Figure B-3. To create a singleton Prediction query, click Mining Model | Singleton Query from the menu bar. Different versions of SQL Server and differing locations of the builder interface have slightly different ways of doing this. Sometimes, you switch to a singleton query using a toolbar button. Sometimes, there is no option to switch from a case table to a singleton query (there you would use a single-record case table to emulate a singleton query). The method given here (Mining Model | Singleton Query) is valid for an SSMS singleton query with SQL Server 2008 R2. You may have to adapt for other interfaces and versions. The Prediction Query Builder for a singleton is shown in Figure B-4.

Later in this appendix, you get to see how to use the query builder to create your queries. Before that, we take a look at other routes to the builder.

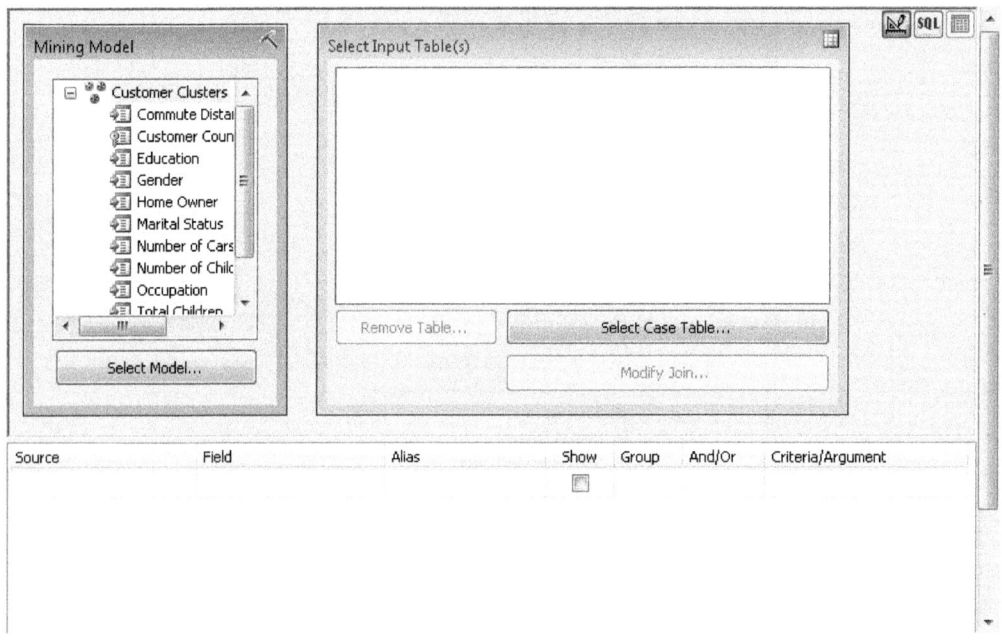

Figure B-2   *Prediction Query Builder in SSMS*

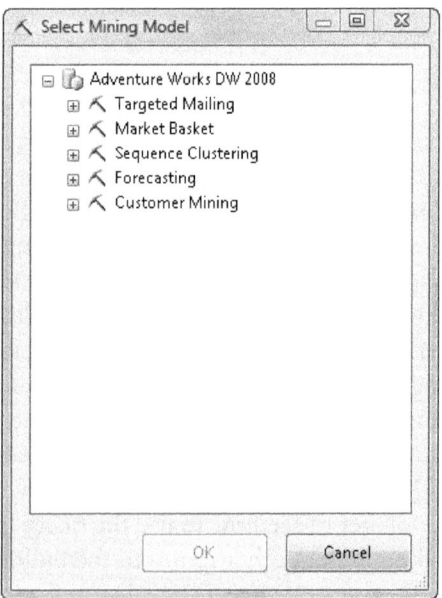

Figure B-3   *Select Mining Model dialog*

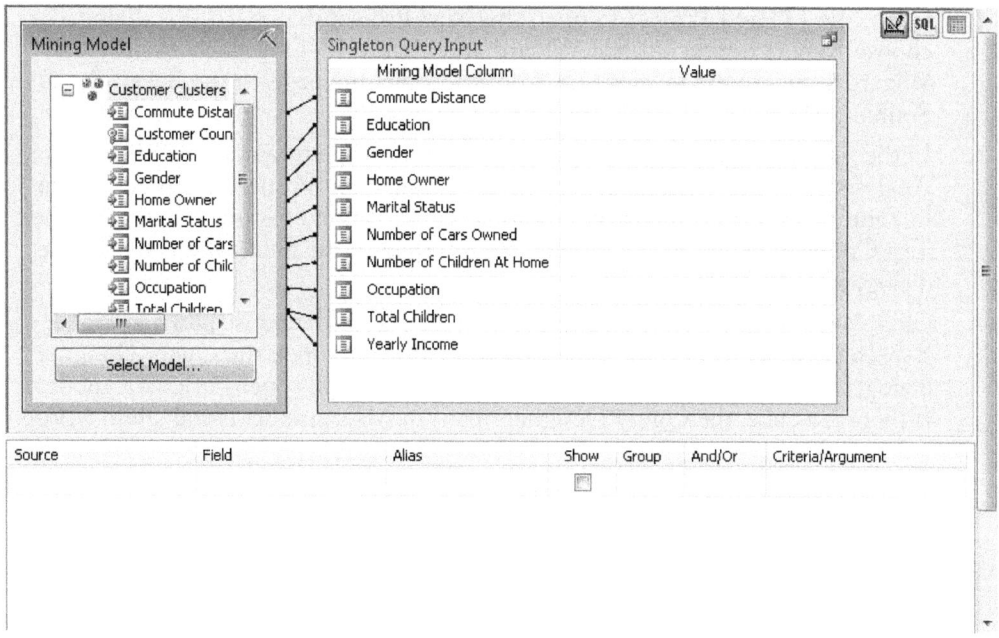

Figure B-4 *Prediction Query Builder for a singleton*

SSRS Prediction Queries

You can build Prediction queries for SSRS in BIDS. This can be done in Report Designer or in the Report Wizard. Whether you use the Report Designer or the Report Wizard, you must take out a connection to SSAS, not the default of SQL Server. BIDS and SSRS are beyond the scope of this book, and only outline instructions are given here. If you are interested in designing SSRS, SSIS, or SSAS objects in BIDS, I refer you to *Delivering Business Intelligence with Microsoft SQL Server 2008* by Brian Larson (McGraw-Hill, 2008). If you are new to SSRS and BIDS, here's an outlined step-by-step procedure to access the Prediction Query Builder (we're using the Report Wizard rather than the Report Designer):

1. Open BIDS (SQL Server Business Intelligence Development Studio in your SQL Server program group).

2. Click File | New | Project to open the New Project dialog. In this dialog, choose Report Server Project Wizard and click OK. This starts the Report Wizard—click Next to move on from the welcome page to the Select the Data Source dialog.

3. In the Select the Data Source dialog, change the Type to Microsoft SQL Server Analysis Services. Click Edit to open the Connection Properties dialog, shown in Figure B-5. Enter the name of your SSAS server and choose a database. Click Test Connection and click OK. You are returned to the Select the Data Source dialog, which is shown in Figure B-6.

4. Click Next to see the Design the Query dialog. This dialog is shown in Figure B-7. In the dialog, click the Query Builder button to open the Query Designer dialog. If there are no cubes in your SSAS database, this opens in DMX mode. If there is a cube, the Query Designer opens in MDX mode. If you are in MDX

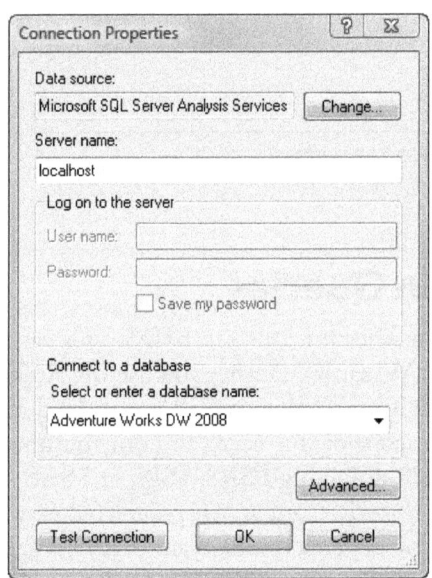

Figure B-5 *Connection Properties dialog*

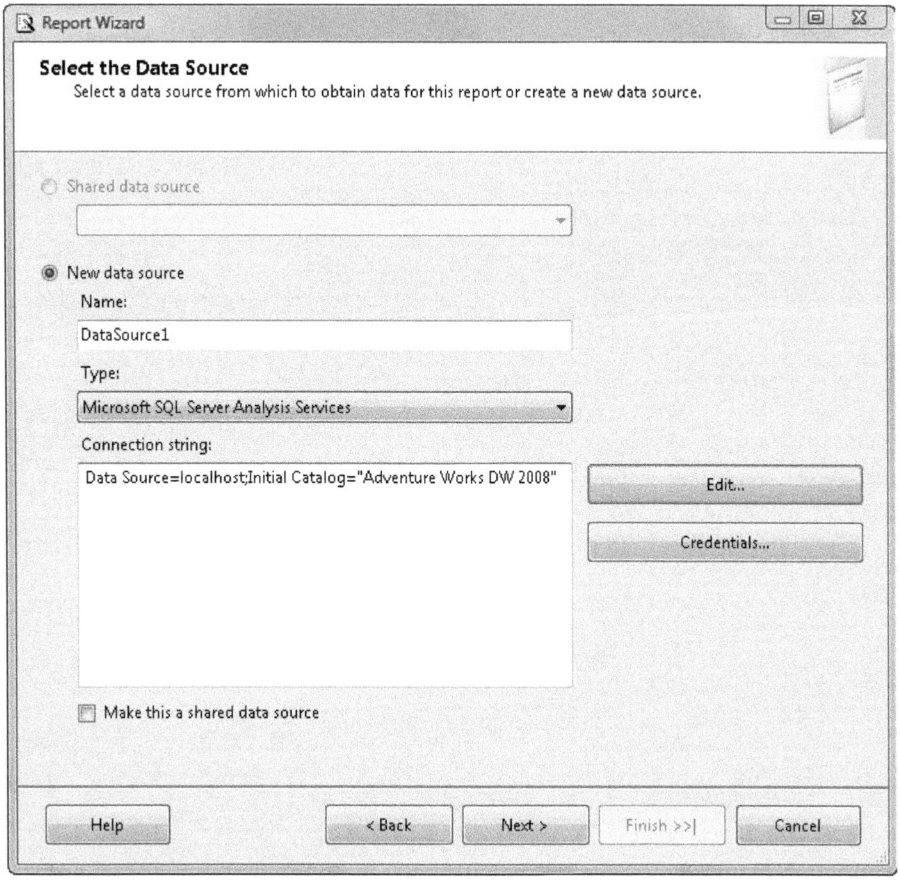

Figure B-6   *Select the Data Source dialog*

mode, you will see a Metadata pane to the left—to switch to DMX mode, click the pick-axe button on the toolbar and click Yes to the warning message. The Query Designer in DMX mode is the Prediction Query Builder. This is shown in Figure B-8. There are a few minor differences from the SSMS version—in particular, there is no option to switch to a singleton query.

Figure B-7 *Design the Query dialog*

The topic of report design is beyond the scope of this book. However, once you have built the query, you can progress through the Report Wizard and create a report based on the results of the DMX query. From there, you can right-click on the report in Solution Explorer and choose Deploy to send the report to your Report Manager or SharePoint web sites.

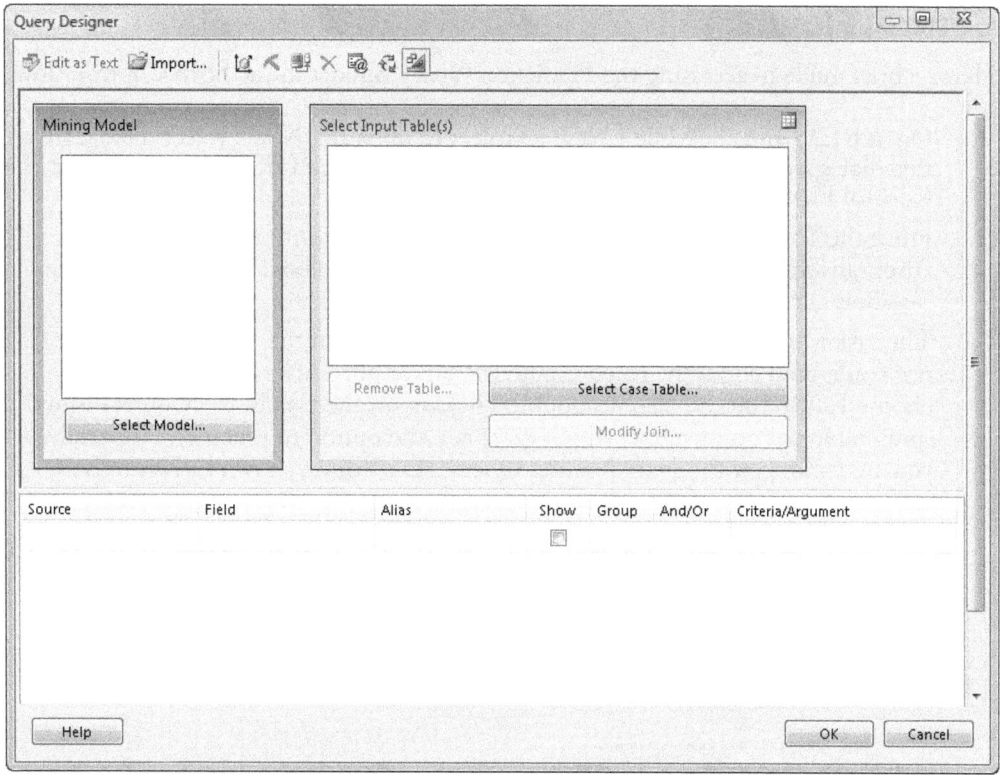

Figure B-8   *Prediction Query Builder in SSRS*

SSIS Prediction Queries

You can build Prediction queries within SSIS in BIDS. This can be done in the Control Flow tab (as a task) or in the Data Flow tab (as a transformation). Whether you use the Control Flow or the Data Flow, you must take out a connection to SSAS. BIDS and SSIS are beyond the scope of this book, and only outline instructions are given here.

A Prediction query in the SSIS Control Flow functions as a task—all of the configuration is done through the task editor. A Prediction query in the SSIS Data Flow functions as a transformation. As such, you must add a source and a destination, before and after the transformation, to create a complete data pipeline within the Data Flow tab. There is no option to switch to a singleton query—you must use a single-record case table instead.

Control Flow

Here's a brief guide to accessing the Prediction Query Builder in the SSIS Control Flow:

1. Open BIDS and click File | New | Project to open the New Project dialog. In this dialog, select Integration Services Project and click OK. This takes you to the Control Flow tab of the SSIS package designer.

2. From the Toolbox, drag the Data Mining Query Task into the Control Flow. Alternatively, you can double-click the task in the Toolbox. If you can't see the Toolbox, click View | Toolbox.

3. The task is now in the Control Flow. The red circle on the task indicates it's not configured correctly. To configure the task, right-click on the task and choose Edit—you can also try double-clicking on the task in the Control Flow (preferably not on its name, which gives you the option to rename). Hopefully, you are looking at the Data Mining Query Task Editor, shown in Figure B-9.

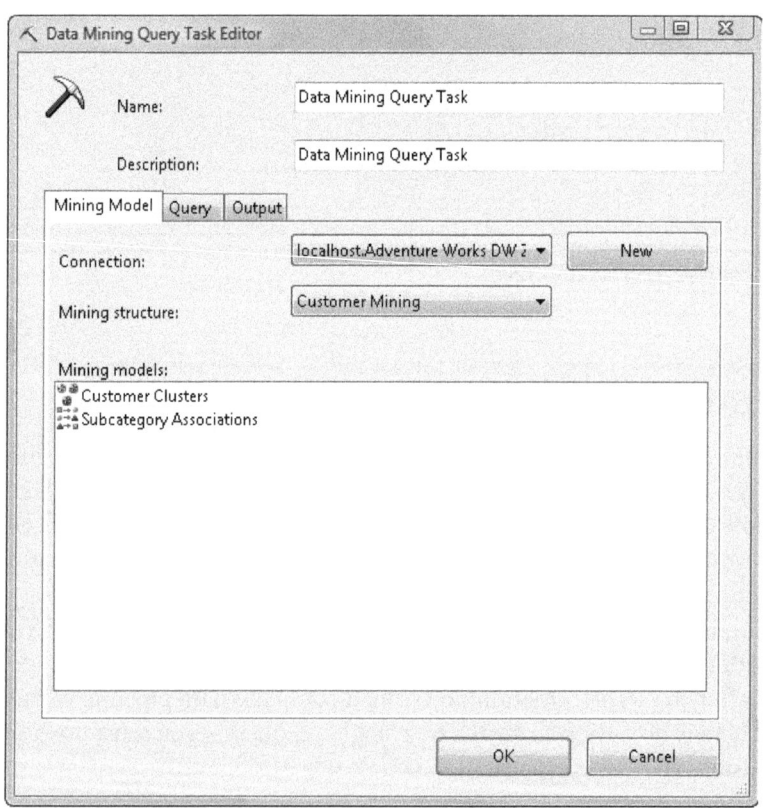

Figure B-9 *Data Mining Query Task Editor*

4. In the editor, click the New button and click New again to take out a connection to your SSAS server and database. Make sure you change the Provider to Microsoft OLE DB Provider for Analysis Services 10.0 (or 9.0 if you have SSAS 2005). Click OK twice to return to the Data Mining Query Task Editor.

5. On the Mining Model tab, choose a structure from the Mining structure drop-down. The mining models in that structure are listed under Mining Models. If you have more than one model, select the model of interest.

6. Click the Query tab. This tab has subtabs. Make sure that the Build Query subtab is current and click Build New Query. This opens the Prediction Query Builder, shown in Figure B-10.

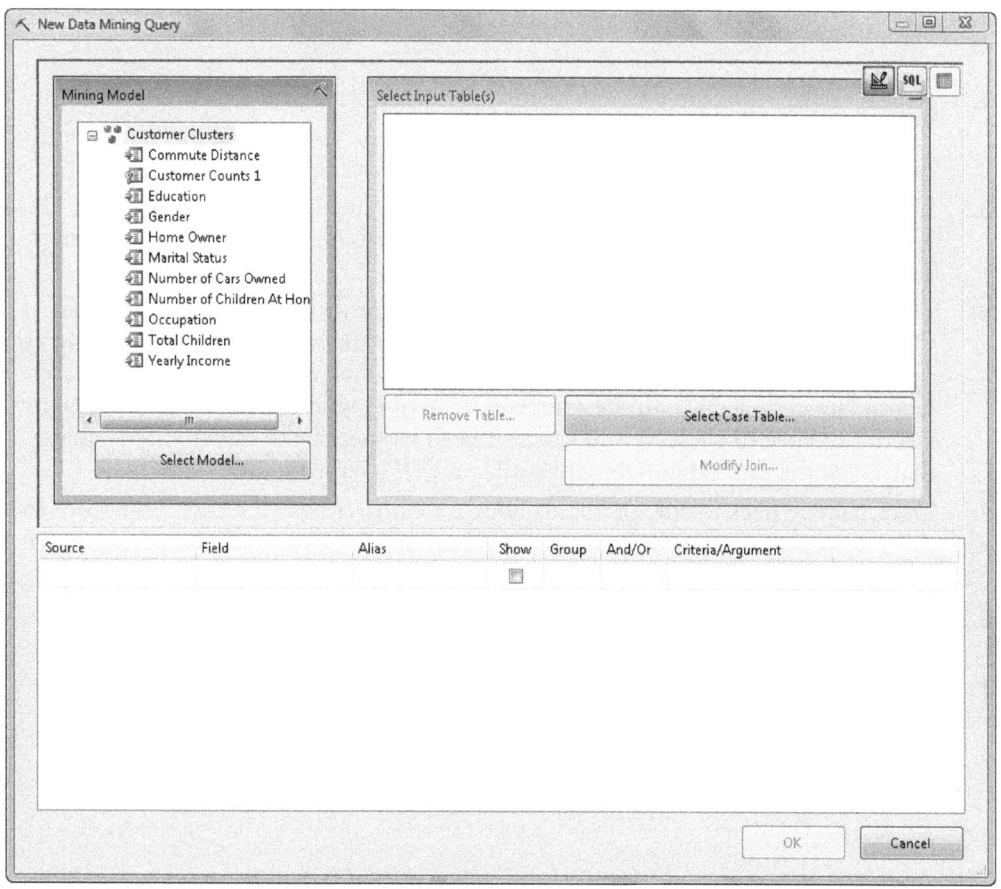

Figure B-10   *Prediction Query Builder in SSIS Control Flow*

7. When you have designed the Prediction query (more on this later in this appendix), click OK to return to the Data Mining Query Task Editor. To complete the process you must specify an output for the DMX query results on the Output tab. On the Output tab, you create a new connection (to a SQL Server database, *not* an SSAS one) and specify the name of the table to hold the results.

8. Execute the package (one way to do this is to right-click on the package file in Solution Explorer and choose Execute Package—by default the package file is called Package.dtsx). Your query results will be saved to the specified output table.

Data Flow

Here's another brief guide, this time to accessing the Prediction Query Builder in the SSIS Data Flow:

1. Repeat step 1 from the previous section on Control Flow to create a new, empty SSIS package.

2. From the Toolbox, add a Data Flow Task to the Control Flow.

3. Double-click the task in the Control Flow (or right-click and choose Edit). This takes you to the Data Flow tab in the package designer. This tab has a different Toolbox from the Control Flow.

4. From the Toolbox (in the Data Flow this time, not the Control Flow), add an OLE DB Source to the Data Flow. Double-click the source in the Data Flow to open the OLE DB Source Editor. In this editor, click the New button. You are taking out a connection to the source of your case table—if the connection is not listed, you have to click New again. You need to specify the server and database that holds the case table—this is possibly a SQL Server source.

5. Once you are back in the OLE DB Source Editor, choose the case table from the third drop-down. A result is shown in Figure B-11. Click on Columns and turn off any columns not required.

6. Click OK to exit the editor. If there is still a red circle in the source, you have to go back and check the configuration.

7. From the Toolbox, add a Data Mining Query to the Data Flow (it's under the Data Flow Transformations section of the Toolbox).

8. Click on the OLE DB Source and drag the green data pipeline onto the Data Mining Query transformation.

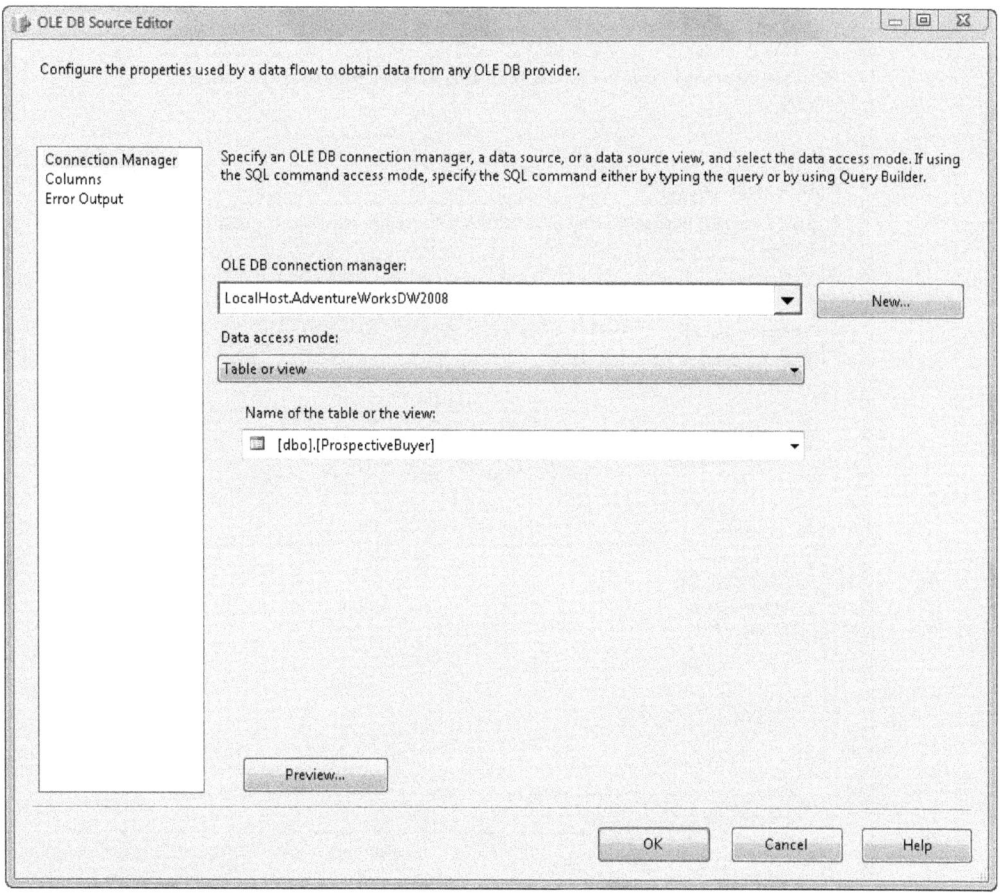

Figure B-11 *OLE DB Source Editor*

9. Double-click the Data Mining Query transformation. This opens the Data Mining Query Transformation Editor. A completed editor screen is shown in Figure B-12.

10. In this editor, you will need an SSAS connection (server and database)—click New followed by Edit (make sure you are using Windows Integrated Security). You can then choose a mining structure from the Mining structure drop-down. Doing so populates the Mining models list. If you have more than one model in the structure, select the appropriate model from the list.

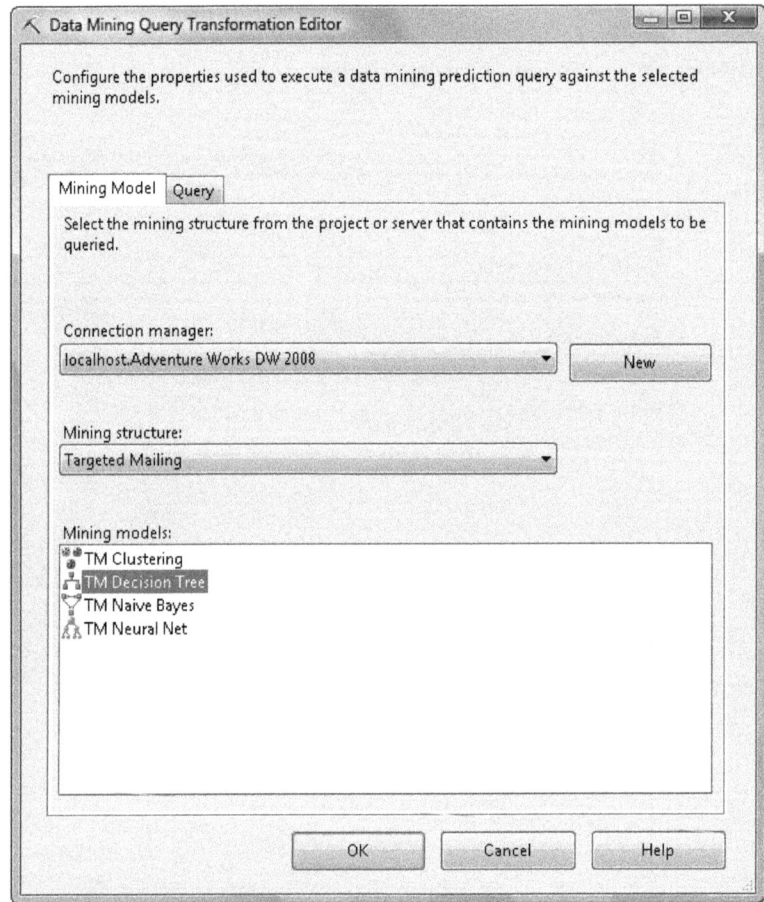

Figure B-12   *Data Mining Query Transformation Editor*

11. Click the Query tab, and in the tab, click Build New Query. This opens the New Data Mining Query dialog—this is the Prediction Query Builder and is shown in Figure B-13.

12. Build your Prediction query (this is covered shortly) and click OK. Click OK again to exit the editor.

13. Add a destination from the Data Flow Destinations section of the Toolbox. This might be an OLE DB Destination (for SQL Server or Excel) or a flat file. If you don't want to commit the query results to a physical destination, you can use the Multicast transformation or a DataReader Destination as a black-hole destination.

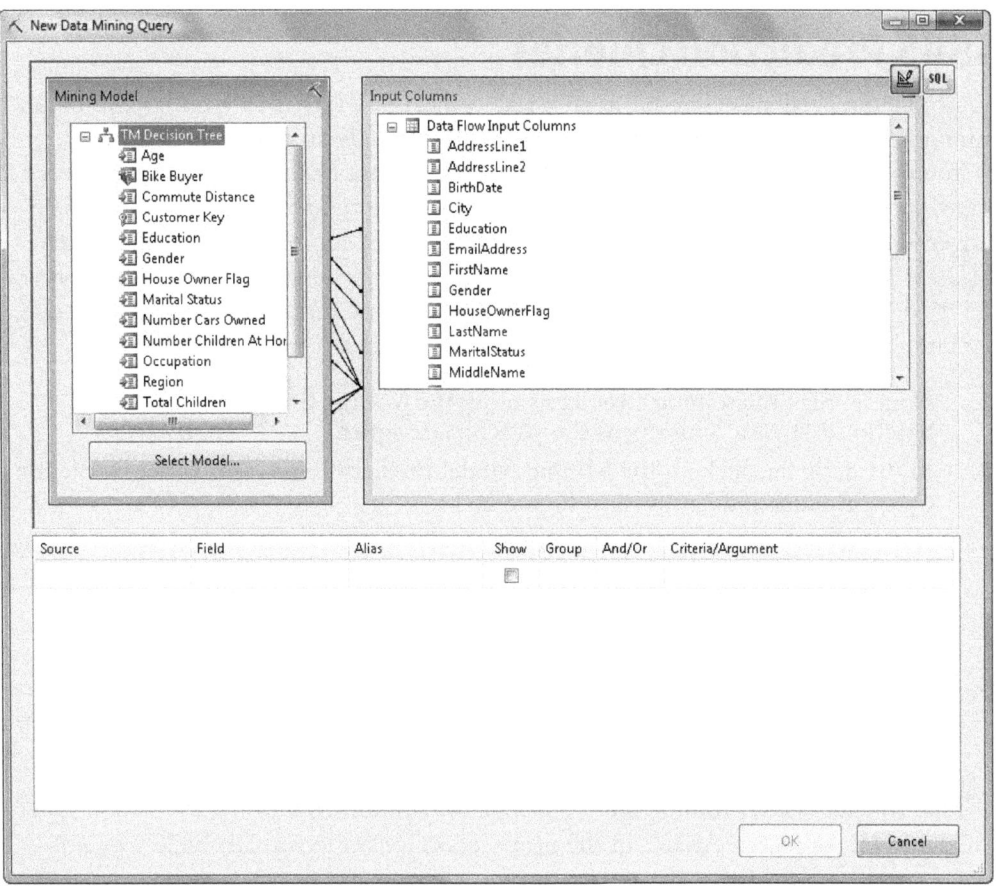

Figure B-13   *Prediction Query Builder in SSIS Data Flow*

14. Drag the green data pipeline from the transformation to the destination. Double-click the destination to configure it—you don't need to do this for a Multicast transformation black-hole destination.

15. Right-click on the lower data pipeline and choose Data Viewers. This opens the Data Flow Path Editor. In this editor, select Data Viewers and click the Add button. Select Grid and click OK twice. The Data Viewer grid lets you see the results of the DMX query in a pop-up window when you execute the package.

16. Execute the package.

SSAS Prediction Queries

You can build Prediction queries in an SSAS project in BIDS. BIDS and SSAS data mining design are beyond the scope of this book, and only an outline is given here.

You will need an SSAS project in BIDS with at least a Data Source, a Data Source View, and a Mining Structure containing a data mining model. If you have the SSAS Adventure Works database, you can use this. Full instructions on how to get this into BIDS as an SSAS project were given in the previous appendix—there are three ways of doing so! The following step-by-step instructions assume that you can see at least one data mining structure in Solution Explorer for an SSAS project in BIDS:

1. Double-click the mining structure (under the Mining Structures folder) in Solution Explorer. This opens the structure designer.

2. In the designer, click on the Mining Model Prediction tab. This is the Prediction Query Builder and is shown in Figure B-14.

3. If the structure contains more than one model, you can switch models by clicking the Select Model button.

4. If you want a singleton, click the singleton query button on the Mining Model Prediction tab's toolbar.

5. Build your Prediction query and view the results. To view the results in this interface, choose Result from the SQL drop-down on the toolbar. Incidentally, the drop-down is labeled SQL as DMX is really an extension to the SQL language.

That concludes our rather lengthy introduction on how to find the Prediction Query Builder in lots of places. At last, in the next section we get to actually build a query!

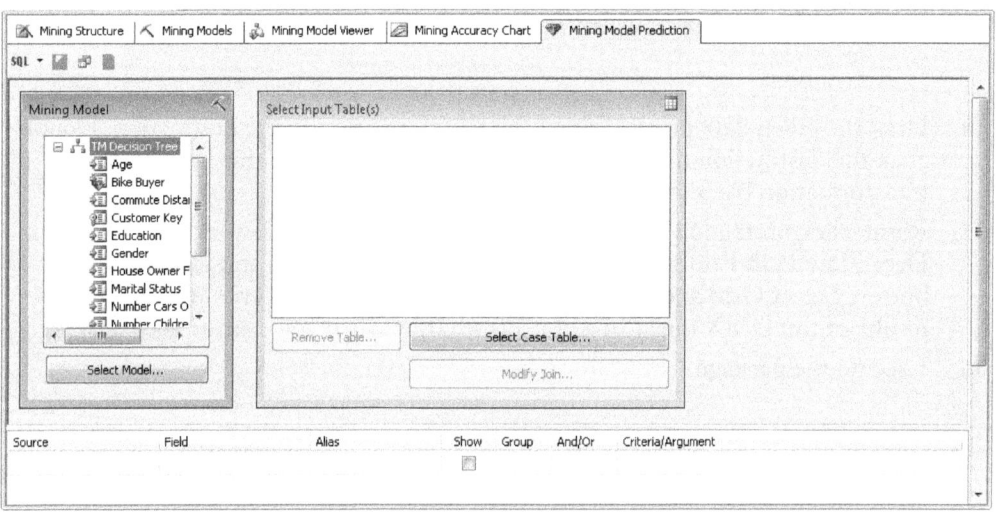

Figure B-14   *Prediction Query Builder in SSAS*

Building a Prediction Query

Of all the methods, perhaps the easiest and most direct way to use the Prediction Query Builder is through SSMS. In the examples that follow, SSMS is used. The principles, however, are the same, no matter which route you take to the builder. There are some minor cosmetic interface differences, but you should be able to adapt the SSMS instructions easily for SSRS or SSIS or SSAS. The only problem arises with singleton queries. The builder only supports these in SSMS and SSAS. If you are using SSRS or SSIS and wish to have a singleton query, you will need a single record case table. Should you do this, be aware that the DMX generated will be for an input case table rather than a DMX singleton query, in which the attribute values are hard-coded in the syntax. We'll take a quick look next at Clustering Prediction queries, Time Series Prediction queries, Association Prediction queries, and Decision Trees Prediction queries—all will use the models in the SSAS Adventure Works database. Later on, we'll have a quick look at the Excel alternative.

Clustering Prediction Queries

This section is based on the Customer Clusters model in the Customer Mining structure. Following is a quick practical to generate Prediction and Cluster queries and view the results:

1. In Object Explorer in SSMS, right-click the Customer Clusters data mining model and choose Build Prediction Query.

2. In the query builder, click Select Case Table. This opens the Select Table dialog, which is shown in Figure B-15. In the Data Source drop-down you will see two connections. One is to the SSAS database, and the other is to the underlying data source for the SSAS database—here it's a connection to the SQL Server AdventureWorksDW2008 database. We need the SQL Server connection to select the input case table—quite possibly, you have to switch in the drop-down. It's the connection with a table called ProspectiveBuyer—choose this table and click OK. You could choose the Customer dimension from the SSAS connection, but that contains the cases already used to train the model. By choosing ProspectiveBuyer, we are analyzing completely new customers.

3. In the builder, mappings are automatically made between model columns and case columns with the same names (it is sometimes clever enough to do this even though one name may contain spaces and the other may not). If you want to add more mappings, for columns where the names are different, simply drag from one to the other. If you want to remove a mapping, click on the mapping line to highlight it and press DELETE.

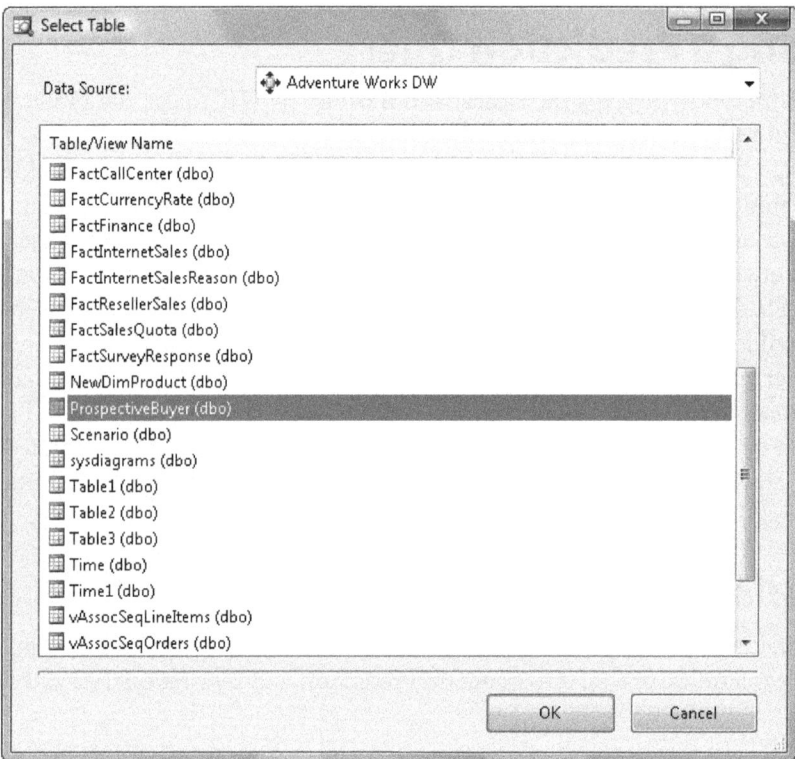

Figure B-15 *Select Table dialog*

4. In the lower part of the builder, select ProspectiveBuyer table in the Source column drop-down. In the Field column drop-down, select LastName.

5. In the second row, select Education as Field.

6. In the third row, select Occupation as Field.

7. In the fourth row, select Prediction Function as Source and Cluster as Field.

8. In the fifth row, select Prediction Function as Source and ClusterProbability as Field. Your builder should look like Figure B-16.

9. Click the third button on the small toolbar at the top right to switch to query result view. Based on education and occupation, it shows the cluster to which the customer is most likely to belong. It also shows the probability of their doing so. If you switch back to design view (first button), you can optionally enter a cluster name in single quotes as the Criteria/Argument for the `ClusterProbability()` function—this will return the likelihood of a customer belonging to the nominated cluster.

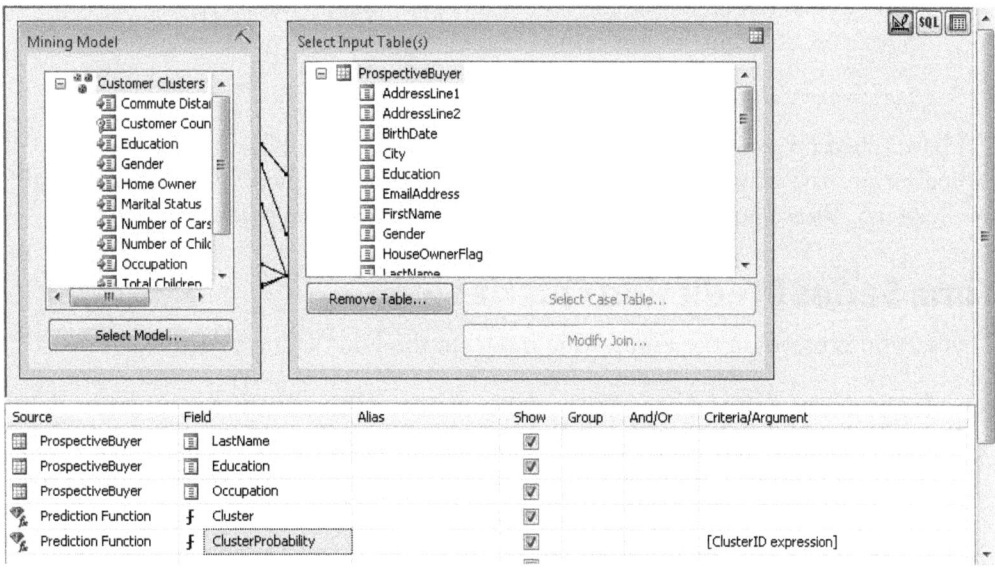

Figure B-16 *Completed Prediction Query Builder*

10. Now switch to text view (the middle SQL button). That's cool DMX you just wrote! You can edit the DMX if you want, but any changes you make are lost if you switch back to design view. My generated DMX looks like the following:

```
SELECT
t.[LastName],
t.[Education],
t.[Occupation],
Cluster(),
ClusterProbability()
From
[Customer Clusters]
PREDICTION JOIN
OPENQUERY([Adventure Works DW],
'SELECT
[LastName],
[Education],
[Occupation],
[MaritalStatus],
[Gender],
[YearlyIncome],
[TotalChildren]
FROM
[dbo].[ProspectiveBuyer]
') AS t
ON
[Customer Clusters].[Marital Status] = t.[MaritalStatus] AND
[Customer Clusters].[Gender] = t.[Gender] AND
```

```
[Customer Clusters].[Yearly Income] = t.[YearlyIncome] AND
[Customer Clusters].[Total Children] = t.[TotalChildren] AND
[Customer Clusters].[Education] = t.[Education] AND
[Customer Clusters].[Occupation] = t.[Occupation]
```

I have tidied up some white space but preserved the original line breaks and capitalization. You may want to compare this to some of the queries we wrote manually in Chapter 5. Please note this is a prediction join, not a natural prediction join.

Time Series Prediction Queries

This section is based on the Forecasting model in the Forecasting structure.

1. Right-click on the Forecasting model and choose Build Prediction Query.
2. In the builder, there is no need for a case table this time—if you recall, the Time Series algorithm is quite happy to make predictions based on existing, rather than new, data.
3. In the Source column drop-down, select the Forecasting mining model. In the Field column, select Model/Region.
4. Add a second row with a Source of Prediction Function and a Field of PredictTimeSeries.
5. Drag the Quantity column from the mining model to the Criteria/Argument column of the second row. Type a comma (,) followed by **3**. My completed builder is shown in Figure B-17.

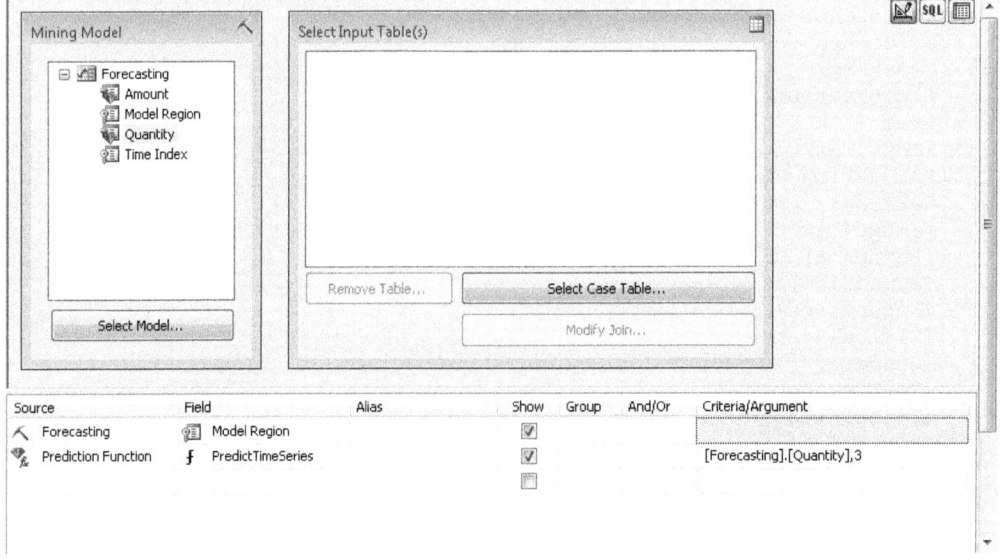

Figure B-17 *Completed Prediction Query Builder*

6. View the results (third button on toolbar). It includes a nested table, which you can expand. It shows the projected future sales quantity for three time periods for each model/region.

7. Switch to text view (the SQL button). The following is the syntax generated:

```
SELECT
[Forecasting].[Model Region],
PredictTimeSeries([Forecasting].[Quantity],3)
From
[Forecasting]
```

This is very similar to some of the hand-written queries in Chapter 4, except this syntax prefixes the column names with the model name to avoid any potential ambiguity. If you would like to test this as a stand-alone DMX query, copy and paste it into the DMX query editor—you may want to also flatten it to expand the nested table and try removing the model name prefix to the two column names.

Association Prediction Queries

This section is based on the Association model in the Market Basket structure. Only the minimal number of steps is given this time. As a change, let's build a singleton query.

1. In the builder for the Association model, click Mining Model | Singleton Query on the menu bar. The focus must be on the builder for this Mining Model menu option to be visible. In some versions of SQL Server, you can also right-click on the background. This changes Select Input Table(s) to Singleton Query Input.

2. Click the ellipsis in the Value column of the first row of Singleton Query Input. This opens the Nested Table Input dialog, shown in Figure B-18.

3. In this dialog, locate and select Water Bottle. Click Add and then OK.

4. In the first row, choose Prediction Function for Source and PredictAssociation for Field.

5. For this row, drag v Assoc Seq Line Items from Mining Model (*not* from Singleton Query Input) to the Criteria/Argument column. Type a comma (,) followed by **5**. The final design is shown in Figure B-19.

6. Have a look at the results of the query—you have to expand the nested table. These are the five most likely products to be bought with a Water Bottle.

7. Switch to text view. The generated syntax is as follows:

```
SELECT
PredictAssociation([Association].[v Assoc Seq Line Items],5)
From
[Association]
NATURAL PREDICTION JOIN
(SELECT (SELECT 'Water Bottle' AS [Model]) AS [v Assoc Seq Line Items]) AS t
```

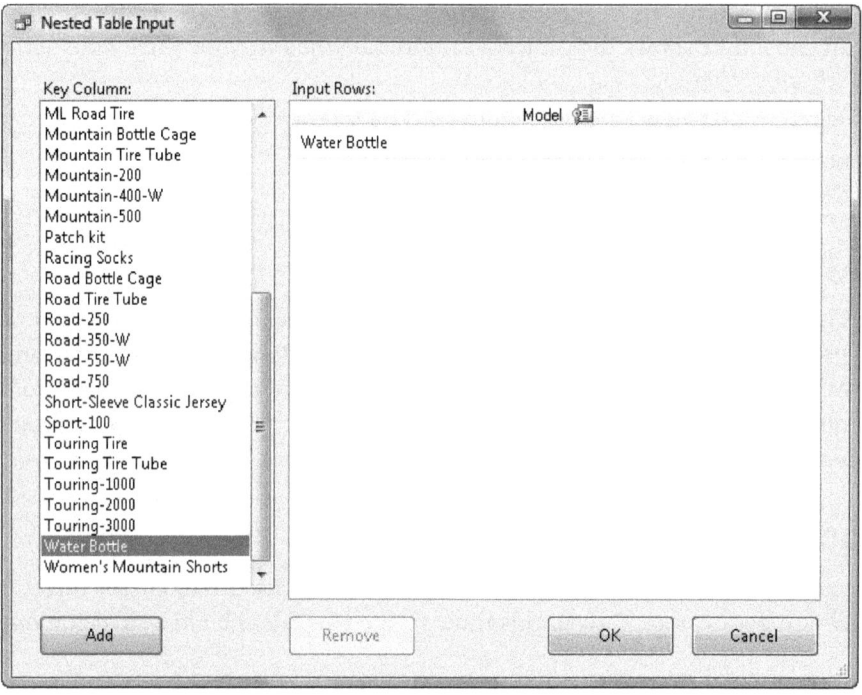

Figure B-18 *Nested Table Input dialog*

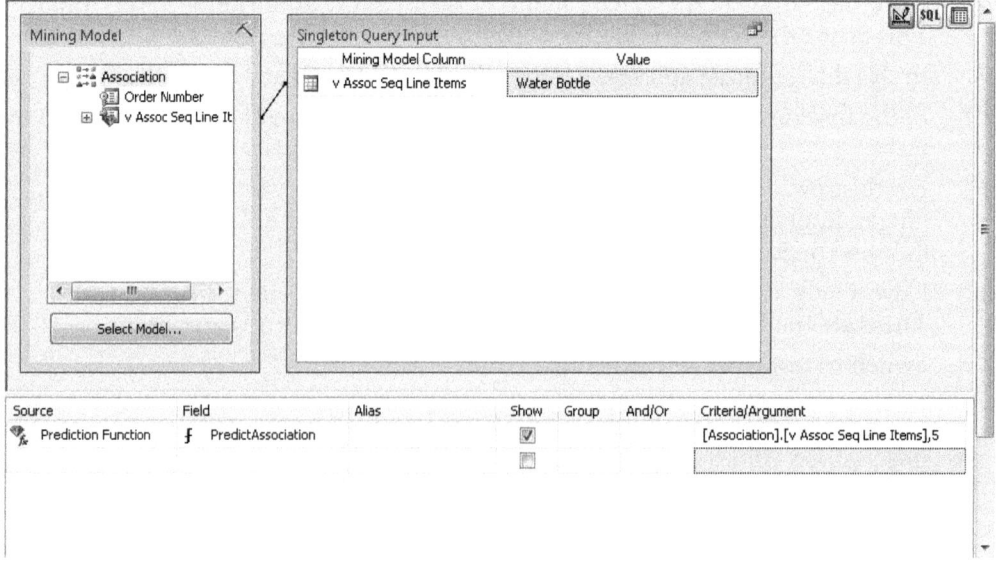

Figure B-19 *Completed Prediction Query Builder*

This is almost identical to the query entitled Cross-selling Prediction 1/7 in Chapter 6. The only differences there are the flattening of the query and the use of the polymorphic `Predict()` function, rather than an explicit `PredictAssociation()` function as in this example.

Decision Trees Prediction Queries

This section is based on the TM Decision Tree model in the Targeted Mailing structure. Here is a short step-by-step procedure:

1. In the builder, click Select Case Table. Switch the Data Source away from SSAS to SQL Server, and choose the ProspectiveBuyer table. Click OK.
2. In the first row, set Source to ProspectiveBuyer table and Field to LastName.
3. In the second row, set Source to ProspectiveBuyer table and Field to FirstName.
4. In the third row, set Source to Prediction Function and Field to Predict (the *first* one). There are two options for Predict—the first accepts a column (scalar) as a parameter, and the second accepts a table.
5. In the fourth row, set Source to Prediction Function and Field to PredictProbability.
6. Drag Bike Buyer from the Mining Model to the Criteria/Argument column for the third (Predict) row.
7. Drag Bike Buyer to the Criteria/Argument column for the fourth (PredictProbability) row. The final design is shown in Figure B-20.

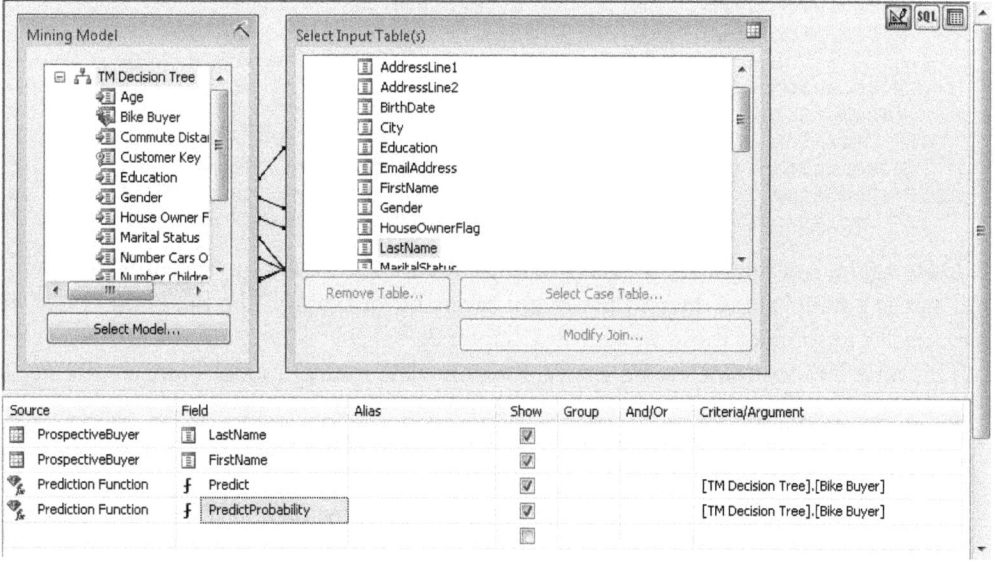

Figure B-20   *Completed Prediction Query Builder*

8. Have a look at the results—they show which new customers are likely to buy a bike (or not) and the probability of their doing so.

9. Finally, check out the DMX syntax.

```
SELECT
t.[LastName],
t.[FirstName],
Predict([TM Decision Tree].[Bike Buyer]),
PredictProbability([TM Decision Tree].[Bike Buyer])
From
[TM Decision Tree]
PREDICTION JOIN
OPENQUERY([Adventure Works DW],
'SELECT
[LastName],
[FirstName],
[MaritalStatus],
[Gender],
[YearlyIncome],
[TotalChildren],
[NumberChildrenAtHome],
[Education],
[Occupation],
[HouseOwnerFlag],
[NumberCarsOwned]
FROM
[dbo].[ProspectiveBuyer]
') AS t
ON
[TM Decision Tree].[Marital Status] = t.[MaritalStatus] AND
[TM Decision Tree].[Gender] = t.[Gender] AND
[TM Decision Tree].[Yearly Income] = t.[YearlyIncome] AND
[TM Decision Tree].[Total Children] = t.[TotalChildren] AND
[TM Decision Tree].[Number Children At Home] =
t.[NumberChildrenAtHome] AND
[TM Decision Tree].[Education] = t.[Education] AND
[TM Decision Tree].[Occupation] = t.[Occupation] AND
[TM Decision Tree].[House Owner Flag] = t.[HouseOwnerFlag] AND
[TM Decision Tree].[Number Cars Owned] = t.[NumberCarsOwned]
```

Once again, you might wish to copy and paste into the DMX query editor in SSMS, and test as a stand-alone query. That might save a bit of typing! The Prediction query is very similar to some of those we met in Chapter 3.

This time, let's try a singleton query on the same data mining model. Here are the steps:

1. Start a new Prediction Query on TM Decision Tree.

2. Switch to a singleton query.

3. In Singleton Query Input, select 37-42 for Age, M for Gender, 0 for Number Cars Owned, and Pacific for Region.

4. In the first row, set Source to Custom Expression, Field to 'Male, Pacific, Youngish, No car', and Alias to Demographics. Please note that the Field entry must be in single quotes unless you are explicitly referencing a column.

5. In the second row, it's Prediction Function and Predict (the first scalar one). Type **Bike Buyer?** as Alias.

6. In the third row, it's Prediction Function and PredictProbability.

7. Drag Bike Buyer from the Mining Model (*not* from Singleton Query Input) to the Criteria/Argument column for *both* the second and the third rows. The final design is shown in Figure B-21.

8. View the results (my result shows a very high probability of this type of customer being a potential bike buyer) and the syntax.

```
SELECT
('Male, Pacific, Youngish, No car') as [Demographics],
(Predict([TM Decision Tree].[Bike Buyer])) as [Bike Buyer?],
(PredictProbability([TM Decision Tree].[Bike Buyer])) as [Probability]
From
[TM Decision Tree]
NATURAL PREDICTION JOIN
(SELECT 40 AS [Age],
'M' AS [Gender],
0 AS [Number Cars Owned],
'Pacific' AS [Region]) AS t
```

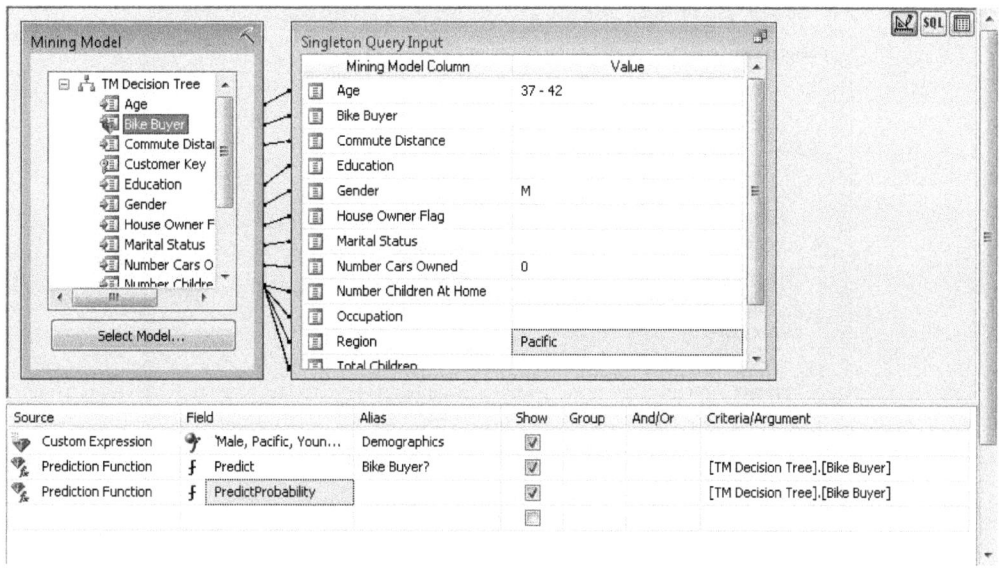

Figure B-21 *Completed Prediction Query Builder*

It might be a good idea to test this in the DMX query editor to verify the syntax and the result. The Prediction Query Builder discretized the Age column. The syntax generated has a value that is approximately in the middle of the discretized range chosen. This query is almost identical (apart from the age of the customer) to the query entitled Singletons 5/6 in Chapter 3.

We have not covered all of the possibilities for DMX Prediction query generation, but you have seen most of the important aspects—and, hopefully, it's enough to get you started.

Excel Prediction Queries

You can also build Prediction queries from the Data Mining ribbon in Excel 2007/2010. You do so by starting the Data Mining Query Wizard. This is only going to work if you already have an SSAS connection in the Connection group of the Data Mining ribbon. Here is a very quick demonstration that assumes you have a connection to the SSAS Adventure Works database already established in the Data Mining ribbon:

1. Click the Query button in the Model Usage group of the Data Mining ribbon. This starts the Data Mining Query Wizard (also called the Query Model Wizard). Click Next to open the Select Model dialog, shown in Figure B-22. For now, notice, but don't click, the Advanced button. Select the Forecasting model and click Next.

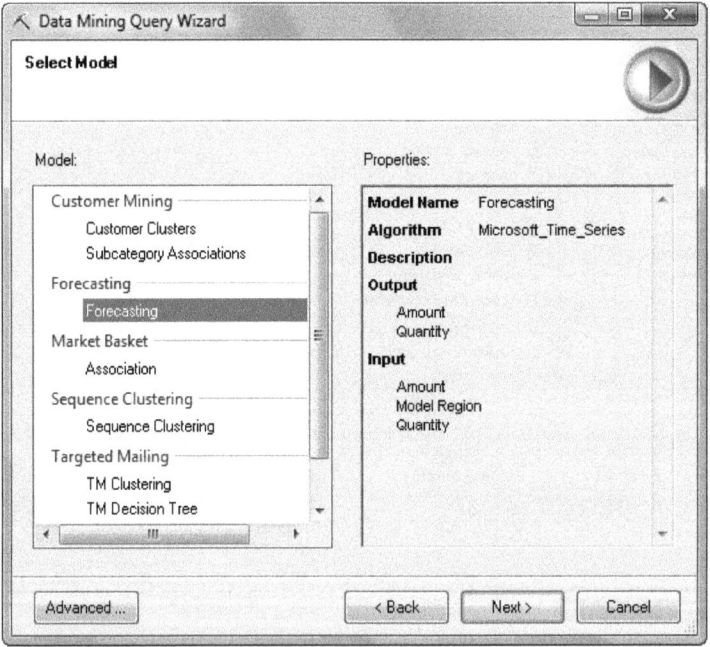

Figure B-22 *Select Model dialog*

2. You are now in the Choose Output dialog of the wizard, shown in Figure B-23. Set the Number of Predictions to 3 and choose Quantity as Column to Predict. Click Next.

3. The next dialog is entitled Choose Destination for Query Results and is shown in Figure B-24. Accept the default destination of New Worksheet and click Finish.

The results are interesting. They are the same as we achieved with the Prediction Query Builder on the Time Series model earlier in this appendix. They are also the same as the results of the query entitled PredictTimeSeries() 2/11 in Chapter 4.

In this Excel example, we didn't get to see the syntax generated. If you wish to dig deeper, try the Advanced button in the Select Model dialog of the wizard. This opens the Data Mining Advanced Query Editor, shown in Figure B-25. In this editor, the drop-down button DMX Templates is incredibly powerful—it can generate lots of useful DMX and not just for Prediction queries. Also, don't forget the equally powerful templates in the DMX query editor in SSMS (View | Template Explorer). If you exploit the Advanced button and the templates in SSMS, and the techniques covered in these three appendixes, you can save a lot of typing and syntax errors and learn even more DMX at the same time. Try the Advanced button, experiment, and have fun with DMX!

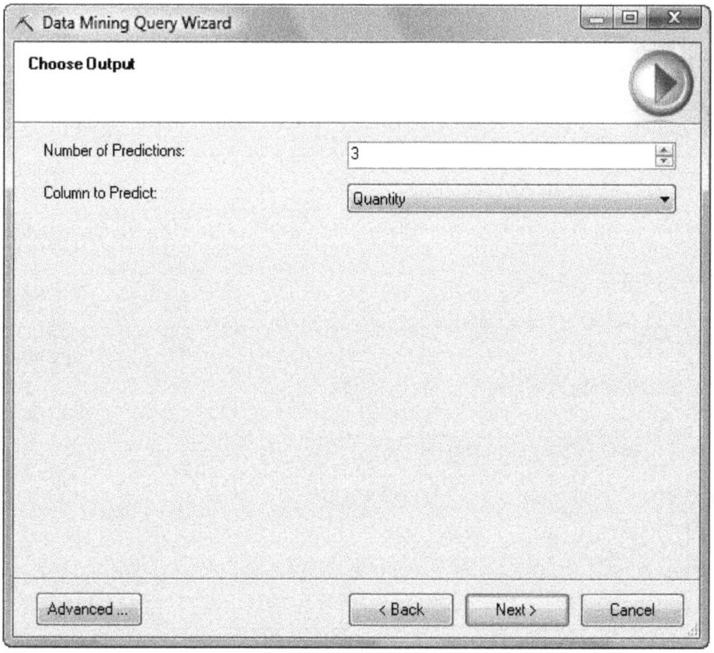

Figure B-23 *Choose Output dialog*

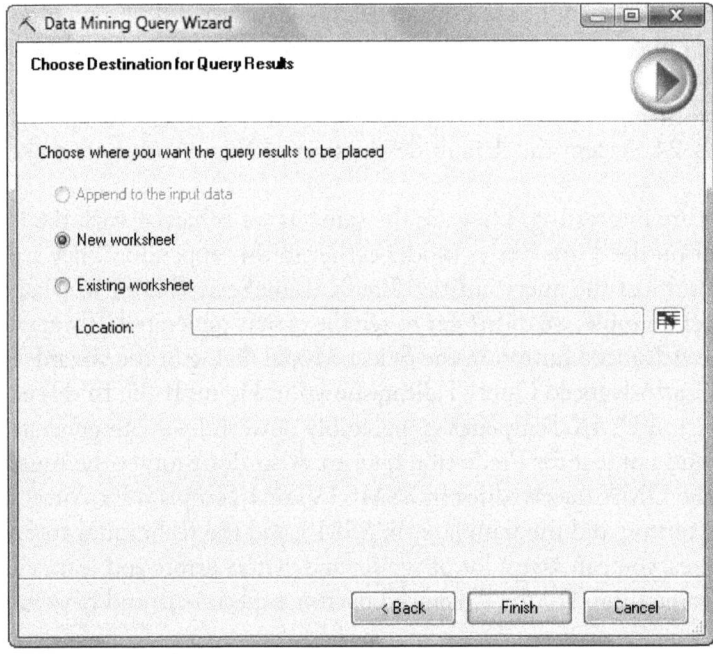

Figure B-24 *Choose Destination for Query Results dialog*

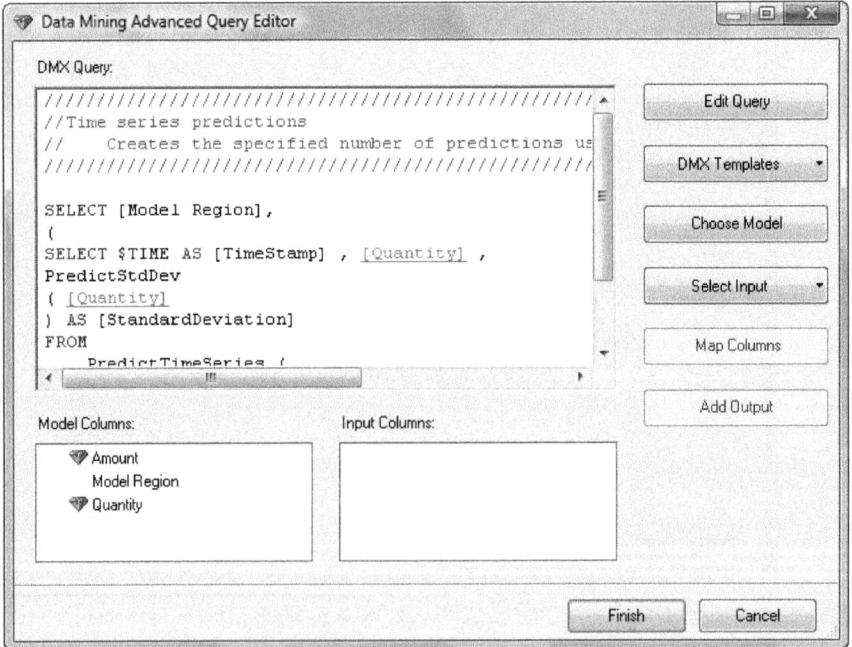

Figure B-25 *Data Mining Advanced Query Editor*

Excel Data Mining Functions

In the previous appendix, we met the Excel DMCONTENTQUERY() function. There are two more Excel data mining functions: DMPREDICT() and DMPREDICTROW().

To conclude this appendix on Prediction query generation, you may want to try the following two formulas in two Excel worksheet cells:

```
=DMPREDICT("","[TM Decision Tree]","Predict([Bike Buyer])",
"40","Age","M","Gender","0","Number Cars Owned","Pacific","Region")
=DMPREDICT("","[TM Decision Tree]","PredictProbability([Bike Buyer])",
"40","Age","M","Gender","0","Number Cars Owned","Pacific","Region")
```

The results are the same as we achieved with the Prediction Query Builder on the Decision Trees model, earlier in this appendix. The first parameter is the connection name; an empty string means the current connection in the Data Mining toolbar. The second parameter is the name of the mining model. The third parameter is a DMX Prediction function. The fourth parameter is a series of column name/value pairs. Instead of hard-coding the values for the columns, you can use cell references. The Predict() and PredictProbability() DMX functions are used in the two examples—you might like to try Cluster() on a Clustering model too. The DMPREDICTROW() function is similar to the DMPREDICT() function, except that it takes a cell range for the values, followed by a comma-separated list of the column names, rather than a series of column name/value pairs.

Appendix C

Graphical DDL Queries

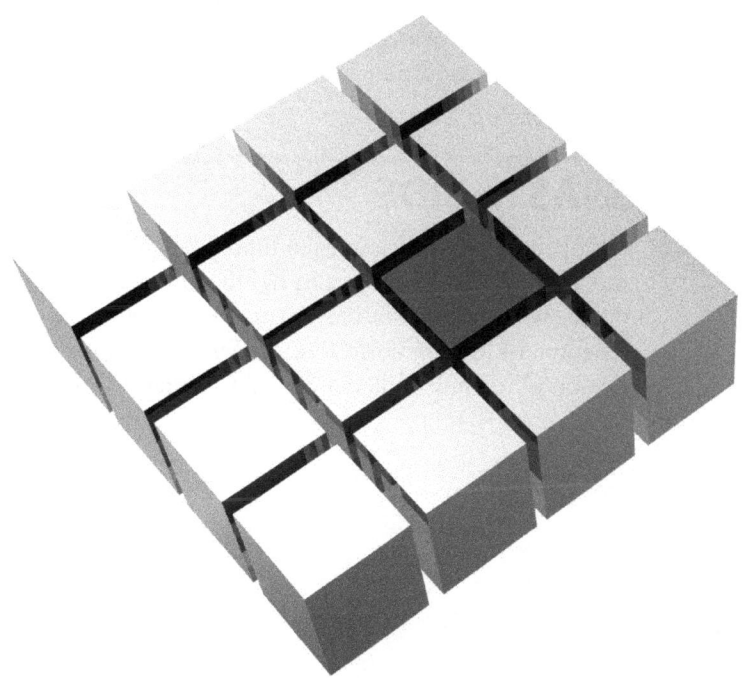

This appendix demonstrates how to generate DDL queries graphically. Such queries are for creating and training data mining models. You can do this from Excel 2007/2010 or from BIDS. There are also a number of features in SSIS that help you create and train data mining models with little or no syntax involved. In this appendix, you get to see how it can be done in Excel 2007/2010, SSAS in BIDS, and SSIS in BIDS.

▶ **Key concepts** Creating data mining models graphically, training data mining models graphically

DDL Queries

DDL queries were covered in Chapter 7 and involved a fair amount of reasonably complex DMX syntax. Such queries are used to create data mining structures and data mining models, train models, and carry out administrative tasks. All of these can also be done graphically without the need to type any syntax at all. If you turn on SQL Server Profiler, you can see the DMX generated—which is a good way to learn. You can generate data mining model scripts from Object Explorer in SSMS (right-click, then click Script Mining Model As | CREATE To | New Query Editor Window), but the language generated is not DMX; it's XMLA. You can use either DMX or XMLA as a DDL language for data mining. However, this is a DMX book, so the SSMS method is outside our scope. Fortunately, there are other ways to generate and examine DMX DDL. This appendix considers a couple of these. In particular, we'll take a look at graphically creating models and training models in SSAS in BIDS and from Excel 2007/2010. In addition, there's a section on how to train models in SSIS in BIDS with no syntax involved.

SSAS in BIDS

Whole books could be written (and probably will be) about how to create data mining models in an SSAS project in BIDS. This section of this appendix is merely a fleeting overview to get you started. If you wish to pursue this topic further, we refer you to Chapter 14 in *Delivering Business Intelligence with Microsoft SQL Server 2008* by Brian Larson (McGraw-Hill, 2008) and Chapter 4 in *Data Mining with Microsoft SQL Server*

2008 by Jamie MacLennan, ZhaoHui Tang, and Bogdan Crivat (Wiley, 2008). The former is an excellent guide to all things BI in SQL Server, and the latter is the SSAS data miner's bible.

To get started, you need a data source and a data source view in your BIDS SSAS project. This example uses the SSAS Adventure Works database as a BIDS project. There are three ways of creating this project and they are fully covered in Appendix A. You will also require the SQL Server AdventureWorksDW2008 (AdventureWorksDW in SQL Server 2005) database as a source for the case table. Let's create and train a model based on the Time Series algorithm:

1. In Solution Explorer, right-click on the Mining Structures folder and choose New Mining Structure. This starts the Data Mining Wizard. Click Next to move on from the welcome screen and see the Select the Definition Method dialog, shown in Figure C-1.

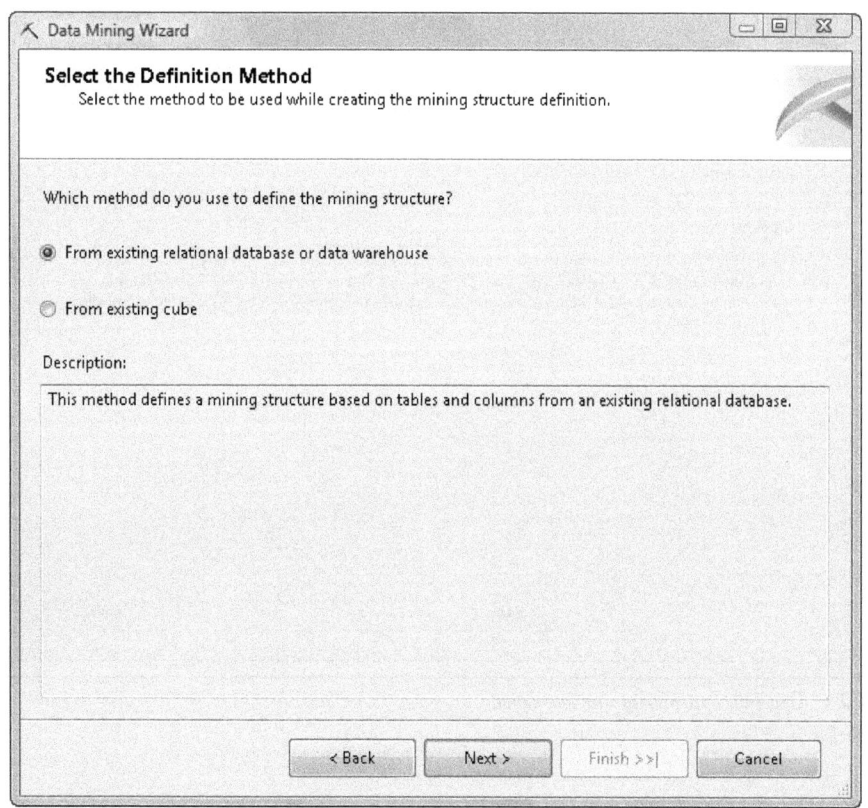

Figure C-1   *Select the Definition Method dialog*

2. In this dialog you choose the source for your case table. You can base a structure, and its constituent models, on either a relational or a multidimensional source. Keep the default setting of From Existing Relational Database or Data Warehouse and click Next to open the Create the Data Mining Structure dialog, as shown in Figure C-2.

3. In this dialog, leave the top option button turned on; we want a model within the structure. From the drop-down, select Microsoft Time Series and click Next. The next dialog, Select Data Source View, is shown in Figure C-3. Accept the data source view, Adventure Works DW, and click Next.

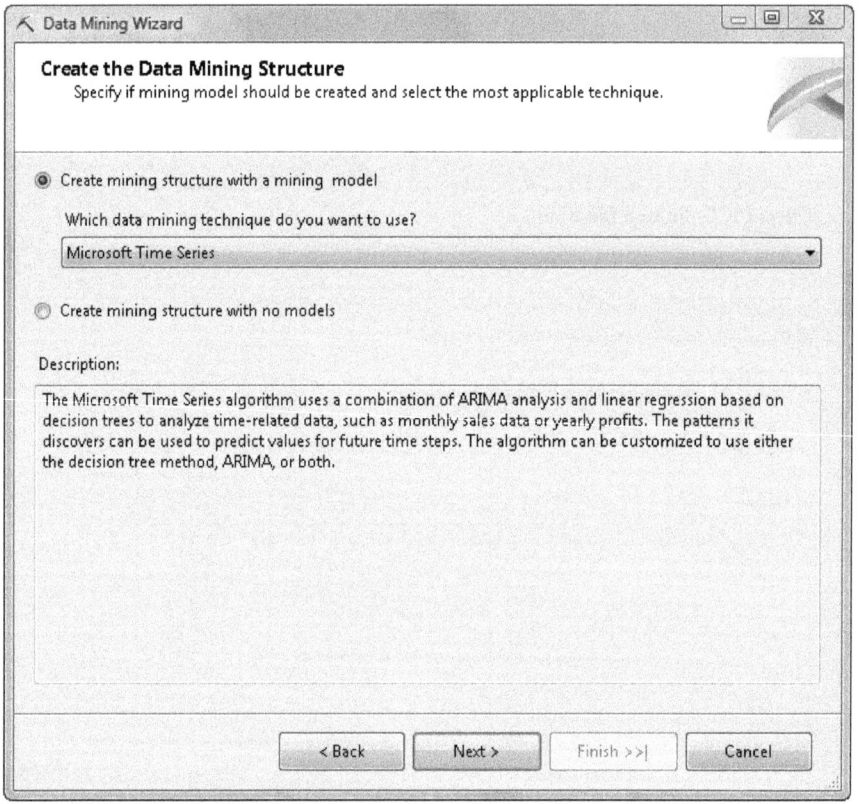

Figure C-2 *Create the Data Mining Structure dialog*

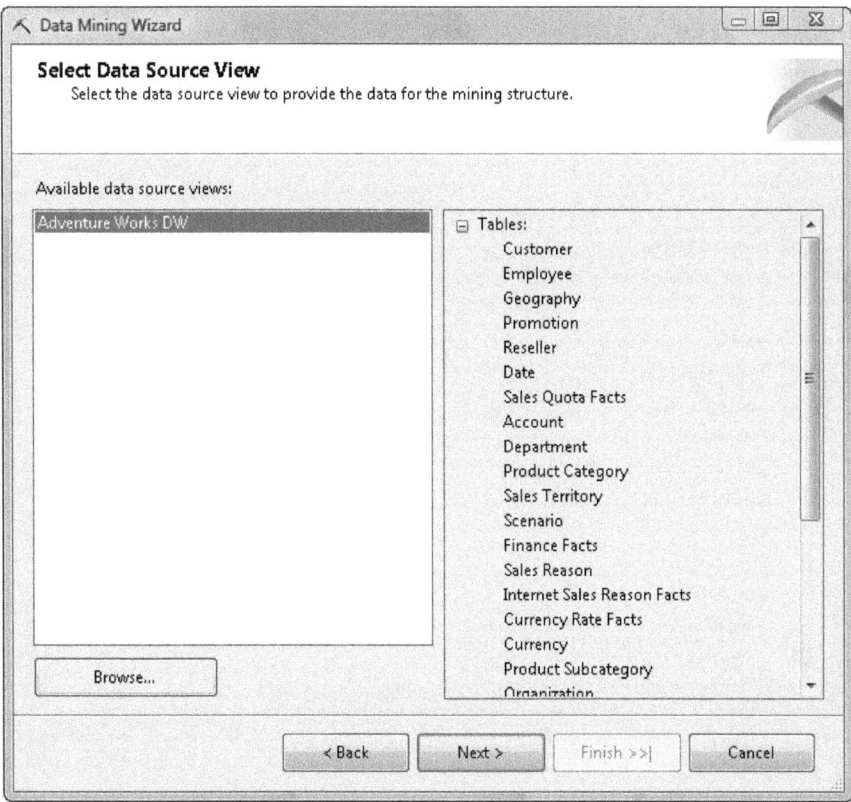

Figure C-3   *Select Data Source View dialog*

4.   You should now be in the Specify Table Types dialog, shown in Figure C-4. This is where you choose the case table (and nested tables, if you need them). Find the table vTimeSeries (it's actually a view), and turn on the check box in the Case column before clicking Next.

5.   The Specify the Training Data dialog is next. This dialog is shown in Figure C-5. This is where you select the columns to use and the nature of each column. Turn on the Key check boxes for both ModelRegion and TimeIndex. Also, turn on the

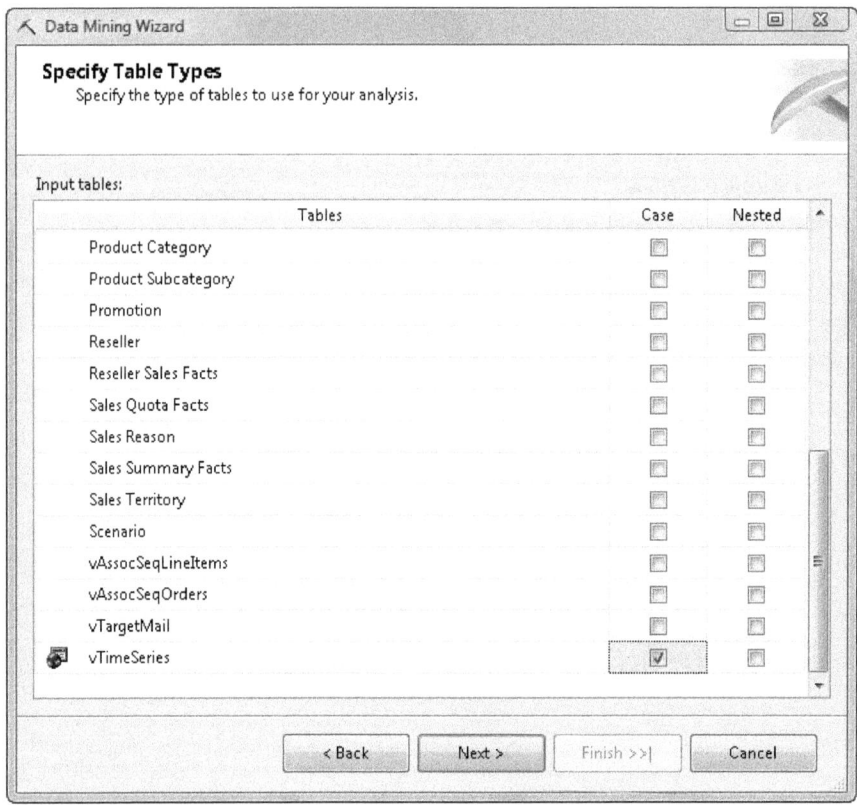

Figure C-4 *Specify Table Types dialog*

Input *and* Predictable check boxes for both Amount and Quantity. We want to predict Amount, for example, based on historic amounts sold—it's an input as well as a predictable column. If a column is both an input and a predictable column, it's the Predict column. If it's only a predictable column, it's PredictOnly—if it's only an input column, it's Input. You can see these settings in the designer when you have finished the wizard. Click Next.

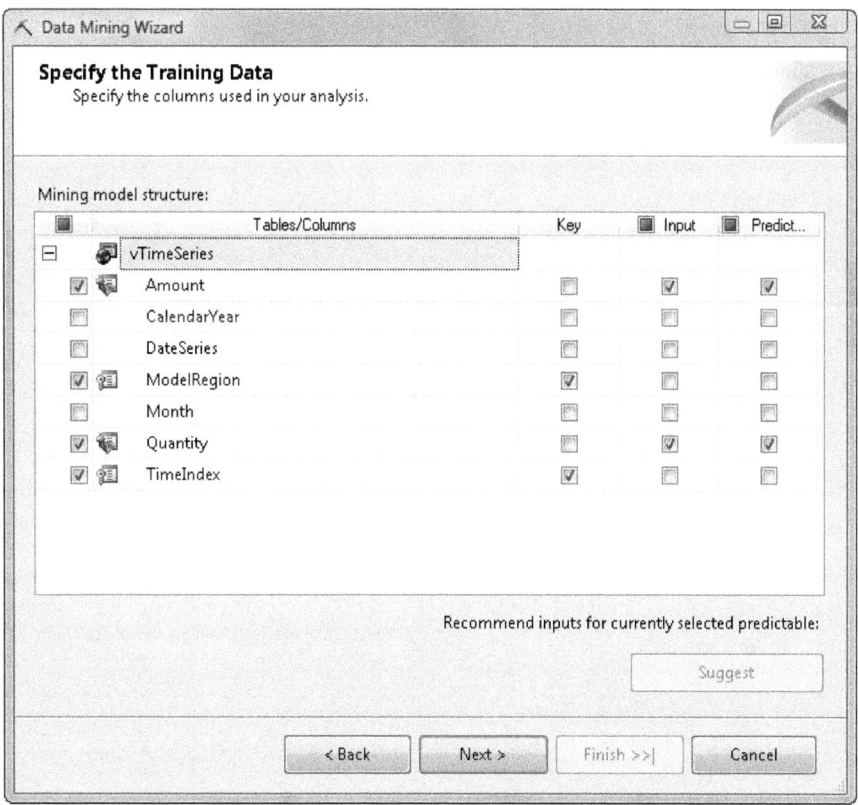

Figure C-5   *Specify the Training Data dialog*

6. Figure C-6 shows the next dialog, Specify Columns' Content and Data Type. Note here that TimeIndex has been renamed to Time Index and its Content Type is Key Time. Click Next.

7. The Completing the Wizard dialog, Figure C-7, is the final dialog of the wizard. In this dialog you can, optionally, enter meaningful and descriptive names for both the structure and the model. Click Finish.

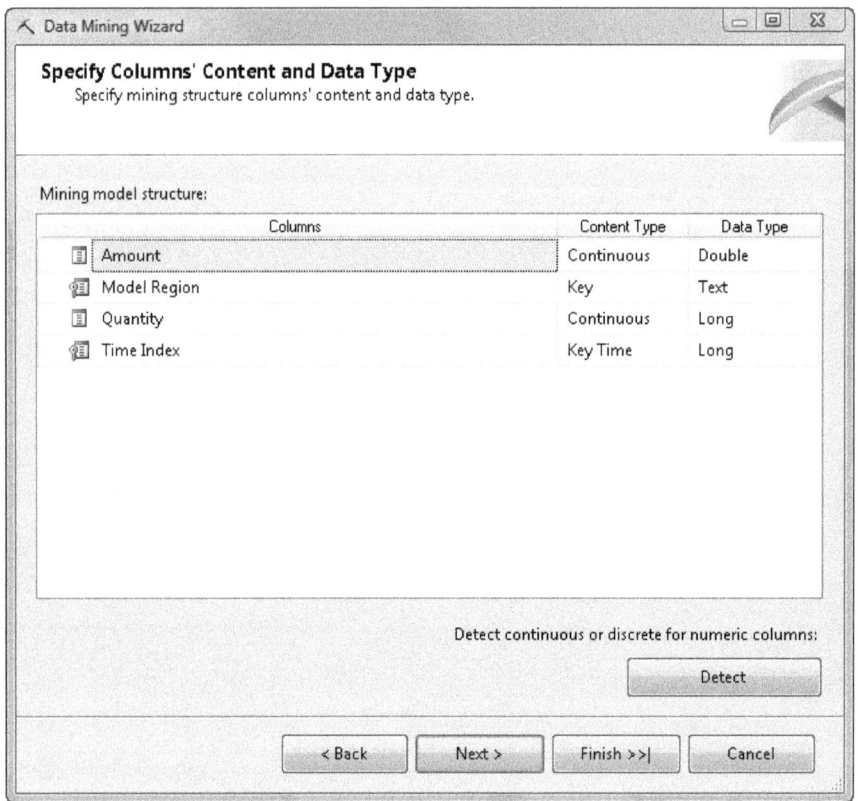

Figure C-6 *Specify Columns' Content and Data Type dialog*

8. The wizard drops you into the designer. The first tab shows the structure. The second tab shows the model. The third tab is for viewing the content. Click on the third tab, Mining Model Viewer. You won't be able to view the content until the model has been created on the server (your model has only been created in BIDS) and trained. In other words, the model must be deployed and processed. Click Yes when prompted (this probably happens twice), and click Run when the Process Mining Model dialog appears. This dialog is shown in Figure C-8. When the processing is completed successfully, click Close twice. The final result should be similar to Figure C-9 (in SSAS 2005, click the Charts tab).

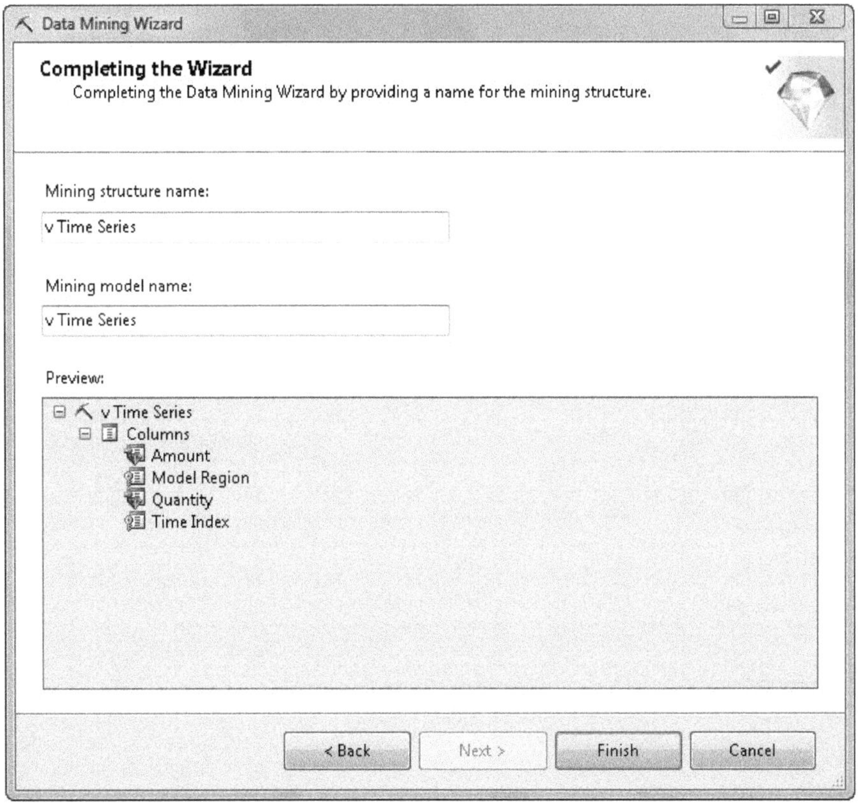

Figure C-7   *Completing the Wizard dialog*

The result is very similar to that of the Forecasting model we saw in Appendix A. There will probably be some minor differences in the two charts. The Forecasting example has a PERIODICITY_HINT of {12}. Setting model parameters in code was mentioned in Chapter 7. If you are interested in how to do this in BIDS, click first on the Mining Models tab. Then right-click on the algorithm name, Microsoft_Time_Series, and choose Set Algorithm Parameters. This opens the Algorithm

Figure C-8 *Process Mining Model dialog*

Parameters dialog, as shown in Figure C-10. If you would like to experiment, try a PERIODICITY_HINT of {12} and reprocess the model. It will now be the same as the Forecasting one.

You can also graphically create and train models from Excel. This is examined in the next section.

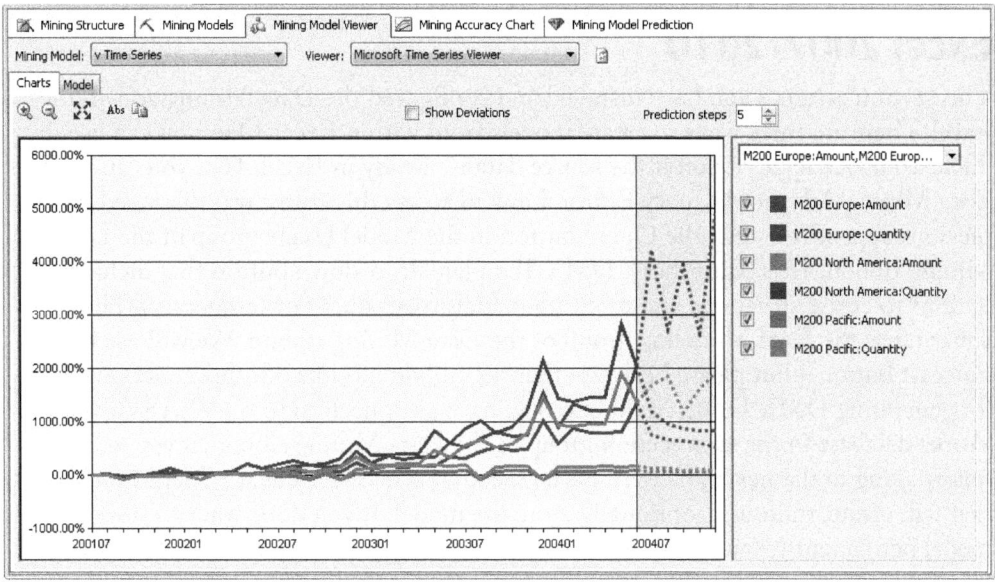

Figure C-9   *Time Series data mining model content*

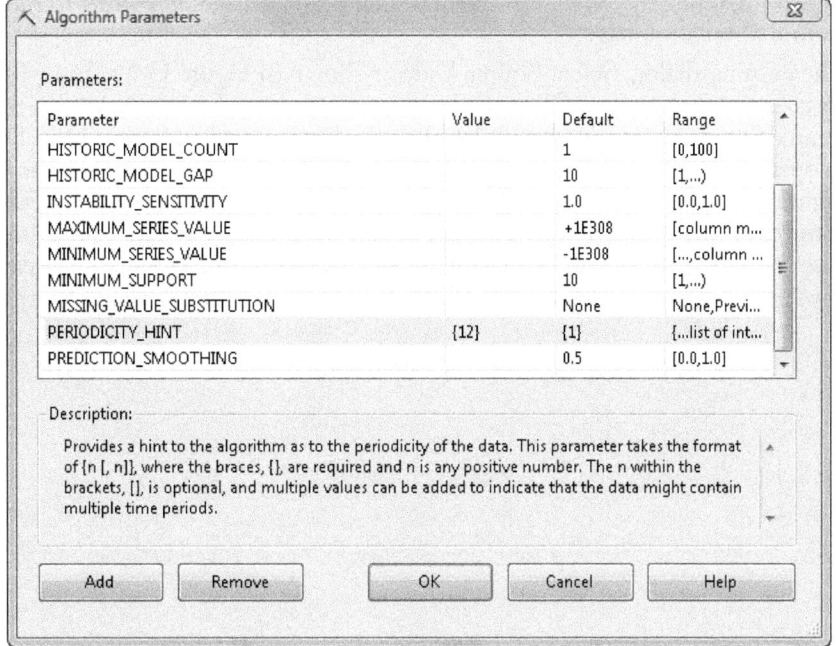

Figure C-10   *Algorithm Parameters dialog*

Excel 2007/2010

This section assumes you have installed and configured the Data Mining add-in for Excel. There are three ways to create models from within Excel. One, you can use the Table Tools/Analyze ribbon if the source data is already in Excel. Two, you can use the Data Mining Advanced Query Editor. How to access this editor was discussed in the previous appendix—click the Query button in the Model Usage group of the Data Mining ribbon. This editor has a DMX Template drop-down button that includes options to create structures and to create models (permanent or temporary). Three, you can use the Data Modeling group of the Data Mining ribbon. We will use the Forecast button—but please be aware that the ribbon has lots of other functionality for generating DMX DDL. Make sure you have a connection to the SSAS Adventure Works database in the Connection group of the Data Mining ribbon, if you want to follow along to the next exercise. This connection is necessary, as it's SSAS (not Excel) that will create, train, and, optionally, store the model. If you don't want to store the model permanently, you can have a connection to any SSAS database. Let's build a Clustering model (some of the steps are only given in outline):

1. Hover your mouse over the Cluster button in the Data Modeling group of the Data Mining ribbon. This verifies that this button uses the Microsoft_Clustering algorithm. Click the button to start the Cluster Wizard. Click Next to move on from the welcome page.

2. The ensuing dialog, Select Source Data, is shown in Figure C-11. You will need an External data source. Click the button next to Data Source Name. In the Data Source Query Editor, Figure C-12, click the button next to Server Data Source to open the New Analysis Services Data Source dialog. This dialog is shown in Figure C-13. Its title is slightly misleading—it's not a connection to SSAS, but a connection to a SQL Server data source that will become a data source for SSAS. The Provider is SQL Server! You will need a Data source name (which can be anything), a Server name for your SQL Server, and a Catalog name for the SQL

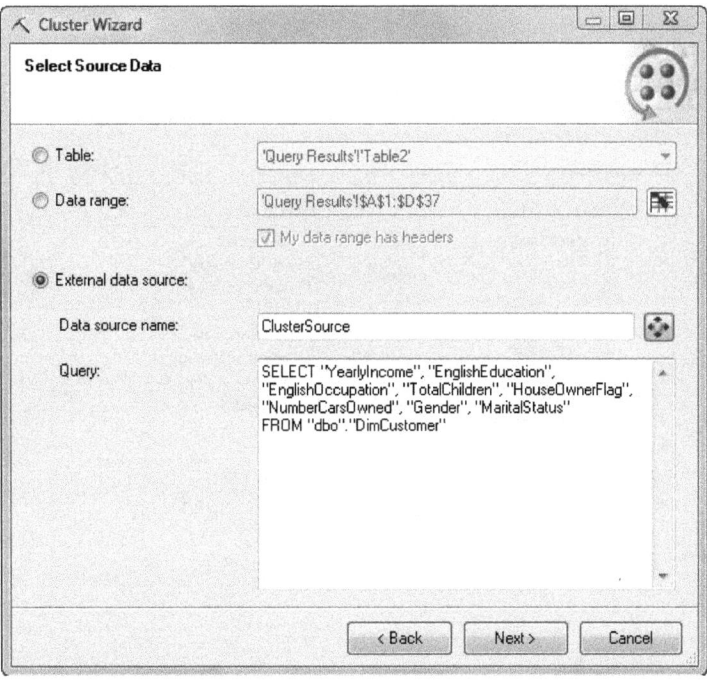

Figure C-11 *Select Source Data dialog*

Server AdventureWorksDW2008 (AdventureWorksDW in SQL Server 2005). Click OK to return to the Data Source Query Editor—you may see a couple of prompts; if so, answer in the affirmative. In the editor, expand DimCustomer, and add about half a dozen suitable demographic columns (for example, EnglishEducation and YearlyIncome). Click OK to return to the Cluster Wizard and click Next.

3. You should be on the Clustering dialog of the wizard. This is shown in Figure C-14. Click Next to accept all the defaults. The next dialog (SQL Server 2008 only) is entitled Split Data into Training and Testing Sets, shown in Figure C-15. Click Next

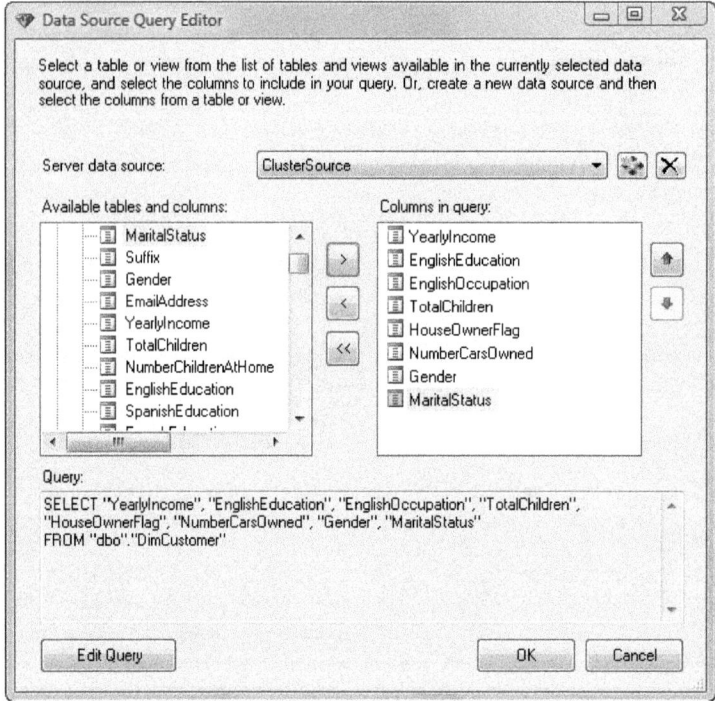

Figure C-12 *Data Source Query Editor dialog*

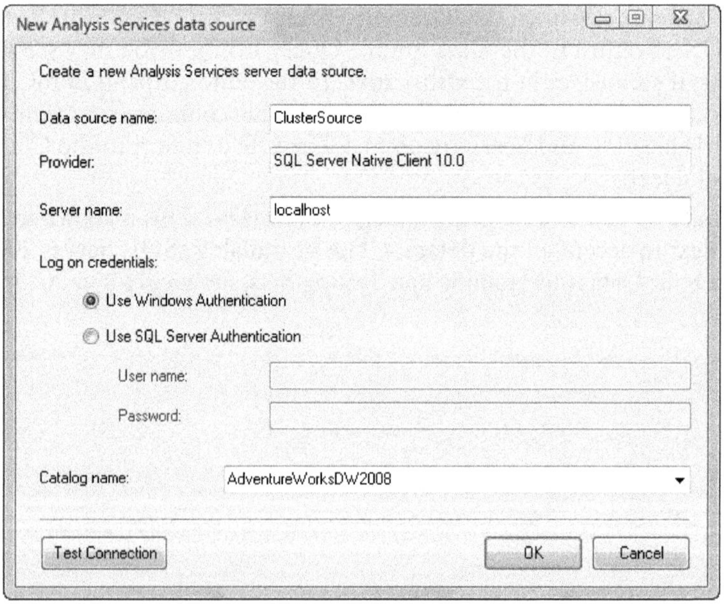

Figure C-13 *New Analysis Services data source dialog*

Figure C-14 *Clustering dialog*

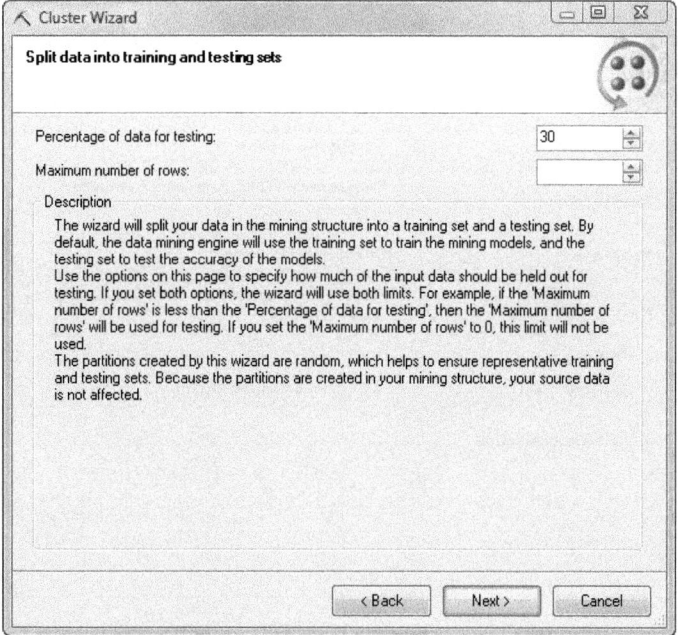

Figure C-15 *Split data into training and testing sets dialog*

to move on to the Finish page dialog. The Finish dialog is shown in Figure C-16. Here, drill-through is enabled by default, and you have the option to create a temporary model only. If you don't choose a temporary model, the model and containing structure become part of your SSAS database. You can only create temporary models if the DataMining \ AllowSessionMiningModels property for SSAS is set to true in SSMS. Click Finish!

4. The final result is shown in Figure C-17. The position and shading of your clusters may well be different. If you created a temporary model, then closing the content viewer will lose the model. If you created a permanent model, you can use the Browse button in the Model Usage group to retrieve it.

There is so much more graphically based data mining functionality in Excel. As well as the Cluster button, the Data Modeling group contains buttons labeled Classify (Decision Trees), Estimate (Decision Trees), Associate (Association), and Forecast (Time Series). The Advanced button, in the same group, allows you to create data mining structures, to which you can add models later. The Manage Models button, in the Management group, can generate administration-based DMX DDL. The Trace button, in the Connection group, is a mini-SQL Server Profiler—you can see some of the DMX generated, but be aware that sometimes it uses XMLA rather than DMX. The Document Model button, in the Model Usage group, is well worth a mention too—you may want to try it on one of your models. It's pretty cool!

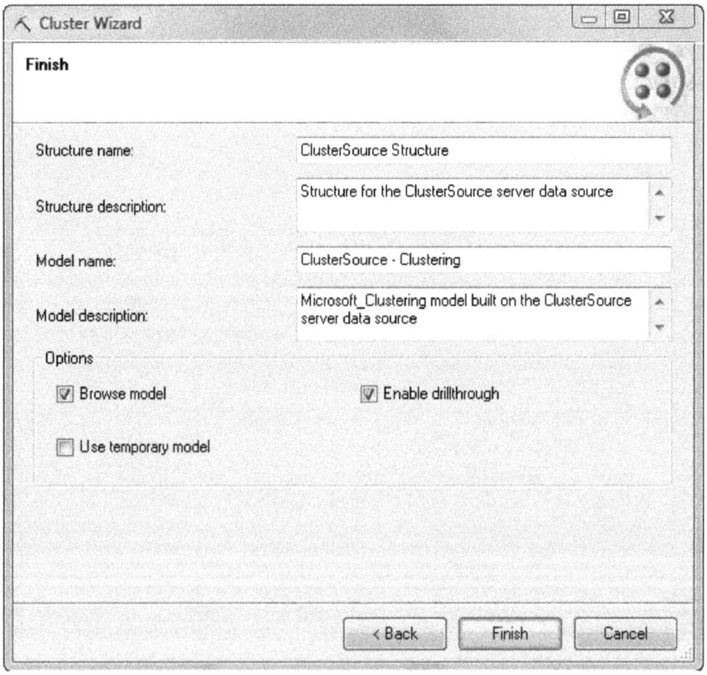

Figure C-16   *Finish dialog*

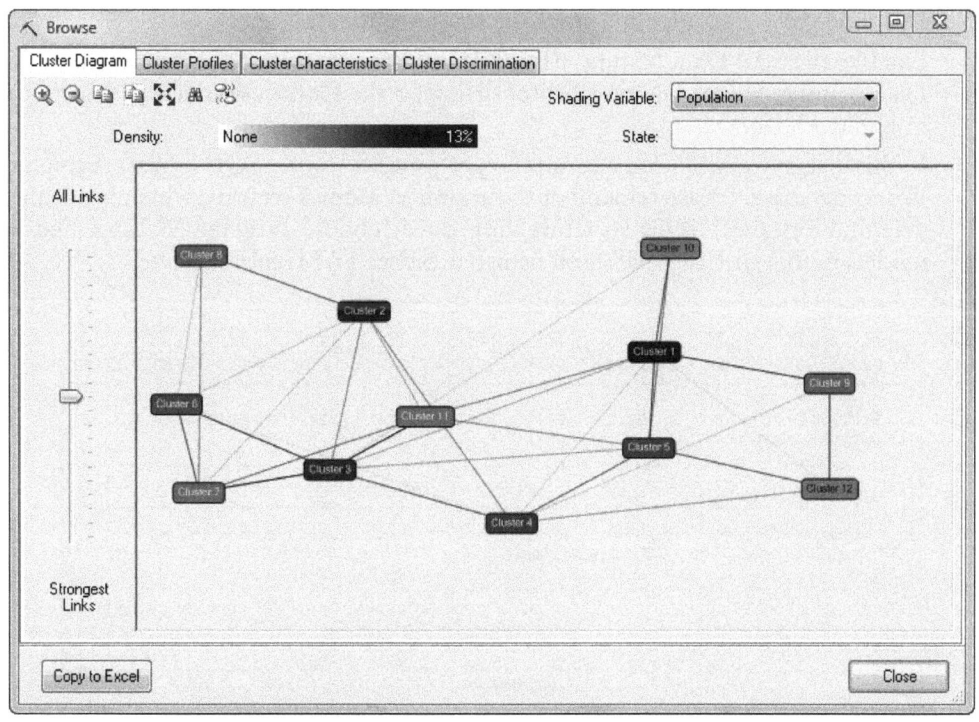

Figure C-17   *A data mining model created from Excel*

SSIS in BIDS

There was a short introduction to SSIS and its Data Flow tab in Appendix B. There, it was used to graphically create Prediction queries. But it can also be used to graphically create DDL queries too—specifically, for training a data mining model. It can save a lot of typing—you can also train a model graphically from SSMS (right-click, Process), and from an SSAS project in BIDS. Here is a short introduction (this is in outline only) to using SSIS to train a model:

1. Add a Data Flow Task to the SSIS Control Flow.

2. Go to the Data Flow tab and add an OLE DB Source (for the case table) and a Data Mining Model Training Destination. For the source, you could use the SQL Server AdventureWorksDW2008 (AdventureWorksDW in SQL Server 2005) database. The case table could be vTargetMail (it's actually a view)—this is the case table for the Targeted Mailing mining structure in the SSAS Adventure Works database. If you try this, make sure you go to the Columns page and check that all columns are turned on.

3. Drag the green data pipeline from the source to the destination.

4. Double-click the Data Mining Model Training destination. This opens the Data Mining Model Training Editor dialog on the Connection tab, as shown in Figure C-18.

5. In this dialog, you will need a connection to your SSAS (*not* SQL Server) Adventure Works database. Please remember to turn on Windows security, which is not the default. From the Mining structure drop-down, choose Targeted Mailing. The models in this structure will then be listed. Select TM Decision Tree.

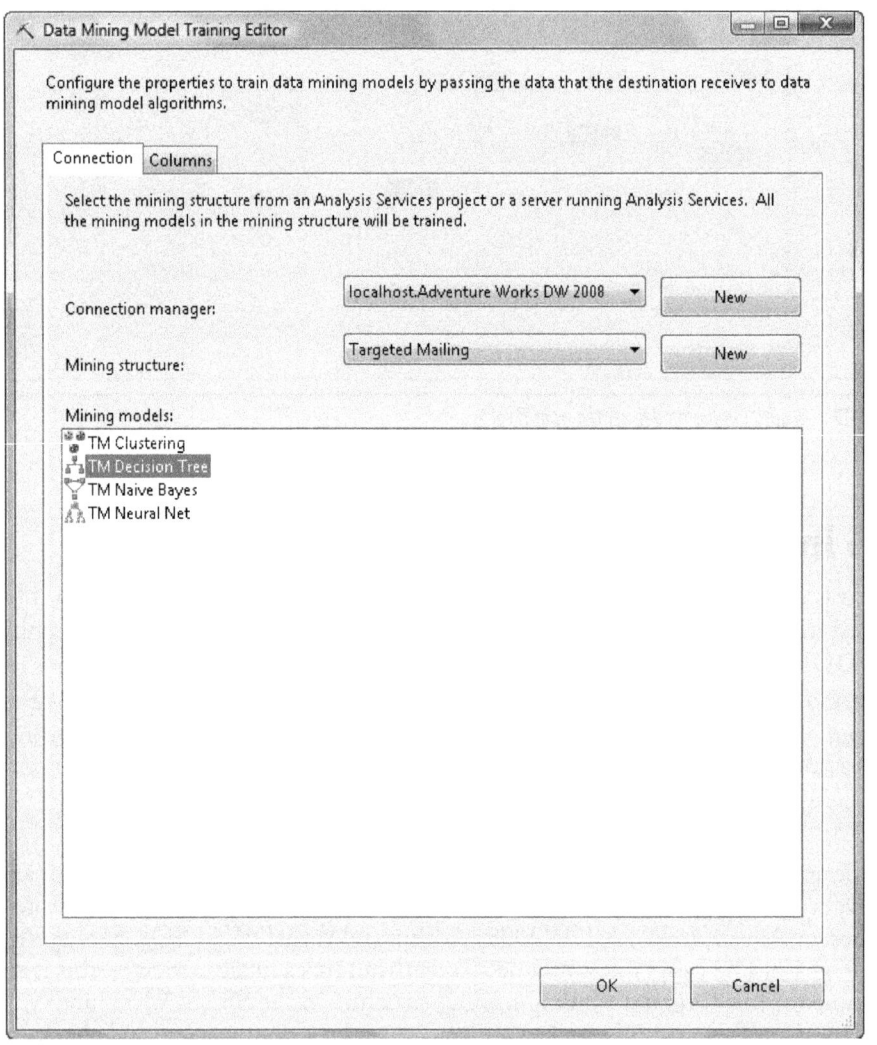

Figure C-18 *Data Mining Model Training Editor dialog, Connection tab*

6. Click on the Columns tab of the editor. Most of the mappings will have been made for you, based on column names—it's clever enough to cope with spaces in names. However, two columns will not be mapped. In the Input Column column, select EnglishEducation to map to Education in the Mining Structure Columns column. Do the same for EnglishOccupation to Occupation. The completed entry is shown in Figure C-19. Click OK.

7. Execute the package.

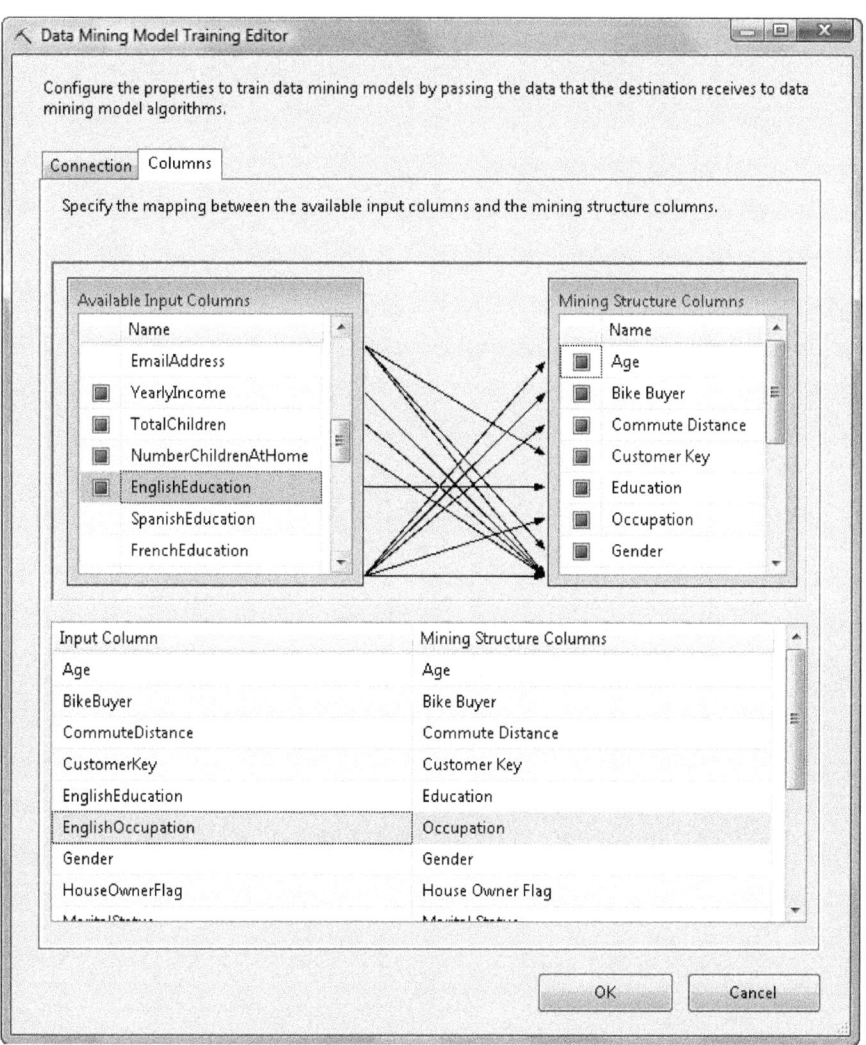

Figure C-19   *Data Mining Model Training Editor dialog, Columns tab*

Didn't that save a bit of work? These three appendixes are designed to make life easier. You may have also consolidated your knowledge of DMX in the process, especially if you have SQL Server Profiler running. Well done, we have finished our tour of all things DMX. Only please remember that there is no substitute, in terms of flexibility and power, for writing your own DMX—even if the GUI tools are quite sexy!

Index

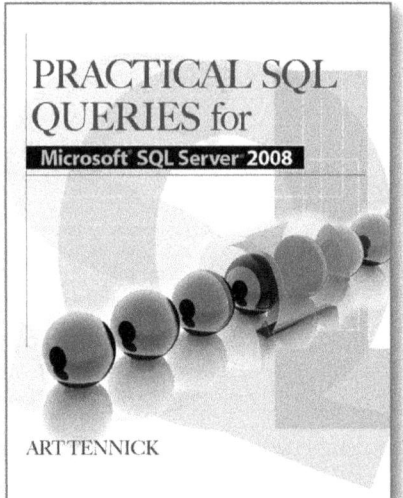

Lightning Source UK Ltd.
Milton Keynes UK
UKHW05f2152050318
318931UK00004B/518/P